D0575912

American River College Library
4700 College Oak Drive
Sacramento, CA 95841

The Very Hungry City

Urban Energy
Efficiency and the
Economic Fate
of Cities

AUSTIN TROY

Yale

UNIVERSITY PRESS

New Haven and London

Copyright © 2012 by Austin Troy.
All rights reserved.
This book may not be reproduced, in whole or in part,
including illustrations, in any form (beyond that copying
permitted by Sections 107 and 108 of the U.S. Copyright
Law and except by reviewers for the public press), without
written permission from the publishers.
Yale University Press books may be purchased in quantity
for educational, business, or promotional use. For
information, please e-mail sales.press@yale.edu (U.S. office)
or sales@yaleup.co.uk (U.K. office).
Designed by Sonia Shannon.
Set in Minion type by Newgen North America.
Printed in the United States of America.

Library of Congress Cataloging-in-Publication Data

Troy, Austin.
The very hungry city : urban energy efficiency and the
economic fate of cities / Austin Troy.
p. cm.
Includes bibliographical references and index.
ISBN 978-0-300-16231-8 (hardback)
1. Cities and towns—Energy consumption.   2. Energy
policy.   3. Urban economics.   4. City planning—
Environmental aspects.   I. Title.
HD9502.A2T76 2012
333.79′13091732—dc23
2011027161

A catalogue record for this book is available
from the British Library.

This paper meets the requirements of
ANSI/NISO Z39.48-1992 (Permanence of Paper).

10 9 8 7 6 5 4 3 2 1

To the memory of Joseph F. Troy

Contents

Preface

It was the late spring of 1979, and third grade was coming to a close at Brentwood Elementary in Los Angeles. Summer vacation was about to begin. The days were getting longer. I had a new ten-speed Schwinn. Life was good.

Nonetheless, at recess each day I was beginning to notice that something odd was happening just across the street at the Union 76. Lines of cars waiting for gasoline mysteriously sprouted and steadily grew at this normally sleepy filling station, until at one point they wrapped around the block. As a nine-year-old, I didn't have the faintest understanding of what caused the pileup—how it related to political upheaval in Iran, price controls in America, or OPEC production quotas. And frankly, it didn't matter much to me, because it had little impact on my daily life; after all, I rode my new bike to school, and the other places I cared to go—the store where I bought baseball cards and my friends' houses—were all within easy walking distance.

But beyond my tiny world, the impacts were momentous. Even though predicted shortfalls in oil supply were modest, just the threat of not being able to fill up whenever needed sent Californians into an irrational frenzy that resulted in hoarding, multi-hour wait times, and physical attacks in the gas lines, including one against a pregnant woman. Why were all these adults acting so crazy?

It's not surprising to me that the 1979 panic began in Southern California, the motherland of urban automobile dependency, before spreading east. Residents of the Los Angeles area knew just how crippling the lack of fuel could be to their way of life. Even though the actual shortages were modest, the fears were real. In Los Angeles, there simply was no substitute for internal combustion.

As I look back on that experience, it strikes me that energy is something we don't notice until there's a crisis. When these crises happen, they can fundamentally change our behaviors—even our whole outlook. When a crisis abates, so too does our attention to the issue. In the years following the 1979 oil crisis, price controls were lifted, oil production dramatically increased, and prices fell as supplies burgeoned. Cars and houses got bigger. People turned up their thermostats in winter. Commuters drove ever longer distances. Energy slowly drifted out of public consciousness.

Fast forward to 2008. After gradually rising for a few years, prices at the pump suddenly skyrocketed to more than four dollars a gallon. Only this time it wasn't due to revolutions, price controls, or embargoes. Rather, far more frighteningly, it was caused by a simple supply-and-demand imbalance. A red-hot global economy was demanding far more fossil fuel than producers could supply. Some would say this was due to insufficient investment in production capacity. Others would contend that we were beginning to reach the physical limits to global oil production. Whatever the cause, it was another awakening in energy consciousness. Just as they had done twenty years earlier, behaviors changed: cars slowly got smaller, investments in energy efficiency increased, and some people moved closer to their work. However, there wasn't a lot of time for these effects to take hold. Within a few months, recession struck, in turn reducing demand and sending energy prices plummeting. Worries about energy use were suddenly replaced by much more immediate concerns about unemployment, mortgage foreclosures, and debt. But eventually the economy limped out of recession and, with this recovery, oil prices rebounded. As I write this preface in mid-2011, those prices are again approaching their 2008 peak.

One thing these oil shocks illustrate is that people can adapt to rising energy prices and reduced energy availability when they have to.

In fact, many were able to reduce their energy consumption without compromising their quality of life.

But there are limits to this adaptability. And the most important determinant of these limitations is where people live. The rate at which people use energy varies across rural, exurban, suburban, and urban contexts, and from one city to another. These variations are due not just to differences in automobile dependency, traffic, and commuting lengths but also to factors like climate, building-stock quality, water delivery and filtration, and waste processing.

The Very Hungry City is about the intensity of energy use in cities, which I refer to as "urban energy metabolism." Typically this has been considered an environmental issue. My premise is that it's equally important as an economic issue. There's strong evidence that long-term energy prices will rise considerably as global demand for energy increases, while supplies face growing constraints—not just geophysical constraints but also regulatory ones related to climate-change mitigation and political ones related to instability in countries that produce fossil fuel. As prices climb and energy costs make up an increasingly large share of the cost of living, urban energy metabolism will go from being just an environmental virtue to a core determinant of urban economic competitiveness. Efficient metropolitan areas—those that are laid out and planned well, have a good mix of land use, have efficient and well-designed building stock, are geographically well located, and have low-energy solutions to providing and delivering essential resources like clean water—will have an ever-increasing competitive advantage over those with a poor metabolism in terms of attracting firms, employment, and investment. Some cities will be able to adapt quickly, but others will face significant hurdles, particularly if they are car-dependent, sprawling, dominated by inefficient buildings, and located in energy-intensive climate zones. This issue is relevant to economic competition not just between cities but also between nations.

This book focuses on why cities have the metabolisms they do, and what they can do to improve them. I believe that predicting the future impacts of energy metabolism on regional economies would be interesting. Such an analysis would, however, be a speculative modeling exercise at best, since history offers no significant long-term energy price increases that we could use for data. But both common sense and economic theory tell us that if something as irreplaceable as energy becomes significantly more expensive, there will be winners and losers, and the losers will most likely be those unable to quickly adapt. Given this, I think it's a safe bet to assume that urban energy metabolism matters.

The book is in two parts. Part One (Chapters 1–5) deals with some of the major determinants of urban energy metabolism: water supply, climate control, and transportation. Chapters 4 and 5 discuss the history of highway and transit development and why certain cities have ended up dominated by one mode versus the other. Part Two (Chapters 6–10) addresses solutions to the energy metabolism problem. Chapters 6 and 7 examine programs and approaches that tackle building and transportation energy efficiency, respectively. Chapter 8 looks at central-city redevelopment as a strategy for reducing energy use. Chapter 9 is about regional solutions to energy metabolism. Chapter 10 is a summary of some of the major policy approaches that I feel could make a big difference with energy metabolism and, in the process, address a whole host of other related urban issues.

In between chapters I have inserted what I call "energy interludes"— brief sections that explore the constraints on energy supply. The first offers a quick synthesis of why I think energy will get more expensive. The next five deal with fossil fuels, while the last three examine alternative sources of energy. If there's a main point that comes out of these interludes, it's that with the depletion of the easily available fossil-fuel deposits, supplies just won't be as responsive in the future as they once were. And with growing demand, that means increasing prices. The other main point is that no alternative energy source offers the silver bullet needed to fill in these growing supply gaps.

The book focuses particularly on American cities and the steep challenges they face following decades of energy profligacy. As a basis for comparison, I look at several cities in Europe that are at the other end of the energy-use spectrum for developed nations. Rather than being an exhaustive inventory of all cities in these areas, this book details just a few cities that are illustrative of particular challenges or opportunities related to energy metabolism. (Readers who are interested in comprehensive rankings of cities' energy metabolisms can turn to such excellent sources as Sustain Lane's *How Green Is Your City* or the Brookings Institution's *Shrinking the Carbon Footprint of Metropolitan America.*)

Finally, as someone who has lived in a wide range of housing and community types, I have tried my best not to be judgmental about people's lifestyle choices or where they live. While I do, for instance, point out the energy consequences of living in more distant and automobile-dependent suburbs or exurbs, I don't in the least bit condemn people who choose to live in such places. Rather, if I have a gripe, it's that Americans have far too few choices when it comes to the type of community or neighborhood in which they can live. While there is a decided preference in the United States for living in so-called "suburbs," Americans are, by and large, not getting the kinds of suburbs that they want. If they were, we'd be using a lot less energy.

I don't expect this book to directly contribute to expanding these choices. But if it can get a conversation started, I'll be happy.

Acknowledgments

Almost five years ago, I had a phone conversation with the literary agent Gillian MacKenzie about some ideas for nonfiction book projects. One of those related to the different ways that cities consume energy and what that could mean as energy gets more expensive. Around this time I'd been frequently reading *The Very Hungry Caterpillar,* by Eric Carle, to my oldest son, Theo, for bedtime. Somehow, synapses in my brain crossed and this nascent idea became *The Very Hungry City.*

This book is almost the same age as Theo, who is nearing the end of kindergarten as the final edits are being made; it feels like writing this has taken almost as much time, effort, and nurturing as raising him. Writing began in earnest in mid-2009, by which time my second child, Ben, was a toddler and my one-semester writing sabbatical from the University of Vermont was over. Needless to say, making this book a reality required some big sacrifices on the home front. So, above all else, my deepest thanks go to my family, particularly my wife, Sheryl Glubok. Not only did she pick up huge amounts of slack with managing kids and household, but she also served as an editor extraordinaire, reading almost every bit of prose I wrote and telling me what worked and what didn't from the perspective of an omnivorous reader. Without her, this book truly never would have happened. To say that I'm in her debt is an understatement.

Another person without whom this book would have been nearly impossible is my sister, Darcy Pollack. She introduced me to my literary agent, Gillian, and also arranged for me to interview Ed Begley Jr., an important character in this book, and to visit his house (a visit she accompanied me on). Additionally, she and her husband, Jeff, were instrumental in connecting me with potential blurbers for the book and offering some great ideas for marketing. Others who provided valuable help with blurbs and publicity include Jan Whitman Ogden and Bill Lofy. I deeply appreciate their assistance.

Three people deserve special thanks for their indispensible help with the editing, organization, and structure of this book: Gillian MacKenzie; Jean Thomson Black, my editor at Yale University Press; Karen Gangel; and Ann-Marie Imbornoni, my production editor at Yale University Press. In the early phases of this project, Gillian deprogrammed me from my previously ingrained academic style of writing and helped me find a literary voice more suited to popular nonfiction (I hope the reader agrees). Jean furthered that education by carefully reading through my subsequent chapters and offering splendid critical feedback, as well as hand-holding me through the highly complicated procedures of publishing a trade title. Karen meticulously read through the entire manuscript and provided indispensible line edits. And Ann-Marie did a fantastic job of coordinating the book's final production.

I am also deeply indebted to everyone I interviewed for this book, each of whom provided extremely valuable content and insights: Murat Armbruster, from the Carbon War Room; Ed Begley Jr., actor and environmental advocate (who not only agreed to be interviewed but showed me all around his home); Kaid Benfield, director of the NRDC Smart Growth program; Mikael Colville-Andersen, Copenhagen filmmaker and bicycle advocate; Duncan Crary, media consultant; Greg Dicum, freelance journalist; Reid Ewing of the University of Utah; Dan Firth of the Stockholm Traffic Administration; Joel Franklin of KTH University in Stockholm; Eric Freudenthall of Hammarby Sjöstad; Stellan Fryxell of Tengbon Architects; Lars Gärde of ByggVesta; Con Howe, former New York and Los Angeles City Planning Chief; Daniel Jonsson of KTH University in Stockholm; Gary Klein, formerly of the California Energy Commission; Sophie Lambert, director of LEED-ND; Shaun McKinnon of the *Arizona Republic*; Sean Patrick Neill, from Transcend Capital; Thomas Sick Nielsen of the University of Copenhagen; John Norquist, director of the Congress on the New Urbanism;

Mark Pisano, former director of the Southern California Association of Governments; Phillip Schneider of Deloitte Consulting; author Paul Sheckel; Llewellyn Wells, of the Living City Block project; and Zev Yaroslavsky, Los Angeles County Supervisor. I also wish to specially acknowledge Blair Hamilton of Efficiency Vermont, who passed away only a few months after I interviewed him. Blair, cofounder of the Vermont Energy Investment Corporation, was one of the great visionaries of the energy efficiency world and made a huge difference in advancing this cause.

A number of additional people deserve thanks for providing feedback on writing and content: Dale Azaria; Eric Garza; Nate Hagens of Theoildrum.org; my mother, Brigitta Troy; David Glubok; my sister, Darcy Pollack; and the numerous graduate students, Fellows, and Affiliates of the Gund Institute for Ecological Economics who offered great suggestions at a presentation I gave on the book. Thanks also go to my cousin Gordon Troy for his expert legal advice; the Rubenstein School of Environment and Natural Resources at the University of Vermont for funding my research trip to Denmark and Sweden; the Baltimore Ecosystem Study and its funder, the National Science Foundation (LTER award DEB-0423476) for enabling my research in Baltimore, which in turn contributed to the portion of Chapter 8 on Baltimore; and the University of Vermont Transportation Research Center, which provided funding for some of my research which informed sections of Chapter 3.

Also, I'm thankful to the many institutions and individuals that granted permission to reproduce the images used in this book, such as the Eisenhower Presidential Library, the William H. Hannon Library at Loyola Marymount University (Cynthia Becht), the Southern California Automobile Club Archives (Morgan Yates), the University of Vermont Libraries Special Collections (Chris Burns), the Airwell-Fedders Corporation, the Stockholm Traffic Administration, Treg Christopher, Anders Flodmark, and Duncan Crary.

Introduction: Why Urban Energy Metabolism Matters

I have yet to see a place where the icons of urban energy use come together on a grander and more poetic scale than around the interchange for Interstates 5 and 210 and Highway 14 in the city of Sylmar, just outside of Los Angeles. For those who love the sight of acres of reinforced concrete and steel, this is the place to be. Here, I-5 expands to up to fifteen lanes in width to accommodate the massive amounts of traffic these interchanges generate. Running every which way around these ribbons of concrete are dozens of high-tension transmission lines supported by a forest of massive steel pylons, which carry electricity to 3 million people. To one side of I-5 is the Sylmar Converter Station, a 35-acre knot of concrete and pulse-valve semiconductors. Adjacent is the energy-hungry Los Angeles Aqueduct Filtration Plant—the largest direct filtration plant in the United States—which daily makes 600 million gallons of water drinkable. Finishing off the scene is the 1,100-acre Sunshine Canyon landfill.[1]

Until one visits a place like this, it's hard to appreciate just how hungry cities are for energy. And it's far harder to appreciate what makes a city energy efficient.

Most people have an idea of what makes a building efficient or inefficient—leaky windows, insulation gaps, old furnaces. But, while a building manager may keep track of energy use, there is no one to monitor overall urban energy use. Further, while the boundaries of

Near the interchange of I-5 and I-210 in Sylmar, California.
(Photo by author)

a building are obvious, the same can't be said for an urban system—
should urban energy efficiency be defined in terms of neighborhoods,
individual municipalities, counties, or whole metropolitan areas?

In the 1960s, inventor and sanitary engineer Abel Wolman coined
the term "urban metabolism" to describe the flows of matter and en-

ergy in an urban system.[2] A generation later, I argue that the time has come for us to talk about urban energy metabolism, which describes the differing rates at which cities consume energy. Any number of factors can cause this metabolism to vary, among them climate, access to water, the quality of the building stock, industrial use, and the linked issues of transportation and urban form.

Having a high-energy metabolism is like having a high metabolism for food. Take, as an example, the former speed-eating champion Sonya "Black Widow" Thomas, who although only ninety-eight pounds, can eat thirty-five bratwursts in ten minutes. She can consume pounds of food in a matter of minutes without gaining a single pound herself. But her insanely high metabolism is a good thing only in the context of cheap and abundant food. If food were suddenly scarce and expensive, that high metabolism would become a liability. That is, a slow metabolism would be a competitive advantage because it would mean being able to do more with less.

Many American cities have metabolisms like those of competitive eaters—they are structurally constrained to require a huge amount of energy per capita to meet their basic functions. From an economic perspective, none of this has mattered while energy has been cheap. But, as I discuss in this book, there are a lot of good reasons why it's unwise to assume that it will remain so.

Energy conservation has long been thought of as an environmental virtue. But as energy becomes more expensive in the long term, urban energy metabolism will become ever more critical to cities' economic well-being and success. This is particularly important for the United States, because it has some of the world's hungriest cities and because Americans are among the highest per capita consumers of energy, with the typical American using twice the energy of a Briton, six times that of a Chinese, and eleven times that of a Salvadoran.[3]

There is a whole branch of economics that addresses the reasons why industries and firms choose one location over another—reasons such as wages, access to natural resources, transportation routes, workforce education, taxation, and preexisting clusters of firms and industries. As energy gets more expensive, urban energy metabolism will rank increasingly high on that list, and cities with a high energy metabolism will find themselves with a significant competitive disadvantage.

One reason for this disadvantage is that in the new world of high energy prices, residents of high-metabolism cities will require compensation for their increased energy-related expenses, such as transportation, heating and cooling, waste processing, and water supply. Phillip Schneider, a principal for Deloitte Consulting's Location Strategy and Site Selection Team, helps firms choose locations. He told me that he believes that firms in cities with long commutes will likely have to increase wages to compensate workers for increased transportation costs as energy gets more expensive: "It does stand to reason that cities that are more compact and that have mass transportation should do better." Higher wages may sound like a good thing, but in this context they're a liability. Employees in the high-metabolism city are no better off than employees earning less in a low-metabolism city, because the former must spend additional income on transportation, and meanwhile the costs for the employer have gone up (some of this compensation would also be accounted for by lowered housing values which, although good for those buying a home for the first time, is disastrous for existing homeowners and highly destabilizing for a regional economy). Practices like locating corporate headquarters in suburban or exurban areas may become unsustainable. According to Schneider, such facilities may eventually have to be relocated or "there will have to be a transportation solution to get people out there once gas prices are high." Consequently, "cities in America that have good mass transit systems . . . stand to be winners when it comes to condensed activities, like headquarters." European cities, by contrast, are better prepared "because they never got rid of their mass transportation and they stopped urban sprawl."[4]

Schneider believes, however, that there is plenty of opportunity for cities to adapt. Those that are currently inefficient "won't give up and go away. The price of fuel will stimulate workarounds." I agree that they will try. But the question is, can they afford to wait until prices rise? Recent experience shows that waiting can be costly.

In Rio Vista, California, at the intersection of Park Place and Hearth Lane, not far from the banks of the lazy Sacramento River, is the ironically named Hearth and Home at Liberty, a subdivision intended for 855 upscale homes that were never built. Today, long after ground was first broken, only 13 lonely model homes sit vacant within an otherwise empty 40-block street grid, complete with pavement, underground utilities, street lights, fire hydrants, sidewalks, bike lanes, crosswalks, a parking lot—and now tumbleweeds.

Hearth and Home was just about the farthest frontier reached by the Bay Area's red-hot housing market. Located about an hour and forty minutes from downtown San Francisco, in typical rush hour traffic, this bedroom community offers an example of energy metabolism gone to its extreme. Once a small rural town, Rio Vista's population exploded as developers built subdivisions such as the 250-unit Homecoming and the 2,000-unit Trilogy. However, by the time Hearth and Home broke ground in 2005, that frontier had become an inhospitable place for new developments. Between 2005 and 2009, median home prices there dropped by almost 45 percent, and by the end of that period, nearly every home for sale in town was a short sale or a foreclosure. With population dropping and property taxes plummeting, the town came close to declaring bankruptcy in 2009.

Rio Vista's situation is by no means unusual for the "exurbs"—that is, commuter communities located beyond the traditional suburban fringe. It and other satellite towns epitomized a phenomenon known as "drive 'til you qualify," which means that if you couldn't afford a home of a certain size and quality in a particular area, you moved to an area where land values were lower. The United States is today littered with the remnants of this trend in the form of so-called zombie subdivisions—distant exurban housing developments where empty lots grow weeds and unfinished houses deteriorate as they await foreclosure sales. Some of these developments are half built; some have just been platted. Many were planned for thousands of residents and today are occupied by only a few dozen homeowners.

Zombie subdivisions can now be found just about anywhere there are exurbs. For instance, in tiny but fast-growing Teton County, Idaho, there are 33 partially built developments nearing the expiration of their permits, involving over 1,800 lots (upon which only 83 have been built) on 5,300 acres, all of which has had such a significant negative impact that the county is considering replanting almost all the land.[5]

But by far the most numerous examples of this phenomenon can be found in the formerly upbeat Sun Belt states. Among these, few have a greater zombie problem than Florida, where a white-hot real estate market fueled by speculation and loose credit led to massive overbuilding of distant exurban housing. Here, in developments like Antillean Isles, over 30 miles south of Miami, lots that were supposed to contain large up-market homes today contain only subtropical weeds. In the nearby Enclave at Black Point Marina, which was recently foreclosed upon by the lenders, there are 40 partially built homes, 180 empty lots, and no residents. Down the road, in Old Biscayne Villas, vagrants live in unfinished cinderblock structures, while in the Mirage subdivision cars are regularly coated with dust and dirt from the vacant home sites comprising 75 percent of the lots. Throughout Miami's far-flung southern suburbs, homes lost on average half their value in just a year, a decline so extreme that brand-new four-bedroom homes are frequently available for around $100,000. And even at that bargain-basement pricing, people aren't buying. In fact, in a recent bulk sale, a large number of new and unoccupied three-bedroom homes in Antillean Isles were sold for just $70,000, even though many neighbors had paid in the mid-$300,000s for the same homes a few years earlier.[6]

Most people would probably blame this on the collapse of the mortgage market and subsequent global recession that started in 2008. But they'd be only half right. If we examine the geographic distribution of abandonments and mass foreclosures, it becomes evident that they're disproportionately found in the outer suburbs and exurbs—the most recently built parts of the American housing frontier.

Several studies have looked at the geographic distribution of price declines in housing. A 2010 report from the Federal Reserve Board found that the stock of distressed "real-estate owned" properties, known as REOs (generally foreclosed properties owned by banks or mortgage companies) is now far greater for so-called boomburbs, or recently established suburbs, than for core cities, and that the concentration of REOs increased greatly in the past few years. By early 2010, the percentage of REOs in boomburbs was almost three times that of core cities, and the percentage of delinquencies was double. Furthermore, the report stated that prices in boomburbs fell on average three times more than those in established cores.[7]

A 2008 study by the economist Joe Cortright, who examined the geographic variation in housing price declines, found that although prices were declining almost everywhere as of 2008, the magnitude of decline was considerably greater for neighborhoods that were distant from the urban core. He attributed these geographic differences in price declines to the steep rise in fuel prices from 2004 to 2008, during which time gas went from an all-time inflation-adjusted low in 1999 to an all-time high in 2008. In other words, cheap gas fueled the expansion of the housing frontier into distant satellite communities like Rio Vista by making multi-hour commutes economically feasible. These areas of the housing market were therefore the most vulnerable to rising gasoline prices.[8]

Another 2010 study from the Federal Reserve Board found that gas prices had a significant effect on suburban housing construction; a 10 percent increase in gas prices resulted in a 10 percent decrease in construction in distant suburbs relative to central cities, meaning that the run-up in prices just between February and June 2008 would have been enough to reduce construction by one-third in these far-flung areas. At least some in the mortgage finance world anticipated this kind of effect well before rising gasoline prices took their toll. A 2006 article from a mortgage-industry trade publication predicted that "there is a possibility that homebuyers will find the price/cost trade-off is no longer feasible. This could drive down the price of housing in far-flung suburbs and put an additional premium on homes that are close in or with access to public transit systems. . . . If energy prices continue their upward climb homeowners are going to be unable to afford the big homes they have been demanding for the last two decades."[9]

One of Cortright's most interesting findings was that the distance of the suburb from the central city mattered less than what sort of metropolitan area it was part of. When looking at the overall health of the regional housing market, metropolitan areas with more "vital" urban cores were found to have fared better in the housing downturn than those without ("vitality" was defined as a high spatial concentration of people with advanced educational levels within the core relative to the periphery). In other words, metropolitan areas where differences between the core and periphery are modest (like Phoenix and Las Vegas) experienced steeper declines in housing prices and greater foreclosure rates overall than those areas with defined centers and clear density gradients (like New York and Portland, Oregon).

None of this proves exactly how rising energy prices will affect the economies of high- versus low-metabolism cities. But it does suggest that the layout of metropolitan areas will begin to matter more as energy becomes more expensive. As John Norquist, president of the Congress on New Urbanism and former mayor of Milwaukee, told me, "If you look at the difference between Europe and the US in terms of energy consumption, it's almost all accounted for with human settlement pattern and the availability of transit. . . . We're completely in favor of energy efficient lightbulbs. Building materials, green building, using insulation appropriately, thermal windows—these things are all spreading and being used like crazy. But human settlement is the one big thing that could be done that would really change things—the one big thing that hasn't been popularly embraced."[10]

Places like Hearth and Home at Rio Vista pushed the outer limits on a certain type of settlement pattern. Maybe this settlement pattern is inherently unsustainable, or maybe we just built too much of it. Whatever the reason, there are lessons to be learned in those lonely, weed-choked streets.

PART 1
Why Cities Are Hungry

CHAPTER 1

The 68° City

I f you drive to Death Valley from the west, there's a good chance you'll pass by—and quickly speed through—an old, half-abandoned mining town called Trona. Its pervasive industrial odor of rotten eggs, the abundance of vacant properties, and signs of recreational arson make it a particularly uninviting locale. Even the leader of the Trona Pride Committee admitted, "Let's face it, the place can't get any worse."[1] But what really strikes you about Trona is that people can actually survive in such a harsh natural environment. With its alkaline desert soils, blazing desert winds, and heat described as a "blast furnace," it's not surprising that grass won't grow here. For this reason Trona has the claim to fame of being one of the only towns in the nation with a dirt-surfaced high school football field.

Another noteworthy fact about Trona is that it was one of the first towns in the country to be almost completely air-conditioned. According to a 1948 advertising brochure from the American Potash and Chemical Corporation, the company that owned the town, most of the community buildings, and all the single residential quarters had air-conditioning, an extraordinary rarity in those days, but a necessity in a locale where temperatures frequently soar into triple digits. The school building, constructed in 1941 and still standing, had such a state-of-

Bicycles parked outside a subway station in Copenhagen, Denmark.

(Photo by author)

the-art climate-control system that the *Saturday Evening Post* wrote a story about it, "Schoolhouse in the Inferno." With its modernist exterior, somewhere between art deco and fifties sci-fi, this building in the middle of nowhere boasted thick glass walls, central air-conditioning, evaporative cooling, refrigerated drinking fountains, and venetian blinds adjusted by light meters, making it one of the most advanced climate-controlled buildings in existence at the time.[2]

In fact, Trona was a harbinger of a monumental change that was about to sweep the entire American Sun Belt. As air-conditioning became more reliable and affordable, it stimulated a massive redistribution of population to hot weather climes, which in turn made air-conditioning one of the biggest sources of power demand in the nation. By 2000, one-fifth of the electricity consumed in the United States went to air-conditioning, an amount exceeding the total electricity consumption of India and Indonesia combined. How did this technology go from being an oddity found in desert outposts to one of the nation's primary determinants of energy consumption?[3]

"Dad can enjoy hot coffee; junior isn't restless; ironing is made pleasant for mom, and the poodle doesn't have to be clipped." So read a 1960 *Saturday Evening Post* article about the benefits of modern air-conditioning, which was just beginning to revolutionize lifestyles in hot climates.[4]

Before air-conditioning, summers in many parts of the country were intolerable. People adapted by wearing sun hats and white linen, taking cold baths, or summering in cooler climes. Even the nation's capitol was so hot and humid that during the summer most government functions shut down, making it seem to many like a ghost town. As the *National Review* columnist Jonah Goldberg observes, in pre-air-conditioning days "a congressman wouldn't be caught dead in Washington during July. Well, actually, they might be caught dead, because they wore all those clothes and were so fat that they might have died while trying to get out."[5] Problems with heat kept many industries from taking root in the Sun Belt. Bread grew mold quickly, items got stuck in vending machines, and industrial machinery overheated. It wasn't surprising that the South had been losing population nonstop since the Civil War.

If there was a watershed moment in the adoption of air-conditioning in the United States, it was probably the scorching summer of 1952. Previously, fewer than 1 percent of US homes had an air conditioner, no large New York hotels had it, and only a small number of apartment and office buildings were cooled. But in the crucible of a massive heat wave that summer, big changes were in the making. The editors of *House and Home* magazine sponsored a national conference on air-conditioning and devoted thirty pages of their inaugural issue to promoting it. They predicted that with dropping prices and increasing reliability, the technology was due for a huge boom. Time proved them right. Even though overall rates of air conditioner ownership were still low in 1952, that summer there was a run on national supplies, with sales of nearly four hundred thousand window units. In fact, when the presidential candidates Dwight Eisenhower and Robert Taft went to Chicago for the Republican National Convention, representatives of the Carrier Corporation had to search high and low to obtain window units for the party's quarters; the Democratic candidates, whose convention was a few weeks later, weren't so lucky. (Perhaps Adlai Stevenson would have ended up president had the air-conditioning tables been turned.) Central air-conditioning was also gaining traction. A 1952 poll indicated that almost no home builders planned to include central air. The next year, 40 percent said they would.[6]

The growth in air-conditioning was complemented by an explosion in other energy-intensive cooling technologies. One was air-conditioning for the automobile. To avoid being parboiled in a car on hot summer days was something of an art form in the pre-air-conditioning days. A 1953 *New York Times* article about tips for driving in desert heat suggests strategies as diverse as going shoeless, wearing cotton gloves ("The gloves . . . serve as insulation between the hot wheel and the hands, and are likely to give the driver a mental lift from the extra fillip they give to his appearance"), using woven straw seat pads, and putting masking tape on the roof to increase reflectance. Another technology without which life in hot regions would have been difficult was refrigeration. A 1935 Frigidaire advertisement, typical of the times, shows refrigeration as a key technology in conquering hot climates. In it, a blazing sun over a desert landscape of cacti and cow skulls is juxtaposed with a couple, each with sun hat in hand, happily ogling their new refrigerator. After describing the "scorching fires of heaven" and "mesquite burned to a crisp," the ad pointed out that the Frigidaire Super Freezer "provided an abundance of ice cubes . . . and swiftly froze desserts." The desert is truly whipped when making frozen desserts is that easy.[7]

The fastest growth in these technologies was in the South. By 1953, southern builders who had previously disparaged air-conditioning were seeing it as mandatory. Dick Hughes, a prominent builder and president of the National Association of Homebuilders, declared that in his state of Texas homes without full air-conditioning will be "as obsolete as a house today without a plug for an electric refrigerator." Hughes was right; over time the South became the showcase region for air-conditioning. In 1966, Texas became the first state to have more than half of its households air-conditioned, and by 1970 the rest of the South followed suit. By the mid-1970s almost all of the South's commercial facilities had the technology, including chicken coops, aircraft hangars, cattle barns, grain elevators, and even outdoor queuing areas at amusement parks. Air-conditioning became so culturally ingrained that supposedly some people would drive around in un-air-conditioned cars in stifling heat with the windows rolled up just so passersby would think they had air-conditioning. By 2005, 96 percent of southern households were air-conditioned, and nearly three quarters of those claimed to use it all summer long. The revolution was complete.[8]

In 1970, a *New York Times* editorial took note of the enormous demographic consequences of the air conditioner: "The census of 1970 was the census of the astronaut and the air-conditioner. . . . The humble air-conditioner has been a powerful influence in circulating people. . . . Its availability explains why increasing numbers of Americans find it

Fedders advertisement for air-conditioning, *Life*, 1957.
(Courtesy of Airwell-Fedders North America)

comfortable to live year around in the semitropical heat of Florida, southern Texas and southern California."[9]

As cooling technologies became widespread and one of the biggest barriers to living in hot climates was erased, there was a flood of population to the Sun Belt. In 1950, just before the revolution began, this region contained less than a third of the nation's population. By 2008, that number was closing in on half. During that time, hot and muggy Florida more than tripled its share of the national population, from 1.8 percent to 6 percent, and Clark County, Nevada (where Las Vegas is located), went from a measly 48,000 people to nearly 2 million! In fact, the Sun Belt is really the only part of the United States where significant growth is still occurring. The ten fastest growing cities for the first decade of the twenty-first century are all in the Sun Belt.

Perhaps no single city enjoyed a bigger boom as a result of cooling technology than Phoenix, today the fifth largest city in America, despite having temperatures that reach or exceed 100°F 110 days out of the year. In a 1961 interview, a prominent local banker was asked what accounted for the boom: "Two things—air conditioning and jet air travel. . . . Jet planes bring you quickly to what was once an isolated state. And modern air conditioning makes it possible for you to live through the summers. . . . Without modern air conditioning, this would still be a small state capital. Now I take my vacation in the spring or fall, because I like it here in summer. I awaken in my air-conditioned home in the morning. I take a dip in my swimming pool. I dress and get into my air-conditioned automobile, and drive to the air-conditioned garage in the basement of this building. I work in an air-conditioned office, eat in air-conditioned restaurant and perhaps go to an air-conditioned theater."[10]

Prior to the air-conditioning era, executives had exhibited interest in Phoenix, which seemed a prime location for new high-tech plants in emerging low-cost areas with strong quality-of-life factors. But Phoenix's heat was seen as enough of a drawback to greatly limit economic development. So, it wasn't surprising that the widespread adoption of air-conditioning correlated with an explosion in investment.

For instance, the manufacturing income of Phoenix increased from a modest $5 million per year in 1940 to more than $435 million in less than twenty-five years. As one of Motorola's vice presidents said in 1954, in justifying his company's move to that city, "Motorola management feels that refrigeration cooling in the plant and in the home is the complete solution to the Phoenix summer heat problem. . . . The occasional superheated periods are as easy to deal with as the short runs of subzero weather in the north. Refrigeration cooling in the home has transformed Phoenix into a year-round city of delightful living."[11]

Far from the Sun Belt and its humming banks of central air units, I zip up my fleece and adjust the legs on my long underwear as I make the morning rounds of the various heating devices that keep my northern Vermont home from becoming an igloo in winter. First I turn up the thermostat on my oil-driven baseboard heaters. Then I hit the "on" button for the propane heater in the room that's not on the baseboard system. Then, in true Vermont fashion, I go outside and grab some firewood and kindling to load into the wood stove. Twenty minutes later the fans on the stove kick on, and we're soon basking in 70° heat, which feels tropical relative to the outside temperature of -20°. I pour a steaming hot beverage and slowly thaw my extremities.

As I sit in my kitchen I wonder about the energy required to keep our family comfortable in winter. The common perception is that cold and northerly places like Vermont consume far more energy for household climate control than do their southerly neighbors. But given the electrical burden of cooling all those sprawling Sun Belt cities, is that still true? In pre-air-conditioning days, when the typical Floridian or Texan didn't use a lot of energy on climate control, such a comparison would inevitably show northerners using far more energy. But today, with the total surrender of hot regions to air-conditioning and the redistribution of population that followed, the calculus is no longer as simple. Far northern climates still use very large amounts of energy per capita to keep warm, but increasingly the differential in total energy for heating and cooling is shrinking.

One would think that figuring out energy use for heating and cooling homes in different regions would be relatively straightforward. But in reality it's maddeningly elusive. Two indicators are frequently used for this purpose: heating degree days (HDDs) and cooling degree days (CDDs). A heating degree day is an index that reflects the demand for energy to heat a home; it is calculated by taking the average temperature for a given day and, if it is lower than the "optimal" indoor temperature of 65°, subtracting it from 65. If, for example, the temperature averages 45° on a given day, then the HDD for that day is 20. In other words, it's an index that combines the amount of time for which heating is needed and the intensity of the heating required. Different parts of the country can then be compared by adding up HDDs for each day to get the yearly number. Cooling degree days work the same, except that that index looks at temperatures higher than 65°.

My chilly state of Vermont had a population-weighted average of 7,723 HDDs during the July–June cycle of 2007–8, as compared to 5,536 for Pennsylvania, 3,957 for Virginia, 1,974 for Arizona, 1,760 for Texas, and 540 for Florida. Only seven states in the lower forty-eight had more HDDs than Vermont for that year, with North Dakota topping the list at 9,551. Of course, even these high numbers are still a far cry from the untouchable 20,370 of Barrow, Alaska. Vermont, however, and other Frost Belt states make up for this addiction to heat somewhat with their relative lack of cooling degree days. Vermont has a paltry 279 CDDs, compared to 1,106 for Virginia, 2,701 for Texas, and a whopping 3,406 for Florida. This means that once it gets warm enough to turn off the heat—say, in early May for my part of Vermont—there is only a relatively minor need for any mechanical climate control until October.[12]

Summing CDDs and HDDs is one of the most commonly used approaches for predicting how expected energy demand for climate control varies by geographic region. The Residential Energy Demand Temperature Index of the National Oceanographic and Atmospheric Administration (NOAA), for instance, is based on CDDs and HDDs, weighted by population. Historically, there is some validity to this—

research has found an extremely tight correlation between HDDs and energy use. Because there tend to be far more HDDs in the Frost Belt than there are CDDs in the Sun Belt, it is frequently assumed that cities in the former implicitly require far more energy for climate control than those in the latter. Data from the US Energy Information Agency's Residential Energy Consumption Survey largely back this up. For example, whereas the typical New England home in their survey spends about $2,400 per year combined on heating and cooling, that number is around $1,750 for the South and only $1,400 for the Pacific West.[13]

But just because the average Frost Belt home currently uses more climate control energy than the average Sun Belt home doesn't mean that the Frost Belt is necessarily more vulnerable to rising energy prices than the Sun Belt. In fact, there are a number of reasons why Sun Belt residents could find themselves paying more than Frost Belt residents in the future to stay comfortable in their homes.

One reason has to do with a phenomenon known as passive heating. Buildings essentially get "free" heating from direct sunlight when the skies are clear, a principle that has been used to warm structures throughout history. The amount of passive heating depends on building design features, like the proportion and area of windows facing south (or windows facing north in the Southern Hemisphere), the color and material properties of absorptive surfaces in and near the sunlight's path, and the circulation of air in a house. Many house designs have good "solar gain" just by accident, while others are consciously designed to maximize passive solar heating. As a society, we're generally not accustomed to passive designs because cheap heating fuels have largely negated their relevance. But a recent rekindling of interest in these designs shows that they can be both effective and economical. Studies in Europe have found that passive houses can be so effective that they use 90 percent less heating energy than a conventional home. In the United States, the added cost of passive designs may increase construction costs by 10 to 15 percent, while in Europe, where passive houses are far more common and needed building materials are far easier to come by, that cost premium is now below 5 percent.[14]

Although passive house designs can reduce the cooling energy burden somewhat as well, their ability to substitute for air-conditioning is minimal compared to their ability to substitute for heat. A passive house can "harvest" the sun's energy to make warmth when it is cold outside, but it cannot create cold air when the weather is warm. In climates where night temperatures drop sharply, passive designs can at least harvest the cool night air and keep it trapped inside during the day as much as possible. But most of the Sun Belt doesn't get cool enough at night during the hot season for this strategy to be effective, and, more important, passive designs don't deal with the humidity that so often accompanies heat. Getting rid of that humidity is essential not only to keeping people comfortable (humidity is a component of "heat index") but also to keeping interiors from developing rot and mold. And doing so requires lots of energy—generally in the form of air-conditioning. Furthermore, typical modern home designs in the Sun Belt tend to be antithetical to passive principles. Before the advent of mass construction, houses in this region were often designed with features like high ceilings, large windows for ventilation, and verandas for shade, but by the 1950s demand was insatiable for "sealed homes," which were essentially unlivable without centralized mechanical air.[15]

That there are so few bona fide passive houses in the United States might suggest that passive heating is and will continue to be insignificant in offsetting energy burdens. But just because a home is not officially designated as passive does not mean it incorporates no elements of passive design. In fact, a large and growing number of homes do incorporate elements like good southern exposure and absorptive surfaces, which means that, although they still require internal heat sources, they're getting at least some "free heat." For this reason, HDDs may overestimate heating energy, and that overestimation will only increase as passive design elements become more commonplace in Frost Belt construction—a trend that is certain to accelerate as volume brings down the price of materials and rising energy costs shrink payback periods. While adoption of passive designs in the Sun Belt might also create a growing differential between CDDs and actual energy use for air-conditioning, that effect is likely to be considerably less because of physics.

Global warming is another reason why the costs of climate control may tip in favor of the Frost Belt. If average temperatures continue to rise throughout the continental United States, the not-so-unexpected result would be that cooling burdens will become even higher in the Sun Belt, while northern areas would experience reduced heating loads. However, Frost Belt cities could also find themselves with significantly higher air-conditioning bills. For instance, it's been estimated that by 2080, New York City could have a climate like that of Raleigh, North Carolina, with far longer summers and many more heat waves. So, making a blanket statement about whether climate change would favor the Frost Belt or Sun Belt is very difficult. Still, there are projections available. A 2006 study predicted that under scenarios for both high- and low-temperature increases, net energy use for climate control would actually be reduced (that is, reductions in heating would outweigh increases in cooling) for the Northeast, the Middle Atlantic, and the East North Central portions of the country. For the West North Central portion of the country, the outcome depended on the scenario, while for the remainder of the country (the Southeast, Southwest, Mountain, and Pacific regions), both warming scenarios would result in net increases in energy use for climate control. In other words, the Frost Belt would see total energy bills for climate control go down, and the Sun Belt would see them go up.[16]

The effect of global warming will likely be exacerbated by the so-called urban heat island effect: it has been shown that urban landscapes tend to be hotter than surrounding vegetated areas, which means that as urbanization increases, so too does the need for cooling relative to heating, an effect that also favors the Frost Belt over the Sun Belt. The difference between urban and rural landscapes has been documented to be between 2° and 6°F for daytime temperatures, depending on the location, size, and pattern of the urbanized area. Nighttime differences (when conditions are calm and clear) can be as much as 22°F. The larger the city, the greater the effect. The heat island effect stems from a number of physical factors. In vegetated landscapes, solar radiation is absorbed and water vapor is released, which results in evaporative cooling. In cities, impervious surfaces have little moisture to release and so there is less evaporative cooling; waste heat from buildings and transportation serves as a giant space heater; and highly absorptive surfaces like tar, asphalt, brick, and roof shingles concentrate solar energy through conduction.[17]

For larger cities, peak utility loads are estimated to increase by 1.2 to 2.2 percent for every increase of 1°F due to the urban heat island effect. A city with a middle-of-the-road 4.5°F heat island effect could therefore have a 10 percent increase in its demand for electricity.[18] As development encroaches on formerly vegetated land, as it is predicted to do, the urban heat island effect will only get more pronounced and will likely compound the effects of global climate change. While this will affect both the Sun Belt and Frost Belt, the effects will likely be disproportionately felt in the Sun Belt, not only because of the greater amount of solar radiation in those lower latitude areas but also because heat islands provide an unexpected benefit by heating up cities slightly in winter, which is of far greater benefit to Frost Belt cities.

Perhaps the biggest reason why the Sun Belt is likely to be more vulnerable to rising climate control costs, however, is the way that heating and air-conditioning are produced from primary fuels. Over 95 percent of air-conditioners in the United States are powered by electricity (natural gas-powered air conditioners exist but are rare due to their fixed costs). Heating devices, on the other hand, work from a variety of sources— for example, cord wood, wood pellets, natural gas, or fuel oil—all of which are combusted on site in a stove or a furnace (electric heat accounts for only about 4 percent of the energy generated by heating devices).

Electricity is most frequently generated from fuels like natural gas, oil, and coal in big, centralized steam-driven power plants. This process involves a great deal of waste; much of the potential energy in fuels is lost as waste heat up the smokestack during the generation process, and once the electricity is produced, some is lost in transmission. The

Energy Information Agency uses a conservative estimate of 33 percent "generation efficiency" for steam-based power (which includes most plants fired by fossil fuels). In other words, it takes an amount of fuel equivalent to three units of energy to provide one unit of energy of usable electricity. Two out of three BTUs (British Thermal Units, a standardized unit of energy equal to the amount of energy required to increase the temperature of one pound of water by 1°F) are lost either as waste heat during combustion or in the transmission process.

By contrast, the fuel utilization efficiency, or ratio of heat output to energy consumed, is quite high for on-site heating furnaces. Oil and gas furnaces, among the most common types of household heating devices, lose only a small amount of their generated heat through the exhaust. The US Department of Energy established guidelines in 1992 that required all furnaces to be at least 78 percent efficient, and in fact many furnaces function as high as 97 percent. Every year, the efficiency of the average furnace goes up.

If we ignore efficiency loss from power plants, warm-weather regions have a big edge over cold in terms of BTUs consumed. The typical northeastern house uses slightly more than twice the BTUs in fuel for combined heating and cooling than the typical southeastern home, and the typical New York State home uses more than three times the BTUs of a Florida home. But if we account for all the energy that goes into *producing* electricity (as well as the much smaller efficiency loss for furnaces), the picture changes dramatically. Using the Energy Information Administration's conservative 33 percent average efficiency rate for fossil fuel–based electricity generation and a 90 percent average efficiency for heating furnaces, the differentials shrink significantly; in this case the typical northeastern home uses only 39 percent more BTUs than the typical southern home, and the typical New York State home uses only 23 percent more than a Texas home. If we then tweak those efficiency factors to account for regional differences in generation, the differentials are narrowed even further. Areas that disproportionately rely on older coal-fired plants for electricity, like the Ohio Valley and parts of the South, have slightly lower average efficiencies.

So, for instance, if we compare New York to Texas but account for the latter's estimated, lower-than-average 30 percent electricity generation efficiency, the difference between them in BTUs consumed shrinks to just 13 percent.[19] Furthermore, generation efficiency measures are based on a fairly circumscribed analysis. Those percentages can get even lower if you start expanding the system boundaries to include energy needed for things like maintaining and repairing a plant, transporting fuel, conducting environmental cleanup, and fighting foreign wars to secure energy sources. How much these factors bring down the actual generation efficiency number depends on the specifics of the situation and what is included, but these corollary costs illustrate just how big the gap is between usable energy and fuel consumed in producing electricity.

This problem of low electrical generation efficiency could become significant for the Sun Belt as fuel prices increase. The incremental cost of cooling will go up disproportionately relative to the cost of heating because those two units of fuel that go wasted up the smokestack for every one utilized will get ever more expensive, assuming continued reliance on fossil fuels for electrical generation. That is, fuel-driven increases in the price of climate control could be three times greater for cooling than for heating.

Whether in the Frost Belt or Sun Belt, cities of all latitudes need to start making a lot of strategic investments to reduce their vulnerability to increased heating and cooling costs. One of the simplest things that can be done is fighting the urban heat island effect. Just as homeowners can retrofit their homes with a passive design, revegetation, tree planting, "green roofs" (that is, roofs planted with vegetation), and light-colored surfaces have all been found to yield significant reductions in the heat island effect and to lower peak energy loads associated with air-conditioning. For instance, it's been estimated that using reflective roofs in major metropolitan areas could bring down cooling use for residential and commercial buildings by 3 percent nationally—roughly the equivalent of fourteen half-gigawatt power plants. Shade trees are particularly useful because they not only intercept sunlight before it can warm a surface but also cool the air through evapotranspiration (the combined effect of evaporation and plant transpiration of water). For Northern California houses, shade trees were found to result in a 30 percent savings in cooling energy. In hotter cities like Houston, Los Angeles, and Phoenix, shade trees can yield between fifteen and thirty-five dollars in savings per thousand square feet of roof space. Trees also have the added advantage of intercepting winds in the winter to keep buildings warmer. Because of this, the energy savings per tree for combined heating and cooling can be as high as two hundred dollars.[20]

One of the leaders in studying this linkage is New York City's Regional Heat Island Initiative, part of the New York State Energy Research and Development Authority. They conducted extensive research which found that conversion of open grassy spaces to trees, street tree planting, installation of green roofs, and making impervious surfaces lighter colors all have significant effects on locally reducing the urban heat island effect. The last three of these were found to be most effective in moderating temperature. Models indicated that if all three were implemented for 50 percent of New York City, peak temperatures could be reduced by 1.2°F, in turn reducing peak electrical demand by 1.6 percent, for a savings of 170 megawatts. Of all these strategies, street trees were found to have the greatest impact per unit area. Every $13 million spent on trees was found to reduce peak power use by a megawatt. Further, trees yield lots of other benefits, like increased property values and uptake of pollutants.[21]

Utilities also need to adapt. They should invest in high-efficiency facilities for power generation, moving away from inefficient coal and oil, adopting waste-reduction technologies like co-generation (where waste heat from the power plant is used for a secondary purpose such as district heating or cooling), or installing more renewable power-generation capacity that, although low in terms of efficiency, does not rely on fossil fuels. Additionally, builders and property owners should move back toward gas-powered air-conditioning (the dominant form of cooling prior to the 1950s), which results in far more cooling for every unit of fuel consumed, keeping down operating costs.

Sun Belt cities should also tap their greatest resource: sunshine. They could learn a thing or two in this respect from a desert city whose temperatures make even a summer in Phoenix seem balmy. The United Arab Emirates contain some of the world's most brutally hot deserts, with summer temperatures regularly over 120°F. So, it's not surprising that this tiny nation has the highest per capita carbon footprint in the world, with 50 to 60 percent of its electricity consumption going to cooling. A few miles outside of the capital of Abu Dhabi, however, a new city is rising out the desert that is intended to counteract this trend.

Masdar City will cost over $16 billion and will be home to more than fifty thousand people when finished. It is also hoped that it will be one of the greenest cities in the world. Its builders plan to generate all needed energy from the sun, including concentrated solar power (systems that use lenses or mirrors to concentrate solar radiation and generate electricity, often through use of a steam turbine, and hot water) and solar photovoltaic cells (which generate electricity by converting sunlight into direct electrical current using semiconductors). They plan to harvest enough solar energy to power the entire city and still have a little left over to sell back to the electric grid. That means all energy needed for air-conditioning will, ironically, come from the source of all that heat. Although such cooling will require an enormous amount of very costly solar generation capacity, efficiency will be high, because the entire city will be on a centralized district cooling system (no individual air conditioners will be allowed), which has been found to result in savings of between 40 and 60 percent in energy use relative to conventional cooling. Masdar's centralized system will work by combining very large-scale efficiency-enhancing mechanical systems that could not be feasibly deployed on a smaller scale. These include a dehumidification system that captures water vapor in the air and collects it for recycling in the cooling process; an electrical chiller that compresses and evaporates a refrigerant; and an industrial-scale absorption chiller that, counterintuitively, uses solar-generated and potentially geothermally generated hot water to cool air (it does so because when hot water is compressed, it can drive a compression-evaporation cycle, and the process of evaporation results in cooling). Of course there is also a demand side to this equation. By centrally coordinating the construction of all buildings, energy efficiency can be kept high through measures like insulation, demand-controlled ventilation, radiant cooling, programmable thermostats, and structural piles that exchange energy with the soil. As a result, the proportion of electricity that a Masdar City household would use on cooling would be about half that of a conventional Emirates home.[22]

Clearly these are very expensive investments. But if fuel prices are to go considerably higher, the business-as-usual scenario of using conventional air-conditioning technology with fossil fuel–generated electricity to cool the Sun Belt could prove to be far more costly. Efficient technology is not currently in place there on any significant scale, because energy is still relatively inexpensive. But that's going to change—it's just a question of when. The problem is that no one is planning for the possibility that energy prices might rise faster than solar farms or district cooling infrastructure can be built. Given how long this type of construction takes and how quickly energy prices can rise, it would seem prudent for America's Sun Belt states to invest a little in the resource that gave them their name in the first place.

There's an urban legend among political conservatives that the Founders purposely located the nation's permanent capital in the hot and muggy site of Washington, D.C., to keep government small. The columnist Jonah Goldberg suggests that the installation of air-conditioning in the capitol in 1928 perfectly correlates with the rise of "big government." Perhaps, he muses, banning air-conditioning in the District would bring back the days of small and restrained government.[23]

Whether or not air-conditioning can actually take credit for such momentous changes in our government, this seemingly innocuous invention is certainly responsible for a paradigm shift in where Americans live and how they use energy. With the widespread adoption of air-conditioning, the nation experienced the largest and most sudden geographic redistribution of population in its history. In the process, warm-weather regions were forever changed and made dependent on this technology. As the historian Raymond Arsenault wrote of air-conditioning in the South: "General Electric has proved a more devastating invader than General Sherman."[24]

A few days before writing this I was in a suburb of Phoenix for a conference and decided to take a walk. The fact that it was December and the sunlight was still blazing hot made it clear just how much energy is needed to keep this and other Sun Belt megacities from overheating in the more challenging summer months. Cooling technology came of age in an era when energy was incredibly cheap. In fact, the cost of cooling was so cheap that many prominent architects at the time believed that soon whole streets and even downtown districts would be air-conditioned using giant tents.[25] But with energy prices what they are today, we're no longer talking about air-conditioning Main Street. So what will happen if energy becomes even more expensive? There are plenty of ways we can adapt. First, people will probably put up with less comfortable indoor temperatures, we'll perspire more in summer, and in winter we'll wear that ugly cable-knit sweater with the reindeer more often. We'll also have to increase the efficiency of our heating and cooling devices, our homes, and our electrical generation facilities. And increasingly we'll need to tie heating and cooling to distributed and renewable power generation. If we look at the first word in "Sun Belt," for instance, it already suggests a potential winning combination; sunny places need more cooling, but they also are the best sites for solar energy. Creating incentives today to get small-scale solar installations into individual residential and commercial buildings that need to be cooled throughout the Sun Belt will not only serve to hedge their requirement for electrical cooling against the risk of energy scarcity and rising average temperatures, but it will also make hot regions more energy independent overall. Sun Belt cities will very likely adopt such changes, but will they do so quickly enough? If not, while it's unlikely that Tampa will end up looking like Trona, the economy of the Sun Belt might some day look slightly more like today's Rust Belt.

The Big Picture on Rising Energy Prices

IN 2008, A HUMMING GLOBAL economy led oil prices to reach a record of nearly $150 a barrel, translating into more than $4 per gallon at the pump. The subsequent recession brought prices back down to earth, and many analysts wrote off the price spike to a speculative blip. But the fact that prices are returning to near-2008 levels as this is being written in 2011 suggests that the fundamental supply constraints that first led to this price increase have not changed. As Jeff Rubin, the former chief economist for CIBC World Markets, writes: "Once the dust settles from the various crises rocking financial markets, we are looking at the same basic demand-supply imbalance that we were looking at before the recession began. . . . Other than lulling us into an unjustified sense of optimism about the future direction of oil prices, a global recession will do absolutely nothing about the unavoidable fact that oil production is nearing a plateau while oil consumption around the world is still rising."[1]

This was once considered a fringe view of energy economics. Today, these concerns are increasingly mainstream. Joining a growing chorus of foreign governments, the United States Military—perhaps the least "fringe" organization imaginable—released a report in mid-2010 warning that by 2012, surplus oil production could entirely disappear, and by 2015 there could significant shortfalls. According to the report, "The discovery rate for new petroleum and gas fields over the past two decades . . . provides little reason for optimism that future efforts will find major new fields." The CEO of Royal Dutch Shell, Jeroen van der Veer, expressed a similar view when he recently stated that "the economy will turn, demand will come back and the overcapacity of supply will disappear. The oil and gas industry cannot supply all this

32

additional demand. . . . This means the next price spike is in the making." And Nobuo Tanaka, executive director of the generally optimistic International Energy Agency, warned in April 2011 that "the age of cheap energy is over."[2]

Many write off these worries because there is still a vast quantity of fossil fuels left in the ground. But depletion is a red herring. What matters is whether the rate of extraction can keep up with demand. Even if demand were to remain flat, which is unlikely in the long term given the rate at which countries like India and China are industrializing and adopting the use of automobiles, our ability to get fossil fuels out of the ground is increasingly constrained. As I discuss in the next three interlude sections of the book, the easily accessible sources of our most valuable fossil fuels—oil and gas—are increasingly being used up. What's left are smaller and more technically challenging deposits. As each successive deposit gets harder to recover, it takes increasing energy to retrieve the same amount of fossil fuel, even with advances in technology. At the first big gusher in the United States, in Spindletop, Texas, discovered in 1901, oil was found just a thousand feet underground and was under such intense pressure that it spewed out 100,000 barrels per day at first and took 9 days to contain. Today's most promising new find, on the other hand, the Tupi field, with an estimated 14 billion barrels, lies 155 miles off the coast of Brazil, beneath as much as 9,000 feet of water, 10,000 feet of rock, and 6,600 feet of salt. Petrobras, Brazil's state oil company, estimates that after about 3 to 4 years of development from initial discovery (around 2010 or 2011), the Tupi field will be pumping 100,000 barrels per day, the same as Spindletop yielded the instant oil was struck.[3] So as each field is depleted, the next discovery gets harder to recover, and technology can do only so much to overcome this, because getting energy requires using energy.

Adding to the supply constraints on fossil fuels is the strong possibility that new greenhouse gas regulations will further raise the cost of using them by imposing either caps with tradable permits or taxes for fossil fuels. The European Union already regulates ten thousand sources of greenhouse gas emission under a cap-and-trade system.

California's Global Warming Solutions Act (AB 32) may implement a cap and trade system as early as 2012, if it's not overturned. The Regional Greenhouse Gas Initiative (RGGI) imposes a cap-and-trade system for CO_2 emissions from power plants in ten northeastern states. And in 2009, the United States House of Representatives passed the Waxman-Markey Bill, which proposed a type of cap-and-trade system. While this bill never made it past the Senate, it's expected that some kind of climate legislation will eventually pass in the next few years and that it will raise the cost of using fossil fuels.

Alternative sources of energy will increase in importance as fossil fuels become more expensive, but as the last three interlude sections of this book describe, none is as easy or inexpensive to harness, transport, and use as fossil fuels. Each alternative energy source has big barriers to major adoption that fossil fuels do not have, which explains why nearly our entire energy infrastructure is based on fossil fuels. Wind and solar energy are diffuse, intermittent, and material-intensive and have transmission and reliability problems. Because wind turbines produce only when the wind is blowing and solar panels only when the sun is shining, lots of additional capacity has to be built to accommodate their unpredictability, which significantly raises their price. This also puts an effective cap on what percentage of our energy portfolio they could account for. Nuclear is constrained by the supply of uranium and by the expense and danger of dealing with its waste. Biofuels are limited by how much land can be planted in energy crops, the huge energy input that is needed to produce them, and, at least for ethanol, the increase in food prices as each acre planted for this purpose displaces food crops.

The magnitude of effort needed to shift the world to alternative sources of energy is monumental. If we tried to replace all fossil fuels with nuclear energy, over ten thousand of the largest nuclear reactors would have to be built, and at that rate the world's uranium supplies would dwindle quickly. If that replacement was wind power, building a million one-megawatt wind turbines would still generate only 12 percent of the world's power.[4]

CHAPTER 2

The Very Thirsty City

"Under no contingency does the natural face of Upper California appear susceptible of supporting a very large population: the country is hilly and mountainous; great dryness prevails during the summers, and occasionally excessive droughts parch up the soil for periods of 12 or 18 months. Only in the plains and valleys where streams are to be found, and even those will have to be watered by artificial irrigation, does there seem the hope of being sufficient tillable land to repay the husbandman and afford subsistence to inhabitants."[1] So wrote Navy lieutenant Henry Augustus Wise, after spending considerable time in the Golden State in 1847.

Although Lieutenant Wise would no doubt be surprised to know that California today is now home to almost 40 million people, the fundamental water constraints that he wrote about still exist. As Los Angeles County Supervisor Zev Yaroslavsky told me, "Water is probably the single most vexing issue that we have in . . . places like Southern California, because it's in such short supply. Water is a more valuable commodity in some respects than oil, or it will be over time."[2]

The Los Angeles metropolitan area couldn't support a fraction of its current population without imported water, which today accounts for nearly three quarters of its supply. Water distribution and treatment alone currently account for about 18 percent of all energy consumed in

The Los Angeles Aqueduct. (Photo by author)

the Los Angeles region, making it the silent energy hog, rarely seen, poorly understood, and always on the verge of crisis.

Throughout the nineteenth century, settlement in California flourished as a result of gravity-fed irrigation. By the time the Los Angeles Aqueduct was completed in 1913, all the gravity-fed supply areas had been exploited. Southern California water planners then started looking farther afield, at inter-basin transfer routes that would require uphill pumping. The first of these was the Colorado River Aqueduct, built in 1933, which carried California's allotment of that river's bounty across 240 miles of scorching desert. But by far the most energy-hungry water project in the state—and among the most energy-intensive pieces of infrastructure in the world—was the last of these aqueducts: the California State Water Project (SWP). To appreciate why it needs so much energy requires a brief lesson in California's geography.

Long before Hollywood Boulevard had its sidewalk stars or 90210 was a ZIP code, the area that was to become the Los Angeles Basin experienced some inconvenient geologic activity. A set of tectonic interactions between the Pacific and North American Plates—complicated by a sharp left turn taken by the San Andreas Fault—compressed and heaved up a large chunk of the Earth's crust, forming one of California's only east-west oriented mountain ranges. This beautiful and unique topography was to have significant consequences for the region's energy footprint.

Known to geologists as the Transverse Range, the mountains form a nearly two-hundred-mile-long barrier. The range has its merits: it shelters Los Angeles from the surrounding desert and has provided a low-cost television and film setting for such places as Africa, New Hampshire, and Hazzard County, Georgia. But this barrier also separates Los Angeles from the part of the state where all the reliable water is located—the western drainage of the Sierra Nevada Mountains. Vast quantities of water—most of it in the form of snowmelt—flows from these mountains into California's Central Valley, the southern half of which is known as the San Joaquin Valley. At the southern end of this valley, a bowl is formed where the Transverse Range meets the Sierra

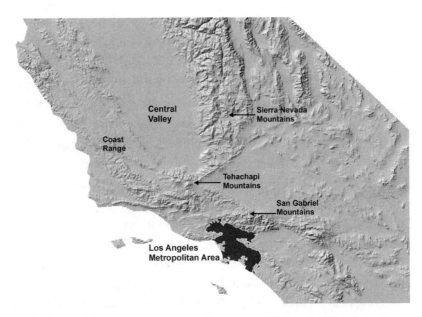

Relief map of the mountain ranges of Southern California. (Map by author, based on digital elevation data from the US Geological Survey)

Nevadas and the Coast Range, the north-south chain forming the western barrier of the Central Valley. The small segment of the Transverse Range that forms the bottom end of the valley, known as the Tehachapi Mountains, presents an unavoidable barrier between Los Angeles and the Sierra Nevada's ample west-side runoff.

The steepness and elevation of the walls of this bowl, combined with the existence of two major underlying faults—the Garlock and the San Andreas—make the Tehachapi Mountains a great place to mountain bike, but a challenging barrier across which to deliver water. Los Angeles, however, didn't have much choice. Drawing water across this barrier using a system of gravity-fed siphons, as with the Los Angeles Aqueduct, would be impossible. The grades are too steep for pipes to sit aboveground and still be fed by the gravity-powered action of siphons. Tunneling, which would have allowed gravity-powered siphons to function, is geologically infeasible because an earthquake on one of these highly active faults could easily crush miles of tunnel under thousands of feet of earth and close the aqueduct for years, or even permanently. The only alternative was to use energy—and gigantic amounts of it—to pump a river-sized aqueduct uphill over this mountain range. The opportunity to build this behemoth came with the initiation of the SWP, begun in the late 1950s. The resulting infrastructure, known as the California Aqueduct, would be not only the most massive infrastructural project in the state's history but also its largest user of energy.

The 444-mile California Aqueduct works by pumping water uphill and then letting it flow downhill by gravity. It begins near sea level, where water is pumped from the Sacramento River Delta, near San Francisco. The water first makes a long and gradual climb to the southern terminus of the Central Valley, at the base of the Tehachapi Mountains. In the course of this 278-mile section, 6 major pumping stations lift the water from sea level to an elevation of about 1,300 feet, using in an average year about the amount of electricity that over half a million typical California households use—more than the number in San Francisco and Oakland combined. Once the water reaches the mountains, the massive Edmonston pumping plant gives the final push, lifting the water up its last ascent of 1,926 vertical feet over the Tehachapi Mountains using 9 gigantic pumps. After this final boost, the liquid can leisurely course downslope, toward faucets, fountains, and swimming pools. Edmonston's pumps, each the height of a five-story building, consume in aggregate as much electricity as nearly three quarters of a million California households, making the plant among the highest single users of energy in the world. The plant can pump an acre-foot of water (that is, one acre of water, one foot deep, or enough to supply between one and three households for a year) in under ten seconds, but to do so requires about the equivalent of the energy in three 55-gallon drums of fuel. In total, to get from the Sacramento River to the crest of the Tehachapi Mountains, one year's worth of water requires just slightly less electricity than the combined amount used by all residences in the city of Los Angeles. Some of this electricity is recovered by turbines that capture the energy of the downward flow of the water after it has been pumped up. But the amount generated as a direct result of hydroelectric recovery is only a quarter of the total amount expended.[3]

In arid regions, here's the big tradeoff: needed water is far away and heavy, and transporting heavy things against gravity means using energy. Add in high mountains, and the energy costs get even worse. According to Gary Klein, a retired water-energy expert formerly of the California Energy Commission, every thousand feet that a megagallon (that's a million gallons) has to be pumped uphill requires about the same amount of energy as that used by a California household in six months. It's for this reason that Southern California uses more than three times as much energy as Northern California in getting a gallon of water from source to tap. It's also for this reason that for the typical Southern California home, water delivery is the third biggest energy user after air-conditioning and refrigeration.[4]

By choosing to grow beyond the limits allowable by a purely gravity-fed water system, the Los Angeles area bound its fate to the price of energy. When energy is expensive, water becomes expensive. The economics of water are so sensitive to the price of electricity that during the California Energy Crisis of 2000–2001, the spike in pumping-cost rates amounted to nearly five hundred thousand dollars more per peak hour for the California Aqueduct. Demand for water in the Los Angeles region currently outstrips supply by about half the volume that Edmonston pumps in a year—an imbalance that has had to be made up with conservation measures. And although demand is expected to increase significantly, the supply of water isn't getting any larger. In fact, it's likely to shrink as the impacts of global climate change worsen.[5]

Any attempt to address this problem through increased supply will be extremely energy intensive: either water must be imported from even farther away (e.g., Oregon or Washington), requiring even more pumps, or undrinkable water must be turned into drinkable water. One such approach is desalination, whereby seawater is turned into freshwater. While this approach is popular in the Persian Gulf states, it is massively energy hungry. Desalination requires even more energy than pumping that same amount of water over the Tehachapis. Using the latest technology, making one acre-foot of saltwater drinkable consumes roughly as much electricity as one California household uses in four months. And because the laws of physics impose theoretical limitations on the energy efficiency of desalination, which the most advanced plants today are quickly approaching, room for future efficiency gains is modest. It is therefore not surprising that even the most ambitious desalination plans for California would account for only 6 percent of the state's freshwater supply.[6] Another energy-hungry approach is wastewater recycling, referred to derisively by its detractors as "toilet to tap." In fact, in mid-2008 Los Angeles started drafting a plan for a $2 billion water program, a central piece of which was to increase wastewater recycling sixfold. Needless to say, drinking former sewage water tends not to be very popular with consumers.

Although engineered solutions are being discussed, there's increasing recognition that such drastic approaches might not be needed if people simply used less. And there is some good news in this respect: in the past thirty years, water use in the City of Los Angeles has remained roughly constant, despite an increase in population of nearly a million people.[7] As described in Chapter 6, a combination of restrictions on lawn watering, voluntary measures like low-flow showerheads and low-flush toilets, and more aggressive pricing has significantly reduced per capita water consumption, saving massive amounts of energy in the process.

While Los Angeles County has made big strides in reducing its average household water use to 168 gallons per day (GPD), it's still only in the middle of the pack for western cities, somewhere between the laggards (such as Las Vegas, Tempe, and Salt Lake City, at 230, 211, and 193 GPD, respectively), and the trendsetters (Tucson, Phoenix, and El Paso, at 107, 142, and 122 GPD, respectively). Of course, even the best-performing American cities are put to shame when consumption is compared to the German household's frugal average of 70 GPD, about as much as a typical American's Slip'n Slide consumes in a few hours.[8]

In the complex world of Southern California water, much has changed, and over time there is little doubt that efficiency will increase. But while politicians and utility managers continue to struggle over what to do, down a lonely service road at the base of the Transverse Range, a river in a pipe will continue to flow uphill.

A few hundred miles away, the main aqueduct of the Central Arizona Project (CAP), the country's largest and most expensive water-delivery system, wends its lonely way through the blazing hot Arizona desert toward millions of homes, vast agricultural fields, silicon-chip plants, and Phoenix's Wet 'n' Wild amusement park. This aqueduct makes an eastward turn from the Colorado River's Lake Havasu Reservoir not too far from the place where California's Colorado Aqueduct—one of the three to supply the Los Angeles Basin—makes its westward turn. Between these two thirsty aqueducts—providing irrigation for California's Imperial Valley farms and the municipal water system for Las Vegas—it's not surprising that by the time the Colorado River reaches its outlet in the Gulf of California, there's nothing left but a rivulet of toxic sludge.

In Arizona, water is such an emotional issue that at the end of a major drought in 1941, Governor Sidney Osborn declared April 26 a "Day of Thanksgiving for Water," complete with an all-day celebration including a chuck wagon lunch and dancing in the streets of Phoenix.[9] So it is not surprising that the history of the water supply for Arizona's two big cities—Phoenix and Tucson—is a roller coaster of alternating abundance and scarcity. Engineered water supplies are what allowed people to inhabit this region, going all the way back to the ancient Hohokam culture, which disappeared most likely due to drought several hundred years before Europeans ever came to the region. One limitation faced by the Hohokam was that their water supply traveled by gravity alone.

Gravity today has been overcome by pumping technology. But coordinating population growth and water supply in Arizona has proven to be far more difficult than lifting water uphill. As Tucson and

The Central Arizona Project Aqueduct in Phoenix, Arizona.
(Photo by author)

Phoenix grew, water-supply engineering and population chased each other in a cycle of increasing cost, dependency, and vulnerability. In this arid environment, water has always been the key limit to population growth, so as improved water-supply infrastructure allowed more reservoirs to be filled and groundwater to be pumped, immigration and urbanization were spurred on. But southern Arizona's climate is characterized by cycles of drought that are hard to predict; as population grows, a larger buffer is needed against that uncertainty. Whether the current buffer is sufficient remains to be seen. As Charlie Ester, the Water Resource Manager for Phoenix's Salt River Project, said to the *High Country News*, "If it does not rain every year, and reservoirs go dry, and there is nothing to pump, we're moving."[10]

The Central Arizona Project is without doubt the grand finale in this unfolding drama. Before it was built, Phoenix depended largely on impounded surface waters stored in large desert reservoirs, while Tucson, with its much smaller watershed, depended on pumping groundwater from its considerable underground aquifer. By the 1920s, despite similarities in the overall amount of municipal water, Phoenix's reservoir system contained three thousand times more water than did Tucson's. To meet demand, Tucson was pumping so much groundwater that by 1935 between 65 and 75 percent of city power use went to that purpose, and by the early 1940s, Tucson was removing groundwater at a rate faster than it could be recharged, leading to a lowering of the water table that would continue for decades.[11] Although construction of aboveground storage tanks did reduce pumping energy somewhat, in the long term this savings was at least partially offset as the water table grew lower, requiring more energy to pump water from greater depths.

By the early postwar years, following on the heels of the drought described above, it was clear that there was precious little wiggle room between demand and supply for both of these communities. On numerous occasions residents were asked to dramatically curtail water use. In one case in 1951, Phoenix supplies were so short that police patrols were dispatched to stop people from watering lawns or washing

Xeriscaping in the Phoenix suburbs. (Photo by author)

cars.[12] With all the "easy water" already appropriated in the region and groundwater levels decreasing substantially, it was becoming clear that a massive project on a scale that only the federal government could mount would be needed to bring in water from the Colorado River.

Authorized in 1968, begun in 1973, and completed to its final connection in Tucson in 1991, the Central Arizona Project would become the icon of Arizona water supply, as well as one of the defining symbols of western water excess. By the time it was finished it would be the largest and most expensive water-transfer project ever undertaken in the United States.[13] Thanks to this massive project, water falling as rain and snow in the distant Rockies as far north as Jackson, Wyoming, would now be finding its way to golf courses and swimming pools in Tucson and Phoenix. In exchange for the Central Arizona Project, Arizona communities were supposed to reduce their withdrawals of groundwater, to prevent the continual overdraft and depletion of the aquifers and the associated subsidence of soil. Associated with the Central Arizona Project was legislation that established a timetable for the gradual elimination of groundwater overdraft in designated areas.

The Central Arizona Project was supposed to permanently free southern Arizona from its chronic water woes. But, as with the California State Water Project, it has inadvertently tied the water supply to the price of energy. Also like the California project, Arizona's water is gravitationally challenged. Fourteen pumping stations are required to keep water moving along this 336-mile Crazy Straw, with its 3,000 feet of elevational lift. Roughly one quarter of the output of the massive coal-fired Navajo Generating Station in Page, Arizona, is used solely for this purpose.

In a year the Central Arizona Project's pumps use the same amount of electricity as is consumed by about 210,000 typical Arizona homes during that same period. Hence, the yearly water bill for the typical Phoenix household incorporates the cost of about 1,100 kilowatt hours of electricity for pumping its share (roughly two-thirds of an acre-foot) of water via the CAP. That's equal to all the electricity used by that household over the course of about five weeks, roughly $125. For every dollar paid in household water bills, about 42 cents go to energy costs.[14]

Rates such as these are an inconvenience at this point, but hardly crippling. According to Shaun McKinnon, a journalist for the *Arizona Republic* and an expert on Arizona water, this hasn't made much of an impact on water use, at least not in Phoenix. Residents there still use water copiously, and the typical household water bill is lower than in many eastern cities.[15]

But all this could change soon. The Central Arizona Project and the communities it supplies are highly vulnerable to future increases in energy prices right now. This vulnerability is even greater than that of thirsty Southern California, for several reasons. First, although the Central Arizona Project may use less power in aggregate than the California State Water Project, it uses more energy per capita, which means that the risk and uncertainty of energy price spikes in Arizona is spread over fewer rate payers.

Second, the California State Water Project is powered by a diversified and relatively sustainable portfolio of power-generation facilities, whereas the Central Arizona Project is dependent on a single power plant fueled by coal. California's project by contrast gets the lion's share of its pumping power from hydroelectric generation within the state; only about 30 percent of the energy used comes from fossil-fuel power.[16] That hydropower is clean, carbon-free, and not subject to volatile fuel prices or emissions regulations. Furthermore, almost all the hydroelectric facilities generating power for the California State Water Project are either part of that project or owned by the California Department of Water Resources, which is also the owner and operator of the State Water Project, giving those massive pumps first dibs for this valuable electricity. Granted, this strategy comes with an opportunity cost; as energy prices rise, California's water managers may find themselves missing out on huge profits that could have been reaped from selling this fuel-free renewable power on the open market. But for better or for worse, this power source has been tied to water delivery through legislative fiat, and, as long as this arrangement continues, water-supply costs will continue to be relatively stable for the State Water Project.

Arizona, on the other hand, with its far lower precipitation and less ideal topography, has no significant hydropower resources. Needing access to a dedicated source of power, the Central Arizona Project turned to the Navajo Generating Station, one of the few plants at the time with adequate spare power to share with this project, in the process securing access to 24 percent of its massive output. This means that the future price of pumping energy—and hence of water rates—is tied to the cost of using coal. Right now that cost is low. But a tightening of future supplies and, more important, the regulation of coal power's pollutants, including greenhouse gases, could dramatically change this. The Central Arizona Project management has made public these concerns. According to them, the Navajo Generating Station emits about two tons of carbon dioxide for each acre-foot of water pumped. Naturally, they are worried about greenhouse gas regulations, which would place a price on each ton of CO_2 emitted.[17] Although the Waxman-Markey Bill (HR 2454) never made it into law, its passage in the House of Representatives suggests that future comprehensive greenhouse gas legislation is a very real possibility.

The key question for the CAP managers is how high those added costs would be if climate change legislation passes. According to a review of the proposed legislation by the Energy Information Administration, had Waxman-Markey passed, the price of carbon would get higher over time, but the starting price and the rate of increase would depend on a number of factors, such as whether there would be sufficient large-scale deployment of carbon-capture technology and carbon-free energy generation to reduce demand for carbon emission allowances. In the low carbon-price scenario, this analysis predicts prices per ton going from $20 in 2020 to $30 in 2030. That would cause the cost of Central Arizona Project water to increase by about 30 percent by 2020 and by 50 percent by 2030 (holding all other price increases constant), representing an 80 percent and 100 percent increase in pumping energy costs respectively. Under the high carbon-price scenario, the price per ton goes to $93 in 2020 and $191 in 2030. In this scenario the 2020 and 2030 cost per acre-foot of water would be 250 percent and 420 percent higher than current costs, respectively.[18] And all of that doesn't even include the added costs of cooling this power plant as water gets more expensive, or the proposed Environmental Protection Agency retrofit requirements to clean up other point-source pollutants from this plant, which, it has been estimated, could cost more than $600 million. And, finally, there is the fact that the Central Arizona Project generates revenues from the sale of the unused portion of its power from the Navajo Generating Station, which they use to offset delivery costs. With carbon legislation, that source of income would likely become negligible, driving up rates even more. Almost all of this added cost would be passed on to the end users; according to McKinnon, the Central Arizona Project "has no other way of generating revenue." In that case, the price of admission to Wet 'n' Wild would have to go up quite a bit.

Although these rate increases will certainly pinch Arizona households (particularly those in Phoenix, where per capita water-use rates are much higher than in Tucson), the effect might not be quite as devastating as it initially sounds; the increases are based on a very low starting price, and households can generally adapt quickly to water scarcity by doing things like making landscaping less dependent on water or taking shorter showers. However, for water-intensive industries, the margins for adaptation are not nearly so big. High-tech manufacturing is what allowed the Phoenix economy to grow to the extent that it did, but many of these industries have insatiable thirst.

Intel, for example, has invested nearly $10 billion in the region and created more than ten thousand jobs in the Phoenix suburb of Chandler. Where subdivisions transition to scrub, three massive chip-fabrication plants glisten like alien landing craft, taking up the equivalent of seventeen football fields. Making chips is extremely water intensive, and by modern standards these plants are big. So it's not surprising that this industrial campus, which consumes 2 million gallons per day (they actually require 7 million, but after recycling the net use is lower), is the largest consumer of water in this suburb of a quarter million people. To deal with the region's water scarcity, Intel has chosen to pump nearly three quarters of the water it uses back into the underground aquifer, where they bank it for future use; over time they've accumulated nearly 3 billion gallons, a feat that contributed to their being designated a "Water Efficiency Leader" by the Environmental Protection Agency (EPA) in 2007. That's good environmental practice and a good economic hedge against future water scarcity, but it begs the question of how far energy prices can go up before this water gets too expensive. All of Intel's water comes at a huge energy cost: it requires extensive filtration to achieve the level of purity required for washing chips, a process that is made more energy-intensive by the mineral content of the desert water; water has to be pumped into the aquifer and out when required; and the CAP supply they use comes with the energy cost described above.[19] With so much infrastructure already sunk in Chandler, and so many other production costs that dwarf water, it seems unlikely that Intel would leave Chandler solely on account of skyrocketing water rates. But the more relevant question is, Might the next Intel, scouting a new location for a chip plant, choose not to locate in Phoenix because of the increasing constraints on water, particularly when there are plenty of competing locations in the country where water is far purer and nearly free?

There's one more important way that Intel's water depends on the price of energy—but this cost affects everyone in the region proportionally. The biggest nonagricultural consumer of water in Arizona is power generation. The dependency of power generation on water is particularly ironic considering how dependent water delivery is on power. Rising costs of energy could create a vicious cycle in which ensuing increases in water costs drive power costs up even further, and so on. That also means that each gallon that Intel or any household directly uses comes at a cost of indirect water use from the power plant that helped pump it there. Most Arizona power plants use recycled water, but that water still needs to come from somewhere, and it could have been recycled for some other purpose. And it's not a trivial amount of water. In one year Phoenix's Palo Verde nuclear plant uses enough recycled water for cooling its turbines to match that consumed by more than two hundred thousand Phoenix households. Even though its water is recycled, it still must compete for that secondhand water with thirsty users like golf courses and parks. Consequently, Palo Verde's ability to expand is limited, because it already takes about as much water as is available.[20]

The effect of rising energy prices on Arizona's ability to provide affordable water really depends on how important the Central Arizona Project ends up being in the overall water-supply mix, relative to less energy-intensive water sources. Currently, the typical Central Arizona Project allocation makes up between 30 percent and 40 percent of a typical Arizona city's water supply. But, McKinnon says, "it only takes one or two dry years and the reservoirs can go down fast." If that happens, it means Phoenix will become increasingly reliant on Central Arizona Project water, and prices will reflect that. The condition for a "perfect storm" that Phoenix water officials fear most is a prolonged drought (scientists studying tree-ring records have found that such patterns are common in this region) that would lower local reservoirs and in turn increase dependence on the Central Arizona Project, in conjunction with increasing CAP water rates due to rising energy prices and greenhouse gas legislation. Even worse would be a prolonged drought of the whole Colorado Basin, as many scientists predict, which would reduce the amount the Central Arizona Project could actually pump, since Arizona is lowest on the priority list among the southern basin signatories to the Colorado River Compact.

Central Arizona Project administrators are aware and worried about these problems. To avoid skyrocketing costs resulting from energy rate increases, they're trying to plan for power sources beyond the Navajo Generating Station. But there is no obvious source out there. The power deal with the Navajo Generating Station was arranged by the federal government to allow for affordable pumping energy. Moving to the open market for power would result in a massive increase in electricity rates for the Central Arizona Project. Additionally, there are no other existing sources of power in Arizona with the spare capacity to serve as a substitute—particularly not any with a low-carbon footprint. To keep Central Arizona Project water affordable in the long term, new sources of low-carbon power need to be developed—and in large quantities. According to McKinnon, one source that is often pointed to is "concentrating solar"—a technology in which a reflector concentrates sunlight to boil water and drive a turbine. But this technology also gulps down a lot of water—far more than coal power does, so it would need cheap water as much as those thirsty Phoenix residents do—and every gallon it took would be one less gallon for a farmer, dishwasher, or Intel.

Ultimately, if western water starts to get scarce and expensive, the tradeoff will be between urban and agricultural users. There's actually plenty of water in the West to keep people hydrated and clean, and even to water lawns and fill swimming pools. But most water in the West currently goes to irrigated agriculture—urban users get what's left over. At a certain point, if water gets too expensive, western water managers will have to start asking the question of whether desert agriculture—a massively important source of the nation's food, but also a massive water sink—is worth the cost. Agriculture in these arid lands has been subsidized for decades through provision of water below the cost of delivery. The question is whether this can continue indefinitely. As city residents start getting squeezed by water prices, more people will start asking it.

Back in my office in Vermont I'm watching sheets of rain cascade onto already saturated ground, and I longingly try to imagine what a southwestern water shortage would feel like. Vermont could hardly be more different from my birth state of California when it comes to water. It rains so much here that I didn't need to water my lawn once this summer. Lake Champlain, into which most of Vermont's water drains, is so immense that it contains over 20 million acre-feet—enough to supply the greater Los Angeles metropolitan area with water for more than four years without any refill. And the nearby Great Lakes, with 20 percent of the world's freshwater (and 95 percent of the United States' water), dwarf Lake Champlain, with nearly a thousand times the volume.

These facts make me realize that the problem with water supply is not about scarcity but about distance and gravity; there's plenty of water on the North American continent, but it takes lots of infrastructure and energy to get it from point A to point B. Another way of thinking about water supply is that ample sunshine attracts residents, but it also happens to be fairly well correlated with water scarcity. Although some parts of the Sun Belt are wetter than others, some of the highest growth rates have been found in the driest regions. That these sun-drenched regions are already at the hydrologic breaking point suggests there may be significant limits to how many more people can make the move from water-rich to water-poor parts of the country.

But what does it really mean to be water-rich? There's a common assumption that every area east of the Great Plains has plenty of water. This was once the case, when populations were lower, but today it is far from the truth. In fact, many mid-Atlantic and southeastern states are on the verge of a water catastrophe. The southeastern United States in particular had such a prolonged and severe period of drought in

2007–8 that boat launches in reservoirs found themselves hundreds of feet from water lines, fights brewed between neighboring states over river allocations, and Governor Sonny Perdue of Georgia resorted to calling for a statewide "day of prayer for rain." Even Florida, once literally covered in freshwater habitat, is experiencing a water crisis; with an astounding 90 percent of its water coming from pumped groundwater, it is depleting its underground aquifers so fast that entire homes are commonly getting swallowed by sinkholes as the ground subsides.[21]

Climate change is going to complicate this a lot. We should expect to see more droughts, more loss to evaporation in reservoirs and canals, and an outward creeping of the "water-poor" zone. Keeping cities in these regions running is going to require ingenuity and conservation; it's also going to require more energy, because if supplies shrink, many cities have nowhere to look for new sources of water but other basins. The good news is that right now water is a very small part of the cost of living and doing business in most places—even arid places—so there's time to prepare.

Finally, there's another, very different way that climate change could affect the water-energy nexus. Warming global temperatures are expected to be accompanied by rising sea levels. This means that low-lying coastal cities will need to embark on expensive public works projects to keep rising water tables and higher storm surges at bay—and the common denominator to all these projects will be energy-hungry pumps. Already, we've seen what storm surges can do to a low-lying city like New Orleans, where much of the developed land area is below sea level and where land is actually sinking at a rate of almost an inch every two years. If sea level were to rise even a little, Katrina-like surges could become commonplace. Even before Katrina hit, New Orleans had a network of 148 large drainage pumps to keep the city from being submerged. These pumps had a combined capacity greater than the flow of the Ohio River. But Katrina showed that even this massive system was inadequate. In response to the failure of the system during Katrina, the Army Corps of Engineers has started work on a $14 billion project to create a system of levees, barriers, gates, and flood pumps that together could protect the city from 16-foot storm surges. This will require use of the world's largest pumping station, a $500 million monster that will have the capacity to spew an astounding 150,000 gallons of water per second—the equivalent of about 15 Olympic-sized pools per minute. It's unclear exactly how much energy this will require, but what is clear is that if sea level does rise, those pumps will spend much more time running, and the energy bill could get ugly. The same goes for plenty of other low-lying coastal cities, from Miami to New York to Venice. But each successive megapump that's installed to fight off these rising waters will only further tie the fate of these cities closer to the price of energy.

Several years ago when visiting Spain, I saw my first ancient Roman aqueduct. The bridge of Ferreras, built during the reign of Augustus and located just outside the Mediterranean city of Tarragona, is a spectacularly preserved 250-meter-long segment of a 25-kilometer aqueduct, spanning a small river valley. Seeing this monument, I couldn't help but think how fundamental water supply has been to nearly all societies, going back to the dawn of civilization. I was also struck by the fact that water-delivery infrastructure is, by necessity, so massive in scale and durable in construction that it is one of the most lasting and evident legacies of civilizations long gone. I was amazed to later learn how much Rome's ancient engineers were able to do with so little technology. Using gravity alone, the aqueducts for the city of Rome were able to supply its hundreds of thousands of citizens (most of whom were rather obsessed with cleanliness by ancient standards) with more than 250 gallons per person per day—more than many of America's desert cities can feasibly supply today. Their water-delivery system was so extensive that few dwellers of that city lived more than 50 meters from a water outlet.[22]

Two thousand years later, many ancient Roman aqueducts are still serviceable (after some retrofitting). Operating with no external energy requirement and reflecting brilliant structural engineering, these mammoth channels functioned for centuries; the only thing that could stop them from working over the extremely long term was seismic activity (the eruption of Vesuvius, for instance) or invading hordes, which was what eventually did most of them in. Despite using the most modern materials and engineering methods, the American West's system of water delivery is, by comparison, highly ephemeral and vulnerable for the sole reason that so much of it is dependent on energy. With the exception of the gravity-fed systems like the Los Angeles Aqueduct, the West's water supply—like the water supply in so many populated arid regions of the world—is inextricably tied up with the availability of energy. Massive cities were built in response to the availability of water, made possible by pumping technology. This network was built at a time when energy was cheap and almost no consideration was given as to whether this energy-intensive model was sustainable in the long run. In the end, energy prices could prove to be far more destructive to today's public water supplies than hordes of sword-wielding Germanic barbarians were to Rome's.

Oil Depletion in the United States

WITH HUGE OIL DEPOSITS in places like Texas and California, the United States was one of the world's predominant exporters of oil in the early twentieth century (the first big "gusher" was located in Spindletop, Texas). Few thought that America would ever have any serious constraints on its supply. But as demand for oil surged, supply dwindled. By 1946, the United States could no longer meet its domestic demand with domestic production, turning it into a net oil importer, a situation that would only get worse over the next sixty years.[1] Although annual US production increased for many years after, it didn't increase as fast as demand. US production reached its peak in 1970. Since then, it's been slowly declining as big oil deposits dry up and new finds fail to replace the lost capacity.

There are significant ramifications to being a net importer of fuels. Until the fossil-fuel age, societies got their energy locally. Even in the coal age, most coal was obtained from nearby, as that resource is far more ubiquitous than oil. But starting in the oil age, the world suddenly found itself divided into net energy consumers and net exporters. Now, countries without the proper geologic legacy (or, as in the case of the United States, countries whose thirst outstripped their legacy) have to look to other countries for their energy. And as demand increases and domestic supplies decrease, that foreign dependency gets even worse. Of course, putting the most developed nations at the mercy of a small group of oil producing nations, most of them in the politically unstable Middle East, has had far-reaching consequences for twentieth-century global politics, but that's a topic for other books.

That fewer and fewer countries are finding themselves as net exporters underscores the crux of the problem: the earth is not making

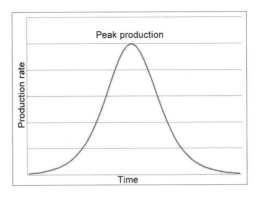

Hubbert's Curve. (Drawing by author)

any more oil. Although this fact may seem obvious to some, society has conveniently ignored it, with potentially dangerous consequences. It takes millions of years for aquatic organisms to get pressure-cooked into oil, so once petroleum deposits are used, they cannot be replaced. The world's stock of oil is like an energy bank account in which, for millions of years, tiny increments of energy were deposited in the form of dead biological material, with relatively little being withdrawn (the exception being oil and gas seeps). This combination of long-term deposits coupled with concentration through heat and pressure turned "energy pennies" into thousand-dollar bills—highly dense and compact sources of energy. But this bank account that nature took millions of years to build up has been precipitously drawn down by humans in the last century and there appears to be no concrete plan for what to do when it runs out.

M. King Hubbert, a geophysicist who worked at Shell in the middle of the twentieth century, built on the earlier work of others to popularize a mathematical theory to predict the pattern in which oil production rates go down as reserves are depleted. "Hubbert's Curve," derived through fancy mathematics, looks a lot like a standard bell curve (earlier versions of this curve were not symmetrical). The x axis represents time, and the y axis the rate of oil production. The peak of the bell represents the year with the highest rate of production. Theoretically it also should equal the point where about half of the world's oil has been consumed. The area under the curve at a given point in time represents the cumulative amount of the resource extracted. In the 1950s, Hubbert calibrated this equation with historical production data and used it to predict the peak of US oil production, coming extremely close to the actual peak year of 1970 (this was his upper-bound estimate). US production has been consistently declining ever since, also just as Hubbert predicted, although the rate of production decline is slightly less than he predicted. This same type of curve could be applied for other exhaustible fuels.

CHAPTER 3
The Very Mobile City

everal years ago, if morning commuters driving into Albany on I-787 glanced eastward, they might have noticed a lone canoeist in the middle of the Hudson River. Although the pilot of the canoe was certainly having fun, his primary purpose on the river was business: he was on his way to work. That paddler was Duncan Crary, a publicity consultant, and his vehicle of choice was a seventeen-foot-long Old Town canoe. About the only similarity his morning "canute" (a commute by canoe) had with the typical American commute was that it began at a place called Starbucks—in this case a Hudson River island referred to locally as Starbuck Island.

Crary admits that this form of commuting, popular with the Mohicans four hundred years ago, isn't the most practical way to get to work in the modern age, which may explain why he did it only six times. The nine-mile paddle took over two hours, plus there was the walking to and from the river (a few times he even wheeled his canoe through rush-hour traffic in downtown Albany while wearing his suit and tie). He had to time his outbound and return voyages to coincide with the ebb or flow tide. And he had to contend with a highly polluted stretch of river that featured the outflow from an out-of-compliance sewage-treatment plant and a frequent rain of litter tossed from overhead bridge traffic (almost always McDonalds wrappers, according to Crary).

Duncan Crary (*right*) and Alison Bates with canoe, on their way to work in Troy, New York. (Photo: John Crary; by permission of Duncan Crary)

Despite all this, Crary claims "it's the most fun I've had getting into work—I had a big blast doing it." While motorists were watching the bumper of the car ahead, he was getting exercise and taking in scenery that occasionally included bald eagles. But most of all, he enjoyed the sense of place it delivered. "There's nothing like arriving in a city by water vessel" he says. "You depart Troy and you can see it behind you. As you approach Albany you can see the skyline ahead. You realize real distances when you're in a canoe. You understand why Albany and Troy are where they are."[1]

Although "canuting" proved to be lots of fun and a good upper-body workout, Crary admits he did it mainly to make a point: Americans are far too dependent on their cars. "I hate driving. Commuting by car is awful to me," he says. "The automobile landscape is so dull. People don't know where things are—they speak of distances in terms of driving time." He refers to the mass of roads and highways surrounding most central cities as "the suburban asteroid belt." Between his "canuting" and a later enterprise in which he partnered with a cruise line to reintroduce river commuting to the New York capital region for a day, he hopes to show that cars, while useful, don't have to be the only way we get around. So far he's fighting an uphill battle.

There are three factors that determine how transportation energy footprints differ from city to city. The first is the way that people get around. The second is how far people have to travel in a given day to get to where they need to go. And third is the amount of traffic delay.

The way people get around, also known as "mode," strongly influences answers to the other two. There certainly are many ways to transport oneself in modern-day cities, including subways, light rail, bicycles, buses, in-line skates, skateboards, rickshaws, scooters, and of course canoes. But for the vast majority of Americans—and increasingly for much of the developed world—the car is the unrivaled mode of choice. An indicator of Americans' devotion to this contraption is the sheer quantity of gasoline we consume: if you walled off a football field, the walls would have to be 50 miles high to contain all the gas used by cars in America in a single year. This translates into a yearly consumption of about 450 gallons per person, about 6 times more than is used by Europeans, 13 times more than South Americans, 36 times more than Chinese, and 238 times more than Tanzanians. In aggregate, the United States consumes about 140 billion gallons per year, nearly three times more oil than the next biggest oil consumer, China. That means when the price of gasoline goes up by a dollar per gallon, it takes a $140 billion chunk out of the national disposable income. Hypothetically, double or triple that increase, and it becomes evident just how tied our well-being is to the price of fuel.[2]

Some have tried to challenge this supremacy with attempted technological paradigm shifts. Remember the Segway? As this new mode of transportation was being unveiled in 2001, the illuminati of Silicon Valley (many of whom happened to also be its investors) were predicting that this pogo stick with wheels would be bigger than the personal computer, revolutionize transportation, reshape our cities, and be "to the car what the car was to the horse and buggy." A decade later, cities remain untransformed, Segways are banned from streets in numerous countries (including the Netherlands, where almost everything is legal, including prostitution and marijuana), and the most prominent place you'll see this "symbol of dorkiness" is under a rotund security guard in the movie *Paul Blart, Mall Cop*.[3]

The car-driving portion of the world, which includes the vast majority of Americans, shows no sign of giving up its devotion any time soon. Currently, almost 88 percent of Americans commute to work by car.[4] Americans in particular love their cars for the same reason their forebears a century ago loved their horses: they make us more mobile, give a sense of independence and freedom, and allow us to go off into the sunset—or to Vegas—on a whim. They're also wrapped up in our identity and self-image; after all, James Bond drives an Aston-Martin and Paul Blart drives a Segway. Try imagining it the other way around and you'll see why there aren't more Segways.

Just because two cities are equally dominated by car transport, though, doesn't mean that their per capita gasoline consumption is necessarily the same. Besides fleet composition (there are slight differences in the average miles per gallon for all vehicles from one city to the next), the big question is how many people typically occupy a car. In the United States, about 87 percent of car commutes are made alone, one of the highest rates in the world.[5] Increasing riders per car is probably one of the easiest sources for achieving big aggregate reductions in energy consumption with relatively little pain; just find someone else going to the same place you are and you've both halved your per capita fuel consumption.

In other countries, people not only drive alone much less often but often cram themselves into vehicles far beyond that carrier's capacity. My most vivid experience of this phenomenon was in Peru in the 1990s. Returning from a mountaineering expedition, my buddies and I needed to hitch a ride back from a small village at the foot of the Cordillera Blanca mountain range to the regional capital of Huaraz, about four hours away. The only car to come by in the course of three hours was a compact-sized 1970s Toyota pickup truck, whose driver took a few dollars for providing a lift. The five of us threw ourselves and our several hundred pounds of gear in the truck bed and, believing the car was already overloaded, thought we'd be the only passengers. Turns out we were wrong. About a dozen more people and several chickens clambered on board. By the time we were ready to go (on sinuous mountain roads that would be highly hazardous even in the best of vehicles), the wheel wells barely cleared the tires and the bed was so crowded that I had to stand on one foot for three hours with my face pressed into the back of an old man's head. It might be an extreme example, but the contrast with American social norms of driving our nice, big, clean SUVs all by ourselves day after day is stark.

So what makes one city have high rates of carpooling versus another? Surprisingly, compact San Francisco, New York, and Boston are all far down the list, with carpooling rates between 6 and 8 percent. At the top of the list are sprawling Mesa and Phoenix, Arizona, and not far below are Fresno, Dallas, and Houston, with rates ranging from 14 to 17 percent.[6] These results probably stem from the negligible level of public transportation in the latter group of cities, which means transit and carpooling are not competing for the same people. In addition, these cities have many large corporate campuses that employ thousands of people. Large, uniform destinations make it easier to organize shared rides.

The automobile's primary competitor as a transportation mode is public transit, which includes buses, light rail, subways, street cars, and so forth (canoes, sadly, are still at the bottom of the list). Public transit should, in theory, be much more energy efficient than personal cars (perhaps with the exception of the Peruvian death-mobile mentioned above), because the idea is that lots of people are being propelled by the same motor at once. And among types of transit, subways are generally considered to be the most efficient because of the volume of people they transport. A study of thirty-seven global cities done in 1997 found that overall rail modes are about four times more energy efficient on a per capita basis than cars but that there's variation around that number because both cars and trains vary in efficiency from place to place.[7] So, for instance, European commuter trains are seven times more energy efficient than single-occupant car travel in the United States, while the Manila rail system, with its incredibly high ridership, is fifty-nine times more energy efficient than US car travel! Buses come in behind rail, with about half the average energy efficiency of trains, but still nearly double the efficiency of private cars.

Given these huge energy advantages, America's low rate of transit ridership has a big impact on our urban energy metabolism. Urban Americans cover about 3 percent of their yearly mileage on transit, while Australians travel 7 percent, Canadians 10 percent, Europeans 23 percent, and East Asians 49 percent. Of course, there is considerable variation among American cities, ranging from New York City, where 54 percent of daily commutes are made by public transit, to Wichita, Kansas, where that number is one half of 1 percent. Of the fifty biggest American cities, about thirty-five have transit commuting rates of less than 10 percent and about fifteen are under 2 percent. If the definition of "city" is expanded to include greater metropolitan areas, then the disparities between America and elsewhere become even more pronounced; for instance, only 10 percent of the miles traveled by greater metropolitan New Yorkers are on transit, compared to 16 percent in Sydney, 27 percent in Stockholm, 30 percent in both London and Paris, 54 percent in Seoul, and 63 percent in Tokyo.[8]

To attract a large ridership, transit must be competitive with cars in terms of speed, ease of use, cost, and dependability. Part of the equation is making transit more available, affordable, and higher in quality. Another part is making regular car use more difficult and expensive. In most American cities, the opposite is true: driving is cheap and easy, thanks to massive subsidies to highways, parking facilities, and fuel prices, and transit either doesn't go where it's needed or is too slow and undependable. It's also frequently expensive. On the other hand, New York, the only American city where transit ridership is on par with Europe, has readily available and fast transit, whereas driving and parking in that city is abysmal and expensive. Numerous research studies have backed up just how sensitive transit ridership is to the cost of driving. For instance, a study in Portland, Oregon, found that boosting parking fees from zero to six dollars per day would boost the number of people riding transit from 22 percent to 50 percent.[9]

In European and Asian cities, by contrast, ownership of a car is far more of a liability than an asset. I recently met an academic from Paris who had just changed careers and gone to work as an executive for a major corporation. His superiors at the company felt it proper that someone of his rank have his own luxury company car. My acquaintance tried to reject it, telling his boss that he really had no use for one since he lived near a metro stop and could get to everything he needed by walking or transit, not to mention that parking in Paris is impossible. His boss insisted that he take the car regardless, but he ended up using it only rarely—mainly for family outings to the country.

Making it harder and more costly to drive in the United States is logistically feasible (although politically it may be a nonstarter). Getting existing transit to run more reliably and faster is not out of the realm of possibility. But far more challenging would be to build enough infrastructure in currently car-dependent cities so that transit could provide a viable alternative. As pointed out in Chapter 4, while American cities (with the exception of New York and Chicago) were building up their street networks for both streetcars and the new-fangled automobile, many European cities were investing in subways and other rail transit. Those systems took generations to build but are now yielding huge benefits. Many American cities today would like to follow Europe's lead but are finding that massive transit investment projects are simply not feasible in this day and age.

Planners love to talk about transit, and municipal offices throughout America are littered with hundreds of discarded plans for public transit expansion. Perhaps one of the best examples is from my home state of Vermont, which in the early 2000s came up with a plan to establish commuter rail service on a freight rail line running right through downtown Burlington, the largest city in the state, with a whopping population of thirty-eight thousand. So was born the "Champlain Flyer," which for a few years was the nation's shortest commuter rail line, at thirteen miles. Unfortunately it also turned out to be the nation's least used rail line. The paltry two cars attached to the diesel locomotive were rarely more than a fraction full. Both capital and operating costs were more than double the projection, and ridership was only 40 percent of the already modest expectations. So, after just a few years, and $18 million later, the plug was pulled and this experiment in micro-commuting ended, little noticed by the world. Perhaps it failed so badly because of the tiny population of the region it was serving or because of the few residents who lived in the two suburban towns where it stopped (roughly ten thousand people between them). Or perhaps it failed because there's little downside to driving in this region, which has ample parking, well-maintained roads, and no traffic congestion. Whatever the reason, it provided a rather extreme example of how transit—particularly rail transit—does not work everywhere. And American cities seem to disproportionately display the characteristics that make transit harder: an automobile-friendly environment plus low population and low job density.

About 5,000 miles south of the southernmost stop of the Champlain Flyer, the worst recorded traffic jam to date occurred on June 10, 2009. Throughout that rainy Wednesday, nearly 25 percent of São Paulo's 6 million vehicles attempted to leave town for the long Corpus Cristi holiday weekend, causing a jaw-dropping 293 kilometers of traffic backups—35 percent of all the monitored roads in the region. As individual traffic backups were compounded, roadways turned into parking lots. The jam was so bad it made the international news and sealed the reputation of São Paulo as one of the worst places to drive on earth.

Traffic is so bad in this Brazilian megalopolis of nearly 20 million that it's in the news almost every day. Some cabbies have video game consoles to keep them amused during backups. Standstills can be so long that motorists get out of their cars and enjoy a leisurely *cafezinho* at a café before traffic moves again. And per capita helicopter use is now the highest in the world (most new office buildings are equipped with helipads). In fact, if you Google the term "São Paolo" along with the Portuguese word for "traffic," the adjective that most frequently accompanies the search results is *caos*, Portuguese for "chaos."

São Paulo is typical of many megacities in the industrializing world, where newfound economic prosperity has brought on a wave of automobile purchases that has pushed inadequate and underinvested street and highway infrastructure to the limit. Another example is Bangkok, where today the average car spends the equivalent of nearly forty-five days stuck in traffic each year, hundreds of babies are delivered in cars, and the police don't consider traffic "bad" until vehicles have been stationary for over an hour.[10]

Megacities like São Paulo or Bangkok reveal something of a paradox when it comes to the second and third determinants of urban transportation energy use: trip length and traffic. Both are theorized to be influenced by urban density, but in opposite ways. In dense cities, by definition, things tend to be closer together, which means that trip lengths should be shorter. But it also means that a greater number of vehicles must share roadways whose capacity is constrained by space. Transit can alleviate this to a certain extent, but in cases where transit is insufficient—which is frequent—highly dense cities can become a nightmare of traffic congestion. Because cars are less efficient when moving very slowly or in stop-and-go conditions, congestion also means wasted fuel. Which effect is more important?

The tradeoff between these two aspects of density has been a source of debate in the planning literature, with some claiming that sprawl results in both long trip lengths and traffic congestion and others suggesting that density is the true culprit of congestion. Two of the foremost proponents of the latter view are economists Peter Gordon and Harry Richardson, who argue that "though mass transit supporters argue for higher densities to reduce congestion . . . in fact the relationship between density and traffic congestion is positive rather than negative."

They also write that "suburbanization has been the dominant and successful mechanism for reducing congestion," in what they refer to as a "safety valve" effect.[11]

While most people concede that high density does breed at least some congestion, those on the other side of the issue believe that the benefits of density and compactness—namely, shorter trips and greater enabling of transit—far outweigh the traffic-related costs. As Anthony Downs, the noted Brookings Institution Fellow and urban economist, noted, "Higher average densities in new-growth areas help to reduce the need for movement generated by future population growth. They do so by accommodating that growth in a smaller added area than would be possible if development continued at the present average density. Consequently, the new residents would have to travel shorter distances to accomplish their normal tasks of living. That would reduce total energy consumed in traveling. . . . Similarly, lower total miles driven might reduce traffic congestion under some circumstances."[12]

Those on this side of the debate cite evidence of growing trip lengths. For instance, between 1983 and 2001, the average number of daily vehicle miles traveled (VMT) per household in the United States shot up from 32 to 58 miles, while the average amount of land used per person increased from 0.31 to 0.36 acres. Also, Americans on average travel much farther than residents of foreign cities where densities are higher—specifically, 1.5 times farther than Canadians, two times farther than Europeans, and three times farther than Asians. Meanwhile, American metropolitan areas are half as dense as those in Canada, between a third and a quarter as dense as those in Europe, and nearly a tenth as dense as those in Asia.[13]

A commonly cited source of evidence for those who prioritize congestion as the bigger problem is Texas Transportation Institute's (TTI) Urban Mobility Report, one of the most important sources of data in transportation policy and the basis for many transportation system investment decisions. According to the most recent version (2009), congestion in the United States results in drivers collectively spending 4.2 billion more hours on the road than needed and purchasing an unnecessary 2.8 billion gallons of gas. The yearly costs of heavy traffic, including time-productivity loss, wasted fuel, increased accidents, and pollution emissions, are estimated at nearly $88 billion, or $757 in avoidable costs per traveler. The report finds that travel delay and wasted fuel have nearly doubled since 1997 and nearly quintupled since 1982 and that the average quantity of wasted fuel per capita in 2007 nearly tripled since 1982, up to 24 gallons—roughly the amount a typical commuter now uses in three weeks. It also finds that the number of metropolitan areas with more than 40 hours in annual per capita delay for peak commutes went from one in 1982 to 23 in 2007.[14]

There's another viewpoint, however, countering that the Urban Mobility Report overstates the costliness of congestion. In a 2010 report, the economist Joe Cortright scrutinized TTI's data, obtained new sources of data for reference, and altered a number of assumptions in the TTI methodology. It suggests that TTI's estimated costs of traffic congestion are overstated by about 70 percent—that is, they are around $22 billion instead of $88 billion. This is significant because if congestion is measured as having a lower cost, then one of the primary arguments against density has less weight. Cortright finds that a larger source of "wasted" fuel and time is actually excessive commuting distances during peak travel hours, which account for $31 billion in unnecessary fuel and time costs, 40 billion in extra miles, and 2 billion extra gallons of gasoline. In other words, residents in all the major metropolitan areas who were able to keep their peak-hour commutes to distances characteristic of more compact cities would save $31 billion annually. This translates into the typical commuter spending forty hours more per year in peak-hour driving in sprawling versus compact cities. He also finds no evidence for TTI's contention that the economic costs of congestion have tripled since the 1980s. Rather, any increases in these costs are due to increased commuting distances.[15]

Many density proponents also counter the traffic congestion argument with the observation that, over time, low-density areas generate their own traffic congestion. In other words, the supposed advantage of low-density areas being free from congestion is only transitory, and eventually that advantage is lost as new, scattered development soaks up highway capacity. Adherents to this perspective believe that road investments designed to serve existing development in lower-density areas simply tend to spur on new development (a process known as "induced growth"), which in turn results in more drivers using those roads until they reach their capacities again (a process known as "induced demand"). Think of it as a classic case of "If you build it, they will come."[16]

A considerable body of research has addressed the relationship between transportation and density. Much of it focuses on average trip distances. A number of studies have found that a theoretical doubling of density can result in reductions in vehicle miles traveled per capita that range from negligible to 40 percent (depending on the starting level of density) and reductions in the number of vehicle trips of over 70 percent. Another found that every 10 percent growth in the extent of an urban area (i.e., sprawl) resulted in a 2.5 percent increase in miles driven, beyond what would be expected just from associated population growth.[17]

Another group of studies looks at the relationship between urban density and actual energy consumption. One found that moving from a neighborhood density of under one thousand people per square mile to over ten thousand caused fuel consumption per person to go down by 40 percent. Another found that a doubling of urban density reduced consumption by a third. Perhaps the most well-known researchers of this question are planning scholars Peter Newman and Jeffrey Kenworthy, who found a very tight negative statistical relationship (explaining 85 percent of variation) between urban density and per capita fuel use for private transportation for fifty global cities. The curve they traced with their data was shaped like an L, with energy use declining first rapidly and then more slowly in response to increasing density. Furthermore, they found significant variation in fuel use within metropolitan areas. For instance, in the greater New York City area, residents of the most centrally located neighborhoods use only a sixth of the energy used by residents of the outer regions of the metropolitan area.

A 1988 study they did focusing on Perth, Australia, found that while reductions in congestion did lower energy use for driving, drivers experiencing the least congestion also used the most energy because their trips were longest, leading to a conclusion that dense development saves energy.[18]

Although the majority of studies do conform with these results, the literature is by no means in perfect agreement. Several researchers have pointed out supposed flaws in Newman and Kenworthy's earlier work, including the failure to control for socioeconomic variables like income or fuel prices (which could be the real cause of less driving), use of coarse measures of density, and overreliance on journey-to-work trips, which in turn makes it hard to establish that density is the actual cause of reduced energy consumption. One study from 2004 reanalyzed Newman and Kenworthy's data in a way that, the authors claim, better controlled for potential confounding effects and found no significant correlation between transportation energy and any measure of density (urban, employment, outer area, inner area). Another study found that London had lower transportation energy efficiency than a number of smaller, less dense urban areas. This was not only because of longer trip times but also because of trip lengths (which contradicts the literature discussed above on trip length and density). And yet another study in Denver found that simulated increases in density in strips along transit and highways led to predictions of both longer trips and greater congestion, which together offset efficiency gains from greater transit use.[19]

While it is acknowledged that accounting for congestion is critical to understanding transportation energy, just how much these differing results presented above relate to methods of accounting for congestion is unclear. Traffic congestion data are notoriously hard to obtain, so it is common for studies to use proxies or models that estimate traffic from other data. Therefore it's not surprising that we lack a clear answer about the tradeoffs of congestion and trip length in response to increasing density. This gap in understanding is becoming ever more important as automobile use explodes in the developing world at rates far greater than road builders can accommodate. The result is that traffic congestion in many global megacities is reaching previously unseen levels. Given this, it's reasonable to question whether much of the existing research (a lot of which is based on data from the 1990s and earlier) is already out of date. It's certainly possible that in the years since much of the research was done, the energy costs of congestion have risen significantly, at least in the developing world.[20]

This raises the question of just how bad traffic needs to be before it really takes a toll on energy consumption. I raised this question with the planning scholar Reid Ewing, one of the nation's foremost experts on the connection between urban form and energy use. According to our discussion and his meta-analysis of nearly two hundred studies, congestion resulting from the average "dense" pattern of development in the United States yields a 10 percent reduction in the energy-efficiency gains accrued from compact development (i.e., that 20 to 40 percent savings is reduced to 18 to 36 percent). That is, the benefits of density greatly outweigh the costs. Ewing attributes the small magnitude of this discount to the fact that American highways and roads are so well developed relative to developing countries like Brazil. A 2010 study also finds only very slight increases in fuel usage due to congestion—in fact so small that it was not statistically significant.[21]

I asked Ewing if he thought, however, that the hypothetical 10 percent discount from congestion could get worse if average traffic speeds in a congested American city were to approach those of a megacity like São Paulo; his answer was yes, because of the way that average speed relates to energy consumption. Congestion wastes energy because when traffic is not free-flowing, cars spend more time on the road burning fuel. For each car, there's an "energy efficiency sweet spot" at which fuel economy is maximized. Averaged across the US fleet, that spot—or, more accurately, zone—ranges between 43 and 55 miles per hour, depending on the vehicle type and conditions (see fig. below). Above that sweet spot, fuel efficiency goes down slightly; for instance, an average car at 75 miles per hour (mph) uses about 30 percent more fuel per

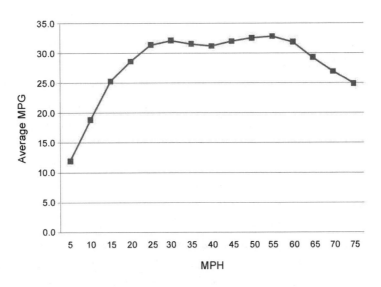

Average fuel efficiency in relation to speed.
(Data from West et al., 1998)

mile than one going 55—one of the reasons why the national speed limit was lowered to 55 in the late 1970s. But what is most interesting is how steeply fuel efficiency drops as cars go much slower. From 25 mph down to 10 mph, average fuel efficiency drops precipitously, from 31 to 19 miles per gallon (mpg). At 5 mph it goes down to 12 mpg. For heavy trucks, the impact of slower speeds is even more pronounced; a truck going 75 mph gets twice the mpg of one going 25 and three times that of one going 10 mph.[22]

In large US metropolitan areas (with more than 3 million people), the average peak-hour speed is about 70 percent of the speed limit, meaning that speeds may average about 40 to 45 mph on the typical urban freeway and 25 to 30 mph on a typical surface street (for smaller metro areas this reduction is even less pronounced). The graph indicating average fuel efficiency in relation to speed shows that these reduced speeds are still generally in the region of the fuel efficiency "sweet spot"—that is, average mpg is still relatively unimpaired even at 25 mph. This indicates that current traffic congestion conditions in

America add relatively little to urban energy metabolism. But if they drop considerably lower—say, to those in São Paulo and other global megacities—average mpg will drop significantly, and energy consumption from traffic delay will consequently rise steeply. If, for example, average speeds were to fall from 30 to 10 mph, we'd see average fuel economy fall by 40 percent, from 31 to 19 mpg. And dropping down further to 5 mph takes us to 12 mpg (if the vehicle fleet were to switch over to hybrids, these results would no longer hold). In other words, there is still time to act before traffic congestion becomes a big contributor to wasted energy. But projections of future traffic speeds for some major metropolitan areas suggest that significant drops in efficiency are not out of the realm of possibility. For instance, the Southern California Area Governments' traffic simulation model predicts that average speeds on Los Angeles area freeways during the morning rush hour will drop from the 2003 level of 54 mph to 31.5 mph in 2030. That may still sound fairly fast, but it's an average, which means that lots of cars will be running at speeds where fuel economy falls steeply. Congestion may have only a minor effect on transportation energy efficiency in the typical American city today, but it might have a much bigger impact in the city of tomorrow unless we have a big jump in the share of more efficient hybrids or electric cars.

During the several months I spent in São Paulo in 1996 and 1997, my lifestyle didn't require much driving. I was staying at a friend's apartment in the centrally located and very dense neighborhood of Vila Mariana. Surrounded by a veritable forest of high-rise residential towers, there was a customer base for retail of every kind within walking distance: five minutes to bakeries, restaurants, grocery stores, ice cream parlors, a subway stop, and, of course, my favorite neighborhood *barzinho*; fifteen minutes to movie and stage theaters, nightclubs, major retail, commercial office districts, and São Paulo's largest park, the beautiful Parque Ibirapuera; thirty minutes to food of any ethnicity on the planet, from sushi to canolis, pierogis, and kimchee. For more distant trips the proximity of the Ana Rosa subway station—which was

One of many high-density neighborhoods
in São Paulo, Brazil. (Photo by author)

one of the cleanest, easiest-to-use, and most modern subway stations
I've ever been in—allowed me to make easy trips to many other parts
of town.

On the surface, this city seems to have all the things that so many
urban planners love—mixed used, a modern subway system, and a
similar density to New York City. So why would a place like this have
such appalling traffic, such long cars trips, and, consequently, such
a horrible transportation energy footprint compared to other dense
places like New York? At first glance its traffic woes would appear to
lend credence to the arguments of those who warn against density.
Does it really?

Simply put, not all density is necessarily good density; just because
homes, businesses, and services are located close to one another doesn't
mean that people will necessarily take advantage of this proximity, that
automobile use will be reduced, or that trips will be any shorter. In fact,
places like São Paulo suggest that density may be a red herring; in fact,

other characteristics, correlated with but distinct from density, may really be what matter.

Reid Ewing agrees. His previously mentioned meta-analysis indicates that density is far less important than other factors that often—but not always—accompany density. In terms of predicting VMT, he told me, "density is actually a disappointing factor when we look across all studies. Jobs-housing balance and 'centeredness' proves to be much more important." By centeredness, Ewing means the extent to which an urban area is organized into distinct, higher-density clusters of activity, as opposed to being uniform across space. According to his research, centeredness, also referred to as "destination accessibility," is four to five times more important in predicting VMT than overall density. Even the overall connectivity of the street network has been found to be more important than density in this respect. Ewing and others have created their own "sprawl index," which integrates these various dimensions. Using this system they find that many cities that have relatively high measured average densities—like Los Angeles, surprisingly—are actually quite sprawling due to lack of a real center. In these places, a sprawl index that factors in centeredness does a much better job in explaining differences in VMT than overall density. So, for instance, while Philadelphia has an average density similar to San Diego's, the latter has 25 percent greater daily VMT than the former. The big difference? Philadelphia has a real, dominant downtown, where lots of people live and work. In other words, what keeps down trip lengths in a metro area is not just cramming buildings together but building an urban landscape that maximizes the probability that people will live near where they work, learn, play, and shop.

Ewing's analysis also addresses what urban design factors determine the likelihood of driving versus walking versus taking transit, which in turn influences traffic and trip lengths. The proximity and availability of transit stops are the biggest determinants of transit use and also correlate with increased walking. Other factors associated with increased walking and transit use include the density of intersections (which leads to shorter and more routing options for transit users and pedestrians), the length of blocks (long blocks reduce walkability), the balance between jobs and housing (a good balance makes it possible to efficiently link transit trips with errands), and the overall mix of land uses.

So-called compact development, Ewing concludes, results in about 20 to 40 percent fewer VMTs than traditional sprawl-style development, at least in the American context. But in his definition of compact development, density plays only a relatively small role. Far more important are characteristics like strong centers, mixed uses, walkability, and connectivity.

These results help clarify what's going on in São Paulo. First, the city badly lacks defined centers. Instead it's like a continuous, never-ending carpet of high-rises, all capped at around the same height limit by local regulations. Thus, rather than having a few dominant destinations that would help orient transit and highways, residents of this city seem to be going everywhere all the time. The lack of centers limits the usability and mode share (ridership) of the subway system—a system which should be far bigger and more heavily used for such a big city. Second, its subway system, while clean and modern, is woefully inadequate, with stops serving just a fraction of this vast city and a relatively low mode share, in part because of the lack of centers for orienting the system, and in part because of a late start in developing it. This in turn leaves the burden of transit services on the bus system, which has to compete for road space with millions of cars, thereby adding to traffic. Third, there are some significant design challenges; for instance, in many neighborhoods blocks are far too big (typically one block measures about five hundred feet on a side) and intersections too far apart. Fourth, although many neighborhoods have a great balance of work to housing, many of São Paulo's jobs are located in uniquely zoned industrial areas on the periphery of the city. And finally, an issue not brought up by Ewing's analysis, São Paulo is massively income segregated. The working poor tend to live far outside the main city in peripheral settlements called *favelas*. Many of these people don't have the choice of working near where they live. So for the millions of working poor to get to their jobs in the more central parts of the city—or potentially to other peripheral locations—they must travel incredibly long distances, putting huge pressure on an already strained transportation network.

The task of designing good density is becoming more complicated over time. Although in past decades the typical urban resident's movements were relatively predictable (home to work, work to home, home to shopping), patterns of daily urban life are becoming increasingly complex as traditional gender and family roles change and more households have two wage earners. These socioeconomic trends mean that yesterday's formula for planning compact development oriented around home, work, and shopping may do little to effectively curb energy-intensive transportation today.

One indicator of this change is that the number and type of trips people make are getting larger and more diverse. As the geographer Helen Jarvis writes, households are increasingly composed of two wage earners "juggling different job types, working conditions, scheduling constraints and mobility imperatives. The practical considerations of securing, combining and maintaining two careers from a single location can be colossal. Many of the 'new economy' jobs . . . routinely require employees to work long hours, travel interstate on business and work to deadlines which demand unpaid overtime. Other service sector jobs are of poor quality, entailing temporary, reduced hours and variable shifts. Both have specific implications for individual and combined household strategies of space-time coordination."[23]

According to the Federal Highway Administration's 2001 National Household Travel Survey, while the average vehicle miles traveled per household went up by about 70 percent between 1969 and 2001, trips between home and work went down slightly, while shopping trips and "other family and personal" trips both doubled (from 7 percent to 13 percent and from 10 percent to 21 percent, respectively).[24] Other family and personal business trips represent those that are part of the daily routine but not part of work or shopping for actual goods—this includes things like trips to school and day care; services like banking, car repair, tax preparation, or haircuts; family business not classified as "social and recreational"; and activities like soccer and karate practice for the kids or yoga and self-help classes for mom and dad.

The truth is that families these days are on the go so much more than they were a few decades ago that it has become harder to predict where individuals are likely to go given where they live. As a result, Jarvis writes, "Evidence . . . suggests that those households living in central neighborhoods are no more likely than those living in more suburban areas to limit and contain movement within a discreet area."[25] In her study areas of Seattle and Portland, Oregon, she found that many centrally located urban families drove as much or more as suburban families because mom and dad worked in different directions, kids went to school in yet another location, and activities were spread out all across town. This situation may prove to be a headache for planners as they try to design new urban forms that will allow people to minimize their vehicle travel. This is not to say that making compact communities where trips are short is impossible, but rather that there are no simple prescriptions for achieving lowered personal car usage. In other words, car use can't be reduced through direct regulation. All that planners can do is provide the necessary context that will allow residents to choose to drive less if desired.

The last car that the San Francisco freelance writer Greg Dicum owned was a 1987 Oldsmobile Firenza—"the worst car that GM ever made," he claims. Ten years ago, as the car's condition was going from bad to worse—in addition to constant engine problems, one of the windows had been replaced with plywood—Greg and his wife, Nina, started to question why they had a car in the first place. "At one point we realized that the only reason we'd been in the car in the last month was to move it so we didn't get a parking ticket." Unlike the case of Duncan Crary, there was nothing ideological about his dislike of owning a car—it was simple math; after adding up all the junker's monthly expenses—insurance, registration, parking, maintenance, and fuel—they realized that for the same amount they could pay for a taxi ride and weekend car rental. Because they generally used the car only once or twice a month, it made no sense to keep the car, so they got rid of it. The money they save on expenses goes toward public transportation and the occasional use of Zipcar, a car-sharing service that allows users to easily pay for the use of a shared car by the hour. When they want to take a long weekend out of town, they plan a few days in advance and arrange a rental. And they weren't deterred by the birth of a child a few years later—often one of the key events triggering car purchase. When it comes to kids, says Dicum, "people assume you need a car as if it's a required piece of child rearing equipment." But getting their son around safely without owning a car has turned out to be a snap.

Greg and Nina's ten years of carlessness have given them a whole new perspective on urban life and transportation, just as Crary's morning canute did for him. For one thing, by making apparent the real costs of moving around, it's made them less wasteful and more efficient when it comes to their travel budget. According to Greg, "With a car you have a constant dribble of expenses so you don't notice it as much. With Zip Car or a rental you actually feel it every time you reach into your pocket. So you can control your costs on a moment to moment basis."[26]

While it's impossible to say what Greg and Nina's precise transportation energy footprint is, there's no question that it's far lower than that of the typical American family. But unfortunately, as Dicum acknowledges, their formula wouldn't work for most. They are able to go carless because they live in one of the few American cities where urban form and public transportation make this possible. Without doubt, the city most epitomizing carless living in America is New York City, with more than half of all households lacking a car. Outside New York, the conditions needed for carless living are exceedingly rare. The Dicums' hometown of San Francisco—where currently about one quarter of all households are without a car and 45 percent commute by noncar means—is one of the few other places where this lifestyle is feasible (some others include Washington, D.C., Chicago, and Boston).[27] This is possible because San Francisco is dense and highly walkable; has a strong mix of land uses; and boasts a subway system (which Nina uses to get to her work on the San Francisco waterfront), a streetcar system, and an extensive bus network. But neighborhoods matter too. And their neighborhood, the Mission District, is one of the best places for being carless in San Francisco—and perhaps in the whole country. According to the website walkscore.com, which rates the walkability of any address in the country, Greg and Nina's house gets a score of 95 out of 100—labeled by the website as a "walker's paradise." According to the site, within a half-mile walk are six transit stops, seven grocery stores, eight restaurants (most of them amazing), seven coffee shops, eight bars, four movie theatres, seven schools, two libraries, two parks, eight bookstores, seven fitness clubs, four hardware stores, and five drug stores.

Go across the San Francisco Bay, however, and this lifestyle is not nearly as feasible. Outside San Francisco, the 5-million-person Bay Area looks not too different from the rest of the nation, with an 8 percent rate of households without cars. Even highly urbanized San Jose (with a larger population than San Francisco's) fails badly, with its 6 percent rate of carless households and its 4 percent rate of public transit commuting. That many of the Bay Area communities with the highest rates of car ownership are also on a subway line (take, for instance, Pleasanton, with a 3 percent carless rate, or Livermore, with a 4 percent rate) provides fairly solid evidence that making public rail transit available is not enough.

If there's anything that Greg and Nina's example demonstrates, it's that reducing our transportation energy footprint is more likely to succeed by simple math than by philosophizing. Cars still make more sense for the vast majority of American cities. The number of people who could run the calculations that Greg did and find the no-car option to be superior is very small. This speaks to a fundamental issue (some might say "problem," others "strength") of how American cities are planned and laid out: most were built for the car.

There's a growing strain of antigovernment sentiment in the United States that perceives planners as seeking to impose a European style of development on American cities against popular will. As the conservative writer Steven Hayward writes, "The new urbanism seeks to mandate high-density, neotraditional neighborhoods as the only development pattern of the future and as the way to redevelop existing cities and suburbs. They approach urban problems with an attitude that could justly be described as 'Planning Über Alles.'"[28] The irony behind this view is that the near opposite is true: historically, land-use planning and policy have given Americans little choice but to live in low-density, auto-oriented suburbs. Greg and Nina are lucky to live and work in one of the few places where carless living is a feasible option. But millions of people who want to live in such "neotraditional," walkable neighborhoods can't, simply because such a choice doesn't exist in their area. And many who do have such neighborhoods in their area can't move to them because of the higher price of housing in them, an indicator both that demand is high and supply is limited for this style of living. So, at the end of the day, promoting compact and walkable development doesn't come down to socialism, bureaucracy, or jackboots but to something that libertarians like Steven Hayward should love: choice.

Before plunging headlong into any kind of paradigm shift in integrated urban and transportation planning, however, Americans need to take a deep breath and look at the big picture. So just as Duncan Crary uses his canute as a chance to gain a new perspective on the urban landscape around him, planners and policy makers need to look at American cities from a new angle.

And to understand where our cities are going, we need to understand where they came from.

Global Oil Depletion

PREDICTING THE DEPLETION curve for the United States, with its well-inventoried geological resources, is relatively straightforward. Doing so for the entire world, however, is much more complicated. At the heart of the problem is uncertainty about the extent of global resources—particularly those under water or ice. In the case of oil, while we know roughly how much has been extracted to date, huge discrepancies exist about how much remains in the ground. Estimates of remaining recoverable conventional petroleum reserves range from 870 billion to 3.2 trillion barrels. This variance is at least in part due to differences in methods of estimating so-called undiscovered resources or petroleum deposits that are not proven but are expected. They also vary based on assumptions about growth in existing reserves and whether product categories like "conventional oil produced by un-conventional means" are included. As a result of all these differences in assumptions, estimates of the peak year of production range from 2001 to nearly 2040.

Chances are that we're either past or very near a peak in global oil production, though. One reason is that most countries tend to exag-gerate their oil reserve estimates for economic and political gain. For instance, in the 1980s an edict by the Organization of the Petroleum Exporting Countries (OPEC) stipulated that the higher a member country's state reserves, the more oil it could export. Conveniently, around that time, the six largest OPEC countries "discovered" that col-lectively they had roughly twice the reserves than previously stated. More recently, with WikiLeak's release of years of confidential US dip-lomatic correspondence in November 2010, it was learned that Saudi Arabia's estimates of reserves may be inflated by up to 40 percent and that production rates are unlikely to ever get near commonly accepted targets.[2]

An even bigger reason for the likely overstatement of recoverable reserves has to do with "energy return on investment" (EROI). This term refers to how much energy input is required to produce a unit of energy output. Oil's extremely high energy return on investment is what makes it such a great fuel. Under good conditions, very little energy is required to extract and process it relative to all other energy sources. However, its EROI has been steadily declining as the "easy oil" has been used up, leaving increasingly hard-to-obtain oil in such locales as deep-ocean environments. This is why in the United States in 1930, one hundred barrels of oil could be extracted using one barrel's worth of energy. But that declined to thirty to one in 1970 and eighteen to one in 2000. This pattern of decline is similar, although delayed, for global oil production, which was estimated to be thirty-five to one in 1999, eighteen to one in 2005 and twelve to one in 2008.[3]

Thus, with each passing year it takes a bit more oil to extract a given amount of oil out of the ground. Therefore, using total oil reserves as an indicator of supply is misleading. A more meaningful metric of supply would subtract out the energy resources required to obtain the remaining oil, taking into account the fact that energy return on investment will continue to decline. If we frame supply this way, the estimate of net oil stocks will shrink at an even faster rate than we're extracting it. Technological advances can help offset some of the decrease in energy return on investment by increasing energy efficiency of exploration and drilling, but the continuous drop in energy return on investment indicates technology's limits. And even if prices of oil go up to near infinity, that doesn't change the fundamental constraints of energy return on investment. High energy prices become a double-edged sword as energy return on investment declines, because although the extractors receive a high price, they also have to pay a high price for the energy required in extraction.

Eventually, the oil left in the ground will be so hard to reach that the energy return on investment could approach one to one. At that point, there may still be billions of barrels left in the ground, but no way to get them without expending more energy than we obtain. As Kenneth Deffeyes, the noted Princeton petroleum geologist, writes: "My prediction is that the remaining half of the oil in most reservoirs will not be economically recoverable, even at high oil prices. Lots of cleverness, time and money have gone into enhanced recovery projects. It doesn't mean that we should stop thinking about enhanced recovery. . . . It does mean that we'd better not count on using the remaining oil for at least a decade. In fact, it may never be recoverable." The increasing cost of getting the remaining oil out of the ground is now being recognized even by the International Energy Agency, an intergovernmental organization founded by the Organization for Economic Cooperation and Development, and among the most sanguine of the energy optimists, which projects that $5.4 trillion in infrastructure investment is needed prior to 2030 to replace failing capacity in oil wells. Without such investment, they contend, long-term prices will be driven up.[4]

Regardless of how much "effective oil" there is in the ground and what the average EROI is, it's likely that the globe is nearing or past its peak of oil production. As mentioned earlier, there are a number of estimates of the peaking date. Teasing them apart can be mind-boggling and reveals why so much confusion exists on the issue. It also reveals how conclusions can vary significantly depending on whom you trust. One of the biggest problems is that you can't know if you've hit a peak until you're well beyond it. As Matthew Simmons, the late energy-industry investment banker and government adviser, said in 2003: "Peaking of oil and gas will occur, if it has not already . . . and we will never know when . . . until we see it 'in our rear view mirrors.'"[5]

Nevertheless, if we examine the historical data and the range of forecasts, it becomes fairly clear that if the peak has not already occurred, it's imminent. The world shows no sign of the dramatic increases in production that are consistent with the optimistic viewpoints. A 2008 review evaluated a large number of forecast models of peak oil production. Of sixty-four scenarios evaluated, all but eleven showed the peak for crude oil production occurring between

2009 and 2031, similar to a 2009 study that found a peak after 2030 unlikely.

The idea that peak oil is imminent became considerably more mainstream when, in late 2010, the normally optimistic International Energy Agency (IEA) released a report that headlined the peak oil, estimating the crude oil production peak at 2006 and the total petroleum production peak at between 2020 and 2035, depending on policies. Their take-home message was unusually grave for this generally upbeat agency: "If governments do nothing or little more than at present, then demand will continue to increase, supply costs will rise, the economic burden of oil use will grow, vulnerability to supply disruptions will increase and the global environment will suffer serious damage." The way to address this problem, they pointed out, is not to ramp up production but to dramatically reduce consumption through efficiency measures.[6]

When it comes to oil, the "rearview mirror" perspective is hard to gauge. The graph below, based on data from British Petroleum, shows how production has leveled off in recent years. The fact that production in 2009, the latest year for which data were available from this source, declined 2.6 percent over the previous year may just be a temporary blip in the data, but it may also indicate the beginning of a long-term decline. More worrisome is the fact that long-term rates of increase have slowed considerably, even as global prices for oil have increased. Taken together with the extensive modeling data, not to mention that world oil discoveries have been declining since the 1960s, it would seem prudent then to give some consideration to the possibility of an imminent oil peak.

The behavior of gasoline prices during the 2009 recession supports the imminence of a peak to a certain extent. This recession might be the first one in which energy prices have been prevented from hitting a natural bottom because of supply constraints. Despite this being the worst financial crisis since the Great Depression, oil prices did not fall nearly as far in relative terms as they had in previous, less severe recessions. As Jeff Rubin, an energy investment analyst, wrote, "What today's skeptics

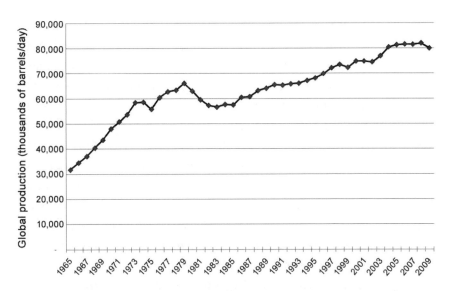

Global production of oil by year. (Data from the BP Statistical
Review of World Energy, 2010)

don't explain is why oil prices aren't $20 per barrel, as they were only
eight years ago, during the last recession . . . even though this recession
is well over three times as severe."[7] Since that statement was written, oil
prices have continued to climb despite a sluggish economic recovery.
These price increases may be partly due to the wave of instability in oil-
producing nations like Libya, currently happening as I write this—
nobody knows exactly how much. But even if price increases were
mostly due to Middle East instability (which they are likely not), the
fact that small supply disruptions can have such a big ripple effect illustrates just how little excess capacity there is in the system of global
oil production.

Furthermore, the thought of an imminent global oil peak is no
longer a fringe idea. Expressing an increasingly common view among
energy ministers, Andris Piebalgs, Energy Commissioner for the European Union, wrote in a 2009 blog posting: "The world is aware that
the production of the existing oil wells is decaying and that new discoveries are more scarce and more expensive. Some experts consider

that global oil production may have peaked. . . . We have to reduce our dependency in all those areas in which black gold is not indispensable, such as heating, or electricity production. . . . One thing is certain, one day we are going to run out of oil, and to prepare for that day we may be running out of time."[8]

Even the IEA is acknowledging that oil production will shortly be outstripped by demand. In their latest World Energy Outlook report, they project conventional crude-oil production will increase only modestly in the future. They point out that to offset increasing decline rates massive investment would be required, but that it is uncertain whether these investments can be implemented fast enough to meet rising demand. They also point out that even if demand remained totally flat, four Saudi Arabias' worth of capacity would have to be built by 2030 to offset declines.[9] Given that large new discoveries of economically recoverable oil deposits are dropping off and opportunities for large oil-field investments are shrinking, these findings can be interpreted as further support that the world is facing fundamental geological supply constraints.

Whether the peak happened in 2005 or will occur in 2015, the precise date doesn't matter except in the short term. What matters with regard to prices is that we are in the general vicinity of a peak. Being near the peak means that increasing production to meet increased demand gets harder and harder, and global energy supply can no longer be as responsive to increased demand. The end result of increased demand and decreased supply is, not surprisingly, higher prices.

CHAPTER 4

From Dirt Tracks to Interstates

D riving across the United States may not sound like much of a feat, but when Horatio Nelson Jackson, a resident of Vermont, accepted a $50 wager to prove that he could do so, people thought he was crazy. It might help to explain that this bet was made in 1903, at which time there were only 150 miles of paved road in the entire United States. In fact, only about 6 percent of the nation's other roads were considered "improved," the rest being little better than dirt tracks. There were no gas stations in the entire country. Fuel had to be purchased in small cans from the shelves of country stores. And cars were so new and poorly understood that some cities banned them, while one state required cars on city streets to be preceded by a man waving a red flag, and another required a week's notice in advance of any automobile trip.[1]

None of this deterred Jackson, a well-to-do Burlington, Vermont, physician and businessman (whose house stands about half a mile from my office). The wager took place while he was visiting San Francisco, only a few days before he was scheduled to return to Vermont by train. With good humor and optimism, but little planning, equipment, or relevant knowledge, he set out from San Francisco with a travelling companion, Sewell Crocker (they later added to their crew a pit bull named "Bud"), in a used two-cylinder Winton, just a few days after the wager, only to blow a tire within fifteen miles. From there on, things went

Horatio Nelson Jackson and the car in which he crossed
the United States. (By permission of the University of
Vermont Library, Special Collections)

from bad to worse as they encountered roads that Nelson described as "a compound of ruts, bumps and 'thank you, m'ams'" and much of their gear jiggled off the car and was lost. In some areas, roads were so bad they preferred to simply drive through untracked sagebrush instead. In others, roads were being used as irrigation channels by ranchers. In Alturas, California, Jackson needed tires and spare parts; ironically, the only way he could get them was by horse-drawn stagecoach—a delivery that took more than a week. And later, in southeastern Oregon, a horse had to tow the Winton back to the nearest town of Lakeview. As for lodging, it ranged from backcountry hotels to the attic of a rural ranch house, where "we found a pile of rags in one corner with two blankets that every settler coming this way since '49 had slept under." On the way farther east, in what is probably one of the most iconic encounters ever between symbols of the new and old West, they encountered some of the last homesteaders in wagon trains, seeking to claim what little free land remained. The homesteaders were so taken aback and baffled by the automobile that several hid under a wagon, thinking that a freight train had derailed and somehow was charging down the prairie. None of those involved in this encounter could have possibly predicted that only a few decades later, the automobile would become perhaps the single most common sight in America.

Eighty-six years later I made my first of ten cross-country drives. By then the United States was crisscrossed by interstate highways to such an extent that the biggest challenge was getting off the beaten path. Being able to drive quickly from coast to coast with ease and comfort was nothing new by 1989. Just one year after Jackson's journey, a cross-country drive could be done in half the time of Jackson's two-month trek, and two years later that was halved again. In 1908 the first truck, a three-ton Packard, would cross the country. And not too long after, work would be begin on linking road segments to form the Lincoln Highway, the first paved transcontinental highway, which would be fully paved in the late thirties. Horatio Nelson Jackson died only one year before the first projects of the national interstate highway system officially broke ground in 1956. About five years later, the country was virtually girded in concrete, with about thirteen thousand miles of interstate highways.

In just over fifty years, the United States went from a system of roads that would not have been out of place in the Middle Ages to having the most advanced and extensive road network of any civilization in human history. In fact, at the time of Jackson's drive, the average highway in America was generally worse than it had been a century earlier—and they were far worse than roads in most European countries, particularly France, which in the nineteenth century had a road system the United States would not rival until the 1920s. A study commissioned by Congress in the early twentieth century found that poor roads forced American farmers to pay 3.5 times as much to haul a ton of produce as their French counterparts, while another study found that it cost a Georgia farmer as much to ship a bushel of peaches twenty miles on roads as it cost a California farmer to ship those peaches across country by rail. Among the reasons for the United States' neglect of roads was that the railroad-building bonanza of the nineteenth century had resulted in so many miles of track that there was little political will to build roads, which were generally funded by local taxes.[2] It also didn't help that throughout the nineteenth century Congress had continually rejected funding a comprehensive national road system in favor of a model that put individual communities—the vast majority of which had no professional or technical staff or expertise—in charge of building roads.

Progress on the nation's road infrastructure was slow in the early automobile years. In 1916 the first ever federal roads bill, the Federal-Aid Road Act, was signed by Woodrow Wilson, authorizing $75 million to be spent over five years in partnership with the states. At the time it was signed, there were almost seven times as many horses as automobiles in the country, and most long-distance transport occurred by railroad, which carried more than one million people and two million tons of freight annually, with their fleet of over sixty thousand locomotives and two million freight cars. This new involvement in roads represented a significant change in philosophy from the federal government's perspective, but there was little to show from this bill owing to the intervention of World War I. By the time the war was over only five hundred thousand dollars had been spent and twelve miles of road built.[3]

Things changed in 1919, when Thomas Harris MacDonald of Iowa took control of the federal Bureau of Public Roads (BPR). This rather colorless engineer, with an all-consuming passion for properly built highways, took an obscure and almost nonexistent federal agency and turned it into a governmental powerhouse that would help set government priorities for decades to come. With his hands on many levers of power in Washington, MacDonald succeeded in quintupling the appropriation of his department in the 1921 Highway Act—and he spent it. Within one year his agency had added ten thousand miles of new highway, yielding, as MacDonald correctly pointed out, greater progress to the nation's highway system than in the entire previous century. By the end of the decade, his agency's count of highway miles built was up to ninety thousand.[4]

All this building would have lacked significance had there been no cars to drive on them. At the time of Nelson's journey, owning a car was out of reach for all but the most wealthy. A top-of-the-line Mercedes cost about $8,000 (around $190,000 in today's dollars), while similar domestic models were about half that. But the assembly-line techniques pioneered by Henry Ford slashed these costs. By 1913, a Model T was going for only $525 and by 1924 that cost was down to about $300 (about $4,000 today). This was the yin to the highway's yang. One could not prosper without the other, and thanks to the impeccable synchronization of MacDonald's rise to power with Henry Ford's revolution, by the late 1920s the United States was leading the global automobile revolution.

These early twentieth-century roads were simple affairs—generally only two lanes with at-grade intersections. MacDonald and most of the general public knew that this type of road would soon become inadequate as automobile traffic increased, but no vision existed for what the road of the future should look like. The new vision came in the late 1930s, in the form of the Pennsylvania Turnpike. Although a state road (with much of the funding coming from Roosevelt's Public Works Administration), it set the standard for the future federal Interstate Highways System. When completed in 1940, its 160 miles and 1.2 million cubic yards of glistening concrete were the engineering wonder of the transportation world. Unlike earlier highways, it offered limited access through designated on- and off-ramps (gated by toll stations). Bridges and underpasses eliminated at-grade crossings, and banked curves eliminated the need to slow down. The ability of cars and trucks to drive at dramatically higher speeds and to avoid stopping cut out five hours of the travel time between Harrisburg and Pittsburgh.

A few years after the completion of the Pennsylvania Turnpike (many more state turnpike systems would follow shortly), General Dwight Eisenhower experienced firsthand Europe's equivalent to Pennsylvania's modern highway marvel. Germany's Autobahn was, at the time, the most advanced national road system on earth. Eisenhower was highly impressed by how efficiently he was able to move military personnel and materiel around the country. Eisenhower was no stranger to bad roads, having grown up in rural Kansas in the late nineteenth century. He was also familiar with the difficulties of long-distance intercity road travel in America, having participated in an epic 1919 military motor convoy across the country—the first of its kind. The motorcade, consisting of eighty-one vehicles, almost three hundred soldiers and officers, and a fifteen-piece brass band, required sixty-two days to cross the country, in the opposite direction traveled by Jackson. Encountering roads ranging from "average to non-existent," the motorcade averaged only five miles an hour and sometimes covered only three miles a day. In the process, army engineers had to rebuild sixty-two bridges that were unable to support the convoy's weight. This journey made an impression on young Lieutenant Colonel Eisenhower, not only because of its difficulty but also because he had to file an official report that included a detailed inventory of the road types and conditions. Conditions were generally favorable, he found, until reaching

Lieutenant Colonel Dwight Eisenhower's 1919 convoy crossing the country.
(Courtesy of the Eisenhower Presidential Library Archives)

Nebraska, where they started to deteriorate. By Utah they were nearly intolerable: "From Orr's Ranch, Utah, to Carson City, Nevada, the road is one succession of dust, ruts, pits, and holes. This stretch was not improved in any way, and consisted only of a track across the desert."[5]

Memories of this trip (not to mention the terrible roads of wartime France and Belgium) were on his mind as he sped over near-perfect stretches of the Autobahn in 1945. In his memoirs he wrote, "The old convoy had started me thinking about good, two-lane highways, but Germany had made me see the wisdom of broader ribbons across the land. . . . This was one of the things that I felt deeply about, and I made a personal and absolute decision to see that the nation would benefit by it."[6]

So when President Eisenhower found himself with a domestic agenda to build and a looming recession to fight as the Korean War wound down, interstate highway construction was the top item on his list. Eisenhower saw this not only as an imperative condition of economic progress but also as a critical element of defense. Military planners of the time felt that an Autobahn-like highway system would allow for mass evacuation of cities and quick transportation of military assets in the event of a nuclear attack. A key component of many military planners' visions was that these highways make a perimeter around cities to allow military convoys to avoid traffic.

After a number of failed attempts at getting a bill through Congress (ironically Vice President Al Gore's father, Albert Gore Sr., was a key Senate architect of this highly carbon-intensive plan), the Federal-Aid Highway Act of 1956 was passed. The most far-reaching highway bill in the history of the country, it authorized $25 billion for twelve years of construction on a vast network of limited-access, divided interstate highways, to be paid for through a trust fund supported by federal fuel taxes. The federal government would cover 90 percent of construction costs, leaving only 10 percent to the states, and would have the authority to acquire rights-of-way. Highway building, once under local and then under state control, was now firmly in federal territory.

By the time Eisenhower was getting ready to leave office, thousands of miles of interstate had been built, and it seemed as if success could be declared. However, one small detail had eluded the president, and it put the entire undertaking in question for him and many others. Never a detail-oriented man (he generally relied on subordinates for such things), Eisenhower had been under the assumption that highways built under the bill he signed would skirt cities, like the Autobahn does. Put another way, he wanted the federal government to have nothing to do with building large highways that penetrated into central cities. Unfortunately, he had failed to read the fine print of the bill. The exact moment when he realized this is a matter of some debate. Some say it was when he was meeting with the planner Harland Bartholomew and the National Capitol Planning Commission in 1959. Others say it was while his limousine was stopped in traffic for interstate construction on the way out of Washington, D.C., at which point he asked an aide who it was that had allowed this interstate to be built in a city (the answer being "you, Mr. President").[7]

However he learned of this, Eisenhower immediately met with his adviser on public-works planning to determine what he could do.

Through a "highest priority" directive, he convened a committee of insiders who were opposed to the concept of intracity federal highways to go up against the BPR, which was firmly entrenched on the side of intracity highways. Recruiting a number of specialists to form study groups, the committee issued sophisticated reports with arguments that sounded not unlike those of modern-day critics of the interstate system: the interstate planning process in place at that time did not coordinate with, and failed to recognize the value of, other modes of transportation; limited-access four-lane highways in rural areas were extravagant and unnecessary; current approaches toward building interstates in urban areas were destructive and unwarranted; there were too many exits in urban areas, compromising the purpose of the system; and they were built with little consideration for urban planning. Based on these findings, the committee issued a demand to the BPR that they immediately delay the approval of all contemplated intra-urban interstates, devise new criteria for building them based on routing around rather than through cities, and establish a comprehensive urban planning process in advance of approvals.[8]

Unfortunately for Eisenhower and his dedicated committee, while their ideas were valid, the legislative record was decidedly not on their side. In fact, intra-urban interstates had been a central part of the BPR's plans since a core 1944 document upon which the current Highway Act was based. And that act was explicit in providing for interstates through the middle of urban areas. A bound book, known as the "Yellow Book," with detailed maps of all the proposed interstate routes, including blow-up maps of all the urban ones, had been distributed in 1955 to the White House and all members of Congress.

In an April 1960 meeting, which included the president; the ad hoc committee chair, General John Stewart Bragdon; and BPR chief Bertram Tallamy, the matter was finally put to rest. According to the official meeting record, Eisenhower stated that running interstates through congested urban areas was "entirely against his original concepts and wishes." The record goes on to say (illustrating perhaps the greatest "the dog ate my homework" moment in White House history) that "he was certainly not aware of any concept of using the program to build up an extensive intra-city route network as part of the program he sponsored. He added that those who had not advised him that such was being done, and those who had steered the program in such a direction, had not followed his wishes." Despite his disappointment, Eisenhower realized that any further effort against intra-urban highways was a losing proposition as soon as Tallamy produced a copy of the Yellow Book—the one that the president was supposed to have looked at several years earlier. Not only did that book make the plan to penetrate major urban areas explicit, but the highway maps it showed made something else clear: a highway bill of this magnitude would never have passed Congress without those intra-urban highways, for they represented valuable capital projects that dozens of urban Congressmen could take home to their constituencies. All participants knew that an earlier version without the publicized intra-urban routes had failed in the Congress. They may or may not have been aware that only one representative whose district included proposed intra-urban highways in the Yellow Book voted against the final bill, and he was not reelected. As the official record of the meeting states: "In other words, the Yellow Book depicting routes in cities had sold the program to Congress."[9]

This new policy of directing massive investments into established urban areas to build infrastructure for cars, made possible by presidential inattention to detail, was to have enormous consequences for the built form of most American cities. Thereafter, if state and local governments wanted their dip at the federal trough, they had to prioritize highway travel. In the long term, this meant not only a dramatic disinvestment in all other modes of transportation but also significant changes in land-use patterns. In the short term, however, this policy entailed the destruction of hundreds of unlucky neighborhoods that new highways happened to plow through. An average mile of urban freeway took twenty-four acres of land, and an average interchange eighty acres. Most of the land needed for such highways was already densely inhabited. Their construction created dead zones where noise and pollution made it hard to live, or they chopped neighborhoods in two, causing isolation, cutting off communities from services, and hastening urban blight. City governments were well aware of this, yet, according to Tom Lewis, a historian of highways, "the fear of losing the ninety percent federal share of the financing—the only substantial help the Eisenhower administration had given them—was so great that they chose to deal with the devil."[10] It should come as no surprise that the communities where planners generally chose to site highways were low income and minority populated—places where, it was believed, resistance would be minimal.

To highway planners of the time, it seemed unthinkable that there could be any discontent with the system they were building. Although engineers of the period could build nearly perfect roadways, they were painfully out of touch with the constituency they were supposedly serving. Perhaps the most classic example of this engineering myopia (some would call it hubris) was a 1963 proposal of highway engineers who were strongly considering detonating twenty-two buried nuclear bombs to obliterate eastern California's Bristol Mountains, which were standing in the way of Interstate 40. Luckily the plan was never executed.

To their surprise, federal highway engineers discovered that not every city or regional government embraced their model of intracity highway construction with equal vigor; nor did all communities in the path of highways accept the process with the expected minimal level of resistance. In many cities, neighborhood groups started to organize, giving birth to a new term: "freeway revolt." A number of early intracity freeway segments had been built with minimal opposition through low-income and mostly African-American neighborhoods. But as plans were publicized to run freeways through more affluent and well-organized neighborhoods, or through important historic or scenic areas, things began to change, particularly after those constituencies saw the impact on the neighborhoods that had already been bulldozed.[11] In cities where the groundswell was sufficient, local and regional governments often followed suit by opposing federal highway plans. Ultimately, these divergent paths of highway development were to have long-lasting consequences on energy metabolism.

Probably the earliest city to have a highway revolt was San Francisco. Highway planners had not anticipated this reaction, because the city had more automobiles per capita than any other at the time. In hindsight, this revolt should not have been surprising considering the aesthetic and cultural values at stake. The construction of a portion of the Embarcadero Freeway in 1959, along the city's eastern waterfront just north of the Bay Bridge, illustrated just how destructive such highways could be; this one cut off residents from the water, isolated iconic waterfront developments like the San Francisco Ferry Building, and spoiled world-class views—all concerns to which highway engineers of the time seemed oblivious. Anxious residents of neighborhoods slated for the bulldozer quickly mobilized, and, within just a few months, the San Francisco Board of Supervisors passed a resolution opposing construction of seven of ten remaining freeway projects. In response to a revised freeway construction plan released in 1964, two hundred thousand people took to the streets for a massive rally.[12] The legacy of this rejection is still felt today in terms of the way San Franciscans get around.

At about the same time, highway revolts began blossoming around the country against numerous ill-planned central-city highway projects: the proposed Vieux Carré Expressway that would have run through the French Quarter of New Orleans; the South Street Crosstown Expressway in Philadelphia; the inner Beltway that would connect Washington, D.C., to Virginia; the plans to run Interstate 40 through a dense and historic portion of midtown Memphis; and the Mount Hood Freeway and Interstate 505 in Portland, Oregon. And then there was New York City, where bulldozing neighborhoods for highways had already become an art form under the guiding hand of Robert Moses, the controversial New York planner, parks commissioner, and highway builder, who was quoted as saying, "When you operate in an overbuilt metropolis you have to hack your way through with a meat axe."[13] Although Moses had successfully built hundreds of miles of parkways in the New York metro area throughout the 1940s and 1950s (he was also the consultant responsible for the designs of many intra-urban highways in other cities), the 1960s brought extensive freeway revolts to the city, leading to the cancellation of projects such as the Lower and Mid-Manhattan Expressways, the Bushwick Expressway in Brooklyn, and the Queens and the Queens-Interboro Expressway. While it's impossible to say how New York City would have been different had these been built, it seems reasonable to assume that today's city is far less dependent on cars than it might have otherwise been.

Another city whose freeway revolts succeeded in tipping the balance slightly away from cars and toward transit was Portland, Oregon. The proposed Mount Hood Freeway (to be part of Interstate 84) was rejected through the election of an anti-freeway mayoral candidate (Neil Goldschmidt) in 1972, following a contentious campaign. The proposed federal funds to have been used for the highway were successfully rerouted into a light-rail line connecting Portland with the suburb of Gresham.

Eventually, the majority of major American cities would experience some kind of freeway revolt. But while many cities' revolts succeeded in halting significant and extensive portions of their intra-urban highway network, others resulted in little more than minor tweaks to the originally planned urban highway layout, if anything at all. According to the historian Raymond Mohl, there were numerous reasons why freeway revolts had such radically different outcomes: the legacy of neighborhood activism and intergroup alliances; the level of support from local politicians and media; and the historical existence of a strong locally based planning tradition.[14] But even more important was the period in which the revolts occurred. Highway segments that were built shortly after the 1956 Act generally met little opposition; those that were delayed into the 1960s—by which time their destructive effects were better known and neighborhood groups had had time to organize—met far more opposition. By the late seventies, freeway revolts were the rule rather than the exception, and highway planners were finding it nearly impossible to build anything in some cities.

But by the time many of these cities began successfully embracing the latter-day freeway revolt, the die was already cast—they were totally dependent on highway travel. For many of these too-little-too-late cities, the revolts were more about keeping specific neighborhoods intact, and less about subduing the dominance of cars and highways. Probably no place illustrates that attitude better than Los Angeles.

According to a 1966 interview in *Cry California* magazine, the Farrier family lived on the freeways of Los Angeles—literally. Following a pregnancy that forced Marilee Farrier to quit her full-time job and that left the couple in debt, they had a choice of selling their house or their motor home. They chose to sell the former. Each day the family, with baby in tow, would leave their parking space in downtown Los Angeles, take the Hollywood Freeway to Burbank to drop Steve off at his job, then drive about 25 miles on the Golden State and San Bernardino Freeways to Marilee's mother's house in El Monte, where she would leave the baby with her mother and take the camper another five miles down the San Bernardino Freeway to West Covina to work a half day at a department store. After work, she'd pick up the baby and do the 25 miles back to Burbank to pick up dad. On the return trip to downtown, dinner would be heated and would eventually be eaten in the peace of the parking lot. All this for a grand total of 128 miles per day.[15]

A number of reporters tried to get interviews with the Farriers after the article appeared but were unsuccessful. It turned out that the article was a hoax. The author William Bronson and the staff of *Cry California*, an environmental magazine, wrote the piece apparently to illustrate the ridiculousness of Los Angeles' freeway culture. That the story was believable enough to pique the interests of reporters was evidence of this.[16]

Los Angeles is associated with the automobile perhaps more than any other place except Detroit. Cars are not just a means of transportation but a centerpiece of culture that is both adored and reviled. Angelenos' ambivalent love affair with the car started early. "How can one

A traffic jam on the 101 Freeway in Los Angeles. (Photo by author)

pursue happiness by any swifter or surer means than by the use of the automobile?" asked a 1926 *Los Angeles Times* article.[17]

Any honeymoon between Los Angeles and the automobile didn't last long. Facing a population explosion that started in the early twentieth century (from 1920 to 1930, it more than doubled, to 2.2 million), Los Angeles' transportation engineers have constantly struggled to keep up with the onslaught of people and cars. Each successive wave of infrastructure development—first surfacing streets, then dividing highways, then creating the freeway system—gave some temporary relief but was soon overwhelmed by increased demand. As only one example of many, one month after the opening of the 1940 Arroyo Seco Parkway, commuters were already experiencing bumper-to-bumper traffic in their Packards and Studebakers.

The Los Angeles metro area consistently gets the worst ranking in terms of annual excess fuel consumed due to stalled traffic, average travel delay, and travel index (the ratio of the time a typical trip actually takes to the time it would take under free-flow conditions).

Postcard of the Arroyo Seco Parkway, 1941, drawn to suggest a rural driving experience. (Department of Archives and Special Collections, William H. Hannon Library, Loyola Marymount University)

And the average person from the Los Angeles region consumes nearly three times the gasoline per year of a New Yorker and twice that of a San Franciscan.[18] Even though these figures don't take into account the non-gasoline energy used for public transit, they still indicate that Los Angeles lags far behind its rival cities in terms of transportation energy use. The reasons for this are complex and multifaceted. But there's no doubt that Los Angeles' decisions to bet all its transportation chips first on the automobile and later on the freeway were among the most important. More than making Angelenos car-dependent, cars and freeways literally made Los Angeles what it is.

During a recent visit to Los Angeles, I took my kids for a walk to a panoramic spot in the Santa Monica Mountains, at the top of Kenter Canyon. On this stunningly clear December day, just after a rainstorm had swept away the smog and haze, I could see not only most of Los Angeles but even distant Orange, Riverside and San Bernardino Counties. Although I'd been to this spot dozens of times growing up, I'd never internalized the pattern that fundamentally defines Los Angeles

Three of the many subcenters of Los Angeles, photographed from
the Santa Monica Mountains. (Photo by author)

until that moment. Now I saw a vast sea of low- to medium-density
urban development, beginning at the coastline and ending at the San
Gabriel Mountains, punctuated by what looked like an archipelago
of isolated skyscraper islands—downtown being just one of many. In
other words, Los Angeles is less like a big metropolis than like a bunch
of small cities occupying the same general vicinity.

This anecdotal characterization of mine has actually been quanti-
fied. First, it turns out that Los Angeles is not sprawling, according
to traditional density-based measures. In fact, a recent report by the
Brookings Institution found it to be the densest metropolitan area in
the country. Rather, the problem lies in how its density is arranged. According to Reid Ewing's multidimensional sprawl index (mentioned in
the last chapter), one particular attribute stands out for Los Angeles—
the variable describing "centeredness." Los Angeles' score is abysmal—
among the worst in the country. It has no concentration of activity like
Manhattan or Chicago that orients people's daily activities. Instead,
true to its individualist nature, Los Angeles is a city where everyone is
going every which way. While Hollywood celebrities are doing yoga to
find their "centers," the city where they live is missing just that.[19]

There's a commonly held perception that Los Angeles was always destined for this style of nontraditional, low-density urbanism—that it simply self-selected the types of people who wanted nothing to do with the old-fashioned eastern vertical city. To a certain extent this is true; the vision for the multinucleated city actually predated the construction of the freeway system. According to the historian Jeremiah Axelrod, many of Los Angeles' early planners pictured the region growing into a series of connected, semibucolic, peripheral "garden cities"—a response, no doubt, to a perception of urban living characterized by shadowy tenements, pollution, crime, and filth. However, by no means was this view universally held in Los Angeles. In fact, in the 1920s, Los Angeles was facing a major identity crisis that could have taken it in either of two radically different directions. Although garden cities were being promoted by some, many of Los Angeles' most prominent business leaders wanted something different: to see the area grow vertically into a dense and compact monocentric city, with all activity focused on downtown, so as to rival the great eastern cities. If you look at promotional materials from this time, you'll see lots of renderings of massive skyscrapers with zeppelins docked on the roof. The "centralizer" faction realized that there would be many other satellite communities in the Los Angeles Basin, but that as those grew, downtown Los Angeles would have to grow proportionally in order to retain its regional dominance. The problem was that by the 1920s, many outlying communities, particularly those on the Westside, were already beginning to get big; to the centralizer faction that meant downtown would have to become enormous quickly. That vision was already well on its way to reality by 1930; while only 16 skyscrapers reached downtown Los Angeles' designated height limit in 1918, that number was up to 103 in 1929, making downtown Los Angeles one of the most extensive urban cores in the country at the time.[20]

But dense downtowns require a way to move people around, and it was transportation that would be the deciding factor in Los Angeles' urban trajectory. By 1920, traffic and parking conditions in downtown Los Angeles were abysmal. As I discuss in more depth in Chapter 5, Los

Angeles had one of the world's largest streetcar systems by the 1920s. But even when streetcars were at their peak, Angelenos were buying cars in droves, with an average of eight residents per automobile in 1915, compared to forty-three per automobile for the United States as a whole and sixty-one per automobile for Chicago. By 1924, the number of cars commuting daily into Los Angeles was greater than all the registered cars in New York State at that time, and the corner of Adams and Figueroa in downtown had the heaviest volume of car traffic in the United States. In 1927, Bruce Bliven, a journalist for the *New Republic*, observed that Los Angeles "is now a completely motorized civilization. Nowhere else in the world have human beings so thoroughly adapted themselves to the automobile." He goes on to describe how the car is not just transportation, but an element of culture: "A great proportion of the male population has no other real interest in life than motor machinery. Bridge and golf mean a little something; but mention air-cooling, or valves-in-head, and behold the sudden warm expansion!" Cars had become so central to life in downtown that surface parking lots occupied a huge proportion of this valuable acreage, as the image on the next page shows. In just a few years, cars had become a defining feature for what set Los Angeles apart. As the 1920s, with its madcap growth rates, came to a close, a showdown was being set up between rails and rubber.[21]

As car ownership increased and downtown congestion grew unbearable, it became evident that there were other, less congested places for businesses to operate while remaining accessible to customers. After all, Los Angeles was located on a vast, flat plain where land was still abundant. This led to a blossoming of low-density, auto-oriented commercial development radiating out from downtown. As Donald Baker, president of the Planning Commission, said in his opening statement to a 1930 city-organized conference on transit planning, "When the carrying capacity of the street system in any section approaches the saturation point, people go elsewhere, and Los Angeles is only beginning to feel the results of this decentralization movement." By 1930, a quarter of all commercial and professional activity in Los Angeles

Aerial view of downtown parking lots in the 1930s, from
the 1937 Traffic Survey Plan. (Courtesy of the Automobile
Club of Southern California Archives)

was taking place outside of established business districts—a proportion that continued to rise throughout the 1930s. Because there was so much open land and so few constraints on where to locate, the pattern of commercial location during this time was haphazard at best. As Baker went on to say, "There is nothing to anchor our central area. In other cities they tear down existing buildings which become obsolete and build new ones. In Los Angeles we allow the old ones to stay and just move on a block." Major thoroughfares radiating from downtown, like Wilshire Boulevard, exhibited a leapfrog pattern of development in which commercial clusters sprang up seemingly overnight, often separated by miles of vacant lots or farmland. These new fringe districts were totally unsuited for any transportation mode other than the automobile. Business owners in peripheral areas adapted to this new reality by including large, centrally placed parking lots in their plans.[22] Many of these stores were miles from the nearest streetcar line, something that would have been previously unthinkable.

For a while, Angelenos thrived on this system of increasingly decentralized commercial activity, served by surface streets. But eventually the congestion that had once been confined to downtown overflowed into these hundreds of miles of peripheral roadways. Surface streets alone could not support the level of auto-mobility required for this new landscape. If this uniquely Southern Californian style of development and mobility was to continue, major limited-access highways would have to be built. But for years the Los Angeles planning establishment had been against these so-called "freeways" (as opposed to less utilitarian and more aesthetically oriented "parkways," which were promoted by planners).[23]

A key institution that propelled the freeway juggernaut was the Automobile Club of Southern California. Their landmark *Traffic Survey* was ostensibly written to spur debate, but in reality it was a detailed construction plan, already backed by many of the city's elite, who now no longer were wedded to the downtown dominance concept. In a sense, this was the first plan to recognize Los Angeles as the chaotic auto-dependent landscape that it was, and to propose a transportation solution that would conform to that reality, rather than battle it. As the plan states in the introduction: "The development of the Los Angeles area was not planned. It just grew by the piecing together through the years of numerous subdivisions. Land use has been determined largely upon the individual owner's guess as to the most profitable use that could be made of his holding. This guess, confused by the widespread use of the automobile as a means of individual transportation, has produced a chaotic intermingling of the various land use throughout the area. . . . There is little stability in either business or residential districts and the streets and highways are congested out of all proportion to service rendered." It then goes on to recognize that automobile-dependence is both the cause and the consequence of this scattershot decentralized pattern: "The widely scattered and intermingled shopping, industrial, cultural and residential districts of metropolitan Los Angeles, a condition for which the automobile is directly responsible, make the area peculiarly and vitally dependent upon the automobile for the major part of its transportation service."[24] Even though streetcars still ran, the die was clearly cast, and the inexorable pull of gravity was toward whatever solution allowed cars to go the fastest. The proposed solution was similar to what was just about to be constructed in Pennsylvania: massive raised and divided motorways without any intersections or interactions with surrounding land uses. And all this was years before the federal Bureau of Public Roads put its plans for intra-urban highways to paper. The design proposed by the Automobile Club is extremely close to what exists on the ground today. While planners at the time had hoped to temper the auto-centrism of the 1937 plan by calling for light rail in the medians of the highways, that element was never implemented.

The 1937 plan launched what became the nation's most ambitious and transformative metropolitan-level highway building campaign. By the time freeway construction petered out in the 1970s, with more than five hundred miles of them in place in Los Angeles County alone, these major arteries had come to define Los Angeles' urban form. According to the author Robert Gottlieb: "The freeway became the new

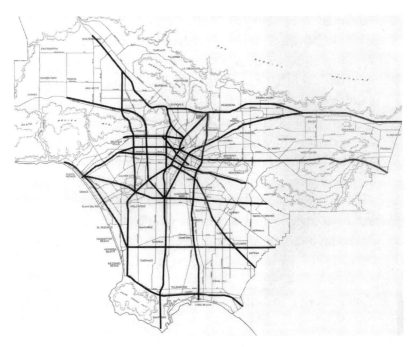

Proposed freeway locations for Los Angeles, from the 1937
Traffic Survey Plan. (Courtesy of the Automobile Club of
Southern California Archives)

center of the city. By the end of the twentieth century, Los Angeles
had indeed become the proverbial string of freeways in search of a
city."[25] Once perceived as a way of reducing congestion by facilitating
long trips (and, amazingly, once believed to be a form of relaxation by
simulating meandering country drives), soon the freeways defined the
city. Minibusiness hubs of gleaming high-rises started popping up at
dozens of freeway interchanges, looking like islands of glass in a sea of
single-family homes. Given an urban form like this, Angelenos had no
choice but to embrace the automobile.

Within a few years, Los Angeles was recognized by the rest of the
nation as the model for highway-oriented urbanism. In 1954 the *Satur-*
day Evening Post summed up this view in an article that reads like an
ethnography of a foreign culture:

[Los Angeles] is a city that rolls on rubber, for public transportation is inadequate to the needs of the population. . . . For some inexplicable reason, few Southern Californians would even consider living near their work. Many drive from twenty to fifty miles daily, to and from jobs. The result is, twice a day, one of the world's champion traffic tangles. Los Angeles commuters don't go into town to work in the morning and out of town in the evening, like New Yorkers or San Franciscans. . . . The motorists go every which way, and automobiles crisscross at 10,000 intersections as they scatter over this vast area. . . . At first, newcomers gaze in awe at the frantic, daring gamble of life and limb and vehicle. Then, after a few days, they catch the spirit and become mad motorists themselves.[26]

What's amazing about this characterization of Los Angeles is the year. Just twenty years earlier, streetcars had completely dominated the region, the unquestioned center of which was downtown. And more strikingly, the interstate highway system was still several years from being authorized by Congress, and divided highways were nonexistent throughout much of the country.

Los Angeles is still considered ground zero for freeways and the car-oriented lifestyle, largely because of the reputation it developed early on. But there's a bit of a twist to this mythology. Although the Los Angeles metro area currently ranks second in the nation in lane miles (after New York), it ranks dead last in terms of lane miles per capita. How could the king of the freeway world come to this? One reason is that just as Southern Californians were early adopters of the freeway, they were highly precocious in the ways of the "highway revolt." Most of the highway miles envisioned in the 1937 plan came to fruition, but only about three-fifths of the mileage proposed in the later, more ambitious 1959 master plan was ever implemented.[27] With this head start on freeway living, Angelenos had many extra years to grow frustrated with their freeways and learn how to oppose new ones. The result is a megalopolis designed for the freeway but with inadequate freeway miles to serve the development pattern they enabled in the first place.

If you ever drive through the suburban town of Essex, Vermont, just fifteen minutes from Burlington, you may end up driving on an odd little segment of limited-access highway, stretching only about three miles and connecting to no other limited-access highways. This is an isolated portion of a proposed federally funded sixteen-mile circumferential highway, known as "the Circ." It was intended to skirt the more heavily settled portions of the greater Burlington metro area, connecting to the region's one interstate (I-89) in two places in something like a half-ring (the segment that was built is isolated from the interstate). Planning began in the late sixties, with the expectation that everyone would love the new roadway. This was not the case. Although the existing segment was built in the early 1990s, progress stalled thereafter due to lack of funds. When the funds became available again, about ten years later, a wide array of opponents organized and galvanized, with the result that construction on two more proposed segments was enjoined by a federal judge just one day before it was scheduled to begin. The reason? The Environmental Impact Statement did not adequately address the extent of the proposed highway's "indirect impacts" on land use, growth, and development. Put simply, the proponents of the highway said that "induced development" would be limited to the immediate vicinity of exits or interchanges, while the opponents claimed that such a highway would significantly affect regional urban form by spurring growth in the sparsely settled exurbs outside the Circ, to the detriment of the central city. The opponents won that argument in court in 2004, and since then, despite a five-year, multimillion-dollar revision to the Environmental Impact Statement process, there appears to be little chance that this highway, or even a lower-impact alternative, will be built any time soon.

The case of the Circ brings up a fundamental chicken-egg question about cities: are highways a response to problems caused by urban form, or do they shape urban form? For much of the twentieth century, planners—particularly highways planners—believed in the former and discounted the latter. Over the past forty years, as highways have transformed the places they were meant to serve, there's been a shift in consciousness.

One vocal representative of this changing view is John Norquist, president of the Congress on New Urbanism and former mayor of Milwaukee. He believes that the historic role of roads has changed from a multipurpose public space to a single-purpose engineering solution to mass movement of goods and people. As he told me,

> The overscaled highways, the theory of congestion reduction as the main purpose for building a road—that departed from thousands of years of practice where you had three purposes for a road: the movement, the marketplace or economic, and social—town square of Main Street. Any time there was a street moving through an urbanized area, whether it was Rome or Constantinople, it would perform these multiple purposes, but in the twentieth century the road was developed with its only purpose being movement—and that's how we ended up with a lot of these big highways in the U.S., not so much in Europe, where they tended to avoid doing that.[28]

The battle against the Circ Highway is one of many that signal this change in consciousness. But unlike so many previous highway revolts, where opposition was motivated by direct impact to people's property, this battle was largely fought not by adjacent landowners but by interested citizens who didn't want to see their region take on a new, more suburban identity, a narrative made abundantly clear throughout all the opposition's outreach materials. This story suggests that cities are not predestined for a particular path of development, as many believe. Rather, it implies that the landscape of cities is a result of some inexorable forces but also of some choices—choices sometimes made administratively, sometimes through the democratic process, and sometimes through grassroots action. It also suggests there are key points in a city's history where radically different trajectories can be taken. And as we'll see, even Los Angeles had just such a window of opportunity.

Tar Sands

WHY DOES OIL MATTER so much if it's not the only source of energy? What about all the other fossil fuels? Can't they take the pressure off price as oil production declines? In short, the answer is no. Oil's role is of such vast importance in the world economy that reductions in its supply are bound to have significant effects on global energy prices in general. All the other fossil fuels have limitations and constraints that prevent them from fully occupying the gap that will be left from oil—that is, there is no "silver bullet solution." And demand will keep growing even as supplies shrink.

In the United States, oil currently accounts for about 37 percent of all energy consumed, making it by far the largest single source of energy, followed by gas and coal, which each account for between 20 and 25 percent.[1] Oil's dominance in the transportation sector is nearly complete, with about 70 percent of all imported oil going toward transportation. The hope is that as conventional oil production rates start to decline, substitutes can start taking up the slack, which would theoretically keep energy prices moderated. But with so much infrastructure geared toward oil, it would be naïve to think that more abundant sources, like coal, could easily be phased in to offset rising energy prices caused by shrinking petroleum supplies, particularly in the face of rising demand. Furthermore, each potential substitute comes with serious limitations. To give an idea of the magnitude of the shift that would have to happen to make up for oil, just to replace the energy capacity from the United States' imported oil, we'd need 750 new nuclear power plants (currently the United States has 104).

Some claim that as traditionally utilized crude oil runs out, we'll simply transition to "nonconventional" (others would say "dirtier") forms of petroleum. According to some, the most auspicious among these (if any could be called that) is tar sands. This is a form of underground oozy bitumen that Mother Nature hasn't cooked long enough to turn into conventional oil. It has a big advantage in that it can be relatively easily refined into synthetic crude oil. Being a liquid at normal temperatures is of enormous importance, because liquids can be stored in tanks, cheaply transported by tankers, trucks, or pipelines, and are essential to the internal combustion engine, the power source for nearly the entire transportation fleet. If tar sands were added to global oil-reserve stocks, they would significantly extend estimated reserves—Canada's tar sands are estimated to contain over 200 billion barrels' worth of oil reserves, which would make Canada the world's second largest possessor of oil reserves, after Saudi Arabia. One problem is that tar sands have a much lower energy return on investment (EROI) than oil or coal because they are diffuse—that is, the bitumen is mixed in with lots of dirt and sand that has to be sifted out, resulting in an estimated energy return on investment for obtaining heavy oil at between five to one and ten to one.[2] Tar sand extraction is also very environmentally destructive. Most tar sands are extracted by strip-mining vast acreages of land, literally denuding it in the process. A newer and less destructive air injection process has been developed but is far less commonly used.

With its low EROI and its destruction of carbon-sequestering forests, it's no wonder that tar sands' carbon footprint is among the worst of all energy sources; heavy oil from tar sands is believed to release about three times as much carbon dioxide as conventional oil, while the boreal forest that is being cut down to extract tar sands is thought to store more carbon per unit area than any other ecosystem in the world. So if greenhouse gas emissions regulations are implemented, the cost of extracting tar sands will dramatically increase relative to other energy sources. Furthermore, building tar sands infrastructure is very slow. Canada started investing forty years ago in this energy source but is only now seeing serious levels of production.

CHAPTER 5

Transit Wars

I

t was July 1959, the height of the Cold War, and the big news
was a two-week visit to the United States by Soviet First
Deputy Premier Frol Kozlov. This severe, unglamorous, and
alcoholic Kremlin functionary made news daily as he visited
low-income housing to see how "the workers" lived, hob-
nobbed with titans of industry at swanky barbeques, sampled mayonnaise for the first time at Woolworth's, and marveled at the
low price of cotton dresses. Among the many prearranged activities
for his delegation was an almost hour-and-a-half ride through New
York's IRT and BMT subways (in a scene that would not have been
out of place in the Borat movie, Kozlov sat next to Shirley Gaskins, a
young black woman on the subway car, telling her in heavily accented
English, "Your skin is colored, just like that of Mme. Nasriddinova—
and she is president of the Uzbek Republic!"). Although Kozlov had
nothing but positive things to say about the United States while in its
borders, his tone changed decidedly when he was back in the USSR
and Vice President Richard Nixon was in town for a reciprocal visit.
Interestingly, one of his loudest critiques—designed to highlight the
inefficiency and inequality of American society—related to the New
York subway system. He called the subways "lousy," telling reporters
that they "are dirty and the air is bad—very bad." By way of contrast, he
gave reporters a brief history of the excellent Moscow and Leningrad
subways. When asked for suggestions on improving New York's, he
said, "You would just have to reconstruct it, I think."[1]

Despite the Cold War hyperbole and Mr. Kozlov's less than stellar credibility, he was right on the subject of subways. At the time, New York's system—along with most of those in America—was lousy. Stations and cars were shabby and poorly maintained, while fares were high. Moscow, by contrast, sported a magnificent metro system, designed under Stalin's megalomaniacal leadership to represent the glory of his regime, resplendent with chandeliers, stained glass, bronze statues, marble masonry, and mosaics of Soviet achievements, not to mention highly subsidized fares.[2] That New York's subway system was—and still is—by far the best in this richest nation on earth, while Moscow's far superior system was built under the iron hand of Joseph Stalin in one of history's most inefficient economies, should be an indication of just how unsuited a nation like the United States is to constructing large public-transit systems. With its diverse mix of stakeholder interests, multitudinous government agencies, laissez-faire capitalist attitude, distrust in higher authority, decentralized and fragmented municipal planning structure, abundant regulatory hurdles, and fiercely independent grassroots democracy, the United States has always faced major challenges in implementing large regional infrastructure projects—particularly if they don't involve cars. Among such projects, subway construction has had among the steepest uphill battles to fight. For this reason, in many cities where subways seemed a natural thing to build, they simply were not.

As discussed in Chapter 3, rail transit tends to consume significantly less energy per capita than a single-occupancy automobile. The most efficient rail transit is the kind that operates on a separate vertical plane from street traffic (either subways or elevated rail), because it doesn't take up street space or contribute to traffic congestion. This type of rail transit also reduces transportation energy in the long-term by focusing new development and making cities more compact, resulting in shorter average trips. The larger the scale of the transit system, the more pronounced these effects are.

With its massive rail system that today carries more passengers than all other US rail transit systems combined (and is fourth in the world in terms of annual ridership), New York City is an excellent case in point. According to a recent study from the group CEOs for Cities, thanks to its massive subway system New Yorkers have the highest transit share in the country, at 57 percent, while they drive only an estimated 9 miles per person per day, as compared with 25 for other large US metro areas (in Houston it's almost 40). This means that New Yorkers drive 133 million miles less per day than they would if they were in an average American metropolitan area, and they require 48 billion fewer gallons of gasoline each year. And all this translates into a net savings of $19 billion per year for New Yorkers in reduced auto-related expenses—or 4 percent of all personal income earned by residents of New York City in 2007. In addition, the parking area saved by New Yorkers' lower car ownership is equivalent to the surface of Manhattan. But most important, the subway system has created the densest and most centered urban landscape in the country, allowing 10 percent of the population to commute by foot, compared to 2.9 percent at the national level.[3]

Reaching this vaunted position as the unquestioned transit leader in the country was far from easy. Manhattan desperately needed this system when construction began at the turn of the century—a time when traffic was horrendous. Thousands of horse-drawn railway cars competed for manure-strewn street space with buggies, wagons, jitneys, and pedestrians, all going less than six miles per hour. The elevated steam-rail system—the largest at the time with ninety-four miles of elevated track—wasn't much better: the trains went only twelve miles per hour on raised structures that generated falling debris and incessant noise and pollution. And even if the horse-drawn or elevated trains could have gone faster, their capacity was totally inadequate. The population and economy were booming but about to get strangled if nothing was done about the transportation problem. Merchants, wholesalers, and manufacturers were beginning to complain about chronic delays in shipments. Furthermore, the island geography of Manhattan meant compressing growing numbers of people into a limited area. If ever there was an American subway system destined to be built, it was this one.

But even with this extreme need, strong cultural, political, and economic barriers stood in the way—barriers that Joseph Stalin would have laughed at as he autocratically dictated the particulars of his pet subway project. After the initial lines were built, the system would continue to face enormous challenges to its needed expansions and, in some cases, its very existence, throughout much of the twentieth century.

On January 31, 1888, Mayor Abram Hewitt, who had recently bested Theodore Roosevelt in the 1886 mayoral race, proposed the construction of a massive rapid-transit system extending from southern Manhattan to the Bronx; yet it took more than twelve years for the ground breaking, and sixteen until the first trains started serving passengers. The plan was opposed by business leaders, who viewed government involvement in a major construction project as a violation of their core laissez-faire principles. Even the real estate industry, which served to benefit from higher land values, thought it was impractical and ill advised.[4]

When bids initially went out for sale of the franchise to run the line, no financier would touch it. Planners eventually realized that the project would have to be publically funded (although privately constructed and operated), but fears of Tammany Hall–style corruption and kickbacks almost derailed the process again. After an agreement was finally hammered out among the city's business leaders, a coalition of nearly one hundred unions intervened, pointing out that the general populace had been totally left out of the process, and calling for a referendum. When that referendum passed, yet another hurdle appeared: the newly formed Board of Rapid Transit Railroad Commissioners (RTC) would have to get consents to build the rail lines from owners of at least half of the properties abutting the projected route—in essence a second, narrowed referendum. The RTC failed to obtain the necessary consents largely because owners of downtown buildings feared structural property damage. At this point the only recourse allowed by law was to petition a panel. If the panel found the transit plan fiscally sound and if the state Supreme Court agreed with that finding, they could overrule the abutting property owners. The panel did so, but the court did not, issuing a scathing decision that dismissed the RTC's cost projections and finding that the subway's cost could not possibly fall under the statutory limit of $50 million. It was only through a compromise crafted by William Steinway (chair of the so-called Steinway Commission) calling for a significantly scaled-down subway route that the plan was able to pass muster with the court.

In the meantime, owners of the streetcar and elevated railway systems attempted their own form of delay by repeatedly proposing major extensions and improvements of their own routes without ever delivering any specifics—a tactic that took many months of the Commissioners' time, which could have been dedicated to advancing the subway plan. Adding to this confusion was the election in 1889 of the pro–Tammany Hall politician Robert Van Wyck as mayor. His ties to the antisubway elevated rail and streetcar monopolies led him to stymie the RTC by amending the law repeatedly and attempting to introduce legislation designed to favor existing railroad interests. Despite this minefield, progress continued. But when contracts were finally put out to bid, it turned out that no one had both the requisite skills and the finances to post the huge bond stipulated by the 1894 New York Rapid Transit Act—one of many stipulations that some felt had been inserted in the law by the railroad and streetcar industry to hobble chances for actual subway construction. While no single bidding entity existed with this combination, the eventual bidder, John B. McDonald, who had the technical skills, found just the right investment partner in the financier August Belmont. Together they formed the Interborough Rapid Transit (IRT) Company.[5]

Construction of the system finally began in 1900, and, despite daunting technical and geological challenges, it was completed on time and apparently with a minimum of graft and corruption. Even Ray Stannard Baker, one of Belmont's staunchest critics in the press, was duly impressed: "Most American works, with which the public has anything to do are marked with more or less official corruption, are scamped in material—where it won't show—are excessively costly, but this Subway, in an engineering sense, has apparently been a thoroughgoing, honest job, well done, with some attention to real beauty, with some effort to protect and satisfy the public." Just 3 days after it opened in 1904, a million people rode the subway on a single Sunday—despite the system's having been designed for a maximum of 350,000 riders per day.[6]

The immediate and obvious need for more subway capacity was so evident that by 1905 the RTC released a plan for a $250 million subway addition—5 times larger than the original—with a proposed 165 route miles, as compared to the 1904 subway's 22. But what seemed like a slam-dunk case for this expansion was quickly shot down by the financier who made initial construction possible. August Belmont, who was, at the time, profiting more than any other individual from the subway's runaway success, used his considerable influence to try to stop any future expansion of the system he helped create. In fact, only days after his IRT subway opened in 1904, Belmont had already gone on record as being against future expansions, stating that crowding was simply a fact of life of rapid transit—and a sign of success. In reality, Belmont had little to gain and much to lose by subway expansion, because the supply-demand imbalance that led to overcrowding generated windfall profits for him without requiring any outlay of additional investment. Belmont also disliked the expansion plan because it included routes to numerous far-flung and sparsely populated areas of New York, where the potential for profit was lower. Belmont dealt with this threat by buying up any competitor that could have bid on the expansion. With his acquisition of the Metropolitan Street Railway, he had created a virtual monopoly on rapid transit in New York City, and the RTC commissioners were essentially outflanked. They couldn't counteract Belmont because the 1894 Rapid Transit Act gave them next to no regulatory power and no ability to threaten a municipal takeover of the system.[7]

While his acquisition of the Metropolitan won him a battle, it may have lost Belmont the war. In 1903, before the first phase of the IRT was even completed, progressive interests were already pushing a piece of state legislation known as the Elsberg Bill, designed to counteract monopolistic tendencies in rapid transit. As proposed, it would limit the power of monopolies, such as Belmont's, by separating the contracts for constructing new subways from those for operating them, by reducing the lease period, and by allowing the municipality to revoke future contracts more easily. It lacked the legislative support to pass until Belmont's IRT acquired the Metropolitan in late 1905, causing an antimonopolistic uproar among the populace. Passage of the Elsberg Bill was followed in 1907 by the creation of a state public-utility commission, replacing the old RTC, which had the authority to investigate, set rates, and order schedule changes for transit.[8]

Although the new Public Service Commission (PSC) was now able to forward a major subway expansion plan—in this case the $150 million Triborough System—the so-called busting of the IRT monopoly by no means ensured its implementation. In fact, some of the antimonopolistic provisions of the Elsberg Bill had to be later amended in order to make bidding on the Triborough System feasible. After years of languishing in political limbo, the Triborough Plan was finally approved by the City's Board of Estimate and Apportionment in 1910. The Public Service Commission advertised two contracts: one for private financing, construction, and operation of this system and, as an insurance policy, a second for construction of a portion of the system using municipal funds. To their great surprise, there was not a single bidder for the private contract. Although twenty-three people bid for the municipally funded contract, that approach was so contentious and divisive that the Public Service Commission had to put it on hold.

For August Belmont, this result was a relief. It confirmed his earlier contention that he had nothing to fear from the Triborough, since it was totally uneconomical and no company would want to operate it. For the people of New York, however, this hold meant that transit would continue to be underprovided, in essence giving Belmont a monopoly. His intention was to wait out the unraveling of the Triborough Plan, at which point he could then dictate his own stiff terms, including municipal construction financing to benefit the IRT. But Belmont's hand was forced by an unexpected proposal for expansion—including to portions of New Jersey—from William McAdoo, of the formerly overlooked Hudson and Manhattan Railroad.

While ultimately unsuccessful, the McAdoo proposal was serious, and it forced Belmont to offer a better deal to the city than he otherwise would have. Belmont's proposal was expected to pass, but deadlock ensued between the mayor and his Board of Estimate. The logjam was finally broken with the offer of competition from another flank: Brooklyn. In 1911, the Brooklyn Regional Transit Company (BRT), a large corporation cobbled together from myriad formerly independent rail lines, entered a proposal for a subway expansion plan, much to the shock and disdain of Belmont. With bombast on all sides of the debate, it took the level head of George McAneny, the Manhattan Borough president, to realize that there was room for a mutually beneficial compromise. He saw that elements of both the IRT and BRT plans could be combined into a far better multiple-company plan, with the IRT focusing on Manhattan and the Bronx, and the BRT focusing on Brooklyn and its rapidly growing population. The city's endorsement of McAneny's plan in 1911 was widely considered to be the turning point in the battle for expansion of the New York subway system. The plan called for a $250 million expansion, to be taken on jointly by the city, the IRT, and the BRT, with half the financing coming from the city, and leases for forty-nine years. Although Belmont initially opposed McAneny's plan, negotiations led to concessions that Belmont realized would not get any better. Finally, in May 1912, the Board of Estimate officially approved the amended plan for this "Dual Contract" system, and in 1913 the ink on the contracts was dry. After nine years of haggling, foot-dragging, and uncertainty, the wait was over. By the time the expansion was completed in the early 1920s, New York's rail-transit system was the largest in the world, with enough tracks to stretch from New York City to Knoxville, Tennessee.[9]

Despite these monumental challenges to its initial development and expansion, the greatest existential challenge to the Big Apple's subway system was still to come. By the time Comrade Kozlov made his visit in 1959, the New York subway was well on its way down a long road of neglect and decline. Trains were old and shabby, air quality was poor, fares were high, and service was declining in quality and reliability. And conditions were only to get worse in the coming decades.

Entrance to the Atlantic Avenue subway station in Brooklyn, New York, ca. 1910. (Courtesy of the Library of Congress)

I still recall the first time I saw a New York subway car, in the late 1970s. It was shocking to see endless lines of them covered in graffiti and to smell the sour odors emanating from subway entrances. Turns out I wasn't the only one with this impression. A 1970 study by the Metropolitan Transit Authority characterized the system not only as "intolerably dirty" but also as unsafe, unreliable, and increasingly unpopular. Technical problems also plagued the subway. Some sections of track were so old and decrepit that trains had to slow to ten miles per hour. Many newer subway cars had problems with cracking trucks, requiring obsolete trains to be taken out of mothballs and used. A 1975 report found that overall the system had lost 20 percent of its ridership over the previous decade; fifteen of Manhattan's sixty-five busiest subway stations had lost more than one-third of their ridership. By 1975, ridership was the lowest it had been since 1918, when the city had 2.5 million fewer residents. And things didn't get any better in the late seventies. Between 1976 and 1977 alone, ridership dropped by 25 million passengers. Had this trend continued, there would have been no riders by 2002.[10]

The slide that began in the 1950s was partly the result of a general disinvestment in urban infrastructure that began at the time, as well as the re-prioritization of public funds toward highways. And despite—or perhaps because of—the unification of all New York subways under public control in the 1940s, financial problems only grew larger. The establishment of the New York Transit Authority in 1953 put in place a system that shielded administrators from electoral accountability, leading to further decline. As investments in municipal infrastructure failed to keep pace with rising costs, a vicious cycle was started in which fare hikes, needed to cover these increasing fiscal gaps, led to ridership declines, in turn reducing revenues, requiring further fare increases. But something more was going on than just a decline in service quality or increase in cost. American society was changing. As central cities were losing their prominence, cars were becoming ascendant. Both families and employers were relocating to the suburbs, and subways were increasingly perceived as the transportation mode of last resort. Said one anonymous transit official to the *New York Times*: "Nobody rides the subway for fun. It doesn't make any difference how plush you make it. You could pump perfumed air down there and it would still be used only by people who had no other way to get around."[11]

Living in New York in the summer of 1989, about ten years after I saw my first New York subway, I found myself riding the subway on a regular basis. Amazingly, the cars were sparkling clean and air-conditioned, the graffiti was mostly gone, service was reliable, stations were generally well ventilated and clean, and I never felt under any threat. What had happened? The story of how the New York transit system emerged from decay to become again one of the best in the world is long and interesting, but beyond the scope of this book. The short answer is that the New York subway met and overcame yet one more in a long history of challenges. Few other American cities were anywhere near as lucky or persistent as New York when it came to delivering on transit. And despite New York's success story, public transit in the United States finds itself in a deep hole. In late 2010, the Federal Transit Administration estimated that existing transit systems have been so neglected through deferred maintenance that it would take almost $78 billion just to rehabilitate them back to full functionality. Given that only about $12 billion goes toward that purpose annually, there's clearly a long road ahead.

It's 2010 and, despite having been born and raised in Los Angeles and having visited the city every year since I moved away in 1988, I've just taken my first subway ride there. While riding the sleek and immaculate train, I can't shake an uncanny feeling that I'm not actually in Los Angeles. Why is it that Los Angeles and rail transit seem so antithetical to so many people?

The car I was riding in was part of Los Angeles' Metrorail system, begun in 1990 and currently serving only a small fraction of commuters of the urban area. There's nothing inherently wrong with the trains or the stops. The system's biggest problem is simply that it developed so late in city's history. And too late meant too little. With only 17 miles of heavy-rail subway, 68 of light rail, and 150,000 daily rides for the heavy transit portion (as compared with 8 million for New York City), Los Angeles' mass-transit system is minute compared to the size of the metropolitan area.

The biggest challenge facing transit administrators hoping to make mass transit work is Los Angeles itself. A fundamentally car-dependent organism built on a skeleton of freeways, Los Angeles' decentralized urban form, made possible by a historical lack of heavy transit coupled with massive investments in freeways, made it precisely the kind of metropolis that transit cannot effectively serve. Because destinations are spread apart, Los Angeles residents travel on average about 40 percent more miles per year than New York residents.[12] Today, Los Angeles' planners are trying to swim upstream against the current of history by investing heavily in transit. The immense expense and limited results of this undertaking have illustrated perhaps the most fundamental lesson in transit: the longer construction of a transit system is put off, the more it costs and the more elusive the benefits become.

So it must be as exasperating to Los Angeles transit planners as it is surprising to most Los Angeles residents that the city of freeways at

The Los Angeles Yellow Line light rail. (Photo by author)

The Los Angeles Red Line subway. (Photo by author)

one point came close to becoming a world-class transit metropolis in its own right, not long after the last tracks of New York's Dual Contracts system were being laid. This window of opportunity was opened for only a short time, and its closing was, many believe, a defining—and forgotten—moment of Los Angeles' history.

For years, automobiles and streetcars had shared the streets of central Los Angeles. As discussed in the last chapter, this coexistence became more difficult as traffic and population increased, resulting in greater delays, more collisions, and a decline in the reliability of the rail streetcar schedules. Initially, planners sided with the streetcar, at least on paper. The 1924 traffic plan for Los Angeles stated that the streetcar, "owing to its economy of space and low cost of operation per passenger, must take precedence over other forms of vehicles in the congested area whenever the traffic capacity of the arteries approaches its limit." (Backing up the economy of space contention, it points to a statistic that passenger cars use 14.3 times as much roadway space per person carried as streetcars.) It goes on to state that "the flexibility of automobile transport effects to some extent its higher unit cost, but mass transportation in whatever form . . . is necessary and desirable to meet present and future needs in congested centers." The primacy of transit was further backed up with their data indicating that traffic within this 90 block "congested area" of downtown included twice as many passenger trips in streetcars as in automobiles during a typical afternoon rush hour. But then the plan goes on to point out potential future courses of action that, in hindsight, appear mutually exclusive. First, they note that streetcars will one day need to be supplanted with "still more intensive mass transportation offered by subways or elevated lines," suggesting greater urban concentration and less automobile dependence. Then, just two pages later, the plan advocates lowered densities and development of outlying subcenters as additional means for battling congestion: "Zoning ordinances, by fixing height limits and the area of the lot which may be covered . . . form a foundation upon which the ultimate solution of traffic congestion will in part depend." Despite its endorsement of transit, the vast majority of the

A Los Angeles streetcar sharing the road in 1946. (Courtesy of
the Automobile Club of Southern California Archives)

1924 plan—and all of its specific recommendations is dedicated to
automobile infrastructure.[13]

The 1924 plan nicely sums up the schizophrenic nature of attitudes
toward planning during this decisive period of Los Angeles' history.
Angelenos of the time really did not know what they wanted their city
to be. But as the streetcar system teetered on total breakdown while
automobile congestion became intolerable, they knew that radical
changes in the transportation system had to be made soon.

The supportive words of city planners were not enough for the
streetcar companies, who were increasingly exasperated. So, in 1924,
the largest of them, the Pacific Electric, decided to act unilaterally by
beginning work on its own subway, known as the "Hollywood Subway,"
more or less absent municipal involvement. Streetcar executives chose
the subway model because they felt that if rail transit was to survive in

Los Angeles, it had to be "grade separated." It was becoming evident to anyone involved in transportation at the time that cars and rail transport simply could not feasibly continue to share the street space because of potential conflicts at intersections, at transit stops, and wherever turns were made. Therefore rail lines had to be either elevated or submerged. Pacific Electric executives promoted this subway explicitly as a critical step in Los Angeles' modernization. Although the initial plan for the Hollywood Subway was not terribly large, they—and many downtown business interests—saw this underground rail system, which had its terminal in the foundation of a twelve-story building (about as high as could be legally built in Los Angeles at the time), as part of a major long-term plan of coupled urban mass-transit development and vertical growth. As D. W. Pontius, president of Pacific Electric, said at the subway opening, "Los Angeles will have more subways. They are the logical answer to traffic congestion, rapid transit of passengers, grade crossing menaces, and other problems."[14]

Unlike the ponderous process of the IRT in New York City, Pacific Electric unilaterally started work on their subway with next to no input from the public or government. Progress was fast, and it opened to great fanfare in 1926. Initial response to the subway was very positive: not only was it profitable, but the route it took saved fifteen minutes over the comparable surface route, owing to lack of competition with automobiles. Thanks to this success, this short subway line was now being seen as "the seed of a vast subterranean system that would solve Los Angeles' travel problems for all times." But within months, all construction on planned extensions came to an abrupt halt, for the city's charter was changed in early 1925, probably in response to this subway, requiring official approval of a full rapid-transit plan prior to construction of any new rail transit.[15]

Despite this setback, Pacific Electric and its allies in government and the downtown business establishment were optimistic. They succeeded in getting the prestigious Chicago engineering firm of Kelker, De Leuw and Company to draft the city's new rail-transit plan, based on an assumption of a "future city population of 3,000,000." The plan, released in 1925, advocated a massive system of regionwide rail transit (see map), including twenty-six single-track miles of subways, eighty-five miles of elevated or depressed tracks, and forty-one of surface street rail for the first phase, at an estimated cost of $134 million. Later phases would include more than two hundred miles of additional track. Its strong pro-transit sentiments were abundantly clear: "The future orderly development of Los Angeles requires the construction of rapid transit lines and the extension and expansion of other transportation facilities."[16] The plan strongly emphasized downtown as the dominant regional center to which all transit would orient but also recognized that the metropolitan area was already quite spread out and that heavy transit would therefore not serve everyone. Instead, it would have to be coordinated with light surface rail and bus lines to give transit access to all.

Despite this forward-thinking framework, the plan and its supporters were naïve in their understanding of the nature of automobile-oriented decentralization. Although today, urban decentralization and heavy transit are seen as incompatible, the plan saw transit as an efficient way to serve a decentralized metropolis: "If the city's unequalled position . . . is to be maintained, it must continue to spread and this spreading can be accomplished only by providing rapid transportation at a reasonable rate of fare." In other words, the authors of the plan had a vision that a region of pleasant, low-density garden communities could coexist with a dominant downtown, served primarily by fixed rail lines. This complemented the view of Donald Baker, president of the Planning Commission, that excessive automobile usage was essentially a response to the failure of rail transit—a second-best approach to transportation: "If you provide these drivers with a rapid and cheap method of reaching their destination you will immediately remove many of the cars which congest our central business district."[17]

Shortly after the plan's release, a totally unrelated conflict arose between the city and the major railroads serving Los Angeles: the Southern Pacific, the Union Pacific, and the Santa Fe. The problem was that each rail line had its own tracks into the central city, and each its own station. As early as 1916, the city had hoped to compel the three

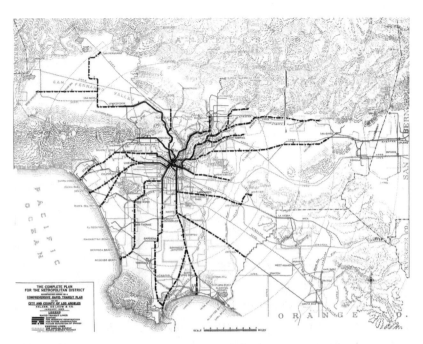

1925 Kelker De Leuw proposal for an extensive regional transit network, from the *Comprehensive Rapid Transit Plan for the City and County of Los Angeles*. (Dorothy Peyton Gray Transportation Library, Los Angeles County Metropolitan Transit Authority)

to make use of a single station, to be known as Union Station. The railroads resisted, and the case went all the way to the United States Supreme Court in 1921, but with no clear judicial remedy. So, by 1925, just as the debate over subways was beginning to brew, the city and the railroads worked out a set of potential compromises to the question of an intercity rail station. The proposal that gained most traction was an offer by the railroads to pay for a system that would link multiple depots in the vicinity of downtown via an elaborate system of elevated rails running electric trains and using existing rights-of-way owned by the railroads—in essence a privately funded circumscribed mass-transit system. This proposal allowed for Pacific Electric to have full access to these tracks, which would connect to the Hollywood Subway.

It also called for the construction of a passenger terminal at Fourth and Central, not far from the heart of downtown. This was a staggering offer: the construction of a full grade-separate mass-transit system throughout central Los Angeles at no public expense. It was expected to remove 1,200 local streetcars from traffic per day. The City Council moved quickly to approve the Kelker plan, but in doing so stripped out its specific route recommendations, to allow for the elevated rail proposal. Most newspapers also supported this seemingly perfect compromise, as did the Chamber of Commerce, commissioners of the Board of Public Utilities, and most elected officials. Los Angeles seemed fated to become the next big transit metropolis.[18]

But one holdout newspaper, the powerful *Los Angeles Times*, did not agree. The *Times* boss, Harry Chandler, did not like the proposed location for Union Station, preferring instead a site known as "The Plaza," located outside the main downtown area. Many have speculated as to the reasons for his strident support of this location and opposition to all others. There were rumors that he had real estate holdings in this area (this was never proved). Another explanation was that he favored the Plaza site because it would break the monopoly of the Santa Fe, Union Pacific, and Southern Pacific in Los Angeles by allowing competitors into the market; this would be possible only if the terminal was outside the center of the city, due to right-of-way constraints in downtown. Alternatively, Chandler's opposition may have really been to the elevated transit proposal itself, with the question of station location being only a proxy battle. It was common knowledge that a Plaza location for a passenger terminal was mutually exclusive of the elevated rail plan, because none of the railroads owned the necessary rights-of-way in this area. In fact, the *Times* frequently used language to conflate the two issues, using such phrases as "the carriers' projected railroad substitute for a Union Station."[19]

Although the *Times'* arguments didn't reflect the views of the majority in the government or business, it was apparent that they reflected the sentiments of many citizens. Following popular blowback in response to a recent downtown parking-ban experiment, many city councilors were gun-shy and wanted to avoid prematurely taking a position on such a difficult issue. With all this in mind, the City Council made the politically expedient choice to put the plan to a nonbinding referendum. The referendum was phrased not to ask directly about the elevated plan, but rather to ask whether there should be a Union Station and, if so, whether it should be at the Plaza location (these were Propositions 8 and 9). But since everyone knew the elevated rail and the Plaza station were mutually exclusive, it was really a proxy vote on the transit plan—and even, as the historian Jeremiah Axelrod put it, about "the future form of urbanism in Southern California." A number of additional propositions bundled into this referendum related to Los Angeles' urban form beyond the Union Station question, including one that concerned lifting zoning restrictions along Wilshire Boulevard (which promoters were hoping to make "the Fifth Avenue of the West") to allow for a major high-rise corridor, and another proposing to waive the city's height restriction for the new City Hall. As a result, this may have been one of the most defining (and forgotten) referendums in the history of Los Angeles' urban development.[20]

Once the referendum was proposed, proponents of transit went on the offensive, bringing twenty local chambers of commerce into their camp. But the *Times'* offensive was even louder and, perhaps, more in tune with popular sentiment. Running up to five pieces per day (ostensibly articles, but really more editorials), the *Times* questioned the motives of the railroads (who were not well trusted in Los Angeles for valid historical reasons) and attacked the concept of elevated railroads in Los Angeles. They drew attention to their noise, safety record, and visual impacts, using terms like "Stygian gloom" to describe the area under the elevated rails. Even though the specific proposal under referendum applied only to 4.5 miles of elevated track, the *Times* conflated that plan with the larger elevated plans of the Kelker proposal. And although the *Times* did claim to support more subway construction in theory, this was probably disingenuous, since they offered no specific proposal, refused to acknowledge that subways are far more expensive to build than elevated lines when denouncing the cost of the latter, and ignored the fact that this elevated system would complement and benefit any future subways. The *Times* may have swayed public opinion, it may have reflected it, or perhaps some of both. Whatever the case, the Plaza proposal was approved, meaning that the elevated plan was defeated.[21]

This turned out to be Los Angeles' last realistic window of opportunity for rail transit on a scale big enough to define the city itself. After the 1926 referendum, attempts at resuscitating transit became increasingly feeble. By the late 1930s, planning bodies had given up their equivocation and placed themselves firmly in the camp of the automobile. In contrast to the 1924 plan, with its advocacy of streetcars as the primary means of transport, the 1937 Highway Traffic Survey prepared by the Los Angeles County Regional Planning Commission opens with a large picture of snarled streetcar and automobile traffic on Broadway, in downtown. The caption reads: "The use of the street by a large number of street cars has a decided effect upon its efficiency as a traffic artery. . . . The obvious crowded condition of this street carrying only 14,000 vehicles per day should be thoughtfully compared with the relatively smooth flowing traffic on Wilshire Boulevard [with no streetcars] with a daily volume of 40,000 vehicles."[22] Disdain for rail transit and praise for the automobile permeated this and most future planning documents, including the Automobile Club's freeway plan, discussed in Chapter 4. And with the construction of each successive freeway segment under that plan, another nail was hammered into transit's coffin.

Although many believe that Los Angeles was fundamentally destined to be an automobile metropolis from the start, the lessons of 1926 suggest otherwise. The referendum may have related only to four miles of elevated rail, but its results condemned the entire mass-transit plan for the Los Angeles region. Had the referendum passed, which it very well might have in the absence of the *Times'* opposition, the elevated would have likely been constructed, and, buoyed by this seed of a transit system, it's very possible that significant elements of the much more ambitious Kelker Plan would have come to fruition, leading to potentially hundreds of miles of grade-separated rail. Had this happened, the fragmented Los Angeles skyline that I described in Chapter 4 would have looked much different.

Although it's almost unthinkable that Los Angeles would have ever achieved the density or centrality of New York, given New York's geographical barriers and Los Angeles' abundance of buildable land, it's also unlikely that Los Angeles would today be characterized by its hodgepodge of freeway-linked subcenters had its initial transit plans come to fruition. Rather, it probably would have been somewhere in between the two extremes—perhaps more like Chicago, which, though surrounded by plenty of sprawl, is distinct from Los Angeles in having a downtown of unquestioned regional dominance, making possible both an extensive heavy-rail system and a monocentric land-use pattern characterized by gradually decreasing densities. Had downtown Los Angeles—like downtown Chicago—been able to maintain its regional dominance as a commercial center through the orientation of transit, the Los Angeles region today would probably have statistics a lot more like Chicago's: 27 percent transit ridership versus 11 percent, and 29 percent of households without a car versus 19 percent.

Of course this is purely speculative. Los Angeles, by nature of its geography, economic base, and self-selected population, may have simply been inexorably drawn toward the car and its associated urban form and repelled by transit. But I think the question of urban predestination is misguided. Rather, the more salient question is when Los Angeles' fate became sealed. It's generally accepted that the suitability of a city for rapid transit is determined by the era in which the city was built. Cities like New York and Boston, which had become well established and well defined before the automobile, had an urban form amenable to transit, as was the case with European cities. On the other hand, post-automobile cities, like Houston or Phoenix, never had a realistic chance. Los Angeles is interesting in that it became a real city of national standing just at the cusp: before the age of automobiles, but only barely. In fact, when the 1926 referendum was held, more people rode the rails than drove cars. But by the 1930s, cars had unquestioned dominance, and by the 1950s the only rail transit left in the region was

Disneyland's monorail. Had the city's development been advanced by a few years, and had the transit plan come in, say, 1915 instead of 1925, this might have all been different.

One of the first things you notice about Stockholm's Tunnelbana Metro system today is how unbelievably clean it is. Stations and subway cars are spotless. Garbage bags are changed so regularly that you rarely see more than a few inches of trash in any receptacle. Cars with graffiti are taken out of service and immediately cleaned. The next thing you notice is that cars arrive with incredible frequency and seem to go everywhere you need. The system is so reliable that since 2002, Stockholm has offered transit commuters a guarantee that they will get full compensation for a taxi ride if there is more than a twenty-minute delay. One would think that this system had been operating for a century, like New York's. In fact it's far younger.

The Stockholm Metro is one of many in Europe that were built in the postwar period, long after cities like Los Angeles had committed fully to freeways. It was begun in 1950 and virtually completed by 1975, with some final construction done in the early 1990s. Yet despite this rather late start, Stockholm is a totally transit-oriented city, with 64 percent of trips to the central city made on transit (two-thirds of which is rail transit) as of 2008 and a whopping 78 percent of trips during the morning rush hour.[23] And rather than resting on their laurels, Swedish transportation planners are constantly doing more. For instance, a four-mile subway tunnel is currently being planned under the entire central-city district to increase future capacity and allow for more subway cars through the center of town.

There are several reasons why Stockholm and other European cities were able to make this late transition to transit. The most commonly recognized reason is that centuries of pre-automobile history had given them a compact and centered urban form that was simultaneously ideal for transit and unsuited to automobiles. This compactness of form is evidenced by the relatively small number of miles traveled per year by the average resident of this city: about 5,300 miles for

The Stockholm Tunnelbana transit system. (Photo by author)

Stockholm (and a similar number for Munich, London, Hamburg, and Brussels), as compared with 7,700 for New York, 10,500 for Los Angeles, and 12,000 for Houston. Furthermore, about 80 percent of trips to work in Stockholm are under 7 miles, and once people are in the central city, its density and pedestrian infrastructure allows for 68 percent of trips within that zone to be by foot or bike.[24]

The second reason is that as automobile use grew dramatically in the 1950s in Stockholm, a consensus was reached between citizens and government that a major investment in transit and a reduction in car dependence were needed for the long-term good of the city. Without the difficulty encountered by Los Angeles or New York, Stockholm was able to plan and then act on the plan fairly quickly, even though Sweden has one of the highest car-ownership rates in Europe.

Third, the plan that was put into place was a good one. The General Plan of 1945–52, devised by the architect Sven Markelius, proposed not only a large-scale system of rail transit but also a corresponding land-use plan based on Ebenezer Howard's model of satellite towns, which was focused around transit stops and anchored by transit lines to a regionally dominant downtown. By coordinating land use and transit, downtown Stockholm could achieve the right mix of uses and densities in both center and satellite. Doing so prevented sprawl while allowing the outward extensions to peripheral areas to maintain a development pattern consistent with more central areas. The result is that today 90 percent of the population of the Stockholm metropolitan area lives within about a thousand feet of a public-transit route with at least hourly service.

Fourth, the government prepared well in advance. Starting in 1904 the City Council began purchasing land for future rights-of-way, so that by 1980 it owned 70 percent of the land within the city limits and hundreds of square kilometers outside those limits.[25]

Finally, transit succeeded in Stockholm because the political culture is simply more conducive to big public-works projects than in the United States. Although a far cry from the Stalinism that enabled the Moscow Metro, Sweden, like so many other European countries, has a hybrid government with elements of both free-market capitalism and welfare-state socialism, making it easier to prioritize large, publicly funded infrastructure projects. From talking to my colleagues and contacts in Europe, it's clear that big projects are more feasible not only because government is more coordinated, centralized, and enabled, but also because citizens tend to trust and defer to their government officials far more than do Americans.

Shortly before leaving on my trip to Scandinavia, I recall watching coverage of the Tax Day Tea Party rally in Washington, D.C. It was one of the angriest ever, with signs calling President Obama a fascist and demanding the dismantling of American "big government." The most beautiful irony was hidden in the Facebook page of the protest organizers, where it was suggested that attendees arrive at the protest site via the Washington, D.C., subway system, whose "staff . . . will be ready to help you with any questions." Apparently "big government" is doing something right.[26] We have to assume that Comrade Kozlov would agree with them.

Coal

COAL IS OFTEN POINTED to as a resource that will last well beyond the effective depletion of oil. Overall, there's agreement that its
production is still far from a peak. Although its solid form makes it
less convenient than oil, it can be used to make electricity and can be
liquefied into synthetic petroleum using the Fischer-Tropsch process,
developed by German scientists between the two world wars. This
method is relatively cost-effective and has been found to become economically feasible at an energy-price equivalent of sixty dollars per
barrel for oil.[1]

But that's where the good news about coal ends. First, supply estimates are almost certainly overblown. Although many energy optimists like to point to the rosy estimate of the United States having
nearly a two-hundred-year supply of coal, this supply horizon doesn't
take into account any increases in demand for coal, particularly those
that would be spurred by drops in oil output. If we take a more realistic view of coal consumption, factoring in increased use through liquefaction, production peaks could be much sooner. Furthermore, the
picture of proven reserves is probably not nearly as optimistic as we've
been led to believe. A recent report by the Energy Watch Group found
that data on coal reserves are extremely poor and probably are greatly
overstated. In many countries, they found that reserve estimates have
not been updated in decades, and for those countries that have recently
updated their reserve data, only two had reassessments that resulted
in upgrades (Australia and India), while all others resulted in down-
grades. The report estimates that the peak of global production could
come around 2025, at roughly 130 percent of current production. As
the report states, "Large reserves formerly seen as proven have been

reassessed as being speculative."[2] So what does that mean for the United States, with its supposed two-century supply of domestic coal? The report concludes that the country's feasibly recoverable supply is quite a bit lower, because much of the remaining coal is of lower quality, lower energy content, and higher sulfur content than what is currently being mined. They point to some indicators of this underlying quality problem: the productivity of mines (tons produced/miner) increased until 2000 and has been in steady decline since; the production of the higher-quality bituminous coal peaked around 1990; and although total production continues to climb, the production of coal in terms of energy content peaked in 1998.

But even if coal was to remain abundant, its cheapness is deceptive. The operating costs of coal-fired plants may appear low due to the cheap fuel, but the capital costs for building a coal plant are exorbitant, generally in the range of $2 billion in the United States, and such plants require about thirty years to pay off. That requirement means that once coal plants are built they can yield cheap power, but the steep cost of building them limits the number that are built in the first place, which in turn limits the ability of coal to substitute for oil. One reason for this high cost is that coal plants in the United States also need scrubbers to get rid of pollutants (such as sulfur dioxide) that form acid rain. This, added to other pollution rules with which coal plants must comply, has discouraged many utilities in the United States and other industrialized countries from building new coal plants in the last two decades, meaning that the ability to ramp up electricity based on coal is limited when these regulations exist.

But even if the optimistic figures of coal reserves were right and coal-fired power plants were cheap to build, there would still be perhaps an even bigger hurdle: carbon. This is the dominant type of atom in a coal molecule, which means that the carbon content of coal is between 60 percent (for lignite) and 80 percent (for anthracite). In terms of greenhouse gases, there simply isn't a dirtier fuel than coal. Coal produces about double the carbon dioxide per unit of energy produced as does natural gas (oil falls somewhere between the two).[3] That means that if greenhouse gas taxes or cap-and-trade programs are passed, coal will undergo the greatest price increases. Under a cap-and-trade system, the prices for those carbon emissions will continue to go up over time as the cap is lowered and outstanding pollution allowances are retired. Hence, coal's only real potential as a major future energy source would require one of two scenarios: either we decide as a society that we don't care about global climate change and effectively give up on any attempt to regulate it, or we can figure out how to implement so-called clean coal technology. Carbon capture and sequestration is a prospective technology in which carbon is scrubbed from power-plant emissions and sequestered deep underground, and it's being touted by many as the way around the carbon problem. But to date, only demonstration projects have been implemented, with nothing proven at the commercial scale.

The issue of legal liability, the tracking of stored carbon, the lack of a commercial-scale operation, and the huge uncertainties about technical feasibility mean that no one really knows what the added cost of clean coal would be. The United Nations' Intergovernmental Panel on Climate Change, however, has estimated conservatively that these problems could nearly double the price per kilowatt hour of coal-generated electricity.[4] Given so many remaining uncertainties about this technology, the price increment could be even higher, and the carbon capture technology simply may not be feasible at the necessary scale. In other words, this technology that is being touted by so many as a silver bullet may just end up being a lump of coal.

PART 2

Taming the Urban Appetite

CHAPTER 6

The Building Energy Diet

T he first thing you notice about the home of Ed Begley Jr. is just how un-Hollywood it is. At slightly under sixteen hundred square feet, it is located in a modest neighborhood of small bungalows. The second thing you notice is that it's more than just a home—it's a living laboratory on energy efficiency.

You may have seen Begley in any of dozens of movies or TV shows going back to the 1970s, like *St. Elsewhere, Arrested Development*, or *A Mighty Wind*. But of late he's best known as one of Hollywood's most prominent—and principled—environmentalists. Begley is the kind of guy who turns up to swanky celebrity events on a bicycle and who rides a specially outfitted stationary bike in the morning to produce electricity to make his morning toast. He's also the star and creator of *Living with Ed*, his own TV reality show about his environmental obsessions, and the author of *Ed Begley's Guide to Green Living*.

Besides Begley and his wife, Rachelle, who bears the brunt of being married to a hell-bent resource miser, the other main character of *Living with Ed* is his house—a place he has such a strong attachment to that he hopes to be composted in its vegetable garden when he dies.

I was lucky enough to tour the house with Begley on an overcast afternoon in December 2009. Even though he'd given hundreds of

Residential redevelopment in the Hammarby Sjöstad neighborhood of Stockholm, Sweden. (Photo by author)

Exterior of the home of Ed Begley Jr. (Photo by author)

tours, his excitement was palpable as he described, with great technical command, every green feature of this retrofitted 1936 house.

One of the first examples of energy efficiency at work was the green belt along the sidewalk in front of his house. Rather than using water-intensive (and hence energy-intensive) grass, Begley uses "xeriscaping," or landscaping with native drought-tolerant plants, even though the city put up nothing but obstacles. "I'd been gently fighting with the city for 20 years: 'please can I get rid of the grass?'—'no you cannot, you must have grass here.' Now [because of water shortages] they're begging people to do what they let me do here."[1]

In the front yard, additional drought-tolerant plants comingle with apple, lemon, avocado, and olive trees. These are irrigated by "graywater," which is recycled from the shower, bathtub, and washing machine using a bank of five filters. As a result, his front yard requires no irrigation from municipal water—one of the single largest consumers of

The solar array on Ed Begley's roof. (Photo by author)

water use for the entire region. And, when there's a drought and other people have to stop watering their yards, Begley's remains lush.

As we enter the front room of the house, sampling delicious ginger cookies sent by his friend Jackson Browne, the background noise of traffic and airplanes disappears as the door closes. This silence is indicative of just how well glazed and insulated the house is, with its double-pane windows, recycled denim in the attic, and recycled cellulose in the walls. Although insulation is neither visible nor sexy, Begley claims that it is fundamental to a green house. "I put in really good insulation before I put any solar on."

Of course everything in the house is state of the art for energy efficiency: compact fluorescent (CFL) bulbs or light emitting diodes (LEDs), "smart" thermostats, Energy Star–rated appliances, and even

Ed Begley showing the charging station for his electric
car, which runs on rooftop solar. (Photo by author)

small skylight solar tubes to let in ample natural light in interior spaces,
reducing the need for indoor lighting.

The backyard sports a solar oven, three composters, and garden
beds, in addition to the hardware for the graywater system. At the back
of the yard stands a structure, added in 1990, that houses Begley's office
and the garage for his electric Toyota. That vehicle is charged by solar
panels leading to an inverter in the garage. In addition to the photovoltaic array, passive solar panels on the back house provide abundant hot
water; heating and cooling are handled by an ultra efficient minisplit
heat pump, a system that produces little waste heat.

Does this mean that Begley can live off the grid? Turns out, not yet.
His electricity use is higher than he'd like, but there's a reason for that.
His home serves as a mini TV studio. "Two hundred days a year either
Living with Ed is here, or CNN is here, or ABC or CBS or KTLA . . .

and they've got bright lights and they've got equipment that uses power. So to be fair, it's not just a home, but a TV studio. And there's an electric car that I'm fueling that does 10,000 miles a year." But even with all that, "the electric bill to run a house for three people and run a TV studio 200 days a year and to drive a car 10,000 miles a year, that figure is $700 a year. And I want it to be lower."

He hopes that will change soon. Right now his solar photovoltaic panel population—currently standing at 108—is limited by being on a one-story building that is partially shaded by a neighbor's house in winter. He'd like to go up one story, which would open up a lot of solar real estate and allow for a proliferation of more panels, and even solar shingles. In that case, Begley speculates that he could be totally off the grid, even with his virtual TV studio consuming significant amounts of power.

Begley's electrical-use strategy is quite sophisticated. Although he doesn't sell back power to the grid via net metering, he does have an electrical storage system that, when combined with a tiered rate structure and "time-of-use" meter, allows him to draw power when it's cheap and abundant and avoid doing so during expensive peak times (as he describes this, he gleefully mentions that his close friend and competing eco-nerd, Bill Nye the Science Guy, has no such electricity storage capacity). By flicking a switch he can move between grid power and stored solar depending on the time of day, allowing him to buy power at rates as cheap as three cents per kilowatt hour. Of course, that can get a bit complicated, so he often has to leave notes for his wife or assistant to flick the switch.

As for hot water, one of the biggest energy hogs in the typical American home, Begley's primary strategy is just not to use much. One strategy is taking what he refers to as "Navy showers," as well as timing his wife's long showers with a stopwatch on his TV show to goad her into using less. But his hot-water thrift is hardly necessary. Putting in two rooftop solar hot-water panels that preheat the water significantly brought down his gas bills. The system is so efficient that even on partly cloudy days it can get the water up to 90° or 100°F. On sunny days the temperature can get to 150°, so that gas-fired hot water is barely needed.

The cost of all this is considerable, but most of Begley's efficiency investments paid off years ago. Further, he points out, most of the materials and equipment he purchased are cheaper today than when he bought them, so payback periods for new adopters have been reduced. So what's keeping more people from following his example?

When it comes to reducing urban energy metabolism, buildings may yield the best return on investment. Residential and commercial buildings consume 41 percent of all end-use energy, the vast majority of which comes in the form of electricity. The second biggest source is natural gas—a big change from 1950, when coal and petroleum were equally big sources of energy in the home or workplace. The fact that buildings are so dependent on electricity is significant, because, as described in Chapter 1, it's an extremely inefficient way of harnessing the energy in fuels. Recall, for instance that over two-thirds of the energy in coal is lost in the process of electrical generation—and some say that number is actually much worse when one looks more comprehensively at sources of efficiency loss in electricity generation and distribution. That means that for most areas (not, for instance, areas using efficient hydropower) savings in electrical consumption amplify reductions in the consumption of electrical generation fuels. This effect is even greater when we consider how inefficient many electrical appliances are. For instance, up to 95 percent of the energy in the coal used to power an incandescent lightbulb is wasted. Taking into account the bulb's waste heat, transmission loss, and generation loss, it takes about 450–650 pounds of good quality coal to keep it lighted for a year.[2]

Buildings in America use far more energy—and particularly electricity—than needed to maintain current standards of living. This is both a problem and an opportunity. As oil companies struggle to drill in eight-thousand-foot-deep waters at great cost to the environment, far too little attention is paid to the fact that the single biggest and easiest source of new energy is sitting under our noses in our homes and offices. The concept of the *negawatt*, coined by Amory Lovins, founder of the Rocky Mountain Institute, refers to an action that conserves energy thereby freeing up energy to be used for other purposes. It turns out that negawatts are the cheapest source of new energy, with every dollar spent saving two dollars in avoided electrical supply investment, not to mention all the other costs associated with fossil-fuel use. As Douglas Foy, a former Massachusetts politician, wrote, "In a way, cities are the Saudi Arabia of energy efficiency, vast mines of potential energy savings that dwarf most of the supply options our country possesses."[3]

And, according to a recent report by the McKinsey Global Institute, the opportunity for efficiency improvements in buildings is huge. Nearly 36 percent of the opportunity for reduction in total energy demand from efficiency-productivity enhancements lies in residential and commercial buildings. The report estimates a 17 percent internal rate of return on all types of investments in future energy savings—a considerable rate in comparison to other investments. But it finds the greatest opportunities when it comes to residential upgrades. For instance, the rate of return on replacing incandescent lightbulbs with CFLs for the United States is estimated at 500 percent.[4]

If improving energy efficiency for buildings makes good long-term financial sense, why aren't building owners doing more of it? Despite all the opportunities McKinsey refers to, the pace of efficiency upgrades has been glacial, particularly in the United States. And the record on efficiency for new construction is mixed at best. One of the biggest problems is awareness; most people simply are oblivious to the energy consumption of buildings and the opportunities for saving money by saving energy. Because energy bills arrive monthly, most of us are desensitized to the energy consumption of the devices we use daily, from the air conditioner to the Nintendo Game Cube. A recent study of residential household behavior found that resource and energy use "have faded so much into the background and become part of the everyday infrastructure in householders' lives that tracking, monitoring and understanding in-the-moment resource consumption is not easy because it is mostly invisible."[5] The study goes on to point out that information is the biggest barrier to energy improvements. Householders feel they lack not only the means to feasibly track and monitor how much energy they are using in real time but also a benchmark that could be used to evaluate their usage.

Increasingly, there are a number of inexpensive tracking devices that consumers can use to get a better grasp on their energy use. I recently purchased one of these from my power company—a Blue Line PowerCost monitor. Sitting behind my kitchen sink, it has a wireless connection to a sensor wrapped around my external electricity meter, allowing me to know how much I'm using per hour—in either kilowatt hour or dollar terms. It also tells me what the monthly bill is likely to be, given power use since the last time I hit "reset." Although it doesn't directly tell me how much each appliance uses, I can infer this by turning things on and off incrementally and looking at the change in per hour costs. Thanks to this method, I was able to calculate the nightly cost of air-conditioning the master bedroom, the hot water for a ten-minute shower (our water heater is electric), or a load of laundry. Now I try to imagine feeding coins into the wall every time I want to turn on a light, do laundry, or add five minutes to my shower. I like to think it's made a difference in the way I behave.

Although an electricity monitor may help change consumer behavior, it's of limited use in detecting or addressing the sources of inefficiency in a building. For that, an energy audit is needed. Energy auditors identify problems that would otherwise go unnoticed, using sophisticated equipment like blower doors and infrared cameras. They spot thermal leaks or sources of unnecessary electrical or fuel consumption and then make recommendations about investment opportunities that would save money in the long term. This professional feedback can help guide homeowners toward high-priority investments by identifying the most cost-effective fixes.

One of the best examples is Ed Begley's house. Long after he had "greened" his home, he got a call from some environmentally oriented real estate agents who wanted to do a free energy audit on this house for publicity purposes. He felt it would be pointless, given how perfectly efficient he thought his house was. But he was curious and hadn't had an audit in many years, at a time when auditing equipment was much more rudimentary. So as the agents started their audit, he blithely commented, "Have some fun. I'm going to grab some lunch. I'll see you in a couple of hours." Returning from lunch, he expected his house to have great results but was totally taken aback when it didn't. He narrates the conversation between him and the agent:

"What are you talking about? I'm Ed Begley Jr. I've got the video tape, I've got the book, I did a lot in this house, I put insulation in the walls, double-pane windows, recycled denim."

"I'm glad you did all that stuff—it would be worse. But you're still leaking a lot. You're leaking like crazy."

"What are you talking about?"

"When did you have your home energy audit done?"

I said it was the late eighties.

"Did they have a thermal imaging device? Did they have a blower door test?"

"No, I guess they didn't."

"You've got to do it with those devices nowadays."

Begley went on to describe how he and the auditors "sealed this and that—lots of stuff"—but there were still leaks. Eventually he found the culprit in the basement. "They had the blower door on, and there was cobweb blowing in the wind. Apparently, a room attached to the back of the house used to be an outside room. There's been a gap there this big since 1988 [he holds his hands about five inches apart]. It's like having a fireplace flue open since 1988 that I never knew about because there's no rain or sunlight getting in. It was blown with a $10 piece of insulation. We did more with a $10 insulation board this big [he shakes his head]. For that meager $10 investment, the difference was 'night and day.' My electric bill, as low as it was, was cut in half. My gas bill, as low as it was, cut in half."

I spoke with Paul Scheckel, author of the *Home Energy Diet*, a book on home energy efficiency, and a former home energy auditor, about the role of audits. Scheckel has done so many that he lost track at three thousand, around six or seven years ago. He agrees that the biggest energy hogs in many homes tend to be things that people are totally unaware of, like a broken well pump or a forgotten dehumidifier that's never been turned off. The worst case he had come across, he said, was a hidden electric radiant-floor heating system that was permanently turned on but that no one was aware of. "They'd been living there and they'd always had high bills and they finally called to figure out why. And the only way I found that out was because I was pointing the infrared camera around, and I saw that striped floor. . . . It was summertime in Vermont, and I couldn't even find the breaker for it. There was no thermostat anywhere. It was just hardwired into a box. That happens all the time. . . . Things get crossed and overlooked."[6]

Auditors also serve as a form of quality control for the inconsistent quality of house construction. Some builders are highly conscientious, whereas others skimp on the parts of the house that are not easily visible to the homeowner. Scheckel says that this kind of corner cutting is commonplace "unless you get a very dedicated builder who is very well informed, has a good crew who is well trained and on board with efficiency, and is willing to go the extra mile. It's a lot of work to get the crew to caulk the bottom plate along the entire perimeter of the building before they nail a wall up. You've got to be on their case all the time." Often these flaws won't be discovered until an audit is performed.

But even when people have the necessary information about opportunities for increasing efficiency, investments rarely follow. Although inexpensive changes like moving from incandescent lights to CFLs has proven relatively easy, big-ticket items like solar water heaters, efficient furnaces, or reinsulation are a much harder sell. Understandable psychological barriers exist that keep owners of homes and commercial buildings from making investments whose returns are in the future but whose costs are borne today. Pedro Haas of McKinsey and Company said to the *New York Times* that his company surveyed people worldwide to see how fast the payback would have to be on efficiency to get them to make those investments. It turns out that most individuals are very wary; one-fourth said under no circumstances would they spend on efficiency, while 50 percent said they would invest only if the payback was under two years—a very tall order.[7] With such a tepid attitude toward spending on efficiency, programs that promote and facilitate efficiency are more important than ever. But there's no consensus yet as to what makes a program work.

Three thousand miles from Ed Begley's house, an energy-efficiency laboratory of a very different sort is bustling with activity. I'm in the offices of Efficiency Vermont, the nation's first statewide "energy efficiency utility," created in 2000 by an act of the Vermont legislature.

Programs abound throughout the world to promote building efficiency, but Efficiency Vermont is among the most innovative. Operated under contract to the Vermont Service Board, the program is funded by a small surcharge on all electric bills in the state—about .03 cents per kilowatt hour. The team took a hodgepodge of small, uncoordinated, and often ineffectual efficiency programs operated by different regional utilities—the way it's traditionally done in most places—and put them under one roof for the whole state, creating what is now a model for the rest of the country. The legislature created Efficiency Vermont not only because they perceived a conflict of interest in having electricity providers deliver efficiency measures but also because of the significant variation in the quality of services from one utility to another. A request for proposals was put out to see who would run this new efficiency utility, and the contract eventually went to the preexisting, nonprofit Vermont Energy Investment Corporation (VEIC), founded in 1986. Today, VEIC's primary responsibilities are administering the Efficiency Vermont contract and providing additional efficiency and renewable energy-consulting services to the public and private sectors, incorporating to a large extent innovations from Efficiency Vermont.

VEIC and Efficiency Vermont are so successful that institutions in other states and countries are increasingly seeking them out for consultation. In fact, days before writing this, VEIC won a major contract to implement programs similar to Efficiency Vermont's for the electricity wholesaler American Municipal Power, Inc., which sells to 128 municipal utilities and over 570,000 customers across six states. According to that organization's president, "We wanted to work with a national leader in energy efficiency like VEIC because of its proven track record of saving energy and money for its customers."[8]

According to Scheckel, who was working at Efficiency Vermont when I interviewed him and has since left, the organization offers a smorgasbord of programs for state ratepayers—both residential and commercial—to reduce their electricity consumption. The range of services is wide, from free compact fluorescent lightbulbs, to interest-rate buydowns on loans for energy-related improvements, rebates on appliances sold in the state, and services for large commercial energy users. While their primary mission is to reduce electricity use, in 2008 they were authorized to begin initiatives involving thermal efficiency upgrades of buildings too.

The data indicate that, despite the state's small size, Vermont's efficiency program is among the most committed and successful of any state program in the nation. In 2007 (the last year for which state-by-state comparison data are available), its expenditures on energy efficiency as a percentage of total utility revenues was the highest in the nation, at 3.4 percent, and, more important, it had the highest incremental electricity savings as a percentage of sales by state, at 1.8 percent (in 2008 it was 2.5 percent). Its innovative approach combined with its dedicated funding source has led to many national awards and produced hard statistics indicating a reduction in energy use. For instance, in 2008 alone Efficiency Vermont programs helped more than 55,000 homes and businesses save 150,000 megawatt hours, equivalent to roughly 2.5 percent of state demand requirements. This was more than the rate of average annual electrical load growth of 1.5 percent, meaning that in 2008 Efficiency Vermont allowed the state to avoid generating or importing any additional power over the previous year, and then some. As the *New York Times* wrote that year, "Vermont is the only state where gains in energy efficiency more than offset the state's projected growth in demand for electricity. That big milestone happened last year—in large part due to the state's efficiency measures." It's no wonder then that according to the National Energy Efficiency Scorecard, Vermont has the highest rank of any state in terms of its "utility and public benefits programs" for efficiency—and this is almost entirely because of Efficiency Vermont.[9]

Efficiency Vermont's successes not only reveal that coordinated efforts can lead to big energy savings but illustrate just how much more cost effective negawatts are than the development of new energy supplies. Although it costs about fourteen cents on average to generate a kilowatt hour of electricity, in 2008 it cost Efficiency Vermont only about three cents on average to save consumers a kilowatt. That translates to about a 65 percent rate of return averaged over the lifetime of the efficiency measures—far better than most other investments imaginable. As a result, Efficiency Vermont got nearly four dollars' worth of benefit in electrical savings for each dollar it spent in 2008.[10] Even though the numbers were down a bit in 2009 because of the tougher economic climate and lower energy prices, Efficiency Vermont still continues to meet or exceed most targets. The explosion of interest in 2008 shows just how responsive the level of efficiency investments is to increases in energy price.

Another way to increase the return on investment is to target programs in geographic areas where demand on the electrical grid is nearing capacity during peak times. In the absence of measures that would reduce demand, these are the areas most likely to soon require expensive new generation and transmission infrastructure. They are also the areas where costly imported power is most likely to be needed during times of peak demand. In conjunction with the Vermont Public Service Board, Efficiency Vermont has mapped out these areas and established an active outreach and incentives program. Efficiency Vermont justifies this targeting of resources because the return on investment in negawatts there is higher than in other areas. The results of the first pilot program were encouraging: summer peak energy savings in targeted zones increased sevenfold over the baseline savings amount, thanks to the program. The second pilot phase was in place as this was being written, to conclude in 2011. Current projections estimate that the success of this program could delay power upgrades by five or more years.

In addition to getting owners of existing buildings to make upgrades, Efficiency Vermont makes a considerable effort to ensure that newly constructed homes and businesses are energy efficient. Between a quarter and a third of new homes built in the state achieve some kind of minimum standard, such as the EPA's Energy Star rating. And it's estimated that between 80 and 90 percent of new large commercial projects in the state work with Efficiency Vermont. One reason for this is that Vermont has a statewide land-use law (Act 250) requiring all large projects to go through a review that includes energy-efficiency criteria. Another is that design professionals in the state now commonly go to Efficiency Vermont at the early stages of a project. According to the late Blair Hamilton, who was cofounder of VEIC and director of Efficiency Vermont, "We rely on them to drive projects to us. Many years ago, I got a memo from the chief of engineering at the biggest engineering firm in the state saying that it's now the policy of this office that whenever you start a new project, you call Efficiency Vermont and find out who the project manager is and get them to the first meeting. Anything, say, over 50,000 square feet—they might not do everything we tell them, but we'll have had a chance to review the blueprints and sometimes be involved from the very beginning in terms even of siting and orientation. We have a dozen engineers doing that kind of stuff." Efficiency Vermont's involvement with the state's building industries is facilitated by various events they sponsor, such as their yearly Better Buildings by Design conference, which generally has more than a thousand attendees, including many of the state's architects and engineers. It also features awards for building design and efficiency, which, Hamilton says, create "a certain amount of peer pressure and expectation that, of course, it's what everyone is doing. We're trying to establish it as the norm."[11]

Efficiency Vermont and VEIC also help organize local energy-efficiency advocacy groups, known as town energy committees, in collaboration with the Vermont Climate Action Network. Activities of these groups include writing town energy plans, soliciting pledges from citizens, organizing community events, raising money for efficiency subsidies, and helping direct the technical outreach of VEIC and other organizations. According to Hamilton, "As Efficiency Vermont, we can leverage the interest and resources of the communities. . . . There's a multiplier effect certainly. And the sense of ownership with community groups is something that really works with us. Of course, it also stimulates interests. And we definitely buy into the notion of building from one single action to larger repeat actions." One of the most memorable interactions they had with a town occurred about eight years ago, when, according to Hamilton, they asked themselves "wouldn't it be cool if we could get absolutely every individual in a town to do at least one thing, like change a light bulb? Every business and every home . . . and be able to brag and be an example?" The town they chose was Poultney, with twenty-three hundred people. In collaboration with a service-learning course at nearby Green Mountain College, they set up a strategy to get every household to switch out at least one incandescent bulb for a compact fluorescent. They announced the program at the Town Fair. They offered one free CFL bulb to each town member at the local hardware store, in addition to six more at a subsidized price. To encourage participation they announced a prize: if 100 percent of households participated, Efficiency Vermont would make free energy efficiency upgrades to one of the town buildings. With the help of the college class, they eventually hit 100 percent.

Although community involvement is an important tool, decisions on efficiency upgrades are made mostly by individual building owners. Much of Efficiency Vermont's activity therefore revolves around searching for hidden opportunities and then pitching the economic case for those upgrades. Because homes tend to have a fairly circumscribed set of energy issues, determining actions that a homeowner or homebuilder needs to take is generally clear-cut. In the commercial sector, however, more detective work and engineering expertise is needed due to the variability of industries. For example, a few years ago Efficiency Vermont installed more efficient blowers to cool the forty lasers used by Green Mountain Coffee Roasters to etch the date and batch onto tiny, single-serve containers of ground coffee, along with other upgrades like better compressors. In another case, they worked with Kennametal, a manufacturer of tungsten-carbide metal-cutting products, to replace three obsolete centrifugal lubricating oil-delivery pumps with vertical turbine pumps, which their research indicated would do the same job more efficiently. The techniques used to identify savings in each case couldn't be more different, but the savings are big and payback periods short in both cases.

Even if there's a positive economic return after a few years, though, many building owners still need additional convincing. According to Hamilton, "We are trying to get better and better at presenting a compelling economic case. Because efficiency is an investment, we're talking about this not as an expenditure, but as an investment. We show them that if you finance it, this is what your cash flow would look like. And in general it's a positive cash flow. . . . Our negotiation's often one of buying down the first cost [cash-in to do the agreement] of the project to where the investment yields the kind of return that allows them to do it. Now, payback is a really bad indicator. If you say, 'This has a ten-year payback,' the business says, 'That's all well and fine but I don't know if I'm going to be in business then.' Then we start negotiating, and we say, 'We'll reduce the additional cost with a grant to bring it down to where it's a four-year payback,' and they say, 'Okay, I'll sign it.' So it's kind of a case-by-case negotiation."

And even with incentives that greatly shorten the payback period, many homeowners or businesses are still reluctant to spend any money on efficiency simply because they don't expect to be in one place very long, they fear they won't get back their investment when they sell, and they tend to discount the value of future savings significantly. Efficiency Vermont's team spends a lot of time thinking about ways municipality can opt into this tax district. And what you agree to is that, in exchange for capitalizing energy efficiency improvements to your property . . . you'll have an assessment fee placed on the property over time up to as long as 20 years. The assessment is a separate line item on your property taxes with the same force of collection . . . and it survives ownership. The municipality would bond for the money. . . . You spread it over 20 years. And hopefully, psychologically, the person agreeing to this will start to approach it very different, as if it's more like a condo fee . . . and [energy] savings are greater than the fee.

The early adopters of PACE have already shown great results. For instance, Boulder County's program, starting in 2009, funded 393 projects totaling $7.5 million in just its first round of funding, and since then applications have been averaging $1 million in proposed upgrades per week.[12] In 2009, VEIC succeeded in getting the Vermont legislature to pass enabling legislation to allow this type of financing, joining 17 other states that now allow this. In March 2010, 6 Vermont communities, including Burlington, enabled Clean Energy Assessment Districts, allowing this approach to go forward. By 2011, 24 states and the District of Columbia had enabled PACE financing, and millions of dollars in grant financing had been administered to launch PACE programs.

As a groundswell was building for PACE nationwide, the federal government was beginning to get interested. In late 2009, the White House developed a Property Assessed Clean Energy Policy Framework with recommended guidelines for the practice. Shortly after releasing the report, Vice President Biden announced that this type of financing would be an official and major component of the national "Recovery through Retrofit" plan, which is part of the larger Recovery Act. In announcing this, the White House committed the Department of Energy to accept state proposals to use State Energy Grants or Energy Efficiency Conservation Block Grants for Property Assessed Clean Energy pilots.

Soon after, however, a major roadblock emerged. In May 2010, Fannie Mae and Freddie Mac, the nation's two largest purchasers of to bypass this psychology. One mechanism they've been exploring is creative use of the mortgage process. About twelve years ago they did a pilot for so-called Energy Improvement Mortgages, in which borrowers took out a slightly larger principal on their mortgage in return for getting a battery of efficiency upgrades on the home, coordinated by Efficiency Vermont. The upgrades were carefully designed and analyzed to ensure that the savings in monthly energy bills would be greater than the increase in the monthly mortgage payment. The pilot yielded more than a hundred test cases, but there were several barriers. First, there was a lot of administrative overhead: each client required on average between seven hundred and eight hundred dollars in "handholding" services through the process. Second, the real estate agents presented significant roadblocks, attempting to dissuade their clients from pursuing this approach. Says Hamilton, "The problem is, once you have identified the buyer, what the realtor wants is to get to the closing as fast as possible and not have anything sour it. What if our energy analysis shows there's a defect that has to be fixed? There are a million things that could wrong. And homebuyers have stardust in their eyes—all they want to do is get through closing." The second barrier was enough to keep that program in check.

Since trying this, however, an even more auspicious financing tool has burst on the national scene. Property Assessed Clean Energy (PACE) financing, first attempted in Berkeley, California, in 2008, is a way of financing major efficiency retrofits on buildings (and in some cases on-site renewable energy generation) in a way that requires no upfront cost for the owner and, in theory, should result in lower net expenses by the homeowner from day one. "It's a potentially game-changing approach to energy investment in existing buildings." Hamilton goes on to explain why:

The fundamental idea is that you can create what, from a legal perspective, would look like a special assessment district [Clean Energy Assessment District] . . . only it's not geographic, it's a virtual district where individual owners within a

The Building Energy Diet   163

mortgages, released "letters of guidance" indicating that they would not purchase mortgages with a PACE lien. Their problem was that the lien under this program would be "senior" to existing mortgage debt, meaning that in the case of default, the municipal debt would be repaid before the bank. Although a spokesperson for the two mortgage giants affirmed his clients' commitment to enhancing energy efficiency, Clif Staton, of Renewable Funding, which administers many PACE programs, points out that "there are 37,000 special assessment districts in the United States for all kinds of things. All of those assessments have the same senior lien status, and Fannie Mae and Freddie Mac have never raised an issue about those special assessment districts."[13] Given the importance of these two institutions—they together guarantee $11 trillion in mortgages—a decision by them to cease buying PACE mortgages is a show stopper, at least for the moment and at least for residential buildings. Most residential PACE programs—including the largest, in San Francisco—have therefore been put on hold as of 2011. Meanwhile the secretary of energy wrote to the mortgage institutions to try to resolve the impasse. If this is really about just a technicality regarding lien seniority, one would expect this to be worked out soon. If it turns into a protracted political battle, American cities will have missed a big opportunity.

Because this impediment applies only to residential mortgages, however, it has not prevented PACE financing from gaining traction in the commercial building sector. As of March 2011, there were four operational commercial PACE programs in the country, accounting for seventy-one PACE building projects worth around $10 million. While this is clearly a very small amount, many expect this amount to rise considerably. Already there are thirteen more commercial PACE programs in planning or development, and a 2010 market research report estimated that the total value of projects could climb to $2.5 billion annually by 2015.[14] Even if PACE doesn't take off, though, there are other inventive approaches to funding efficiency upgrades that don't necessarily require policy intervention. A relatively new approach involves privately investing in building upgrades to commercialize the energy savings. One of three or four such companies is Transcend Equity, founded in 2003, whose managed energy service agreements (MESAs) work by establishing the baseline energy usage for a commercial building, funding efficiency upgrades, and then earning revenues based on the difference between the old and new energy bills. Under this system, Transcend assumes responsibility for paying energy bills. The building owner pays an operating fee to Transcend based on historical energy use, while Transcend pays to the utility the new post-upgrade energy bills, which, ideally, are much lower than the old bills. In the process they pocket the difference. This arrangement continues for the life of a contract, generally ten years, after which the building owner goes back to paying his or her own utility bill. Transcend has applied this approach to about forty buildings, and results have been excellent so far. According to Transcend's managing director, Sean Patrick Neill, overall their portfolio has performed "very, very well." [15]

This model comes with a number of advantages for building owners. First, when the contract expires, they own the upgrades outright and will see their operating costs decrease significantly. Second, during the contract period, building owners avoid the need to repair or replace many aging systems. And finally, the upgrades can improve the work environment and be used as a valuable marketing tool. In fact, one tenant of a building Transcend worked on was so pleased with the improvements to the office that they asked if the company would work with the landlord of one of their other offices in another state.

This approach also comes with a big advantage for cities, because the most inefficient buildings are targeted first, since they can yield the greatest cost savings. According to Neill, this has the potential to truly change how efficiency is dealt with in real estate: "What debt and equity need to be doing is chasing poor performing buildings. And we've never had a market that worked that way . . . not in private real estate. It's exciting to think that we're soon going to have capital pursuing inefficiency."

Although this model may be mutually beneficial for property owners, financiers, and city governments, promoting its wide-scale adoption is challenging. The Carbon War Room, a nonprofit group cofounded by Sir Richard Branson that seeks to tackle climate change through business and markets, is one organization that has taken up this challenge head-on. According to Murat Armbruster, the head of their energy efficiency operation, the War Room's strategy is to catalyze action by bringing together as many key players as possible, highlighting common interests, and serving as a trusted third party. "We're trying to help configure the pieces in such a way so that people can make good decisions quickly and get it done. . . . We've mapped out the ecology of the industry and looked at where we saw there could be real market potential. And then we help the cities and building owners understand what the difference between the different mechanisms and technologies is so that, when they go to make a decision, they can feel that they've had a trusted third party that helps them vet and distinguish their options." Municipal governments are a key element to this process because, according to Armbruster, "cities are amazing conveners, particularly of building owners."[16]

Despite all these promising mechanisms, the relatively slow pace of upgrading building efficiency in the United States suggests that there are limits to voluntary programs, particularly in terms of their adequacy for meeting potential future regulations for greenhouse gas (GHG) emissions. According to Blair Hamilton, "At a certain point in time, very likely, if we're going to meet GHG goals, we will reach the point where we realize that voluntary isn't going to do it. . . . What we probably have to get to, say by 2020, would be mandatory energy improvements at time of property transfer. So when you buy and sell property, you basically have to bring it up to a level which is consistent with achieving GHG goals." Hamilton sees a mandatory program as entailing some hardship at first, but then making everyone better off in the longer term, because once the work is done in the short term, all property owners will accrue benefits greater than that investment. And as energy prices go up, those benefits will only be amplified.

Mandatory efficiency programs are controversial in the United States but have become commonplace in Europe. In 2002, the European

Union passed the Energy Performance of Buildings Directive (EPBD), requiring increases in building efficiency in member states. By 2009, however, it was becoming evident that this directive was having relatively little effect, partly due to a lack of qualified technical personnel in member countries, and partly because of several loopholes in the law. So the European Commission worked to create a stronger directive, which was passed into law in May 2010. Under this law, all member countries are required to draw up minimum efficiency standards that can vary somewhat by country but are constrained by a prescribed methodology for calculating them based on "cost-optimality." All new or renovated buildings have to comply with these minimum standards regardless of size (in the old law, renovation requirements applied only to buildings over roughly ten thousand square feet). "Energy performance certifications" are required for all new buildings at the time of sale and for existing buildings at the time of transfer or renovation. Regular inspections are also required. Certifications not only rate performance but suggest upgrades to the building. The certificates have to be made viewable in a "prominent" part of a building after construction or renovation and have to be included in sales or rental documents and advertisements. Similarly, "smart meters" displaying electricity use have to be installed in new or refurbished buildings. The law also includes a controversial provision that new buildings constructed as of 2019 have to be net-zero energy—in other words, they must generate as much as they use. Further, wherever there is municipal efficiency infrastructure in place, like district heating and combined heat and power generation, developers of larger buildings must at least consider its use. The European Union (EU) expects that compliance with the law will result in a 5 to 6 percent reduction in energy consumption for the entire bloc. They expect that the elimination of the approximately ten-thousand-square-foot threshold alone will result in an additional $35 billion in annual benefits, for a yearly investment of just $11 billion.

It remains to be seen how variable the results of this law will be in different member states. Already, several have successful preexisting mandatory efficiency programs, like Denmark's Green Accounts for Public Buildings program, which sets performance standards for public buildings, and its Large Building Energy Audit scheme, which requires owners of buildings larger than roughly sixteen thousand square feet to meet certain water- and energy-efficiency goals set by a certified consultant. Some European cities have also passed energy ordinances that are far more stringent than the laws of the EU or the countries they're in. In 2000, for instance, Barcelona adopted a Solar Thermal Ordinance (strengthened in 2006) mandating that solar energy supply 60 percent of running hot water in all new or renovated buildings—not a bad idea considering the city's twenty-eight thousand average hours of annual sunshine. It's estimated that, as a result, Barcelona saves as much electric power as is consumed by more than four thousand typical Spanish households and that the amount of solar hot water produced is enough to serve completely the demand of forty-five thousand people.[17]

In the United States, building efficiency regulations are far more modest. As of 2009, ninety-two cities had enacted ordinances requiring newly constructed buildings over a certain size to meet some kind of minimum efficiency standard. Many cities are coupling requirements with tax incentives, expedited permits, subsidies, loans, and technical assistance.[18]

The most common efficiency standard used in these municipal requirements is the US Green Building Council's (USGBC) Leadership in Energy and Environmental Design (LEED) rating, a popular certification scheme that is also pursued voluntarily by many commercial building owners. LEED certification comes with several added advantages. Not only can it help lower long-term operating costs, but as an internationally recognized designation, certification carries caché that can provide a significant edge in the marketing and leasing of new buildings. According to a 2008 survey, two-thirds of respondents from the design and construction industry felt that having a green building yielded higher asking rents, while half felt that it yielded higher occupancy rates and a higher return on investment. In terms of the specific LEED certification for green buildings, one-third found it to be "extremely" or "very" valuable while an additional 50 percent found it to be at least "somewhat valuable." A study by Rosenberg Real Estate Equity Funds validated these perceptions: it found that average rents per square foot for Class A office space were one-third higher in LEED-certified buildings than in noncertified buildings, while vacancy rates in LEED buildings averaged only two-thirds of those in noncertified buildings.[19]

LEED certification, however, is not without its critics. One of the most common critiques is that energy savings from LEED certified buildings tend to be rather modest, because energy efficiency is just one of five thematic areas in which buildings can earn certification points and because LEED certification does not require tracking energy use. A recent study of LEED buildings found, in fact, that not only were purported energy savings of LEED buildings misleading, but that when a real "apples to apples" comparison is made between LEED buildings and similar non-LEED buildings of the same vintage, LEED buildings use on average slightly more energy. These concerns gained further traction in 2008 when a USGBC study of 121 buildings that they certified through 2006 found that 53 percent of them did not qualify for the EPA's Energy Star label, and that the lowest 15 percent used more energy than 70 percent of comparable, noncertified national building stock. Their research also found that a quarter of new, certified buildings do not save as much energy as the designs predicted. A 2009 *New York Times* article widely publicized these findings, also highlighting the lack of a requirement for building owners to provide energy performance data to maintain certification.[20]

The USGBC has, however, responded to these concerns to a large extent. In general, their energy standards for certification have been growing stricter over time. In one round of revisions to the standard in 2009 they started requiring all newly constructed certified buildings to provide energy and water bills for the first five years as a condition of certification. Another round of revisions started in late 2010, with the release of new draft standards followed by an extensive public comment period (final standards stemming from this process are expected in November 2012). The draft wording includes a number of changes that tighten up energy efficiency standards. Among them are more stringent benchmarking for the minimum energy performance prerequisite, more points given for the energy performance credit, a new credit for energy-demand response programs (such as plans to shift electrical loads from peak to off-peak hours), a new prerequisite for building-level metering, and tougher requirements for getting credits for measurement and verification plans.

One of the more comprehensive municipal building energy policies in the United States is in New York City. Its Greener, Greater Buildings Plan seeks to retrofit all buildings larger than fifty thousand square feet. Because those buildings account for nearly half the floor space and consume 45 percent of all energy used in New York City, regulation of this class of buildings has the potential to be far-reaching.[21] Furthermore, because relatively few individuals own these large buildings, there is great potential for coordinating and leveraging efforts. The measures being required are fairly modest, however; according to the city they will have a payback period of less than a year. These improvements include calibrating heating, ventilation, and air-conditioning (HVAC) sensors and controls to optimize performance; cleaning and servicing HVAC systems; tuning boilers; and insulating pipes, among other similar measures. Though modest, the plan does affect a large area of floor space, so it's expected to result in $700 million in annual energy savings and reduce greenhouse gas emissions for the city by 5 percent.

Of course, many Manhattan buildings have gone far beyond these minimum requirements voluntarily, just because they think it's good business. The most high-profile of these "Cadillac retrofits" is, without doubt, the Empire State Building. With the help of the Clinton Climate Initiative, the Rocky Mountain Institute, Johnson Controls, and the developers Jones, Lang, La Salle, the New York monument is undergoing a massive retrofit that includes upgrading more than sixty-five hundred windows, installing a similar number of radiator barriers, retrofitting the chiller plant, upgrading HVAC controls and sensors, and improving air handlers, all at a cost of about $20 million. The resulting package of upgrades is expected to reduce energy consumption by 38 percent, saving $4.4 million annually from the usual $11 million budget.

New York City has also worked to help address structural disincentives to energy efficiency investment. In April 2011 the New York City mayor's office, in conjunction with Natural Resource Defense Council's Green Lease Forum, released a new model for lease language that has the potential to eliminate a significant historical barrier to efficiency upgrades in commercial buildings. The Energy-Aligned Lease, also known as the "Green Lease," deals with what's been called the "split incentive" problem. Essentially, under standard class-A office-leasing language, landlords bear most of the cost of energy efficiency improvements but do not reap the benefits of lower operating costs because leases require that tenants pay those costs. Furthermore, while owners can pass the costs of capital improvements onto tenants, standard leases require that those costs be recouped over the lifetime of the improvement, which can be in the range of decades. The first implementation of this new lease template occurred to great fanfare at the prestigious Seven World Trade Center building for the law firm of WilmerHale, which had leased 210,000 square feet. The tenant and developer agreed to share the costs of upgrades by counting utility savings only over the length of the projected payback period, allowing capital costs to be passed on to the tenant over a relatively short period. Many in the building industry feel that this approach, which has also been tried in Portland, Oregon, Winnipeg, Canada, and cities in Australia, has considerable potential to spur green investment in the commercial building sector.

These policy approaches are all steps in the right direction, but many believe that there's no quicker or more effective way to spur efficiency and reduce waste than through pricing. In the case of building energy, history has shown that individuals are a lot more effective at reducing costs on their own initiative (when those costs go above a certain point) than at following government rules. When prices for all fuels spiked in 2008, there was a flurry of activity to improve home thermal efficiency (from insulation to weatherizing) and to purchase efficient furnaces and solar hot-water systems. According to Paul Scheckel, formerly of Efficiency Vermont, "As energy prices rise [Efficiency Vermont's] phones start ringing more often, our website hits go up, my book sales go up and people drive less. So it's all about the money."

But even more effective is the judicious combining of pricing and regulation—that is, joining policies that coordinate mandatory efficiency measures with rates that better reflect the full cost. Perhaps the best illustration of this approach is from the realm of water use in the West. Southern California, for instance, has had a two-pronged approach for many years. On the regulatory side, local municipalities have passed an array of water-conservation ordinances. Los Angeles' ordinance, which builds on those going back to the droughts of the late seventies, forbids hosing down hard surfaces to an extent that runoff results, sprinkler irrigation between 9 A.M. and 4 P.M. or on certain days of the week based on address, and serving water in restaurants without a direct request for it, among many other prohibitions. Violations come with stiff fines. On the pricing side, the Los Angeles Department of Water and Power (DWP) is constantly changing its rate structure to encourage greater conservation.

A lot of economists believe that no amount of regulation or voluntary programs will solve the problem of overconsumption of water as long as the price of water remains so low. The logic goes that if its price better reflected the cost of getting water to market and the demand among its many users, frivolous use of water would be reduced because people would monitor their water consumption more wisely. There are some challenges to this approach, though. One problem, according to Con Howe, former director of City Planning for Los Angeles, is regional equity. With such variable temperature and precipitation within the Los Angeles Basin, any rate hike is politically contentious because hotter and dryer inland areas require much more water than more moderate coastal areas. Another problem is socioeconomic equity. Because water is a necessity of life, care must be taken not to price low-income people out of the market for water.

To address these issues of geographic and socio-economic fairness, the Los Angeles DWP, like many water utilities elsewhere, uses a tiered rate structure, first implemented in 1993, that allows households to consume a stipulated amount of water at a lower rate (Tier 1). That amount is listed on a household's water bill and varies based on the size of the property (the allotment per square foot goes down with property size), the climate in that location (there are huge variations in temperature and precipitation within the City of Los Angeles), and household size. Tier 1 quantities are set to roughly meet the basic needs of a household and therefore allow lower-income households to get adequate freshwater at an affordable price. Once a household exceeds its Tier 1 allotment, all subsequent water is bought at the higher Tier 2 price. Tier 2 water is for luxuries like long showers, irrigated lawns, and pools. Currently the Tier 2 rate is nearly twice that of Tier 1. So pricing is controlled not only by the baseline rates for each tier but also by the size of the allotment allowed in Tier 1. Under so-called Shortage Year Water Rates (which were still in effect for Los Angeles DWP customers as of May 2011, although debate had started on ending them in the City Council), that allotment is reduced by 15 percent. As a result of this type of coordinated pricing and regulation, Los Angeles' 2010 water use is now as low as it was in 1979, despite the city's having grown by about one million people. Between 2007 and 2010 alone, water use by a single-family home declined by 30 percent, in a downward trend that continued for thirty-one consecutive months.[22]

In total, conservation measures today are estimated to save almost three times what they saved in 1990. According to Zev Yaroslavsky, through pricing "people are forced to do things like turn the faucet off when they're shaving and only turn it on when they need to rinse or limit the amount of time using the washing machine each week— things that really produce huge savings in water without really inconveniencing anybody or changing their quality of life. The trick is to find a way through the pricing mechanism to incentivize people to conserve without fundamentally changing their quality of life. I think they've done a pretty good job so far."[23]

I still recall the sense of unease as I waited to hear the results of my first energy audit, which took place in my previous residence, around 2004. This was almost certainly the first audit ever done on our 110-year-old Victorian home in downtown Burlington, Vermont. The results showed that the home leaked like a sieve and barely produced heat. It would need everything from new windows on the second floor, to replacement of rotted siding and frames, to a new gas furnace, to a new water heater, to blowing insulation into the hollow walls. As I heard this, the already considerable pit in my stomach became a virtual black hole. With the audit report in one hand and a checkbook in the other, I faced the difficult part: deciding what to do next.

Millions of homeowners find themselves in this situation every year. And no matter how much data or analysis goes into the payback projections, the decision to invest is always a leap of faith. We decided to make all recommended investments. From an altruistic perspective, there's no question that these will redound positively for years to any number of future owners and, in a very small way, to the planet. From a comfort perspective, there's also no question that our experience in the house was much improved by the investments. From a personal financial perspective, though, the story is a bit different. With only three years in the house between upgrading and selling it, a weak housing market upon sale, and a neighborhood with a firm price ceiling, we never really recouped our investment.

Does this mean that I think that investment in energy efficiency is a bad deal? Absolutely not. All it means is that, like crossing the street, energy upgrades are not always risk free. And as Efficiency Vermont, the Carbon War Room, and other visionary organizations in energy efficiency work on developing new mechanisms to reduce that risk (and I watch solar hot-water panels go up on roofs all around the neighborhood), I'm already reviewing the audit report for my new house and scheming about what efficiency project comes next.

Natural Gas

NATURAL GAS HAS BEEN promoted by many as a cheap, clean, abundant, and domestically available fuel.

Certainly, it has many big advantages over oil alternatives like coal and tar sands. It works not only for home heating and electricity generation but also as a fuel in vehicles with converted engines (this has been done for 20 percent of American bus fleets).[1] It is cheaper and easier to convert into a synthetic liquid fuel using the Fischer-Tropsch method than is coal. In addition, in the United States and many other countries there is an extensive infrastructure for delivering natural gas for the purposes of home heating and cooking. Finally, it's generally easy to extract because its low viscosity means that it flows out of the earth's surface with less friction than oil or water. For all these reasons, it's been touted by many as the "bridge fuel" from oil and coal to renewable energy. It's also one of the cornerstones of energy security in President Obama's "Blueprint for a Secure Energy Future." But just how cheap, clean, and abundant is it really?

The biggest question may be its abundance. Finding new supplies is critical to maintaining steady supplies of natural gas. The problem is that the production of US gas wells decline, on average, by more than 30 percent per year—far faster than for oil wells. Therefore, new wells have to be drilled at an incredibly rapid pace to keep up with decline. Unfortunately, newer finds tend to be less productive. Gas production in the United States peaked in 1971, and the average size of new North American finds is consistently decreasing; in 2003 about 50 percent less gas was found per foot drilled in the United States than a decade earlier. The average well in 2010 produced 40 percent less gas than in 1990. To fight against these diminishing returns, it has been estimated that the United States will need roughly 30,000 new wells per year to keep production increasing. Luckily, the extensive pipeline system in the United States, comprising more than 305,000 miles of long-distance transmission pipes, makes tapping of these smaller gas deposits more economically feasible than in most other countries.[2]

You wouldn't suspect there's any supply constraint from listening to the rhetoric on natural gas. And the main reason for this has to do with "shale gas," an unconventional source of natural gas that is now being called "a revolution." Exploitation of this resource has been allowed only very recently because of technical advances that have brought together two older technologies: horizontal drilling and hydraulic fracturing (known as fracking). This combination of technologies releases gas trapped in shale by drilling lateral holes that follow a thin stratum of shale rock from a single surface platform. The well is injected with a slurry composed of mixed water, sand, and chemicals that fracture the rock, releasing the gas. These shale formations are huge—occupying vast swaths of the country. Therefore this technology has opened up drilling to large areas once thought to be uneconomical. As a result the US Energy Information Administration has dramatically adjusted upward proved reserves of gas. For instance, just between 2008 and 2009, reserves went up by 11 percent largely because discoveries of new shale deposits in 2009 alone added 75 percent to proved shale reserves. Hence it's not surprising that the Energy Information Administration predicts that US shale gas production will quadruple by 2035.[3]

The problem is that almost all growth in gas production is expected to come from shale. Without the shale reserves, US domestic production is projected to fall by 20 percent by 2035. So US Energy Information Administration projections of ample future gas reserves are largely based on an assumption of increasing reliance on shale. In their 2010 forecast, they projected that 26 percent of gas production would be from shale by 2035. In their 2011 forecast, that number was increased to 45 percent. Hence, a lot of eggs are being put in one basket. Just how reliable is this basket?[4]

The biggest concern is over the environmental impacts of this method. First, it uses enormous amounts of water, often millions of gallons per well, which can be a major problem in some of the arid regions where shale deposits are common (e.g., Texas, Wyoming, and North Dakota). Second, the slurry that is pumped into the shale formations includes any number of chemicals. Fracking is currently almost totally unregulated because of a 2005 statutory exemption from the Safe Drinking Water Act. But a 2011 Congressional report documented finding up to 750 compounds in fracking slurries, 650 of which contain known or possible toxins or carcinogenic chemicals, like benzene or lead.[5] With shale wells increasingly being drilled near towns and drinking-water supplies, there is fear of drinking-water contamination. Groundwater contamination is feared as a result of leaks in wellbores and casings. Surface water contamination is feared as a result of improper disposal of toxic drilling fluids, often detained in waste pits.

While there have been numerous anecdotal reports of polluted well water resulting from fracking, research is still nascent on this topic, and the EPA is expected to release preliminary study results in 2012. Nonetheless, the *New York Times* did conduct an investigative report of this issue in early 2011. Their review of thousands of pages of government documents, some of them leaked, suggests that officials have far more significant concerns about the effects of gas drilling techniques on water supplies and public health than they have publicly acknowledged. One concern expressed in these documents is the potential for contamination from improperly abandoned shale wells to migrate upward to shallower depths, where they could interact with drinking-water supplies. This is not a small issue considering the dizzying rate at which wells are established and then abandoned. Another concern is that because this wastewater is not regulated, it's often sent to facilities, like sewage treatment plants, that are unable to adequately treat its contaminants (some of them radioactive) and discharge them into rivers that serve as major drinking-water supplies. And these concerns go on and on, over the course of hundreds of pages of government documents.[6] Besides the environmental impacts, shale also has potential production issues. First, the rate of production decline for shale wells, which is between 63 and 83 percent in their first year, is far steeper than with conventional wells, which is between 25 and 40 percent. Hence, reliance on shale means an ever increasing number of new wells to make up for production declines. And second, projections on the growth of shale production are based on extrapolations that all shale gas wells would be equally productive, regardless of where drilled. In fact, experience in recent years has proven this to be false. For instance, of seventeen counties in the Barnett Shale region, once thought to be equally productive, today only two and a half are recognized as highly productive. In other words, production forecasts may be far too rosy.[7]

For all these reasons, overreliance on shale for natural gas supplies is very risky. Not only are long-term production prospects uncertain, but there is a growing chorus of opposition to fracking among environmental and public health advocates. In fact, as of 2011 New York State and the Province of Quebec had temporary moratoriums on fracking, and in May 2011 the French Parliament voted overwhelmingly to ban the practice. Furthermore, a number of local jurisdictions have banned it. While the same fate may not follow in the United States, new information on the health and environmental effects of this method is emerging every day, and it would not be surprising to see significant restrictions enacted—restrictions that could boost costs and shut down production in many areas. In other words, the prospect of cheap and abundant domestic natural gas far into the future rests upon the use of methods whose consequences are considered intolerable by many. Just how long they will continue to be tolerated in the United States is uncertain.

The other alternative to keeping domestic production constant through fracking of shale is to increase imports. Currently, almost 85 percent of US gas imports come from Canada (which is connected to the same pipeline system). But as that source nears its limits, the United States will have to look farther afield.

There are many large, actively managed gas fields outside of North America, but according to the late energy investor Matthew Simmons—someone who made a fortune in predicting trends in energy supply and pricing—most have rates of production decline that are far steeper than those for oil fields, and most of the large mega–gas fields are nearly depleted. In the remaining, smaller fields, the economics of extracting gas is far more sensitive to geography than for oil or coal, because pipelines are the only viable way to move large amounts of gas across land. Large gas fields economically justify the construction of pipelines, but small and isolated fields in countries with poor pipeline infrastructure do not, so they remain unrecoverable. This means that the estimates of existing gas resources in the ground are deceiving, because so much exists as small isolated deposits that could never economically justify a pipeline connection, even at high energy prices. In fact, it is estimated that as much as 60 percent of the world's gas reserves are inaccessible for human use by pipelines.[8] Another problem with relying on global gas supplies is that transporting it across oceans presents a significant barrier, for it must be supercooled into liquid natural gas (LNG) typically at −259°F, requiring expensive supply-chain infrastructure. Known as an "LNG train," this infrastructure consists of a liquefaction terminal and pipeline for the producer, giant cryogenic tankers, and regassification terminals in the user country, which together can cost between $3 and $10 billion. Furthermore, the process of using liquid natural gas has a dramatic negative impact on energy return on investment, because so much energy is required to supercool the product. All this may explain why imported liquid gas accounted for only 1 percent of US gas use in 2003 (and 5 percent of its imports), and why only four US ports have facilities for this limited energy source.[9]

Hence, while markets for oil are global, those for natural gas are still largely dictated by pipeline connections, meaning that prices are more strongly influenced by regional supply than by global supply.[10]

Liquid natural gas has the potential to make markets for gas more global, but so far it is a long way from demonstrating that feasibility. In summary, natural gas is hobbled by far too many uncertainties to reliably fill the supply gaps expected to be left as production rates of oil decline.

CHAPTER 7

Smart Mobility

I t's a Monday morning in Copenhagen and I'm tearing down a street called Rolighedsvej on my clunky steel rental bike, trying to make it to a meeting to which I'm nearly certain I'll be late. Shifting into the highest of my three gears, I pass bakeries, corner markets, small boutiques, and plenty of other bikers whose more leisurely pace indicates they aren't late for meetings. Although they pay no attention to me, I imagine they must know I'm American by my haste. As I zip along the beautifully maintained bike lanes, it strikes me that I've never had a city biking experience quite like this. Not only do I feel safe and secure, but I'm able to get to my destination faster, more economically, and with less difficulty than if I were driving a car. And all the while I'm having a blast.

I'm able to do this because Copenhagen has arguably the most advanced network of bicycle infrastructure in the world, including hundreds of miles of beautifully maintained bike lanes, designated crossing areas in major intersections, bicycle traffic lights, enormous parking complexes, and free bike-sharing services. Elements of this infrastructure are present not just on a few streets but on almost every street I traverse, big and small.

A few things struck me about biking in Copenhagen. First, there appear to be more bikes than cars. To someone who grew up in Los Angeles, this feels a little like a Twilight Zone episode. Second, people primarily bike to get places, not to exercise or joyride, as indicated by the press of riders wearing business attire during rush hour. Fancy Lycra

A cyclist in Copenhagen riding in a dedicated lane
while passing cycle parking. (Photo by author)

suits, Oakley shades, and even helmets are nearly absent. Third, people
of all ages ride bicycles. I saw plenty of small kids (who are allowed to
ride on sidewalks until age six) on two-wheelers, cyclists in the grand-
parental age bracket, and everything in between. Often, families cycle
together in a multigenerational peloton. For kids too young to bike
longer distances, parents use any one of dozens of child trailers or special seats. Fourth, Copenhageners have cargo biking down to an art
form, from stashing a few groceries in handlebar baskets to carrying
a new television on a cargo-bike platform or bike trailer. Fifth, much
of this hardy population of cyclists seems insensitive to bad weather.
Although I was in Copenhagen only during May, there were almost as
many bikers when it was near 40°F and raining as when it was warm
and sunny. And finally, biking culture is evident in every corner of the
city and all aspects of daily life. An apartment building will typically
have several times as many bikes parked outside as there are housing
units within. Some newer buildings sport extremely fancy enclosed

Clearly delineated bicycle lanes in Copenhagen that make cycling feasible for commuting. (Photo by author)

Signalization that facilitates the flow of cars, pedestrians, and cyclists at Copenhagen intersections. (Photo: Anders Flodmark; used by permission)

One of Copenhagen's digital bicycle counters, which helps generate
data on cycling. (Photo: Anders Flodmark; used by permission)

bike-parking facilities. Subway stations have bike-parking facilities
that often fill up with thousands of bikes. And small mom-and-pop
bicycle stores are found on almost every block.

My hunches about the importance of biking in Copenhagen are
confirmed by data. It turns out that 90 percent of Copenhageners
own a bike (only 53 percent of Copenhagen households own a car);
approximately 58 percent use a bike daily for at least small trips, and
37 percent make their daily commute on bikes, up from 30 percent in
1996 (the city's target is 50 percent by 2015). Many government service
providers now use bicycles, like mail carriers and police officers. Even
the crown prince of Denmark regularly gets around by bicycle. With a
robust public transportation network to complement the biking routes,
only 31 percent need commute by car in this city. As for infrastructure

Mikael Colville-Andersen with his cargo
bicycle in Copenhagen. (Photo by author)

statistics, in 2008 Copenhagen boasted 246 miles of combined cycle tracks, lanes, and greenways and almost 35,000 bike-parking spaces on roads.[1]

The energy impact of this is huge. Even though subways definitely reduce the energy footprint of the average commuter, nothing can beat bicycling, whose only energy input is the food the cyclist ate for breakfast or lunch. By getting bicycle mode shares to where they are, Copenhagen has in essence eliminated over a third of all transportation fossil-fuel use and, in the process, eliminated ninety thousand tons of greenhouse gas emissions per year.[2]

The destination I was aiming for on my rental bike was the apartment of Mikael Colville-Andersen, known to many as Denmark's unofficial ambassador of bicycle culture. In addition to being a journalist, filmmaker, and photographer, Colville-Andersen is a frequent consultant to the Copenhagen government on bicycle issues, and author of the internationally famous bicycle blogs, Copenhagenize.com and Cyclechic.com (the latter of which spawned an international movement of blogs documenting fashionably dressed people on bikes).

He explained to me that biking in Copenhagen is a natural part of everyday life, not something people do to burn calories or make a statement. "When I lecture I have four rules for promoting urban cycling. And rule # 1 is what I call 'A to Bism,' and that is, if you make it the quickest way to get around town, everyone and their dog will do it. Men in suits, mothers with children. . . . The basic anthropology of encouraging people to ride is to make it easier." Data back up his contention. A 2006 survey found that 54 percent of Copenhagen cyclists ride because it's easy and fast. Nineteen percent do it for exercise, and only 1 percent do it for environmental reasons.[3] The irony is that for many people, the roles of cars and bikes are essentially reversed in Denmark and North America. Says Colville-Andersen: "I was in Washington speaking there and somebody asked me a question: 'You know in the States we go for bike rides in the weekend. What do you guys do?' And I said, 'We go for car drives.' And people laughed. We'll get a car and drive out to see my mother-in-law, or somewhere we don't normally go. Cars are for the weekend."[4]

Biking in Copenhagen is easy and fast partly because of the city's amazing investment in bicycle infrastructure. With over $10 million in annual investments (20 to 25 percent of the road budget), the results are stunning. In addition to the mileage of lanes and the system of bicycle traffic signals, mentioned above, the city has implemented some innovations for bikes, such as the so-called green wave, in which traffic lights on several main arteries into the city center are synchronized during rush hours for the benefit of bikes. This means that bikers can maintain a comfortable 12 miles per hour cruising speed without putting a foot down to stop for a light for up to four miles. The synchronization switches from morning to afternoon so that this pattern can be maintained for inbound and outbound journeys. According to Colville-Andersen, this system has increased cycling on these routes by 10 to 15 percent. And on one of the busiest of those routes they've closed down the road to car traffic. Another perk for bicyclists is the "pre-green" signalization that allows bicycle traffic lights to turn green a few seconds before car traffic lights do, giving cyclists time to avoid dangerous automobile traffic in intersections. To further this sense of safety, bicycle lanes that cross intersections are painted bright blue, giving a clear indication of where bikes should be in the most dangerous areas; further, the lines where cars must stop have been pulled back fifteen feet behind bike lines in 120 intersections to give cyclists a head start.

Copenhagen also has a system of free shared bikes that are parked throughout the city and can be used by a deposit of about three dollars. In the winter, bike lanes get priority in terms of snow clearance and salting. And perhaps most important, the considerable public transit system in Copenhagen is designed to complement bicycling to an extent seen in few other palces. All underground stations on the Metro have large indoor bike-park facilities, and many have large outdoor facilities. Bicycles can be taken on metro trains, many of which have so-called flex rooms designed for bicycles.

Beyond all this municipal support, cycling in Copenhagen is furthered by Danes' long historical affinity for bicycles. According to Colville-Andersen, Danes took to the bicycle right after it was invented, in the 1880s, "because it really appeals to our design sensibilities: it's practical, it's efficient, it's simple and it's enjoyable." Biking also appeals to Danish cultural sensibilities. There's an amorphous concept in Danish culture called *hygge*, referring to things that are comforting, soothing, familiar, positively atmospheric, and lacking in any annoyance or irritation. In a documentary film made by the Copenhagen City Council Department of Roads and Parks, two young women are interviewed about what they love about biking in the city; their answer was "hygge," an attitude that's been validated in other studies of Danish biking culture.[5]

Although cars became popular during the fifties and sixties and bicycle mode share dropped from about 55 percent after the Second World War to 20 percent in the seventies, the oil crises of that decade spurred Danes to recall their biking roots and eventually led to a popular movement advocating the return to bicycle transportation—something that certainly never happened in the United States. Says Colville-Anderson, "There were 20,000 people on the city hall square saying 'we want bicycle infrastructure like we used to have. We used to have bike lanes 70 years ago.' And finally the city, to its credit said 'OK,' and in the eighties was the first separated bicycle lane with a curb down to the street. And then we never looked back."

One of the biggest obstacles to bike commuting in North America is a perception about personal hygiene. According to Colville-Andersen, this obstacle is largely absent in Denmark and other European countries. This is not, he jokes, because "the State has removed our sweat glands." Rather, the idea that low-exertion bike commuting is unhygienic is a total myth—one spawned by the marketing of bicycles as exercise equipment in North America. "Even if it's 35°C [95°F] in the summer, you just ride a bit slower—we've invented deodorant. It's not that Danes sweat less—you know, you have cities in Spain, Seville, Barcelona, that are booming with bicycle culture, and it's bloody hot there. In the States—because the bicycle as a means of everyday transport disappeared at least in the fifties or sixties—the marketing of bicycles in North America has been sports and recreation or kids in the driveway and nothing in between. Forty years of marketing bicycling as a sport or recreation has made it impossible for people to think 'wow, I could ride a bike and not sweat.' It's a cultural thing, but you guys have always had this focus on sports and vigor." This belief was one of the motivations leading to his founding of the first "Cycle Chic" blog, which spawned a movement of websites dedicated to photodocumenting fashionable people on bikes doing ordinary, everyday activities. According to the blog, "Cycle Chic aims to take back the bike culture by showing how the bicycle once again can be an integral, respectable and feasible transport form, free of sports clothes and gear, and how it can play a vital role in increasing the life quality in cities." The popularity of this site and the dozens of sites it has spawned are an indication that this notion has traction.[6]

Perceptions of safety are also a significant barrier to cycling in most places. Numerous surveys have found that one of the primary reasons people in North America avoid bike commuting is because they tend to see it as dangerous, largely because of car traffic. Certainly, I felt far safer riding my bicycle in Copenhagen than I ever did in the American cities where I've ridden (such as Boston, Los Angeles, and Oakland; even tiny Burlington doesn't feel very safe). In contrast, a recent survey found that 62 percent of cyclists in Copenhagen feel secure while riding in traffic.[7]

One reason why cyclists in Denmark feel safer than in more car-dependent countries is that safety comes in numbers. According to studies conducted in America, Europe, and Australia, as the number of cyclists in a city goes up, the rate of injuries goes down. This is borne out by the data in Copenhagen: while distance ridden between 1990 and 2000 increased by 40 percent, cycling injuries declined by 30 percent. The explanation is that in cities where bicycle commuters are few, drivers do not expect them or adequately prepare for sharing the road. Further, because drivers in these cities have little experience with cyclists and are less likely to cycle-commute themselves, they are more likely to make incorrect assumptions about what cyclists will do on the road.[8]

Increased biking therefore begets biking safety. But the numbers won't come until enough bicycle infrastructure is constructed. Properly designed infrastructure increases not only objective measures of safety but also perceptions of it. For instance, where cycle lanes are present on existing Copenhagen streets (the dominant cycle infrastructure for Copenhagen, as opposed to bike paths), about 72 percent of cyclists feel either very or moderately safe. Only about 2 percent feel "very unsafe" on those lanes (by contrast, nearly half of Copenhagen riders feel slightly, moderately, or very unsafe on streets without bike lanes). These perceptions are consistent with the literature, which has mostly found that on-road marked bike lanes significantly improve safety outcomes. Interestingly, the separated recreational multiuse paths that so many Americans are used to are in fact much more dangerous than on-street

A metro station in Copenhagen with ample parking for bicycles,
a commonplace mode of transportation. (Photo by author)

bicycle lanes because of their unmarked turns, obstacles, confusing mid-block intersections, poor maintenance, and multiplicity of users going at different speeds.[9]

A sign of the more relaxed attitudes of Europeans in general toward bicycle safety is the relatively low use of helmets. According to Colville-Andersen, wherever helmets are promoted, bicycle commuting goes down, because they are essentially a mobile advertisement of the perceived risks of cycling. Not only that, but cycling becomes just a bit more complicated in that something must be put on, taken off, and stored, which goes against "A to Bism." "I have a problem with seeing any city that promotes helmets reaching any respectable level of cycling because you're telling people, 'O my God, it's dangerous,' but statistically it's not. Sweden has had bad experiences from promoting helmets in the late eighties and levels of kids riding bikes have just plummeted after they made it mandatory for kids." To him, helmets are a bit of a red herring when it comes to safety: "A helmet is designed for solo accidents under 20 km [12.5 miles] per hour where you land on the top of your head. They're not even tested for impact on the sides or the back." He goes on to say that almost no cycling federation in Europe promotes them, "because there's no conclusive scientific proof that they help and it scares people off bikes." Ironically, one of the only big-city cycle federations that does is in Copenhagen, and since this policy began, he claims, there has already been a slight decline in ridership. Nonetheless, anecdotally based on my few days of experience in Copenhagen, I would say that helmets are still exceedingly rare there in comparison to highly safety-conscious North America.

No matter how safe, fast, convenient, and inexpensive bike commuting can be made, however, it won't be adopted if it can't at least partially out-compete cars. Beyond the "carrot" of incentivizing bicycle commuting, many European cities and countries have also put into place policy "sticks" designed to discourage driving by increasing its cost and difficulty. Denmark, for instance, imposes a tax of 180 percent on car sales (which is not as bad as it sounds, given the high wages in Denmark), and gas there costs almost ten dollars per gallon. Every year 2 to 3 percent of parking spaces are removed to gradually wean residents from auto-dependency. In addition to being scarce, parking is expensive—around five dollars per hour in the city center. And as the time, and therefore the expense, of parking increases, so too does the rate of cycling.

The success of cycling in Denmark raises the question of why America, with its massive resources, lags so far behind on something that could be so beneficial to cities. For the United States as a whole, only 0.4 percent commute by bicycle. The highest mode share in the country is found in Portland, Oregon, at 6 percent, still a far cry from Copenhagen's 37 percent. This question of why cycling is not more common is particularly vexing for the American Sun Belt, where biking weather is often ideal for most of the year. Although Copenhagen (which is at the same latitude as Moscow) manages to keep 80 percent of its biking population during its long and difficult winters (even during snow storms, that level drops only to 50 percent, thanks in part to the active plowing of bike lanes), cities like Los Angeles, San Diego, or Phoenix, with their ample sunshine, can barely manage to break a 2 percent bicycle mode share. In other words, Mother Nature has granted these American cities a natural advantage that has not been exploited. But it wasn't always like this. According to Colville-Andersen, after the invention of the bicycle and before the onslaught of the car, it was commonly thought that bicycles would become dominant in Sun Belt cities. In a guest blog for the *Los Angeles Times*, he quotes an 1897 newspaper article: "There is no part of the world where cycling is in greater favor than in Southern California, and nowhere on the American continent are conditions so favorable the year round for wheeling." At the time, he points out, the world's most impressive separated bike path was located not in Europe but between Los Angeles and Pasadena. The Arroyo Seco Cycleway (also known as the Dobbins Veloway) was a wooden, elevated, multilane bike path replete with features like lighting and gazebo turnouts. Ironically, after being abandoned, it became the right-of-way for the Arroyo Seco Freeway, the first in California.[10]

With a much larger land area dominated by rugged hills and forests and a population obsessed with owning country vacation cabins, Denmark's northern neighbor, Sweden, is a more car-oriented country. Although greater Stockholm bucks this trend somewhat with only about one-third of residents commuting by car, its geographically challenged network of streets and highways has historically not been able to handle even this relatively modest amount of traffic. With a street layout dating from the late Middle Ages and a landscape of islands connected by bottleneck-prone bridges, Stockholm was perfect for the era of sea travel but poorly designed for the age of rubber tires. The recent development of far-flung suburbs has only exacerbated this problem, with the result that the city can accommodate only a fraction of car traffic that other similarly sized metropolitan areas can.

Stockholm planners provided a powerful incentive to get the populace out of their cars by developing one of the world's best metro systems, as described in Chapter 5. Today, a staggering 90 percent of rush-hour trips to and from the inner city are made by public transportation (mostly rail). For the larger Stockholm metropolitan area, however, the statistics are not as good: about 46 percent of travel is by car and 27 percent by public transit.[11]

But regardless of how many people are using public transit, car commuters have long been unhappy with traffic congestion or the unpredictability of travel times. According to a survey done several years ago, 40 percent of respondents perceived "big problems" and another 34 percent "certain problems" when asked about traffic congestion. And the annual cost of this congestion was estimated at between $400 million and $1.1 billion.[12]

That's beginning to change, though, thanks to an approach known as congestion charging. Under this approach, drivers in highly congested areas of a city are charged for access during times of peak demand. From the economist's point of view, the purpose is to charge drivers for the marginal cost they exact on society just by being on the road and adding to congestion or pollution. Because these costs are spread across the public at large but benefits of driving accrue privately, people tend to drive too much. If those costs were internalized for individual drivers, people would, on average, drive less. Or, more precisely, those with a very high need to drive would be willing to pay to do so, while those who were more indifferent between modes or destinations would switch.[13]

To date, Stockholm is one of only four major international cities (London, Singapore, and Milan being the others) to attempt a large-scale coordinated congestion pricing scheme for an entire central city area. London was the first large city to do so, although others, such as Oslo, have older toll systems that to a certain extent approximate congestion pricing.[14]

I had the opportunity to talk with Daniel Firth, a transportation planner for the City of Stockholm Traffic Administration; Firth not only worked on implementing and evaluating Stockholm's congestion charge but also managed London's Transport Office while it was implementing theirs. He told me that the charge in Stockholm faced many political hurdles to become a reality. Although it was first implemented by his employer, the City of Stockholm, Sweden's Parliament soon got involved when it determined that the so-called charge was really a tax, since it applied to people from multiple jurisdictions. Under the Swedish Constitution, taxes fall under the control of Parliament, which meant that a parliamentary coalition had to be formed to gain passage.[15]

Despite this political road bump, a pilot program was approved, and upon implementation it became evident that Stockholm had an important natural advantage for this type of scheme. Because of its island geography (the majority of central Stockholm falls on four major islands), there are only eighteen entry points into the central city, making it easy to design a cordon. According to Firth, "This makes operating a system like this very much cheaper because you can cover this zone with a relatively few number of charge points . . . and you can limit this infrastructure to mainly bridges and highways." By comparison, he points out, London has a congestion area of about the same size, but it requires monitoring of between 350 and 400 entrance points, making both the capital costs of implementation and the charges themselves much higher than in Stockholm (while the charge is approximately $12 in London it ranges from about $1.25 to $2.50 in Stockholm). The overall cost for Stockholm's pilot ended up being only about $400 million which, Firth points out, could have been less if it hadn't been a pilot project, but "is a whole lot cheaper than building a new motorway."[16]

Little physical infrastructure went into creating Stockholm's cordon. There were no booths, gates, or physical barriers. Rather, IBM helped the city set up a system of cameras that, with stunning accuracy, was able to digitally photograph license plates of cars entering and leaving the central city. No transaction takes place upon entering or leaving. Rather, the digital photographs pass through a program capable of optical character recognition, and the plate numbers are then cross-referenced against a database of car registrations, allowing bills to be sent to the owners. The charge is in place between 6:30 A.M. and

The Stockholm cordon consists simply of these cameras.
(Photo: Svartpunkt AB/City of Stockholm; used by permission)

6:30 P.M. on weekdays and varies depending on the time of day. The charge applies only to those entering or exiting, so the 250,000 people who live in the zone don't have to pay unless they leave it. Certain types of vehicles are exempt, such as alternative fuel vehicles (although that's being phased out), motorcycles, and cars from foreign countries. The charge is also coordinated with enhanced transportation alternatives, including extra public transit routes and new park-and-ride facilities.

After a seven-month trial in 2006, the tax became official in early 2007. Since then, the program has greatly exceeded expectations. The city set a target of reducing traffic volume into and out of the city center by 10 to 15 percent. In fact, the congestion tax ended up reducing volume by 20 to 25 percent, similar to London's level of success.[17] The results were so immediate that vehicles crossing the cordon dropped by 25 percent the day after it was implemented. On inner radial routes and inner-city main roads the congestion tax resulted in between 30 and 50 percent less delay (that is, the proportion of actual travel time relative to free-flow travel time) due to congestion. And, according to Firth, "more significant is that it's reduced variance between the very worst days and the very best days—it's the unpredictability in journey times that's the real cost of congestion not just the total travel time, because people say 'my journey can take up to this long, so I always have to leave this long even if it doesn't end up taking that long.'" In other words, a reduction in variance between good days and bad days means that commuters know with more certainty how long their trips are likely to take and don't have to add in a buffer.

As for where these displaced commuters are going, data indicate that the slack is mainly being taken up by public transit. Between the metro, buses, and commuter or light rail, daily passenger trips on transit increased by 9 percent between 2005 (the year before the pilot program) and 2008, while population increased only by 5 percent during that time. Despite the increase in journeys, the level of congestion on transit hasn't gotten much worse. Averaged across the whole day, public transit still has about 55 to 60 percent of seats unoccupied, and during peak hours all modes except for the metro have ample unoccupied seats. Even though the metro does have more riders than seats during peak hours, the increases associated with the congestion tax are negligible (I personally experienced several peak-hour rides on the metro, and it was not bad). But this increase in public transit does not explain all of the decrease in car travel across the cordon, which is more than twice as large. The Traffic Administration estimates that between 60 and 70 percent of this decrease is accounted for by a change in destination, cancelling trips altogether, or combining trips. In other words, the demand for transport into the central city is flexible and sensitive to pricing. By increasing price, people are being more efficient in planning where they go for basic services and how they combine tasks to minimize the number of journeys into crowded areas.

In terms of energy and the environment, the congestion tax has had an impact on air quality, reducing particulate concentrations by between 8 and 14 percent in the inner city. As for energy use, combined gasoline and diesel deliveries in Stockholm County stayed about even between 2006 and 2008, even though population increased by almost

4 percent during that time, and carbon dioxide emissions in the inner city were calculated to have dropped by 8 percent between 2006 and 2008.[18]

Public support was not always strong for this plan, which had many detractors at first. Surveys found that only about 35 percent of the population supported the idea in 2005, prior to the trial. During the trial, support rose to about 53 percent, just barely enough to secure support in the 2006 referendum. But by 2007, that number was up to 67 percent. This is probably because it has succeeded in greatly cleaning up traffic at a small cost. A survey found that the typical driver spent only about ten dollars (eighty-three kronor) on cordon crossings in a two-week period—overall a small price to pay for eliminating congestion.

All these positive results make congestion pricing sound like a pretty good idea. Given its use of market mechanisms and avoidance of direct regulation, many planners think that this strategy is ripe for America.[19] So why isn't it being implemented? In fact, there have been some recent attempts to explore this initiative, though most people have probably never heard of them. In 2007, the US Department of Transportation initiated demonstration projects for congestion pricing in five metropolitan areas, under the Urban Partnerships Congestion Initiative. With $1 billion in funding, pilot projects were initially selected for San Francisco, Seattle, Miami–Fort Lauderdale, Minneapolis, and New York. In addition to congestion pricing, these projects include a wide range of measures designed to fight congestion, from variably priced parking to telecommuting incentives. None of the current congestion-pricing schemes come anywhere close to the scale of Stockholm's or London's, with their whole-city cordons; rather, they focus on relieving congestion in individual arteries.

Among these projects are a twenty-one-mile managed lane on I-95 between Miami and Fort Lauderdale. Project planners aim to use variable demand-based pricing, adjustable up to once every three minutes, to maintain free-flow conditions; revenues will be used to subsidize a bus rapid-transit system. It is envisioned that this route will serve as the starting point for a much larger network of managed lanes throughout the congested region. Minneapolis has a plan to introduce "priced dynamic shoulder lanes" (PDSLs) along fifteen miles of I-35 running through the city, with prices also set variably to ensure the free flow of travel and free access for high-occupancy vehicles. Revenues will be used to provide fare discounts for buses using these lanes. This system will use high-tech instrumentation for dynamic lane assignment, including LED arrows and in-pavement markings that will direct motorists to the appropriate part of the highway, as well as a dynamic messaging feedback system that informs travelers about lane availability, rates, and speeds, among other things. Seattle has proposed demand-based tolls on one of its main freeways (SR-520), accessing downtown. Revenues will fund the cost of replacing the increasingly decrepit bridge where SR-520 crosses Lake Washington. All these projects would collect charges through electronic transponder systems, eliminating the need for vehicles to stop.[20]

The most notable thing about the Urban Partnerships program, however, is the city that is absent. New York was one of the five original participants, but it was withdrawn in 2008. Few places in North America have a bigger congestion problem than Manhattan, with its dense grid of streets and innumerable bottlenecks. But few places also have such natural advantages for a road-pricing scheme. Like Stockholm, Manhattan is surrounded by water and accessed by only a limited number of bridges and tunnels, making development of a tight cordon highly feasible and cost-effective. But despite the best efforts of a large coalition, including Mayor Michael Bloomberg, the effort failed.

Details of the plan were first unveiled on Earth Day (April 22) 2007. It was massive and sweeping in its scope—on the same scale as the plan for London. Prices would have been considerable: $8 to enter Manhattan south of 86th St. and $4 for trips inside the zone. Fees were to go toward improvements in mass transit. Had it been approved, the federal government had also agreed to pitch in an addition $350 million in grants, and the city would have become eligible for nearly half a billion dollars annually in additional federal-transit improvement funds. However, the plan stirred up a hornet's nest of opposition, right from the start. Residents of the city's outer boroughs, a large number of whom commute into Manhattan daily, worried that they would bear a disproportionate amount of the charges. People also feared that parking problems would overrun neighborhoods near transit hubs. Although the mayor, the governor, the city council, the Republican-led state senate, a specially appointed state commission, and even the Bush Administration were all in favor of this proposal (the normally unanimous council was split thirty votes to twenty on this), the stumbling block came in the state assembly, where it was never brought to a vote owing to a supposed lack of supporters, effectively dooming it as of April 2008. Mayor Bloomberg's apoplexy was scarcely contained. In a statement that wouldn't have been out of place during the subway debates of a century prior, he said: "It takes true leadership and courage to embrace new concepts and ideas and to be willing to try something. Unfortunately, both are lacking in the Assembly today. If that wasn't shameful enough, it takes a special type of cowardice for elected officials to refuse to stand up and vote their conscience."[21] Bloomberg vows to continue to fight for congestion pricing, but, just as it was with the subway over a century ago, it is unclear when the politics of Albany will allow that to happen.

Times may finally be changing in the city that made freeways famous. Traffic has been bad in Los Angeles since I was in diapers. Complaining about it has been a fine art for just as long. But recently I've noticed a change. Traffic problems are no longer just annoying, but literally crippling. Life in this mega-region has become circumscribed as traffic confines people to increasingly smaller territories. Residents now define their geographic space in terms of freeways that they won't go past, and as traffic continues to worsen, those boundaries shrink.

The severity of the problem seems to be finally shifting deeply held attitudes about the irreplaceability of the automobile to life in Southern California. Though I have yet to see a decent survey on attitudes toward cars and transit in Los Angeles, changes are at least anecdotally evident in the opinion pages of the press. Take, for instance, the Angeleno Joel Epstein, who wrote for the Huffington Post that clogged freeways "have become a powerful octopus slowly tightening its unforgiving grip around the heart of this city" and that "mass transit . . . has to be expanded if we ever want to leave the house after breakfast and get home from work before the kids have logged off Facebook and put themselves to bed." And public comments in response to many traffic-related blogs or news stories—while hardly a scientific sample— are revealing of the vehemence of many people's attitudes. In response to a 2010 *Los Angeles Times* article indicating that Los Angeles ranks worst among surveyed American cities in terms of "commuter pain," "Emon" writes, "Thank you to the 'visionary' Los Angeles civic leaders throughout the mid to late 20th Century for dismantling Los Angeles' superior public transit system and irreparably scarring the city with freeways that now resemble parking lots. You've helped make this the true (3rd) world-class city it is today." And "TM" writes: "Public transportation here sucks, yeah, thanks a lot to the shortsighted politicians who dismantled the system many decades ago. May they rot in Hell."[22] Another indicator in this change in attitude comes from Beverly Hills, which once firmly opposed running a subway through its borders and now is a strong advocate.

A far more important indicator of the sea change in attitudes, though, was the passage of Measure R in 2008. Approved by 68 percent of voters (it required two-thirds to pass), this ballot measure originally proposed by the Los Angeles County Metro Transit Authority (MTA) allocates roughly $40 billion for road and transit projects over the course of thirty years, funded through a half-cent increase in the sales tax. Forty percent of that amount is earmarked for transit-related projects, including large subway and light-rail expansions. And although initial plans had the large subway extensions completed in the frustratingly distant 2030s, that time frame may be shifted forward dramatically if Mayor Antonio Villaraigosa's proposed "30/10 Plan" is accepted by Congress (which seems likely now, given the strong support from the White House and key congressional leaders). The plan proposes to leverage long-term revenues from Measure R's half-cent sales tax as collateral for a federal loan. Doing this would allow twelve core mass-transit projects in Measure R to be built in ten years rather than thirty. Under the accelerated plan, some of the most ambitious subway line extensions could be completed by 2017, as opposed to 2036. This would not only result in more immediate realization of benefits but would also bring down project costs by between 15 and 30 percent due to the currently lower cost of construction, potentially allowing more to be built. And there's good reason why Angelenos would want to accelerate the realization of those benefits. According to the MTA, construction of those twelve projects would reduce annual particulate emissions by half a million pounds, gasoline consumption by 10.3 million barrels and automobile miles by 208 million.[23] But even more important, moving nebulous long-term benefits into the more immediate future could provide a model for other cities as to how to make costly transit investment far more popular with the public.

The proposed subway and rail expansions would significantly scale up the current transit system. As discussed in Chapter 5, Los Angeles started work on the seed of the Metro Rail network in the late eighties. The resulting system is believed by many to be woefully inadequate, primarily because it's absent from some of the densest and most economically important parts of the region, which dramatically limits its usefulness. The proposal currently under consideration aims to send new lines into many of these areas. This includes an extension of the Purple Line, to run from downtown, under Wilshire Boulevard, through Beverly Hills, Century City, and all the way out to Westwood and UCLA, as well as the Exposition Light Rail line, which will run from downtown through Culver City to Santa Monica. It's a bold plan with some significant risks. But if successful, it could be a game changer for transportation and land use in Los Angeles.

For an insider's perspective on this, I spoke to Zev Yaroslavsky, the Los Angeles county supervisor who has represented nearly two million people on the west side of the county since 1994 and who supports the current plans for expansion of transit. Yaroslavsky's views on encouraging transit use are very similar to Colville-Andersen's about bicycling: "Our public transportation strategy should be to offer people an alternative to being struck in traffic. If we can reduce the amount of time that it takes a commuter to get from point A to point B—people are not stupid—they're going to vote their interests with their feet and they'll take public transportation. If on the other hand we build a public transit system that doesn't respond to the needs of the commuting public and doesn't quantitatively change their commute, then they have no reason to get out of their cars." Yaroslavsky believes in the convenience of the system enough to be a user of it. Several times a week he takes a combination of rapid bus and subway from his Fairfax neighborhood to his office in downtown, with a commuting time that is typically competitive with and sometimes better than driving.[24]

Experience has shown that when a new transit line is added, many new individuals are able to make a choice like his. As he told me, "We estimated when it opened five years ago that 20 percent of the people riding the Orange Line [bus way] were brand new users of the public transportation system—they are people who got out of their cars." And with each additional expansion, the impact is magnified. "The whole is bigger than the sum of its parts. When you add another line to a sector of the county that has previously not been part of the regional transportation network you get an exponential increase in ridership."

Yaroslavsky believes that eventually this type of investment in transit, in concert with other factors like rising energy prices, could fundamentally transform location decisions and the built environment of Los Angeles. "People don't want to spend the kind of money they're spending on gasoline. They don't want to spend the kind of time they have to spend to get to and from work. So the region that invented the word 'sprawl,' and 'suburban,' and 'exurban' I think is seeing a real looking-inward to see how it can do urban infill. There's a growing demand for residential living in the urban core so that people don't have to shuttle long distances. I think that transportation can facilitate that but what's driving it more than transportation is economics." One place where this type of infill is already happening is downtown Los Angeles, which also happens to be the hub of almost all of the existing rail-transit lines. "Tens of thousands of people have moved into downtown, hundreds of buildings have been built, both modern residential buildings and adaptive reuse of old buildings along the river. It's been a response to the demand of people who want to live close to work, or close to the theatre, or in an urban core." Although there are not a lot of families with children living there, recent investments in transit, other infrastructure, and cultural facilities—like the Staples Center, Walt Disney Concert Hall, and LA Live—have turned a declining core that used to empty at night into a vibrant hub of activity with a steadily increasingly population. Residents are being drawn there from less central locations because they "want to be able to walk to the restaurant, the theatre, the museum, to buy goods and services." But Yaroslavsky also believes they are being drawn there by "public transportation that gives them access to the rest of the region."

Los Angeles' massive plan to ramp up transit is significant for a few reasons. First, if successful, it will show that it's never too late to make a paradigm shift in a city's transportation infrastructure. In fact, many of the most stereotypically car-dependent cities have recently embarked on their own rail-transit experiments, like Dallas' DART and Houston's METRORail. These are small (METRORail currently has only 7.5 track miles, DART has over 40), but without the smaller initial investments, it's impossible to leverage the big long-term projects. Second, Measure R shows that large transit investments can happen when least expected. Just as everyone in Los Angeles assumed transit was dead after the last street cars shut down in 1963, it was again assumed that the era of large transit expansion was dead after the first wave of subway and light-rail construction came to a close in the late nineties. In fact, in 1998 Los Angeles County voters approved a ballot measure that banned the use of the MTA's dedicated county sales-tax revenues for the tunneling of new subways (the bill was actually sponsored by Zev Yaroslavsky, who has stated subsequently that it was motivated not by an inherent opposition to subways but by a preexisting federal ban on tunneling across the county due to methane concerns and by his belief that, in that environment, sales-tax revenue should go into other worthy transit projects that don't involve new tunnels). Even in the months just before Measure R was proposed, few in politics or the media believed that large transit expansions were remotely likely. But the 68 percent affirmative vote on Measure R showed that seemingly dead ideas can rise from the ashes very quickly as attitudes change. As the transit historian Robert P. Sechler wrote, "If . . . transit planning in Los Angeles tells us anything, it is that there is nothing new under the sun, and today's dead idea is tomorrow's bright new one."[25]

Back in Copenhagen, my meeting with Mikael Colville-Andersen has come to an end. We finish our lattes and head to our respective bicycles. As we bid each other goodbye, I begin a half-day odyssey that will end at my hotel in Stockholm. Through it all I will never set foot in a car. I start with a pleasurable return trip on Copenhagen's stunning bicycle lanes. With a little more geographical knowledge on my side, I'm back at the hotel in no time. I quickly return the bike, check out, and walk about one thousand feet to the nearby Dybbølsbro Metro station, where I wait about thirty seconds before catching an uncongested inbound train. I do a quick transfer at Nørreport to the airport-bound train (which, incidentally, continues on to Malmö, Sweden). A few minutes later the train stops at the airport, where I take an escalator to the ticketing floor. After a thirty-minute flight to Stockholm's Arlanda Airport that barely gives me time to crack a book, I stop by an airport kiosk and purchase a pass for the entire Stockholm public transit system plus a ticket for the high-speed Arlanda Express airport train. In twenty minutes I'm at the T-Centralen station right in the middle of Stockholm, and after a quick transfer to the subway I arrive at the Odenplan Metro station, where a pleasant five-minute walk takes me to my hotel. In the world of "A to Bism," this is as good as it gets. And not only that, the combined cost of all my public transit tickets and passes—enough to give me free access to all transit in two of the world's most expensive cities for about six days—was considerably less than a roundtrip taxi ride between Los Angeles International Airport and downtown Los Angeles.

Of course, all this comes at a cost to society: high taxes, high expenses for drivers, and extensive regulation. To many Americans this is a deal-killer. But before writing off this kind of paradigm shift in transportation, skeptics might want to take a closer look at a place like Denmark. Despite an income tax as high as 63 percent, many large bureaucracies, and significant limitations on automobile use, multiple global surveys have found it to be the "happiest" country on earth. And not only that, but in 2009 it was ranked as the fifth most economically competitive.[26] Now that's hygge.

Biofuels

TODAY, RENEWABLE SOURCES of energy account for a relatively small percentage of all energy consumed in the United States. As of 2010, about 8 percent of all energy consumed and about 13 percent of all electricity generated came from renewables. Currently the two biggest sources of renewable energy are hydroelectric (a resource with little potential for future growth because almost all the good sites are already being used; hence it is not discussed in these interludes) and biofuels and biomass.[1] There are many good reasons why we don't have more sources of renewable energy to choose from right now. Although renewables are more environmentally friendly than other energy sources, they are also far more diffuse in energy content and difficult to harness. Each alternative comes with limitations that compromise their ability to be adopted on a large scale.

Biofuels and biomass (wood waste, wood pellets, etc.) together accounted for about 4 percent of all energy consumed in the United States as of 2008. Biofuels in particular are among the most frequently touted renewable alternatives, because, as a refinable liquid, they can be directly substituted for oil. They're also popular because the corn from which they're commonly made can be grown in midwestern states with lots of votes in Congress. Biofuels include gasoline substitutes like ethanol, which can be produced relatively easily from edible crops (corn ethanol), or with considerable difficulty from more abundant nonfood crops, like switchgrass (cellulosic ethanol). But any in-depth analysis of ethanol reveals that it is essentially worthless in combating oil scarcity. Corn ethanol is constrained by its low energy content and bottom-of-the-barrel energy return on investment (EROI), which under some conditions is less than 1:1 (in which case it

207

requires more energy to make than it produces). This is complicated somewhat by the fact that the EROI of corn is variable depending on where it is grown. As one moves away from the center of the Corn Belt in the United States, EROI drops significantly. EROI for corn ethanol has been estimated to range from a maximum of 1.11:1 in Minnesota to as low as 0.97 (that is, more energy goes in than comes out) in Texas.[2]

Why is EROI generally so low for ethanol? Think of all the energy that has to go into growing corn, from fossil-fuel-based fertilizers, to irrigation, to transportation of pesticides, not to mention that every acre of corn dedicated to energy displaces acreage for growing food and raises its price. This tradeoff became only too evident during the 2008 oil price spike, when ethanol production went through the roof (largely as a result of subsidies), with the corresponding result that the price of a loaf of bread followed suit. And although renewable corn might seem to be more environmentally friendly than fossil fuels, recent research has found this to be far from the truth. Mass cultivation of corn for biofuels has been found to increase water pollution significantly, and its greenhouse gas footprint has been found to be worse than that of gasoline when agricultural land-use conversions are taken into account.

Cellulosic ethanol has many advantages over corn ethanol, in particular because it is made from nonedible plant materials, including plant wastes and fast-growing biomass crops, like switchgrass. This allows it to be grown on more marginal land that might otherwise not support food production. Because its cultivation is less intensive, it's been found to have a much better energy return on investment of 5:1. But there are good reasons why it's not being used at all in commercial fuels. First, there are technical barriers that limit its adoptability. Cellulose is very tough to break down and turn into a fuel, requiring the use of complex enzymes. Small amounts of enzymes can be manufactured on an experimental basis, but no one has yet figured out how to produce them in industrial quantities. But even if this technical barrier is overcome—and it probably will be eventually—the diffuse nature of this energy source means that a vast landscape transformation would have to occur; one hundred million acres of cropland and pasture would need to be devoted to cellulosic ethanol crops to offset just 25 percent of current petroleum use—as of now only about eighty million acres of US farmland is in corn, and only about 20 percent of that is for ethanol production. And depending on what land use that cropland is transformed from (for instance, forest), it could result in a worse greenhouse gas footprint than oil. Nonetheless, cellulosic ethanol is one of the most promising renewable alternatives on the horizon.[3]

CHAPTER 8

Reinventing Neighborhoods

I t's a sweltering day as I drive through Sandtown-Winchester, one of several gritty Baltimore neighborhoods portrayed in *The Wire*, the hit TV series about urban decay. It's an area I've been to before, but the landscape that confronts me is just as sobering as the first time I saw it: abandoned, boarded-up row houses are seemingly everywhere; vacant buildings, their window frames covered in plywood, outnumber occupied ones on most blocks; empty lots sit overgrown with weeds and the highly invasive, ironically named "tree of heaven"; retail is practically absent except for a few corner liquor stores whose windows generally have enough protective bars to look like army outposts in Afghanistan; garbage sits in piles on nearly every sidewalk, thanks to an ongoing sanitation workers' strike; and the population is just a fraction of what it was in this neighborhood's heyday.

As we turn a corner where some kids are playing in the spray of a fire hydrant, the high-rises of downtown Baltimore come clearly into view; astonishingly, we're less than two miles from Baltimore's thriving commercial center, where more than 110,000 people work every day.[1] Yet hardly anyone who works in these gleaming office towers lives in Sandtown or dozens of other similarly run-down Baltimore neighborhoods in its vicinity. Why is it that thousands of commuters are willing to endure heavy traffic and long distances while the neighborhoods they pass daily remain underpopulated?

Abandoned row houses in west Baltimore. (Photo by author)

Like so many other cities in the American Rust Belt, Baltimore has seen its share of urban decay. Its population has been in constant decline since its peak in 1950, when nearly a million people lived there. Blue-collar African-American neighborhoods like Sandtown were thriving and bustling with activity. Older Sandtown residents recall a neighborhood in which African-American lawyers' and doctors' offices could be found alongside specialized retail such as pet stores, and where music legends like Cab Calloway and Billie Holiday could often be found playing in local clubs. But today the population of Baltimore is down to around 650,000. As those who could afford to move to the suburbs did so, spurred on by the construction of new highways and the decentralization of employers, a downward spiral ensued: a lower tax base meant declining city services, which drove even more people away, leaving only a few remnant middle-class communities among an increasingly low-income population. Neighborhoods gradually decayed and became blighted. Beautiful turn-of-the-century row houses were abandoned by the thousands. Retail vanished. Weeds flourished where once there were well-maintained yards and gardens. The result is that today there are 42,000 vacant housing units in Baltimore, of which approximately 15,000 are so dilapidated that they are uninhabitable. Sandtown was hit by this process about as badly as any neighborhood in Baltimore.[2]

When it comes to finding sources of negawatts, there are few better proven reserves out there than redeveloping and revitalizing underutilized inner-city neighborhoods like Sandtown, which are close to employment centers, near transit, serviced by existing infrastructure, and dominated by energy-sparing row house architecture. A recent report from the EPA found that infill developments significantly outperform suburban or "edge" developments in terms of transportation energy (average trip distance, vehicle miles traveled and travel time), greenhouse gas emissions, and the costs and efficiency of infrastructure. These benefits are not just limited to residences. Another report found that industrial-commercial uses can attain up to 30 percent reductions in their greenhouse gas emissions (which are directly correlated with energy use) by choosing infill over Greenfield sites, thanks to efficiencies in supply chains and transportation. And not only that, but industrial infill real estate markets have outperformed their suburban counterparts for the previous ten years.[3]

The opportunities for development of underutilized infill land are vast given how much of it there is. A study in 2000 found that the amount of vacant land in 83 cities averaged 15 percent, translating into an average of more than 12,000 acres of usable vacant land per city. They also found an average of 2.6 abandoned structures per 1,000 inhabitants (Baltimore was up at 22).[4]

In the latter half of the twentieth century almost all American central cities experienced consistent declines in population and average incomes relative to their surrounding suburbs. Today the average incomes for central city residents are only 40 percent of those for suburban residents. Between 1950 and 1990, the percentage of Americans living in large (greater than 500,000 people) cities shrunk from 17.5 percent to 12 percent. But with only a few exceptions (Buffalo, New York, for one), the city's loss was the suburbs' gain. For instance, Cleveland and Detroit both lost almost half their population between 1950 and 2000. But in that time, the populations of their greater metropolitan regions grew by 22 and 39 percent, respectively. The toll that such demographic reshifting takes on cities is severe; between 1930 and 1980 the value of property in downtown Cleveland fell from $600 million to $45 million (both in 1980 dollars); in Detroit today nearly one-third of all residential lots are vacant. Some Rust Belt cities have experienced so much abandonment that a movement has sprung up to return hard-hit neighborhoods to nature.[5]

But there are signs that in recent years things have slowly started changing for the better in Baltimore. Population decline over the decade from 2000 to 2009 was down to 2.1 percent, the lowest rate of loss since the decline began sixty years ago. While this shift may not sound like a reason to throw a parade, it's good news in relative terms after years of hemorrhaging people, and it represents some real results of decades of concerted effort to rebuild at least a few of Baltimore's core urban neighborhoods.

We see increasing signs of investment and revitalization as we drive toward the waterfront. A few minutes past Sandtown, and just about three blocks from the edge of downtown, we pass by the new 338-unit Albemarle Square redevelopment project, partially funded with federal Hope VI housing dollars, with a mix of affordable and market-rate townhome units. The new units are a breath of fresh air relative to the Stalinist-looking Flag House Courts high-rise housing projects that it replaced. Thanks in part to active citizen participation, its 15-block area sports a wide variety of townhome designs, tastefully done in Baltimore's historic architectural vernacular, with a strong pedestrian orientation and a mix of uses that includes needed retail space, all of which helped it win awards from the Congress for the New Urbanism and the American Institute for Architects. Just a few blocks farther we pass another federally funded townhome redevelopment called Lexington Terrace. Replacing another battered high-rise public housing project, this project has 303 row houses in the traditional Baltimore style and contains nearly 700 housing units, two-thirds of which are rented at subsidized rates. Neither neighborhood looks anything like a public housing project.

Driving farther toward downtown, we see what made this and other similar redevelopment projects possible. Baltimore's formerly crumbling downtown and adjacent Inner Harbor are now among the most appealing central-city districts on the East Coast thanks to billions of dollars in public and private investment over the past forty years. In the 1960s, these areas were on the verge of abandonment; today they sport a stunning new National Aquarium, the massive and trendy Harborplace Mall, dozens of upscale restaurants and hotels, tall ships, museums, and historic districts with restored brick buildings and quaint cobblestone streets, all of which have helped attract businesses, tourists, and eventually residents. In the wake of the successful commercial reinvention of central Baltimore, a wave of dense high-end residential development spread outward from the most desirable waterfront locations into neighboring areas. Thanks to this type of redevelopment, the population of downtown and the half-mile buffer around it increased 78.5 percent between 1980 and 1999.

But growth hasn't gone much beyond that area. Expand the radius to 1.5 miles from downtown and population change drops to -8 percent. In other words, the scale of the problem is far bigger than the scale of investment. Consequently, despite valiant financial efforts, the overall balance between central city and suburban population changed little during this period of urban renewal. People are still leaving the city for the suburbs or elsewhere faster than they are returning to it.[6]

The lesson is that decentralization is not going to be effectively reversed until the scale of central-city redevelopment is ramped up significantly. And although poverty, crime, failing schools, and fiscal mismanagement certainly limit demand for housing in the urban core, there are increasing indications of a significant unmet demand for

High-end waterfront development along Baltimore's
Inner Harbor. (Photo by author)

high-quality urban housing in the United States. The problem in many cities is that not nearly enough of such housing is being built.

One of the largest barriers to ramping up the scale of urban redevelopment is the terrible impression left by decades of failed public housing megaprojects. Because of these ugly and ineffective behemoths that became the norm throughout the sixties and seventies, "large" has become synonymous with "unlivable" when it comes to residential redevelopment.

I myself believed this too until I took a trip to Scandinavia and experienced firsthand how scale need not be mutually exclusive with design, efficiency, and livability.

It's a stunningly beautiful day in the master-planned neighborhood of Hammarby Sjöstad (if you're not Scandinavian, don't even try pronouncing it; I spent about ten minutes being coached by a Swede and then gave up). As I descend from the light-rail car at the Sikla Kaj station, situated in the middle of a street populated with far more pedestrians and cyclists than cars, I look up to see rows of diverse-looking modernist buildings of six and seven stories, amply fenestrated and adorned with sleek metal balconies. Along the ground floor of each building is a wide array of retail, from markets, to toy stores, to restaurants. My hunch that there are no vacancies is confirmed when I look in the window of a real estate office and see almost every listing marked as "Såld." As I walk into a side street, the buildings open up into stunningly landscaped courtyards with beautiful water features, including large fountain arrays, constructed wetlands, and networks of small decorative storm-water canals. Many of the housing units have patios or porches built out into the courtyards, making the public and private spaces merge seamlessly. As I keep walking, I pass through a number of different sections of the project, each designed by a different developer and each with a totally distinct and very Scandinavian architectural style. The result of this visual diversity is that what I'm looking at appears organic—not master-planned. The inviting nature of the building mix and landscaping is validated by the large numbers of residents—mostly parents with kids—strolling about, chatting, and playing, even though it's a Tuesday afternoon. Eventually I hit the waterfront, where a beautiful boardwalk and marina sit across the narrow Sickla Channel from the historic buildings of Södermalm Island.

Hammarby Sjöstad, first dreamed up in 1990 and occupied starting in 2000, is no ordinary urban redevelopment project. If it were, it wouldn't be drawing the nearly thirteen thousand visitors a year who come to learn from its innovations, including the vice president of China, the governor of Maryland, and myriad cabinet ministers, mayors, and business leaders from around the world. It's widely seen as Sweden's flagship example of sustainable urban infill development. And with Sweden's incredible record in this area, that's saying a lot.

For an urban redevelopment project, the scale is huge, comprising six hundred acres of former industrial land. When the last blocks are

Ample balconies at a housing block of Hammarby
Sjöstad, which maximize views. (Photo by author)

completed in 2017, there will be eleven thousand housing units (almost
eight thousand units have been completed) and enough commercial
space for roughly ten thousand workers. It took thirty developers,
an equal number of architects, twenty-five construction companies,
and strong public-private partnerships, all coordinated by the City of
Stockholm, to make this vision into a reality.

Its scale has paid big dividends not only in housing many people
but also in the efficiency of its infrastructure. SymbioCity is a trade-
mark for environmentally synergistic urban development, established
in 2008 by the Swedish Trade Council, supported by a network of
Swedish building and supply professionals, and based on the concept
that one infrastructure system's trash is another's treasure. Hammarby
follows the SymbioCity model by creating synergies among all elements of its infrastructure. As Stellan Fryxell of Tengbon Architects,
one of the designers on the project, told me: "It's about coordinated
infrastructure and master planning. It takes more than a group of
green buildings to make a green area."[7] Hammarby Sjöstad achieves
these synergies through what its developers refer to as an "ecocycle."
Crucial to this concept is the repurposing of waste to serve other

infrastructural needs. As Erik Freudenthal, Hammarby's information officer, said, "In Sweden we don't look at garbage as garbage but as a resource." Each building has an array of pneumatic tubes that suck away different types of waste for different purposes through an underground network of tubes. One tube takes combustible waste to a combined heat and power plant that in turn feeds a district heating system for the development. This fuel provides most of its heat requirement. Another takes food and organic waste to a compost facility that makes fertilizer. And a third takes recyclables to a sorting facility. For big and bulky waste, there are centralized collection points at each apartment block. As a result of the efficiency attained, Hammarby residents get a 50 percent discount on their waste-collection bills. Wastewater is transported to a nearby treatment plant (that provides service for almost a million people), which in turn uses a methane digester to create energy-rich "biogas," most of which goes to power Stockholm's bus fleet, but some of which is returned to Hammarby as cooking gas. The remaining sludge from the process is used to create nutrient-rich soil. The heat in the wastewater is also extracted by heat pumps in a separate plant to further add to the district heating network and to heat tap water. After the heat extraction, the resulting wastewater is cold and so is used to feed a district cooling network that serves offices and retail (including grocery refrigeration) in the development. Solar hot-water panels are found on most roofs and satisfy nearly half the development's demands.[8]

Although most of the energy savings for this development comes from the centralization and coordination of infrastructure, the design of the individual housing units adds to the savings through features like triple-glazed windows, heavy-duty insulation, low-flush toilets, and low-energy lighting fixtures. Some individual housing units also have their own on-demand ventilation and heat-exchange systems that cut down on energy needs even further.

Reputedly, these higher-efficiency building materials and components don't add much to the cost of construction. A case study of a block at Hammarby found that the added costs of "environmentally

Pneumatic tubes used for garbage, compost, and
recycling at Hammarby Sjöstad. (Photo by author)

friendly" improvements were only 5 percent over baseline construction costs. Lars Gärde of ByggVesta, one of the block developers, was
even more optimistic: "As a private developer I would say that it doesn't
add a krona [Swedish currency] extra to build a building that consumes 50 percent less than the official norm [in Sweden]. When we
constructed the low energy buildings, we would say that the money
that we save from an investment point of view when we take out the ra-
diators from the apartments exactly corresponds to the extra amount
we paid for the heat exchanger on the roof, the better insulated walls
and the low emission windows, more or less. But many developers say
it should cost extra. Look at the price of low energy windows. It cost
the same to get U values [lower U values are higher efficiency] of 1.2 or
1.3 two or three years ago as it does now to get windows at 0.9 because
the industry is focused today just on low energy. One of the important
factors from the city was increased requirements. Because as soon as
they do that, the industry starts to change. They develop new products
and you get the price going down on the new low energy produce."[9]

The developers' goal was initially for each housing unit to have half
the environmental impact of standard Swedish housing of the 1990s
era. Although a recent audit found that the development has not yet
met this ambitious goal, it's generally close, with water-consumption

rates ranging between 55 and 60 percent of the baseline, and nonre-newable energy consumption ranging between 53 and 70 percent of the baseline, depending on apartment block. The key to Hammarby's success, though, is that by putting the infrastructure in the background, residents can dramatically cut their environmental footprint without even knowing they're doing it. Says Freudenthal, "Remember this is not an eco-village in the sense that you have to sign a contract, that you have to behave in certain ways. The more we can put it in the buildings and infrastructure, the better it is, because then people don't need to change their behaviors—it takes a long time to change behaviors."

Despite all the fancy infrastructure and green credentials, how-ever, what really draws residents—even though there are almost no vacancies currently—are more practical attributes: aesthetics, design, location. While walking through a courtyard garden, I spoke to a web programmer named Sebastian, who was out playing with his four-year-old son. Sebastian, who has lived in Hammarby for five years, used to live in a suburb twelve miles outside of Stockholm. When I asked him if the environmental attributes of the development were one of the things that attracted him, his answer was "not at all." Rather, what drew him and his family was the availability of nicely built, well-located rental apartments in the otherwise tight Stockholm housing market: "There's an apartment shortage in Stockholm, so when they build a lot of apartments at the same time [as in Hammarby], you can actually get an apartment quite easily. So that's why we moved here, we couldn't move anywhere else if we didn't buy—we have a rental apartment here." What he likes most about the development is that he can get to his work or other activities in the central city easily by train, bicycle, or bus. It's also a great place for kids, with minimal car traffic and ample open space.

The design attributes that make it appealing to families are evident the moment you set foot in Hammarby. Courtyards, patios, and bal-conies are constructed to maximize social interaction and a sense of common ownership. Because each courtyard is distinct in its design, they don't look or feel master-planned or antiseptic but, rather, seem

A highly landscaped courtyard of a housing block
at Hammarby Sjöstad. (Photo by author)

to belong to surrounding housing units. According to Stellan Fryxell, "There's a sort of hierarchy with the private apartment, the part-
private balconies, the part-public courtyards and the public parks. So
the courtyard is a shared space for 150 or 170 apartments. The bigger
children can move around easily and see friends in the neighboring
block. There's a scale factor in the green space. If you take a particular
block, people living in this block . . . know the other families more or
less so they feel secure. So this is very much about making a dense area
family friendly. And it works. We have double the number of children
in this area of other areas." Furthermore, the retail areas, located on
the main street, add to the sense of neighborhood vitality by providing
additional nearby destinations and opportunities for walking—unlike
some residential developments that become ghost towns during the
workday.

An additional attraction is the ample opportunity for recreation.
There are more than a hundred mooring spots for boats on the Sickla
Kaj channel, a large landscaped park in the middle of the development,

Abundant restaurants and cafés provide a venue for neighbors
to socialize in Hammarby Sjöstad, particularly in the
warm summer months. (Photo by author)

extensive jogging trails, a nearby forested nature reserve, access to a
nearby swimming lake, a constructed ski slope just on the edge of the
development, and a number of theaters and libraries.

But even with all this high design and technology, the single most
important asset that this development has in its favor—both in terms
of environmental and real estate value—is its location: it is less than
two miles as the crow flies from downtown Stockholm, just across a
narrow channel from the densely populated Södermalm Island, and a
little more than one mile from a major metro station. Commuters can
be in downtown Stockholm in under twenty minutes through a variety
of modes: a free ferry that runs every fifteen minutes, bicycling using
Stockholm's excellent system of dedicated lanes, buses, or the Tvärbanan light-rail line that runs right through the center of the development and offers a quick transfer to the metro at Gullmarsplan station.
More than one-third of Hammarby residents use light rail, and a quarter use the ferry—many with their bicycles. The energy benefits of this

are enormous: it is estimated that Hammarby residents emit less than half the carbon dioxide of other residents of greater Stockholm.[10] As of 2010, only about 21 percent of Hammarby residents used a car for daily commuting, as opposed to about 35 percent for greater Stockholm; cars are instead used for excursions and errands. The number of cars used by Hammarby residents for noncommuting purposes took planners by surprise. They had initially planned on only one parking space per three housing units but eventually had to revise that up to slightly more than two per three units. However, many Hammarby residents get the benefits of a car without owning one: three car-sharing services in Hammarby for nonwork activities serve the community, totaling about 550 members and 35 cars.

Freudenthal attributes the success of Hammarby's implementation to several factors. First was the active cooperation between the private and public sectors: "The key success was because of the integrated planning, or Symbiocity. It's to take both the public and private stakeholders sitting around the same table and saying how can we make this new area as sustainable as possible before the master plan? And what kind of technology and scale are we going to have?" A collaborative spirit alone, however, was not sufficient. The city needed to take a leadership role in setting strict environmental ground rules at the outset, to be followed by everyone: "In the first area they built, they [city government] asked the developers to participate. When they found out that they had this environmental program, they said 'we can't do it.' But the politicians said if you would like to build there you have to follow it. And they complied. And now, to them, it's nothing, because they've done it. It wasn't such a big thing to do this even though they said we can't do it. I think to succeed with this you have to have the political will. And then you need to commit the developer in some way or another."

Finally, perhaps the most important ingredient for success was that the city had owned the land for generations. Having exclusive say in what was to happen with this extraordinarily well-located piece of land gave the city enormous bargaining power. As Lars Gärde told me,

One of two stations for the Tvärbanan light-rail line
in Hammarby Sjöstad. (Photo by author)

"The City of Stockholm owns quite a lot of land in attractive locations, so the city can really influence and set these programs. If you're invited [as a developer], it's for the city to set the standards." In other words, the City of Stockholm today is reaping huge benefits from its decision to buy large amounts of centrally located land in the earlier part of the twentieth century. Not only Hammarby, but other large eco-developments, such as the soon to be constructed Stockholm Royal Seaport, would likely not have been possible without this. Finally, Hammarby succeeded because of a political culture in Sweden that rewards this type of activity. Not only do politicians gain political points from the success of projects like Hammarby and the Stockholm Royal Seaport, but, according to Garde, "they also know that companies that are developing, for instance, new windows and new heat exchangers for these eco-cities will have excellent export opportunities."

But not all the political and economic factors that made Hammarby's success feasible would necessarily be palatable to many outside of

Scandinavia. Vacancies in Hammarby are near zero not only because of its desirability but also because rental housing is in short supply in Stockholm. The real estate sector is highly regulated and there is a nationwide system of rent control that, many economists believe, stifles new construction and keeps supply limited. In fact, there is currently a waiting list for rental housing in most of Sweden. In Stockholm, that wait can average two years, and for some attractive districts it can be more than a decade—a trend that is absent in most other European countries.[11] But not everyone believes that rent control is the culprit for the housing shortage. Stellan Fryxell cites other causes: "I don't think there is a housing shortage because of rent control. The main reason is that it's complicated to construct and to get planning and building permission and the process is quite long. And to be honest, some of the biggest developers in Sweden . . . don't take risks." Beyond keeping vacancies near zero, there are some additional pluses to rent control. In addition to the obvious one of housing equity, rent control also means that there is no need for subsidized "affordable housing units," which commonly complicate the construction of so many new central-city housing developments. Nor is there a need for the large public housing projects that so frequently blighted American cities. Rather, rent control results in new projects naturally having a diverse mix of income groups without any complex social engineering. In other words, rent control appears pretty appealing when you're sitting in an apartment, and pretty bad when you're waiting for one.

Regardless of the reasons for its success, Hammarby Sjöstad's model is already being replicated and improved upon on an even grander scale, just a few miles away at the Stockholm Royal Seaport. Whether it's a model that can successfully escape the confines of Sweden has yet to be seen.

Given tens of thousands of jurisdictions, each writing its own land-use codes, exporting the Hammarby Sjöstad model broadly to the United States would be no easy task. That's why, up until now, most attempts to change development paradigms in the United States have relied on incentives, something that Americans like much better than rules and regulations.

LEED, discussed in Chapter 7, is an incentive system to make buildings green. But although certification grew to be a powerful incentive to builders, many planning experts began to worry that LEED was failing to incentivize development in the right places and perhaps even doing so in the wrong ones. For John Norquist, executive director of the Congress on the New Urbanism (CNU) and former mayor of Milwaukee, a stark illustration of this problem was the "Gold" level accreditation by LEED of the North American headquarters for financial giant HSBC, in suburban Illinois. As he told me, "They had moved their headquarters from right next to a metro suburban transit line where a lot of their employees were able to take the train to a site that was far away from any transit stop. They got the gold award for having some vegetation on the roof, using some recycled materials in the building. But then almost all of their employees were car-dependent after the move was made. So it really wasn't a green project. The net result of the move was negative—it was bad. We found that just awful." Seeing this yawning gap in the LEED system, Norquist contacted the Natural Resources Defense Council's (NRDC) Smart Growth Program, and together they confronted LEED's parent organization, the US Green Building Council (USGBC). According to Norquist, "We said 'what are you doing? You shouldn't be giving a gold award to this project. You need to do something else.' And they said, 'You're right. OK, let's do something about it.'"[12]

From that and subsequent conversations, the LEED-Neighborhood Design (LEED-ND) program was born. LEED-ND is a rating system, like LEED, but it applies to large developments, or whole neighborhoods, rather than just buildings. LEED-ND began as a pilot in 2007, with 240 participating projects. Following feedback from pilot participants, the system was fine-tuned and began officially in April 2009. NRDC and CNU have served as key partners to USGBC in designing this system and its extensive rating criteria.

An affordable Housing LEED-ND project near
downtown Denver. (Photo by author)

LEED-ND certification incorporates not only the composition of a
development and the efficiency of its infrastructure into the rating but
also its location. As its marketing materials state: "The rating system
encourages smart growth and New Urbanist best practices by promoting the location and design of neighborhood-scale developments that
reduce vehicle miles traveled (VMT) and creating developments where
jobs and services are accessible by foot or public transit. It also promotes an array of green building and green infrastructure practices,
particularly more efficient energy and water use."[13] Criteria can be expressed as either credits, which advance a project toward its minimum
point total, or as prerequisites, which stop the show if not met. Of the
LEED-ND prerequisites, a number relate to the natural environment,
such as exclusion from zones sheltering endangered species, important ecological communities, prime agricultural land, wetlands, or
floodplains. Others relate to New Urbanist principles, such as requirements for walkable streets, compact development, and connectivity.
Still others relate to building performance measures similar to LEED's:
the presence of certified green buildings, building energy and water

efficiency, and prevention of pollution associated with construction work. But the most important—and most elusive—of them all is the prerequisite for "smart location."

In theory smart location seems intuitive. In a place like Hammarby or Albemarle Square, you know you're seeing it, but quantifying the experience is challenging. At its most basic, smart location means being near existing development. But what if that existing development is in a distant satellite suburb, or surrounded by nothing but tract homes, or totally car-dependent? As Sophie Lambert, director of the LEED-ND program told me, there wasn't always clear agreement on these location criteria. In response to proposals for LEED-ND projects in less-developed "Greenfield" areas, "there was a tension within the core committee [the body that helped define rating criteria] between the Smart Growth group representatives and the New Urbanists. The New Urbanists felt that Greenfield development if done in a certain way could be appropriate and I think some of the Smart Growth advocates did not want Greenfield development unless there was going to be transit there. So there were definitely a lot of interesting conversations and debates and compromises." As it reads now, the intent of the smart location prerequisite, according to USGBC's literature, is as follows: "To encourage development within and near existing communities and public transit infrastructure. To encourage improvement and redevelopment of existing cities, suburbs, and towns while limiting the expansion of the development footprint in the region to appropriate circumstances. To reduce vehicle trips and vehicle miles traveled (VMT)."[14]

The rules for designating smart location take the form of a complex flowchart populated with if-then options. First, all projects must be either on sites currently served by water and wastewater infrastructure or on sites where publicly owned water and wastewater services are planned. If not, developers are out of luck. Second, projects must be on sites defined as one of the following: "infill," "adjacent sites with connectivity," "transit corridor route with adequate transit service," or "sites with nearby neighborhood assets." Each of these is elusive to define.

For instance, sites can qualify as "infill" by meeting one of four conditions having to do with the site's proximity, adjacency, or connectivity with previously developed land. Because of these multiple options for defining infill, Lambert says, "our definition of infill is probably looser than people realize. There are four different ways that we define infill and because of that there are definitely some situations where a Greenfield project in the outer part of a region could qualify." For instance, the rules would likely not preclude so-called leapfrog development, in which new construction goes into an already built-up satellite area that is isolated from its central city by large swaths of vacant land.[15] In other words, writing a set of rules that can be broadly applied to define a good development location is no easy task.

LEED-ND certification helps developers not only with their marketing but potentially with their permitting. Greenfield development has been popular among developers because it's easier and more predictable than development in established urban areas. According to Kaid Benfield, director of the Natural Resources Defense Council's Smart Growth program, one of the co-originators of the LEED-ND standard, "Smart infill development needs some help. It's harder for the developer to do, it's harder to assemble land, there's more approvals, there's concerned neighbors, there tends to be more regulations in existing populated places, for a lot of reasons they have a bit of a tougher lift than some of the development that's not so well located." One of the big culprits in this respect is outdated municipal planning and zoning codes that, according to Lambert, are "an impediment to infill development in general." Because of this "it's so much easier to buy this huge tract of land, this Greenfield site, because you're not going to have any of those issues." In fact, according to Lambert, LEED-ND projects are illegal in many towns.[16]

In the short term, the planning credibility that comes with LEED-ND designation can in some cases help developers get variances—permission to circumvent zoning rules on a case-by-case basis—for infill development that might otherwise violate outdated codes. In the longer term, as municipal planners observe the positive outcome of

LEED-ND projects, it's hoped that its example will encourage some cities to rethink the way they write planning codes. Says Benfield, "What I hope we'll see is that municipalities, perhaps even federal and state governments, will find a lot to borrow from in our criteria. I think we've basically created a template for evaluating development." For instance, South Grand Rapids, Michigan, used LEED-ND to inform the updating of its zoning ordinance. And municipal governments may be even further incentivized to incorporate principles of LEED-ND into their planning since the Department of Housing and Urban Development (HUD) started using LEED-ND as a criterion for scoring the location efficiency of grant applications to their agency, totaling over $3 billion. As HUD secretary Shaun Donovan stated in announcing this program in mid-2010, "One of the most important ways we can drive funding toward sustainable development and the plans is through our grant competitions. . . . It's time that federal dollars stopped encouraging sprawl and started lowering the barriers to the kind of sustainable development our country needs and our communities want."[17]

Currently in the United States, a large number of barriers make construction of a development like Hammarby very difficult to impossible, from outdated planning regulations, to financing limitations, to infrastructure constraints, to local opposition. LEED-ND doesn't solve all these problems, but it is an important first step along what is probably a long road toward a new paradigm of urban real estate development in America.

On a recent walk through the twenty-three-block Lower Downtown, or "LoDo" neighborhood of Denver, I saw one of America's best examples of central-city redevelopment. Before this visit I had never heard of the place. After walking around for a few hours, I was practically ready to move there. Buildings are elegantly shared between residential and commercial uses, like restaurants, bars, shops, and offices. Inviting streetscapes support bustling crowds of pedestrians, landscaped vegetation, artfully designed lighting, ample outdoor café seating, bike

Restored historic buildings in Denver's Lower Downtown, known as LoDo,
one of the city's most popular neighborhoods. (Photo by author)

lanes, and wide sidewalks. But most notable is its historic architecture
and urban form. With the streetscape and the majority of the building stock dating from the nineteenth century, it quickly becomes
evident just how desirable and livable these traditional city layouts
can be.

New Urbanism is an approach that calls for a return to the traditional way many cities were built before the advent of the automobile.
According to John Norquist, New Urbanism is really just "urbanism"
in its traditional sense; the word "new" was added "to overcome the
negative image that urbanism had back in 1993, when the organization
was formed." This "return to roots" approach viewed historic buildings, traditional street layouts, and orientation toward pedestrians not
as liabilities but as key resources for making urban neighborhoods
more vital, livable, and desirable. Part of this strategy of promoting

desirability and livability was making neighborhoods walkable, just as historic cities are.

Amazingly, LoDo was a wasteland just a few decades ago. Although it was the original core settlement area of Denver, by the mid-twentieth century it was the city's skid row, replete with vandalism, crime, abandonment, and graffiti. By 1987 LoDo reached a vacancy rate of 50 percent, with one-third of buildings under foreclosure. But, miraculously, most of its historic buildings had escaped demolition, in contrast to many of the surrounding historic neighborhoods, which were leveled as part of the "redevelopment" plans of the Denver Urban Renewal Authority. And the preservation of this historical architectural heritage proved to be the key to its resurrection. In 1988, following a contentious and bitter hearing that lasted until after 2 A.M., the city council passed an ordinance designating LoDo as a historic district, over the objections of almost all the property owners. Under the plan, strict design guidelines were set forth on rehabilitation of existing structures and construction of new ones, including a review process for architectural design. Zoning was set to encourage mixed-use development and higher densities while setting a cap on building heights to maintain a human scale. Investments were made by the city in streetscapes and public spaces. A light-rail line was constructed skirting the northern end of the neighborhood (Denver's planned Union Station multimodel transportation hub will be on the edge of this district when completed). And, of perhaps greatest importance, Coors Field, home of the Colorado Rockies, was constructed in 1995 just at the eastern edge of LoDo, making the area a destination for tens of thousands of sports fans on game days.

Something about this combination of regulation, investment, design review, historic preservation, and economic forces worked. Despite the fears of the building owners in 1988 that the proposed plan would handcuff them, LoDo has turned out to be one of the most vibrant, high-value, and sought-after addresses in the city. In fact, so much of LoDo has already been rehabbed that there are hardly any lots left there to redevelop. As a result, high-end redevelopment is spilling over

New mixed-use development adjacent to Lower
Downtown, Denver. (Photo by author)

into neighboring areas, such as the central downtown, Central Platte
Valley, and ballpark districts, all of which has helped to once again
make greater downtown Denver the center of gravity for the city after
years of decentralization. The spatial extent of this redevelopment is so
great that I was able to walk through LoDo and then continue north

Extensive new development to the north of downtown Denver, which was facilitated by the redevelopment of Lower Downtown and the refurbishment of park lands along the South Platte River. (Photo by author)

for another half hour without coming to the end of it. Now thousands of residents who once would have had little choice but to live in the suburbs can walk just a few blocks to work, shopping, and entertainment. And that centralization of people has been key to making Denver's light-rail system feasible, which in turn is helping spur on more centrally located development. In other words, it's a virtuous cycle.

In the process of revitalizing itself, LoDo has spawned a project that has the potential to change how central-city redevelopment occurs. The Living City Block (LCB) program, working in partnership with building owners and business and residential tenants, seeks to transform one city block of LoDo into a replicable model of efficiency in urban resource use. The block chosen is dominated by attractive historical structures containing a range of land uses, including retail, offices, restaurants, and mixed-income housing.

The idea of LCB is to develop a mechanism and framework that will facilitate the coordinated upgrading of contiguous, small-to-medium-sized buildings. Says Llewellyn Wells, founder and president of LCB, "It's starting to become proven in the marketplace that if you retrofit a big building and do it well, you have a really strong return on investment in a reasonable number of years. . . . But we saw that the case for doing smaller buildings was not nearly as strong in the commercial sense. It became clear quickly that when you don't have as much aggregate square footage to work on, the return on your investment is not as strong on energy efficiency and renewable integration retrofit work. So it occurred to us that we needed to examine why that is and what we might be able to do to help change that paradigm." LCB's idea was to choose one well-located city block that was ripe for upgrades and to essentially use it as a laboratory to determine how coordinated, cost-effective energy upgrades could best be made, and then export that model. "We decided that if we found a block or a couple of blocks and worked to bring the building owners together in some sort of consortium model, that they then would have enough square footage available and have some of the advantages that larger building owners have."[18]

To participate, owners commit to foot the bill for the retrofits and upgrades that apply to their building. As of early 2011, 80 percent of property owners, representing 90 percent of the square footage on the block, had committed to be part of the project. The remaining 20 percent were not actively against it but, rather, lacked the resources or were adopting a "wait and see" approach. LCB's role is that of coordinator. They fund work in a variety of areas: analysis to support the design process and monitor and synthesize results; coordination of building owners; facilitation of creative financing; and communication to help spread the model elsewhere.

The project leaders hope that upgrades will result in an energy savings of 50 percent by 2012, net zero energy use by 2014, and more power produced than consumed by 2016. The financial payback period is estimated at five years. Upgrades to buildings on the block in the short term will include efficiency measures such as maximizing insulation, optimizing mechanical systems, and installing high-efficiency lighting fixtures. Longer-term measures will include updated infrastructure such as onsite wastewater treatment, composting, rooftop gardens, solar panels, and ground-source heating and cooling. Many of these resources will be shared among buildings and so will result in scale advantages, as in Hammarby. To Wells, this is crucial. Although an energy savings of 50 percent can be achieved within an individual building, "that other 50 percent—since we're aiming for net zero over time—can only happen through district wide, shared solutions." LCB recently received an award from the US Department of Energy's National Renewable Laboratory that will allow them to analyze the feasibility of different configurations of these shared systems in their particular context.

The upgrades to this block are intended to go beyond just energy efficiency for buildings. LCB also intends to do what it can to promote more sustainable transportation alternatives for the block, which, luckily is well located. But they feel they can go further. According to Wells, "We will be working on the mobility integration issue even still to make a more walkable, bikable community and to address what's missing in the public transport system so that we can have input to change those things." They're also dedicated to using design to enhance the livability and desirability of the block. "It became evident to us quickly that we didn't just need to create energy and resource efficient buildings. We needed to create economically sustainable livable communities."

Once implemented, they hope to use this model to systematically quantify and communicate the many benefits of this style of centrally located, renovation-based development. These include not just building energy savings but also reduced automobile dependency, lower obesity rates as people begin to walk again, and increased social capital. With these data in hand, the LCB team plans to reach out to other neighborhoods in Denver, the United States, and the world. (They already have a "sister city" project in the planning phases in Washington, D.C.) But, perhaps most important, they want to demonstrate that this type of development brings tangible benefits to building owners, whether it's in the form of higher rents, lower vacancies, or lower operating costs. If they can make that case, this model will sell itself without the help of any nonprofit intermediaries. Says Wells, "Hopefully sooner rather than later the commercial market will step in—there will be companies that pop up that will figure out how to make money off this, and that's what takes it to scale."

Meanwhile, back in Sandtown, Gerry's Goods has recently had its grand opening. This café-bakery, which serves gourmet coffee, lattes, and macchiatos, provides a welcome contrast to the typical retail establishment in this neighborhood. Rather than sitting behind an inch of bullet-proof Plexiglas, clerks and baristas can enjoy a pleasant indoor environment where they freely interact with their customers, who in many cases are also their neighbors. Although it's a far cry from the multibillion-dollar LoDo renaissance, a place like Gerry's Goods represents an important symbolic first step for a neighborhood that's gone through many tough times. And there are other promising signs. The local ministry, called "New Song," which spawned Gerry's Goods, has also sponsored the construction of a church, a health center co-op, a transitional housing facility, a community arts program, and a brand-new school in Sandtown. Habitat for Humanity now has a neighborhood chapter that has worked with residents to reclaim dozens of blocks and hundreds of homes, all outside the purview of the public housing system (in fact they received a grant from the Home Depot Foundation to add "green" elements to forty-five homes). A network of beautiful urban gardens is taking shape in the neighborhood. And crime has been reduced by about 15 percent.

But even with all this progress, Sandtown has a monumental uphill battle. Although you can now get a latte there, vacant units still abound, weeds still grow from empty lots, drug gangs and violence still dominate many blocks, and employment is still scarce. The causes of this have deep roots in racism, income inequality, and globalization, but I like to think that the design of neighborhoods can play some small part in turning a downward spiral into an upward cycle. Only further investment and time will tell if that holds true for Sandtown. In the meantime, it will continue to be one of the many blighted neighborhoods that commuters pass by daily without ever stopping.

Nuclear

NUCLEAR POWER HAS BEEN talked about a lot in the political realm as a potential alternative to imported oil. It currently accounts for about 11 percent of electricity produced and about 8 percent of energy consumed in the United States. Countries lacking in fossil fuels, however, are far more dependent on nuclear power. France, for instance, gets 80 percent of its power from that source.

Nuclear power has some big advantages over both renewables and fossil fuels. First, nothing else even remotely compares in terms of energy density. The amount of energy released from just one kilogram of uranium-235 undergoing nuclear fission is equivalent to burning 5.5 million pounds of coal.[1] And because it produces the steam used to drive its turbines through fission and not through burning a carbon-containing fuel, it is essentially free of greenhouse gas.

But the sight of smoldering reactors in places like Chernobyl and Fukushima underscores just how high the risks are. Not only is there a threat of meltdown due to accidents, malfunction, or natural disasters, but thermal nuclear fission produces large amounts of radioactive waste, particularly in the form of spent fuel. This waste must be disposed of at enormous cost, and increasingly this wayward waste is having a hard time finding a place to call home. For instance, the US Department of Energy spent twenty-two years, between 1987 and 2009, trying to get clearance to create a deep underground storage facility for nuclear waste at Yucca Mountain, Nevada, until the project was defunded under pressure from the Obama administration in 2011. The fact that this multi-decade process led to almost nothing revealed just how hard it is to find a location that is geologically safe, environmentally appropriate, far from populations, and free from major opposition. As a result, in the United States there is currently no long-term home for high-level nuclear waste, most of which continues to be stored on-site at nuclear plants. There are no indications that this will be resolved in the near future (in France, work is under way on a controversial disposal site that is nearly a third of a mile underground and, once open, will be the world's largest geological nuclear repository). What this also shows is that no one really knows the true cost of safely disposing of such waste, and until we do, we can't know what the cost of production of a kilowatt hour of electricity from nuclear fission really is.

Supply is either not a constraint or a major constraint on nuclear production, depending on how you look at the data. According to the Organization for Economic Cooperation and Development (OECD), it is estimated that there is enough feasibly recoverable uranium left to last until about 2090 at current rates of consumption and using current reactor technology.[2] The problem is that U-235, which is what is used in conventional open-cycle thermal nuclear fission, accounts for 0.7 percent of mined uranium. The remaining 99.3 percent, U-238, is simply disposed of—and at great cost because of its radioactivity. Therefore, the estimates of uranium depletion time frames move forward dramatically when assumptions are changed about which type of uranium could be used. It has been estimated that the supply horizon for uranium could be extended by fiftyfold or more if there was wide-scale deployment of new so-called fast neutron reactors, which are able to use the more common U-238 in addition to U-235, all the while generating reactions that "breed" new nuclear fuel in the form of plutonium.

Here's where things start to get highly uncertain. If we're stuck with the current standard nuclear-generating technologies and we expect nuclear power to ramp up significantly to meet the supply gaps left by fossil fuels, then not only do we fail to see that fiftyfold boost in supply, but we could see the current eighty- to ninety-year supply horizon drop dramatically to a fraction of that as consumption increases beyond current forecasts. On the other hand, if fast breeder reactor technology becomes economically feasible, deployable, and safe on a large scale, then suddenly nuclear energy seems almost infinite. Furthermore, if they worked correctly, fast reactors would deal with much of the waste stream by reprocessing it into new fuel, which would dramatically reduce the amount of waste to be buried. In particular, long-lived plutonium would be converted into radionuclides with a much shorter half-life.

But if this were such a "silver bullet" solution, why don't we have more fast neutron reactors in production now, especially considering that the general technology has been around since 1951? Many experts see these reactors as largely experimental and, at this point, uneconomical and unsafe. Fast neutron reactors use high-speed neutrons and operate at higher temperatures than conventional reactors, making them subject to additional stresses that require significant design complexities and more expensive materials. This leads to considerable uncertainties in design and operation that compromise the ability of the technology to move from small-scale experimental to commercial-scale deployment. As a result, the research and development and capital costs for building a new fast reactor are exorbitant. For instance, the Superphenix reactor in France cost $9.1 billion in 1996 ($12.3 billion in 2011 dollars), and even with these extraordinary costs, fast reactors have operated below capacity and have yet to show significant potential for large-scale commercial viability. Furthermore, the conversion of waste into additional fuel is plagued with problems and uncertainties. Many reactors are subject to low rates of conversion, and even when successful, significant fission products are left in the waste, including dangerous radionuclides like technicium-99 and iodine-129. All these concerns have kept fast reactors on the fringes of an industry where new plant construction is already exceedingly difficult. According to Professor Matthew Bunn of Harvard, fast neutron reactors "are not today's technologies. None of them will be ready for commercial deployment for something like 20 years, if not more. Moreover, I have not yet seen a convincing end-to-end systems analysis that would indicate that these technologies, judged overall (including cost, waste management, safety, security against terrorism, proliferation risks, public acceptance, and use of resources) are superior to the once-through approaches that are likely to be available several decades hence."[3]

In fact, the prospect of building a new commercial-scale nuclear power plant of any kind, even for the far more tried-and-true conventional thermal technology, is becoming increasingly remote, particularly in the United States, but also in many other countries. In fact, as of 2011, no new nuclear power plant had gone online in the United States since 1996, and the last order for a new plant that was actually built was placed in 1973. A 2002 report on the financial feasibility of expanding nuclear power, commissioned by US Department of Energy's Office of Nuclear Energy, Science and Technology, found that significant government assistance would be required to pursue the construction of any further nuclear plants in the near future and that high capital costs will limit the economic feasibility of new nuclear plants for some time to come. The report also pointed out several "show-stopper" risks so significant that, unless resolved, will prevent any new plants from being constructed. These include waste disposal, transportation, accident risks, terrorism risks, and regulatory uncertainty. In particular, the report said that there is general consensus among utility and financial executives that no new plant will be built in the United States until the issue of a permanent repository for nuclear waste is resolved. The report went on to assure readers that with an agreement on Yucca Mountain looming near, that issue was settled and no longer a concern. But now Yucca Mountain appears to be off the table, at least temporarily. According to Dr. Bunn, "Cancelling it will throw the entire nuclear waste management program into doubt, and it is likely to be decades before the United States can settle on another site."[4]

In other words, it is highly unlikely that anything more than a handful of new nuclear plants will be built in the United States anytime soon—and certainly whatever is built will have only a modest effect on the total energy supply. For instance, it's been estimated that if every vehicle in the United States were converted from gasoline to electric-derived power (e.g., hydrogen), it would take the construction of one thousand new large nuclear plants to provide all that electricity.[5] Beyond the unimaginable challenges and uncertainties associated with handling all that waste and decommissioning the plants, the fact that US nuclear developers haven't seen a single new nuclear plant completed in over fifteen years, despite soaring energy prices, should give us pause about relying too much on nuclear energy as the solution.

CHAPTER 9

The Very Regional City

One of the earliest writers to describe the trend of suburbanization in America was Lewis Mumford. In 1925, just as this phenomenon was in its earliest stages, he released a short essay entitled "The Fourth Migration," in which he contextualized the growth of the suburbs relative to three previous technology-driven migrations: pioneers settling the continent; resettlement from farms to factory towns; and the move to large metropolitan areas.[1] Mumford saw the move to the suburbs as a tremendous opportunity for American society. According to his vision, shared by many of his colleagues in the now defunct Regional Planning Association of America, roads and automobiles would free Americans from the blight of overcrowded industrialized cities by allowing them to work in those cities while living in idyllic satellite garden villages. He envisioned these as utopian communities, similar to New England farming towns of the early nineteenth century, with ample access to nature and vibrant social dynamics. For this vision to be achieved, Mumford and his colleagues argued strenuously for an extensive system of divided highways and smaller roads, along with expansion of electricity, phone, and gas networks. This would simultaneously allow people to access employment in the city and enjoy a bucolic lifestyle.

While Mumford and the Regional Planning Association of America were clearly prescient in terms of the extent to which automobiles would transform society, they were quite far off in terms of what im-

244

pact automobiles would have on metropolitan areas—a miscalculation that Mumford acknowledged in his later writings. Clearly, the strip malls, big box stores, and subdivisions of modern American suburbia would not fit the bill of their vision of quaint New England village life. As the planner Philip D'Anieri asks: "How did it happen that [the American Regional Planning Association's] ends went so completely unaddressed while its means were embraced?"[2]

The simple answer is that the association got only half of what it wanted: although it did get the expanded technological infrastructure it desired, it never got the authority to plan and regulate land use regionally. The closest it came to implementing its vision was when one of its members chaired the New York State Commission of Housing and Regional Planning in 1926. But that commission's recommendations for extensive regional planning along the Hudson River corridor went nowhere, because, as the author and planner Carl Sussman wrote, they "demanded massive public intervention in the private market. If the state actually implemented the commission's recommendations, urban property values would have been seriously undermined. . . . Such ideas encountered strong and unified opposition from the business community."[3]

Another answer is that the association's vision may have been infeasible even with adequate planning mechanisms.

Regardless of which is correct, the irony is that this first concerted effort at regional planning was intended to help metropolitan areas suburbanize. Today, on the other hand, regional planning probably holds out the greatest hope for keeping cities from decentralizing too far and for restoring urban centers.

Eighty years after "The Fourth Migration" came out, the planning scholar Robert Fishman suggested that a "fifth migration" may currently be under way. According to him, there is strong evidence that decline in many core cities has undergone a sustained reversal, spearheaded particularly by empty nesters, young professionals, and immigrants. One of the driving forces he posits behind this trend is the increasing livability of city centers—particularly a reduction in crime. He sees these urban improvements as being generated through a "virtuous cycle" in which small investments in inner-city neighborhoods—particularly by immigrant and minority communities—serve to leverage more substantial investments, in a process referred to by Jane Jacobs as "unslumming." But he also sees reurbanization as the result of evolving cultural perceptions, such as the realization in recent decades among corporations in industries like law and financial services that no office park could ever substitute for a marquee location downtown.[4]

There is some evidence that the suburban juggernaut may have been slowing even before the onset of the recession of 2008. Since roughly 2003, per capita vehicle miles traveled has leveled off. Demand for housing in urban cores has increased significantly relative to demand for suburban housing since the early 1990s, following decades of decline. As a consequence, in the 1990s, for the first time in decades, property values and population shares began to rise for many urban cores relative to suburbs. For the past two decades, two-thirds of large metropolitan areas have experienced gains in the populations of their primary cities. And, since 2006, suburban growth rates have slowed considerably for over half of metropolitan areas, particularly for Sunbelt cities, while the growth of many primary cities has increased. One of the most detailed studies of this "reversal" phenomenon, undertaken in the New York Tri-State area, found that although there was significant decentralization between 1969 and the early 1990s, this trend was reversed for population and income distribution starting in 1990, for building permits in 1994, and for job location in 1996.[5]

Joe Cortright, a real estate expert, sees the housing market shocks of 2008 as a further evidence of a recentralization trend. To him, declines in the price of suburban housing relative to central-city housing "signal more than just a temporary disruption in housing markets. The resilience, and in many markets appreciation of housing prices in close-in neighborhoods, point the way to a new, more economically and environmentally sustainable pattern of development for the nation."[6]

If a fifth migration is really in the making, it has potentially sweeping implications for urban energy metabolism. Such a shift could mean smaller dwellings, more efficient infrastructure, shorter trips, and less dependence on automobiles.

But will the fifth migration just continue to happen on its own, and will it be of sufficient magnitude to make a difference? Unfortunately, half a century of decision making regarding land use and transportation has put both of these outcomes in doubt. If there's to be any significant reshaping of the American urban landscape, this legacy will have to be dealt with head on.

There's a commonly held view that decentralization is a result of the land market working in the absence of regulation, or, as Professor Jonathan Levine states in his book *Zoned Out*, that "planning interventions tend to counter any sprawling tendencies of the land-development market." Yet, Levine goes on to point out that there is considerable evidence that "zoning and other municipal interventions actually do the opposite: they lead both to development that is lower in density and to communities that are more exclusive than would arise in the absence of such regulation." He also suggests that "rather than mitigating the market's sprawling tendencies, the ubiquitous interventions of municipal land-use regulation actually exacerbate them." As a result, attempts at compact development "are thwarted by municipal regulation."[7]

One manifestation of this phenomenon is the prevalence of restrictions on mixed-use development, which in turn makes it harder to live near where you work. According to John Norquist of the Congress for the New Urbanism, "Most cities in America have prohibitions on mixed use development in commercial zones. If you count all the suburbs, a lot of them don't allow housing mixed with retail. And then you have Fannie Mae and Freddy Mac, which discriminate against mixed used housing by having caps on non-residential in their mortgage products and the secondary mortgage market. . . . The same kind of discrimination happens in other federal housing programs. . . .

These things create sprawl. Separate use zoning creates sprawl." In fact, a study of thousands of municipal and county governments in Illinois lent backing to this claim when it found that while the term "mixed use" is often mentioned in plans, in almost no cases have mixed-use or traditional neighborhood design ordinances taken effect.[8]

But an even more significant contributor to urban decentralization is the prevalence of low-density, or large-lot, zoning. A considerable number of economic studies have found that such zoning regulations tend to push housing densities to what Levine refers to as a "below-market level," meaning that density would be higher in the absence of regulation, and that constraining the market in this way spreads cities out farther, facilitating sprawl. A 1999 study found that, of fifteen hundred county jurisdictions sampled, 20 percent of the average county land area was subject to low-density-only zoning and 25 percent of counties had more than a quarter of their land in this category. As a result, in 2000 nearly ten times as much land in the United States was settled at lower densities (defined as between ten and forty acres per household) as was settled at urban densities (just under one house per acre).[9]

Low-density zoning is a pragmatic thing to do from the local point of view, but when everyone does it, it's harmful to the entire region. The economist William Fischel provides a succinct and convincing explanation of how zoning restrictions designed to manage population and provision of services—known as "fiscal zoning"—have led to decentralization of land use.[10] According to Fischel, different types of municipal jurisdictions have different interests when it comes to fiscal zoning. Predominantly residential suburban jurisdictions, also known as "bedroom communities," tend to be the most restrictive in their zoning, requiring relatively large lot sizes, low densities, and separation of uses. Such zoning serves a number of pragmatic purposes. First is protection of home value. For most people, a home represents by far the greatest share of nonretirement assets. Although a home can be insured against fire or flood, it can't be insured against a decline in desirability or quality of the neighborhood. Fischel believes that restrictive zoning serves as a form of home-value insurance by limiting the potential for bigger developments, which many homeowners fear can impact neighborhood desirability and lead to lowered property values. Homeowners therefore fight change in their neighborhoods, particularly the construction of multifamily residential dwellings, because they don't like exposing their most valuable asset to uncertainty—even if the probabilities of a negative impact on that asset are small.

But Fischel's explanation goes well beyond property values. Property-tax revenues fund municipal services, like schools. Since those revenues are based on property valuations, properties of higher value contribute more to city coffers per municipal "customer" than do those of low value. It would be tempting for a city to require all homes to be of high value for this reason, but that's illegal. Cities can, however, proxy this effect by requiring large lots, since lot size is strongly correlated with home valuation (both in terms of land and improvement value). So requiring large lots not only keeps property-tax revenues per household elevated but also keeps a check on the number of people who will be consuming city services. In other words, it results in greater service provision per household.

Also, requiring large lots reduces transfers of wealth from high- to lower-income people. Every resident of a municipality is entitled to equal access to city services, regardless of how much property tax he or she pays. Therefore, if income is highly heterogeneous in a town, the wealthy are in essence subsidizing lower-income families. By making housing expensive in a community, large-lot zoning effectively keeps out low-income people and in turn reduces the transfer of wealth.

Fischel's framework goes on to show how the timing of large-lot zoning regulations varies based on where a jurisdiction is located and how far along it is in its development trajectory. In municipalities that are considered rural, where economic opportunities are few, zoning is generally absent or very permissive, because economic development is a far higher priority than minimizing crowding or congestion. Hence, though lots may be large in a rural area, that may not be due to any zoning requirements. Suburban jurisdictions, on the other hand, are generally located within commuting distance of major employment centers, where demand for land is much higher. The goal in those communities is to maintain access to those jobs while keeping enough distance to be removed from the negative effects associated with economic activity, such as overcrowding, traffic congestion, noise, traffic, pollution, and crime. Suburban jurisdictions, however, are likely to be more permissive the newer and less populated they are, the reason being that a suburban jurisdiction that is too small (like with a rural jurisdiction) may have an insufficient tax base to pay for the fixed costs of city services (e.g., a new fire truck or school building). Hence, the addition of new residents in a municipality is desirable up to a certain point. But when it reaches a population where just one additional person will add more in terms of congestion costs than he or she contributes in property-tax revenue, the incentive to grow population disappears. Of course, it's not possible to determine exactly when this point occurs, and even if it were, town policies can be slow and imprecise in their response. In general, however, towns tend to start off with policies that invite new residents and then to clamp down on growth when congestion starts to be an issue.

One may rightfully ask how this large number of small and fragmented municipal jurisdictions developed in the first place. Why aren't there just a few large municipalities in each large metropolitan area, as opposed to hundreds? One mechanism common throughout the West is the incorporation of a new jurisdiction on unincorporated county land, frequently following the construction of new developments. The other approach is through secession. As big jurisdictions grow, individual neighborhoods may grow disenchanted with membership in that city. This frequently happens to higher-income, higher-amenity neighborhoods. Many residents of these neighborhoods see themselves as assuming too much of the property-tax burden and getting too little in return in the form of city services—particularly schools. Secessions are often found in cities where school quality is declining and where schoolchildren are forcibly bussed to schools outside their neighborhoods, or where outsiders from poorer districts are bussed in. Secession solves these problems by creating a more homogeneous jurisdiction where upper-income residents receive more in services relative to what they pay in taxes by avoiding transfers to lower-income people. This situation also ends up creating many jurisdictions with differing service and tax levels, from which households can essentially "shop" or "vote with their feet" when they are considering moves—constrained, of course, by what they can afford.[11] This comes at a tremendous cost to the larger jurisdiction, as the secession of multiple wealthy neighborhoods slowly erodes the tax base, making the quality of local services even worse and driving out ever more people.

The result of this situation has been the dramatic growth of suburban jurisdictions and the relative decline of many central-city jurisdictions over the past fifty years (that is, until this trend began a slow reversal in the early 2000s). Between 1950 and 2000, 75 percent of newly developed land and 80 percent of the added population were in jurisdictions located outside of established central cities.[12] A by-product of this is the proliferation of municipal jurisdictions. In the United States there are around 20,000 incorporated local jurisdictions, and 39,000 "general purpose" local governments (which includes sub-municipal entities, like boroughs). Most large metropolitan areas are now composed of numerous individual jurisdictions. For instance, the greater Los Angeles–Riverside–San Bernardino–Orange County metropolitan area has 190 incorporated municipalities.

According to Fischel's summary, restrictive zoning leads to urban decentralization (and hence longer travel distances) by influencing housing supply and prices. If only one small jurisdiction within a region was to zone restrictively, there would likely be little impact on the supply and price of housing regionally. Prices might rise locally, but that's only because restrictive zoning would increase desirability and hence demand for that jurisdiction. But what often happens when one jurisdiction in a region zones restrictively is that surrounding jurisdictions become "copycats," emboldened to enact restrictions that they once thought might not pass judicial review.[13] If enough jurisdictions start zoning restrictively, this will not only restrict land supply but also cause prices to rise regionally (in this case prices go up because of reduced supply; in the previously mentioned case, they go up because of increased demand). Because of constricted land supply and because land prices typically decline in proportion to distance from the urban core, people need to move farther and farther out to afford housing—particularly if they want a detached single-family home. That is, the distance necessary to "drive until you qualify" increases. A pattern that frequently emerges is "leapfrog" development, described in the previous chapter. This is often caused by speculators holding on to large pieces of land to take advantage of the rising prices caused by restricted supply. It may also be caused by jurisdictions zoning large areas as agricultural preserves or open space.

A counterargument often given in response to the proposition that the traditional American system of zoning contributes to sprawl is that Houston has no zoning yet is considered one of the most sprawling urban areas in the country—therefore zoning is not the problem. This is a misleading argument for several reasons. First, Houston is just one of dozens of municipalities in its region, many of which have restrictive zoning. Take neighboring Sugar Land, for instance, which has over half its land zoned as single-family residential. Second, Houston makes up for a lack of zoning with other sprawl-inducing regulations. Until 1999, it required all single-family houses to occupy at least a five-thousand-square-foot lot (98 percent of the city's housing was built before this law was changed). Houston's city code also requires large amounts of parking for both residential and commercial buildings. Rights-of-way for streets are required to be extremely large, and intersections on major streets must be six hundred feet apart. And finally, Houston has the second highest number of highway lane miles per capita in the United States.[14] In other words, the example of Houston by no means exculpates traditional zoning; rather, it just illustrates that there are many other pathways to sprawl too.

Another argument counters that the preponderance of suburban development is simply a result of an overwhelming preference of Americans for suburban living. There is some truth to this. Suburbanites in the United States have been found to be more satisfied overall with their communities. A recent Pew survey found that 68 percent of suburban residents rate their communities as being "excellent" or "very good," as compared to 52 percent for city dwellers, and suburban residents tend to be more content with issues like recreational opportunities, raising a family, traffic, and crime. But these surveys fail to account for the fact that there is much variation within that broad "suburban" category. A different survey, by Smart Growth America, found that the characteristics of suburbs do matter to people. The following were among its findings: respondents favor suburbs near cities over distant suburbs by a nearly two-to-one margin; six out of ten potential homebuyers would prefer to buy in communities with smart growth principles (e.g., mixed use, greater density, less automobile dependence, pedestrian usability, nearby transit, etc.) over communities without; nearly nine out of ten potential homebuyers say that having a short commute is an important consideration in where they choose to buy; and half of respondents cite being within walking distance of stores and restaurants as important.

So, while Americans tend to like living in suburbs, the types of suburbs most commonly being built in recent years—distant, automobile-dependent, and homogeneous in land use—are largely at odds with most people's preferences. Given this, it's totally reasonable to assert that our current fragmented regulatory system is failing not only to deliver more efficient, compact development, but also to deliver on people's preferences.[15]

The debate over whether the current, flawed pattern of land use is the result of too much regulation, or not enough is, I believe, a red herring. The relevant question, rather, is what's the right system of regulation? Fundamental to answering this is first determining the proper spatial scale of land use governance. As a former city Planning Commissioner, I'm acutely aware of the importance of local control of land use in the United States, and I believe that local government must continue to be involved in land use decisions. However, I also recognize that many of the problems I've mentioned above could be plausibly dealt with through the intervention of higher levels of government. Already there is some amount of state and federal intervention in land use (for instance, floodplain development restrictions, via the National Flood Insurance Program, or adequate water supply requirements for new developments, in the case of a California state law). How much more should there be? And, what is the appropriate governmental level at which this regulation should occur?

Many planners believe that the right level is the region—something corresponding to a greater metropolitan area. This approach is pragmatic not only because it coordinates and reconciles the often mutually antagonistic actions of autonomous jurisdictions, but also because the metropolitan scale is functionally meaningful. According to authors William Fulton and Peter Calthorpe, coherent regions are defined by economic, ecological, and social commonalities and by connections that spring from sharing space.[16]

This leads to a spatial mismatch problem; the most vexing urban problems are increasingly metropolitan in scale, while most regulations are local. For instance, while large-scale transit projects are generally coordinated regionally, the fact that land use is locally-controlled compromises the effectiveness of those projects, as automobile-based development patterns continue to be the norm, making it hard for people to shift over to transit. Likewise, there is often a "race to the bottom" phenomenon among competing local jurisdictions. For instance, if a centrally located jurisdiction tries to cap parking spaces for retail so as to encourage walking and transit, less centrally located jurisdictions in that metropolitan area might use this as an opportunity to lure businesses away with the promise of ample parking. The end result is that whether or not the first jurisdiction sticks with the regulation, the intended policy shift (encourage transit and walking) fails because its enactment by only one jurisdiction provides a perverse incentive for other jurisdictions to go against that intended policy outcome.

In other words, because jurisdictions are competing with each other for residents and businesses, it's nearly impossible to accomplish the types of big, regional goals that require not only collaboration, but some mutual sacrifice. And mutual sacrifice simply doesn't happen naturally under the current dog-eat-dog system of municipal interaction. As the planning scholar Frank J. Popper wrote in a seminal 1988 article, "It would help if planners grasped the real nature of the American federalist system of land use controls. It is so loose, so deliberately disjointed and open ended, that it is barely a system in the sense that the European elite civil service bureaucracies understand the term. . . . It is more often a matter of the inevitably uncertain catch-as-catch-can pluralism of democratic power politics."[17]

While many believe that implementing regional land use controls is practically infeasible in the United States, Calthorpe and Fulton point out that an institutional framework for regional governance already exists through the Metropolitan Planning Organizations (MPOs), of which there are currently about 385. MPOs are federally mandated agencies whose purpose is to channel, plan for, and coordinate federal transportation funds and projects within each metropolitan area. Because they work regionally, their jurisdiction cuts across municipal borders and they include representatives from all participating municipalities. MPOs have significant power over the planning, evaluation, and implementation of regional transportation projects. And increasingly, there is recognition among MPOs of the inextricable relationship between transportation and land use.[18] But the ability to act on that recognition is limited. The vast majority of MPOs that actively incorporate land use into their planning process do so in an advisory capacity and generally limit their activities to providing technical support or funding land-use studies. No clear regulatory framework exists for MPOs to make decisions about land-use issues like zoning or open-space protection. Many metropolitan areas also have regional planning agencies generically known as Regional Councils, Councils of Governments, Regional Planning Commissions, or Associations of Governments, among other titles. These are sometimes combined with MPOs into a single large agency, or they may be institutionally distinct, in which case they often occupy the same office space.

Today, more than thirty-nine thousand general-purpose government agencies (comprising cities, counties, townships, boroughs, etc.) are represented by some kind of regional council.[19] Regional councils are more comprehensive in their scope than MPOs and tend to have greater emphasis on regional land use and governance issues. Nonetheless, they have little regulatory authority and lack MPOs' control of federal transportation funds. Both MPOs and regional councils generally have boards that are composed of representatives from constituent municipalities. As such, they tend to be reactive to local desires rather than to proactively set regional goals. Calthorpe and Fulton point out that local elected officials—the primary drivers of land-use decisions—have a tough time representing regional goals when they conflict with immediate local interests, even if those regional goals yield significant indirect benefits. The result is that although there is a lot of regional institutional structure and bureaucracy, there's little regional decision making power.

There is one notable exception, however: Oregon, which has a statutory regional government structure with elected representatives and regulatory authority. In 1973, a law was passed that required each city and county in Oregon to adopt a comprehensive plan meeting fourteen statewide goals. Most significantly, each incorporated city was required to adopt an urban growth boundary that would delineate urbanized from nonurbanized areas and constrain future development. Five years after this law, a ballot measure was passed providing for the regional governance of the greater Portland area, constituting three counties and twenty-seven municipalities. The newly created institution, Portland Metro, is now the most powerful regional planning agency in the country, with statutory responsibility for land-use and transportation planning (it is also an MPO), implementation of the regional urban-growth boundary, habitat protection, large-facility management, and mapping. It has a regionally elected council president plus six councilors elected by individual district.

There are a number of planning advantages that flow from the Portland Metro's regional regulatory powers. For instance, the coordination of land use and transit is greatly facilitated. While in many metropolitan areas, transit-oriented developments (TODs)—the kind that help make transit lines feasible—have to fight for approvals individually against outdated zoning codes, regional planning in Portland allows for a coordinated approach. Each transit corridor where TODs are deemed necessary utilizes a master developer, a consultant who provides proposals for all TODs in a corridor. Rather than requests for approvals being submitted in an ad hoc manner, approvals for TODs are submitted as a package, greatly streamlining the regulatory process and facilitating the coordination of TOD plans across the region. In the absence of this mechanism, TODs might otherwise have been planned in isolation.[20]

From the perspective of urban energy metabolism, an even more important outcome of regional government is Oregon's system of urban growth boundaries. These are lines drawn on a map around distinct urban areas. Outside of the boundaries, land is designated for non-urban uses such as agriculture and forestry and new development over "rural densities" is not allowed. Within boundaries, densities are expected to be higher, not only because of the constrained land supply, but also because development approvals are theoretically easier and, in the case of the Portland region, because there are minimum density requirements. Most of Oregon's urban growth boundaries are small—some less than a mile across for smaller towns. But the Portland urban growth boundary covers a large area and is designed to accommodate a 20-year supply of land based on population projections. It currently includes land from 24 cities and 3 counties, totaling 237,000 acres and more than 1.3 million people.

In theory, a well-designed urban growth boundary is supposed to constrain the spatial extent of urban growth, protect large areas of open space and farmland, reduce sprawl, and make the established urban core more compact. While a glance at aerial imagery clearly indicates that development patterns do change dramatically at the urban growth boundary, quantifying the extent to which these larger goals have been achieved is very difficult. The literature yields some mixed results. One study, which was confined to just the Washington County portion of the region, found that following the implementation of many of the region's growth-management policies with the adoption of the "2040 Growth Concept," trends in many development indicators, which had been toward sprawl, were reversed. Among the changes measured were increases in density, street connectivity, pedestrian access, and proximity of residences to commercial uses (no significant increase was measured in the mix of uses). Because this Growth Concept includes many policy components beyond just the urban growth boundary, the authors point out that it is hard to isolate the effects of any individual policy. Yet in aggregate, they appear to have an impact.[21]

A number of other studies agree that the urban growth boundary, combined with other planning mechanisms, has focused development and reduced sprawl. One study found that the average density of new housing in Portland increased from five to eight dwelling units per acre within about five years of implementing this plan and that multifamily housing starts rose from 35 to 50 percent. Another study, however, found that results were sensitive to the geographic scope of the analysis. By increasing the area from just the three-county growth boundary planning region to a nearby fourth county (Clark County), not included within the boundary because it's in Washington State, the results showed that greater Portland experienced significant suburbanization during the 1990s. The urban growth boundary was found to divert growth to Clark County, which is located just across the Columbia River from Portland, because its growth controls are more lax. According to this study, Clark County therefore acted as a "safety valve" for unmet housing demand and in the process compromised the intentions of the urban growth boundary. And Clark County is likely not the only such safety valve. So-called "leakage" of development also occurs in small, scattered pieces of land located outside the growth boundary that fall under some kind of regulatory exception, such as for lots recorded before the establishment of the boundary.[22]

Despite the safety valve and leakage problems, there is little question that Oregon's growth boundary system is by far the most success-

Light-rail line in downtown Portland, Oregon.
(Photo: Treg Christopher; used by permission)

ful in the country. And the most important factor behind that success is the existence of a powerful regional government that can coordinate and regulate growth boundaries. Lacking regional empowerment, most other growth boundary planning areas are geographically limited to either city or county lines, leading to leapfrog sprawl, as development just gets channeled to whatever nearby jurisdiction has sufficiently lax regulation. The only way to avoid the leapfrog problem is to ensure that the planning area around a growth boundary (that is, the area where development can be restricted) includes everything within reasonable commuting distance around the greater metropolitan area, something that is extremely hard to do without regional governance.

Beyond the existence of sufficiently powerful regional government, though, Oregon's system is also successful because its policies are well designed. For instance, one of the keys to success of Portland's

An aerial image of Portland's periphery, showing the sudden end of
development at the Urban Growth Boundary (outlined in black). (Map by
author; aerial image from National Agricultural Imagery Program; growth
boundary data from Oregon Dept. of Land Conservation and Development)

boundary has been its minimum density requirement for the urban
core. A common problem, written about by planner Douglas Porter,
is that communities without such requirements envision a dense core,
but find it difficult to effectively increase density within the growth
boundary. As a result, boundaries often have to be expanded to accommodate growth. For instance, he details Sarasota, Florida, where "opposition to high-density development from NIMBY (Not In My Back
Yard) project neighborhoods persuaded county officials to turn down
such projects, undercutting the density policy and necessitating a significant expansion of the boundary." This kind of "pressure to expand
the boundary," he finds, "is typical rather than unusual." Another problem he points out is when jurisdictions draw such a large boundary
that there is little incentive for compact development, as is the case in

Minneapolis–St. Paul, where "Planners at the Metropolitan Council . . . acknowledge that development in most of the area within the decades-old regional boundary can be characterized as urban sprawl."[23]

Without doubt, however, the greatest challenges to regional growth boundary systems are political. Regionalism establishes potentially severe constraints on what can be done with private property and hence can undermine property values, particularly along the urban periphery. Whether or not it's fair, anything that negatively affects property owners' ability to do what they want with their land tends to run into steep resistance in the United States. Planners often point out that property ownership comes with nearly as many responsibilities as it does privileges, and that government generally "gives" far more in the form of services and infrastructure than it takes in the form of regulation.[24] But this knowledge is not enough to overcome the suspicion of regional planning—or the inertia—that has kept most land-use planning local.

An indication of the political challenges faced by regionalism was the passage of Oregon's Measure 37 in 2004. This ballot measure, which was largely seen as a backlash to centralized planning in Oregon, required the state to either compensate landowners for lost development opportunities due to land-use restrictions related to the growth boundary or forgo enforcement of those restrictions. The largest group to which it applied owned land outside the urban growth boundaries. As of 2007, there were close to 7,500 claims under Measure 37, covering nearly 750,000 acres and accounting for $19.8 billion. Given the infeasibility of paying all these claims, development restrictions went unenforced for many areas. But in 2007, voters overwhelmingly passed a measure that overturned at least parts of this law and moved back toward stronger regionalism. Measure 49 allows landowners outside the urban growth boundaries to build a small number of homes—generally between one and three per lot, depending on lot size, assuming that such development was allowable at the time of property transfer. If owners can prove that the restrictions significantly devalued their property, then the state allows the construction of up to ten homes. It does, however, restrict development of large subdivisions and industrial developments in these areas. Under the new law, the state expects to see less than 15 percent of the expected number of homes built as would have been allowed under Measure 37. A number of rural subdivisions have in fact been halted as a result of this law.[25]

Some planning approaches have been proposed to deal with concerns over property rights. For instance, Transfers of Development rights (TDRs) allow government to sell the right to develop at higher density within established urban areas and to use the proceeds from these density credits to compensate owners of property in the periphery whose value has been reduced due to development restrictions. It's a great idea in theory, but experience has shown that TDRs are challenging to implement and are a long way from being a solution to this distributional problem.

With few other potential solutions to the compensation problem on the horizon, regionalism has largely been a nonstarter in most parts of the country. Many have declared regional planning effectively dead in the United States and have given up hope for its future. But the nearly two-thirds majority vote for Measure 49 in Oregon suggests that this conclusion might be premature. Regionalism in the United States is as much a victim of the commonly held assumption that it will never work as it is a victim of its actual constraints. One day someone outside of Oregon will notice that.

Regionalism is concerned not only about limiting growth on the periphery but also about figuring out how the established urban landscape will be filled in—and there's far less agreement on this issue than on stopping sprawl. According to Mark Pisano, who served for thirty-one years as the executive director of the Southern California Area Governments (the entity responsible for coordination of regional transportation planning and intercity land-use planning for six of the ten counties in Southern California), "The politics around infill are the most intense government policy debates we're facing now."[26]

Most planners believe that the New York–style monocentric model (in which one very dense commercial center clearly dominates) is efficient because it allows for relatively short average trips and a high share of transit ridership. But, with the possible exception of Chicago, it's doubtful whether any other US city has the option to feasibly duplicate that model. As Pisano said, "If Los Angeles emulates New York or Chicago, we won't make it. We don't have the cost structure for performing services like transportation." So what other model of urban infill can be followed?

Commercial centers largely provide structure and definition to urban areas. In the absence of coherent metropolitan planning, it's increasingly common to see continuous, low-density, automobile-oriented commercial development (often in linear strips), a pattern that the author Robert Lang refers to as "office sprawl" or "edgeless cities." Today, this style of commercial development accounts for nearly two-thirds of non-downtown office space in the United States, and in eleven of the thirteen largest metropolitan areas it accounts for more space than any other style of commercial development, including core downtowns and secondary downtowns.[27] Characterized by a lack of clustering, it makes transit nearly impossible and automobile use nearly mandatory.

But there are other models of regional urban form somewhere between New York City and office sprawl. One is the polycentric model, in which metropolitan areas are made up of an assortment of smaller subcenters, none of which is dominant. While this model clearly does not allow the same economies of scale in transit provision as a monocentric city like New York, it may have some potential advantages that are overlooked. We've seen some of these advantages unexpectedly crop up in Los Angeles as worsening traffic conditions have encouraged residents to work and shop nearer to where they live—in essence, fostering the development of something like an "urban village." With this in mind, many planners in large megalopolises like Los Angeles are focusing less on figuring out how to make a single downtown dominant, and more on how to make regional subcenters have some of the characteristics of a traditional downtown. According to Christopher Leinberger, successful subcenters, which he refers to as "walkable urban places," can function like a downtown as long as they have sufficient density (five times more floor-to-area ratio than what is considered suburban), mixed uses, compact form, access to multiple transportation modes, and walkable pedestrian infrastructure. He sees a number of types of walkable urban places outside of traditional downtowns, ranging from those adjacent to downtowns, suburban town centers, suburban redevelopments, and even appropriately developed Greenfield communities.[28]

Pisano told me that he thinks the Los Angeles region consists of many subcenters, or urban villages, and that this decentralized and multinucleated pattern is potentially more efficient than having a single regional center, because it creates the greatest opportunity for more people to live near their work. "This is a long standing issue that I've been coming to grips with. Is Southern California sprawl, or is it ahead of its time? I've personally come to the conclusion that it's ahead of its time. . . . We will probably evolve ourselves into a more efficient region—possibly more so than those cities in Europe." He believes that the movement of people and businesses to these centers is fundamentally changing the face of Los Angeles and should be big news, but that it falls under most people's radar because "it's around this 'distributed centers' concept and it's not in one place." His agency conducted studies and concluded that if only 2 percent more of the urban land mass could be converted to these types of mixed-used centers, vehicle trips would be reduced by 7 to 10 percent and energy use by 10 to 15 percent.

Con Howe has the rare distinction of having been the head city planner of New York City before occupying the same position for Los Angeles. Howe, who retired from city planning in 2006, strongly agrees that Los Angeles is defined by its multiple centers and that its downtown has far less dominance than those in eastern cities, like New York. He also agrees with Pisano that having multiple centers doesn't necessarily disadvantage a city in terms of transportation efficiency. "I know that it's easy to say that concentric [single center] cities with density are good for mass transit, but it doesn't mean that cities with a different form can't be efficient." He cites recent changes in Los Angeles' development pattern to back this up. For instance, in 2001, 20 percent of the city's new housing units were built in commercial zones. But by 2006, after a concerted planning effort, that figure had risen to 60 percent.

Studies suggest that this strategy may be starting to pay off. In a 2010 article, the urban geographer Ali Modarres found that residents of many of Los Angeles' growing subcenters are now experiencing shorter average commutes. The more balanced jobs and housing are within a subcenter, the lower the commuting times. Modarres gives as an example the Orange County subcenter of Irvine, where nearly 40 percent of residents also work. However, the study also found that lower average commuting time comes with some tradeoffs. First, in a place like Los Angeles, lower-income people are still highly concentrated in neighborhoods that are often far from these subcenters, in turn leading to income inequity in average commuting distances. Second, short commutes reduce the likelihood that people will give up cars in favor of transit.[29]

In other words, in the Los Angeles area, for those who can afford it, cars are the definitive mode of choice, and living in a villagelike subcenter reduces only the probable length of commutes—not the probability of using a car. This is progress over Los Angeles' historic pattern of office sprawl, but it's still a far cry from what the urban-village model could achieve. Many believe that the missing link is transit.

Peter Newman and Jeffrey Kenworthy give examples of some of the world's most successful urban villages, in Munich, Stockholm, Vancouver, and Sydney. What all these have in common is centrally located transit stations around which activities are concentrated and which offer easy connections to other employment centers. Urban villages can benefit enormously from being serviced by transit for a number of reasons. First, transit access reduces the inequity described above by giving lower-income people easier access to more-distant jobs. Second, without transit, the subcenter model is limited in reducing transportation energy, because in our increasingly specialized and income-segregated world, only so many people can be expected to live and work in the same neighborhood. Most urban villages are not all-purpose subcenters of employment. Rather, as the planners Christopher Leinberger and Charles Lockwood pointed out in their seminal article on urban villages, subcenters become more and more specialized over time. For instance, in Los Angeles, the Pasadena subcenter has historically specialized in financial services, while aerospace has clustered in the Torrance region, and much of the film industry is found in Burbank and Glendale. Whenever there is geographic specialization in employment, people will come from afar. It would be unrealistic, for instance, to expect all those in the aerospace industry to live in Torrance.[30]

This type of transit-oriented polycentrism is beginning to spring up all around the United States. Excellent examples can be found in places like the Rosslyn-Ballston Corridor, Tysons Corner, Bethesda, and Silver Spring, all outside of Washington D.C.; the Pearl District and Goose Hollow in Portland, Oregon; Fruitvale in Oakland, California; and the Lindbergh Center in Atlanta, Georgia. Even in the Los Angeles area, several subcenters, like Meridian Village in South Pasadena, have embraced the transit-oriented development paradigm by anchoring major uses around light rail. One of the most interesting examples of transit-oriented subcenters comes from Atlanta, where BellSouth, Atlanta's second-largest employer, decided to concentrate 60 percent of their employees from twenty-five regionally scattered buildings into three large new centers on redevelopment sites. The company mapped the residential locations of their thousands of employees and situated their three complexes as close to the geographic center as possible, putting two of them directly at transit stations. In other words, they created their own subcenters that were geographically optimized to be as close to their employees as possible and to be on transit.[31]

The struggle over regional planning is as much about words as it is about densities, use tables, or growth boundaries. The imprecision of language, the need to categorize things, and the frequent conflation of form and function all serve to flummox communication to the extent that two planners who think they are agreeing may in fact have visions that are diametrically opposed or vice versa. Baggage-laden terms like "suburban," "urban," "metropolitan," "village," "center," "sub-center," or "downtown" often lead to more misunderstanding than clarity. Robert Lang put together a list of nearly fifty such names of urban form categories that have been coined by different authors since the 1960s. He notes that this list "certainly supports the observation that we cannot agree on what to call these places or even on which places need labeling."[32]

In his later writings, Mumford shows a keen awareness of this battle for words, perhaps in tacit recognition of his own misperceptions about suburbia in his earlier writings. For instance, in discussing the intent of Ebenezer Howard in proposing his "garden cities" concept and how that idea has been misappropriated, he writes: "Superficial students patently ignorant of Howard's work still unfortunately make the error of calling suburbs garden cities, or the suburban open plan a 'garden city type of plan': even worse, critics who should know better often refer to the classic garden cities . . . as if they were mere suburbs, because they were all laid out in an open—perhaps too open— framework. But the garden city, in Howard's view, was first of all a city. . . . It was in its urbanity, not in its horticulture, that the Garden City made a bold departure from the established method of building and planning."[33]

A more recent example of the imprecision of language comes from a 2008 article by Christopher Leinberger, in which he suggested that "walkable urban places" would be at a huge advantage over automobile-oriented suburbia in dealing with the aftermath of rising oil prices and the subprime mortgage crisis. A rival planning voice, Joel Kotkin, countered in the *Los Angeles Times* that Leinberger was unfairly demonizing the suburbs and that there was no evidence to support Leinberger's contentions. As evidence for his counterargument, Kotkin offered areas that he classified as "suburbs," such as Burbank, Ontario, and West Los Angeles, all of which were thriving in the aftermath of high oil prices and the mortgage crisis. Kotkin automatically classified these places as "suburbs," probably because they are relatively far from downtown Los Angeles and peripheral to the urban core. But many of the districts that he cited as proof that "suburbia is not dead" were the same districts that Leinberger had used as examples of nonsuburban "walkable urban places" in his earlier writings. In other words, the two authors categorized the same places completely differently. In a 2008 blog posting, the planning writer Bill Fulton commented on this semantic kerfuffle: "Kotkin is about 30 years out of date. His mind lives in a ring of older suburbs that circle downtown L.A.–Burbank, the San Gabriel Valley, the Westside, Irvine, all built between the 1920s and the 1960s as residential suburbs. Kotkin always casts the 'urban v. suburban' battle as a battle between Downtown Los Angeles and these 'suburbs.' But Burbank and Westwood are no more suburbs than is Downtown."[34]

To me, language may be an even greater challenge to regionalism than political obstacles like property rights. If planners are consistently misunderstanding one another, how can they be expected to clearly communicate their ideas to their constituency—the public? The more regional the scale of the planning, the more challenging the communication barrier. Regional planning is fundamentally about applying general concepts to large areas. Although these concepts often are defined in terms of specific and quantifiable metrics such as floor-to-area ratios, it is the generalities that are the subject of public debate and the way that policies are sold. And even when goals for quantifiable metrics are met, there's no guarantee that the result will look anything like what the planners or the public intended. Early planners of Los Angeles thought that its system of "motorways" would lead to idyllic garden suburbs separated from urban blight by pleasant greenbelts. Instead residents got hundreds of miles of mini-mall-style commercial strip development. With planning, the devil truly is in the details.

Renewable Energy Generation

SOLAR- AND WIND-GENERATION technologies have enormous potential to provide clean, decentralized, and sustainable energy. And if you watch advertisements during the evening news, you'd think the whole country is running on them. But their ubiquity in the media is far out of proportion to their actual use.

As of early 2011, wind accounted for 2.8 percent and solar (photovoltaic and thermal) for 0.02 percent of all US electricity generated. There is little doubt that both power sources will come to account for a far larger share of the energy mix in the future. Already, the signs are very encouraging. For instance, between 2010 and 2011, there was a 54 percent increase in wind and 229 percent in solar generation. But there are limitations as to how big a share that can be, and getting to that maximum is going to take a long time. Both have an awful lot of ramping up to do before they can provide sufficient energy to even slightly offset declines in fossil fuels. How much can they offset? To give an idea of the order of magnitude, if a million 1-megawatt wind turbines were built by 2020—a gargantuan task—that would still account for only 12 percent of the world's electrical demand.[1]

The root of the problem is that wind and sunshine are extremely diffuse forms of energy compared to fossil fuels, which pack large amounts of energy per unit of volume. Therefore, energy from these sources is more expensive to produce than the electricity we are accustomed to. Obtaining exact differentials is hard, because the cost of solar and wind generation varies greatly, based on site suitability (everything from wind and sun conditions to required site-preparation work to permitting and public outreach costs). For instance, according to the solar market research website, Solarbuzz.com, prices per installed

269

kilowatt of solar power can vary by over 100 percent depending on whether the climate of a location is cloudy or sunny. The retail price of "backstop" sources (that is, the cheapest source on the market at the time), such as gas- and coal-fired power, also varies greatly, based on market conditions and local and regional factors. For instance, in the first half of 2009, the average price per kilowatt hour for electricity in the United States was 11.4 cents, but there was huge variation around that average—from 7.6 cents in hydropower-rich Washington State to 19.5 cents in Connecticut.[2]

This variability in both the cost of production and the backstop price of power (plus some subsidies) is what allows solar and wind to operate commercially in some areas even though they are not economically feasible in others; for example, in areas with limited electrical generating capacity from fossil fuels (and hence high electricity rates) but with excellent sun or wind resources, solar or wind are more cost-competitive. When the variation is averaged out, however, experts estimate that the cost of wind power is currently about 50 percent more per unit of power output than that of coal. The Electric Power Research Institute (EPRI) estimates that there will be a smaller price differential in the future but that even in 2015 wind will still cost a third more than coal power and about 15 percent more than gas. Solar is far worse: EPRI estimated that in 2015 solar thermal power (which generates electricity by heating water whose steam is used to drive a turbine) will cost nearly three times more than coal power and two times more than gas. Solar photovoltaics (which generate power by converting sunlight directly into electrical current using semiconductors) were estimated to have an even higher price differential. In the United States, as of mid-2009, the average retail price per kilowatt hour for residential solar energy, absent subsidies, was around thirty-seven cents, more than three times the average price for power from conventional sources.[3]

One reason that wind and solar generation is more expensive is a problem known as intermittency. Unlike gas- or coal-fired power plants, wind turbines and solar panels can't simply be turned on and off when power is needed. And when they are producing, it's often not at

maximum power because of low wind, cloud cover, or time of year. Because solar cells depend on sunlight, they're able to work at maximum
capacity only about 22 percent of the time in sunny regions, compared
to about 90 percent for coal plants. And the intermittency and uncertainty gets much worse as one moves into higher latitudes and areas
with greater cloud cover. The capacity of wind farms varies greatly with
the frequency of high winds but is typically around 33 percent for average areas and up to 45 percent for high-wind areas. Wind has an added
problem: areas with the best capacity factors tend to be developed first,
so that subsequent wind farms end up with decreasing capacity. Germany, for example, with its extremely well-developed wind industry,
has a low capacity factor of around 17 percent for its remaining potential sites; by comparison, the factor for the United States, with its vast
unexploited wind resources, is much higher, 28.8 percent.[4]

Intermittency requires either some other power source as a baseload power backup—typically a gas-fired power plant that sits idle
until needed—or considerable surplus renewable generation capacity, known as "overbuild." Consequently, if fossil-fuel power is to be
avoided, many more megawatts' worth of turbines or solar panels must
be installed to achieve a dependable level of power. Thus, if a utility
wants to provide one hundred megawatts of reliable solar power with a
20 percent capacity factor, it must build five hundred megawatts' worth
of panels; for a wind farm to provide one hundred megawatts at 33 percent capacity, it would require the installation of three hundred megawatts' worth of turbines. Overbuild is less a problem when renewables
are generating at a small scale to fill in minor energy gaps, because in
this case there is plenty of generation redundancy and the system can
meet demand without the renewables. But if solar and wind were to
suddenly account for a significant portion of the energy mix, overbuild
would become a more serious obstacle. For this reason, many experts
believe that wind and solar could not feasibly exceed 20 percent of a
region's power mix; above this level it is expected that either intermittency would cause too many power disruptions or the cost of maintaining backup baseload power would become very steep.[5] In other

words, the cost of production per kilowatt hour would be expected to rise significantly as the market share for wind and solar got big enough that their production started to significantly exceed the redundancy factor in the power grid, because avoiding blackouts would require increasingly large amounts of overbuild. At this point, the highest rates for intermittent power-source penetration in the United States are under 15 percent, for small portions of California and New Mexico, and in a number of geographic regions wind-farm generation has been curtailed due to lack of backup generation capacity.[6]

Overbuild is just one reason why installing solar and wind systems is so expensive. The sizable capital investment for wind turbines and solar panels is another. These costs are coming down significantly for wind as economies of scale in production are developed (and this might somewhat counter the increase in the cost of production due to overbuild that accompanies larger scale). For solar, however, costs pose a significant problem, because capturing such a diffuse source of energy requires lots of durable and expensive raw materials, even in the absence of overbuild. For instance, solar panels require significant amounts of high-value metals like silver and copper (which are getting scarcer), as well as high-quality crystalline silicon that must be batch-produced in expensive clean rooms. These high capital costs are compounded by the fact that photovoltaic assembly plants are currently too small to support significant economies of scale that could bring down costs. As of 2006, the largest manufacturing plant of solar panels in the United States had the capacity to deliver only enough panels per year to produce about one hundred megawatts of power. Such a plant would take ten years to produce sufficient equipment to match the electricity output of a single large coal-fired power plant. It is hoped that manufacturing capacity will rise significantly, but these statistics illustrate what a steep hill solar power has to climb.[7]

Start-up costs for wind and solar are also high because they require so much space. While a run-of-the-mill coal-fired plant might have a footprint of 20 or 30 acres, a wind farm with half the generation capacity might cover close to a hundred square miles. A city of a million people would need 45 square miles of solar panels or 25 square miles of wind farms to power it. And providing electricity for the entire United States would conservatively require more than 12,500 square miles of solar panels. Centralized renewable power generation, which will be necessary to meet gaps left by fossil fuels, will therefore involve potentially steep land costs, huge legal, environmental, and social battles in securing the needed land, and enormous expenses associated with servicing such large areas with roads, security, and other infrastructure. So what about just adopting a decentralized model and having a solar panel on every rooftop? Unfortunately a roof panel here or there—or even a few hundred thousand roof panels here or there—is not going to make much of a difference. To give an idea of how monumental rooftop solar would have to be, a 2005 analysis found that to meet the primary energy consumption of the country with nothing but direct rooftop solar power would require construction of solar panels on every square foot of rooftop for every residential and commercial building in the country! This, of course, assumes that one could feasibly build solar panels and generate power on every rooftop, which is far from true.[8]

Another reason for the paucity of wind and solar sources (and why they fail the test of economic feasibility in so many geographic areas) is the inherent difficulty of distribution. Gas- or coal-fired power plants can easily be built next to an existing transmission line. The sites with the best solar and wind potential, on the other hand, are frequently inconveniently located far from existing lines, further burdening capital costs beyond overbuild. According to John Geesman, former commissioner of the California Energy Commission, "One of the challenges in developing these [renewable] resources is that they tend to be transmission-remote. . . . In California we expect to derive more than 4000 MW of new wind capacity from the Tehachapi area, but it will cost well in excess of a billion dollars to build the transmission system necessary to harvest that resource."[9] In other words, the supply of easy solar and wind energy that can be harvested near existing transmission infrastructure is relatively limited. Once those good sites are used up, exploiting the vast areas that don't currently have that access to transmission will require vast investments that will likely drive up the average cost of energy from these renewable technologies.

The linked problems of intermittency, overbuild, and distribution would be greatly mitigated if there was a cheap and effective way of storing energy produced by these renewable sources, then transporting and using it when needed. The most commonly touted example of this type of storage is pure hydrogen (although there are other prospective technologies, such as compressed-air energy storage and ultracapacitors, none is as feasible as hydrogen technology). Hydrogen is essentially a form of stored energy. It doesn't exist in its pure form in nature but can be created by running an electrical current through water using an electrolizer. The resulting hydrogen pairs carry the energy charge from the electrical current used to produce it. That hydrogen can then be transported to where it's needed and recombined with oxygen to yield an electrical current, with water as the only by-product. In addition to generating electrical current with no pollution, hydrogen has the big advantage of being directly usable as a vehicle fuel. Eventually cars could run on fuel cells that turn liquid hydrogen into electricity. These vehicles would get more than three times the fuel efficiency of a gasoline-powered car, because fuel is not combusted, so energy is not lost as heat. That technology is a long time off, however. In the near term, internal combustion engines could actually be modified to run on hydrogen, which would allow a transition to hydrogen fuel without requiring the entire automobile industry to dramatically retool.[10]

A hydrogen distribution system would turn the intermittency problem into a potential benefit. Under the current system, a wind farm or solar array might be producing excess power at a time when it's not being demanded by the grid. This energy simply gets wasted. Meanwhile, during times of peak demand, those renewable generation facilities might be producing very little. Hydrogen storage would allow solar and wind facilities to store any excess energy they generate during peak times for distribution to power generators when demand is high. This technology would dramatically increase the feasibility of wind and solar and greatly increase their potential market penetration. But is hydrogen storage really feasible?

For all intents and purposes, the infrastructure for hydrogen storage and transportation is not only nonexistent at this time, but it would be tremendously expensive and technically challenging to build. Although hydrogen could slash some of the costs associated with overbuild and intermittency, the costs of setting up a workable system could theoretically cost far more than the savings. Each step in the process of producing usable hydrogen comes with significant costs, like the electrolysis stage, which in 2005 was estimated to have an installed capital cost of $730 per kilowatt. For this reason, the US Department of Energy estimated that, as of 2005, a best-case scenario had the gasoline-gallon equivalent of wind-derived hydrogen costing about $5.70, although that is projected to come down to $3.10 by 2015.[11] Another significant cost—and uncertainty—in the hydrogen process is storage. Hydrogen gas is very hard to handle, leaks from just about any container, and is highly flammable and very diffuse. Even in compressed state, its volume is huge, requiring about ten times the volume per energy equivalent as gasoline. The solution to this problem is to supercool the gas into a liquid. But again, this requires the input of considerable amounts of energy, which, in turn, would raise the cost of production and greatly complicate its storage and safety, particularly in consumer end uses, like cars. So at this point, a hydrogen economy is a long way off and may, in fact, prove not to be feasible at the scale needed.

A final problem for wind and solar is that the ability to build wind turbines and solar panels is not limitless. Increasing constraints are being felt on the rare-earth minerals that are required to make solar and wind hardware—elements like dysprosium or neodymium, used in turbine magnets, and indium or tellurium, in photovoltaic films (there are seventeen such elements, some of which also are necessary for compact fluorescent bulbs and hybrid vehicles). Not only is there a limited supply of these deposits, but most deposits are found in China.

A December 2010 report from the US Department of Energy warned that because 96 percent of its rare-earth minerals come from China, the United States' renewable energy sector is extremely vulnerable. In fact, China controls about 95 percent of the world market. At the end of 2010, China announced that it would be slashing its export ceiling on these elements for the first half of 2011 by 35 percent from the previous year. Further, China plans to increase export taxes on many of them. Although there is a possibility that some domestic supplies will increase, the Department of Energy report predicts that at least five rare-earth elements will remain highly vulnerable to supply disruptions for the next fifteen years. The department report and other experts on the subject predict that shortages and significant price volatility are likely in the near future and that these could set back the manufacture of clean-energy technology. Although there are some deposits of these minerals in the United States and other countries outside of China, the report warns that significant hurdles exist for the small mining companies that are interested in developing these resources.[12]

Overall, then, solar and wind technologies have tremendous potential. The limitations pointed out in this interlude don't mean that solar and wind are doomed to fail. Both power sources will grow considerably. But the limitations are real, and they mean that these two technologies can go only so far in substituting for fossil fuels as they grow scarcer and pricier. Put simply, like all the other energy sources I've discussed, they're no silver bullet, and they won't keep energy eternally cheap. But they are an important piece of ammunition.

CHAPTER 10

The Very Efficient City

I t's the day after Thanksgiving as I start writing this final chapter and, like most Americans, I've got a lot of things to be thankful for—a great family, a wonderful community, a full pantry . . . and the list goes on.

I wouldn't actually say this at the dinner table, but I'm also thankful for cheap energy.

Everyone should be. Without the wealth of energy from fossil fuel, our guests wouldn't have been able to make the ten-mile trek to our Thanksgiving dinner; we wouldn't have California pecans for the pecan pie or the bottle of Cabernet Franc from France; we wouldn't have the electric light in the dining room or kitchen appliances that allowed us to make dinner for fifteen without servants; we wouldn't have the plasma TV that kept the kids entertained with *A Charlie Brown Thanksgiving*; and we wouldn't be able to afford a weather-tight house big enough to fit this many dinner guests.

In fact, without fossil fuels, our lifestyles would probably be a lot more like those of the Pilgrims who celebrated the first Thanksgiving almost 400 years ago. When they settled Plymouth, the Industrial Revolution was still nearly 150 years away. The fastest forms of transport at the time were no better than those of the Roman Empire, 1,500 years earlier. All of the food at the first Thanksgiving meal in 1621 was grown, hunted, fished, or gathered locally, and not because it was fashionable to "eat local." In fact, the lack of ground transportation alternatives meant that with the exception of a few manufactured goods brought from Europe, everything had to be local—fiber, building materials, heating fuel, and even the tallow that allowed for the minimal indoor lighting of the time.

Simply put, the Pilgrims and most others of their time were energy poor. They possessed the know-how to harvest energy only from running water, wind, biomass, and muscles (those of humans and draft animals). To visualize this, consider Buckminster Fuller's concept of "energy slaves," which is a little like horsepower, except that it quantifies the amount of work required for a task in terms of human rather than horse equivalents (a human harnesses between one-tenth and one-twentieth of a horsepower, enough to keep one seventy-five-watt lightbulb burning using a stationary cycle). In other words, it's a way of characterizing the amount of energy used to maintain a standard of living not in abstract units like calories or joules but in terms of human work and sweat.

In the distant past, humans could rely on only one energy slave—themselves. With the adoption of draft animals and advances in farming technology, the typical preindustrial agriculturalist was able to exploit around three to four energy slaves. In the modern-day United States, thanks to several centuries of advances in fossil—fuel technology, the typical person uses between 100 and 150 energy slaves. This jump in per capita energy use has been made possible by the recovery of fossil fuels on a massive scale, coupled with the development of technologies that efficiently put these fuels to work. In the United States in 2005, roughly 20 minutes of minimum-wage work purchased one gallon of gasoline, a fuel that contains an energy potential equivalent to 200 hours of a preindustrial farmhand's labor. Put these figures together, and it means that a Pilgrim farmer using draft animals could harness in 50 hours of work the amount of energy contained in just one measly gallon of gasoline.

The history of lighting is particularly illustrative. According to a study by the economist William Nordhaus, a typical tallow candle, a common source of lighting in the time of the Pilgrims, required lots of work to make and produced little light. In fact, it required about

190 times more work per unit of light emitted than a modern incandescent light (that number is 900 for a compact fluorescent bulb). Thus, 5 hours of physical labor would be required to make enough candles to produce the same amount of light provided by a 75-watt incandescent bulb shining for one hour. By comparison, the average American in the early twenty-first century requires less than a second's worth of work to obtain the same amount of light. If fossil fuels aren't something to be thankful for, I don't know what is.[1]

But we haven't been thankful or even aware as a society. Rather, as the fossil-fuel age has progressed, we've increasingly taken cheap and abundant energy for granted. The preindustrial past, with its low-energy lifestyle, seems quaint, alien, and unreal. The current status quo of cheap and abundant energy feels like a permanent state. But it's not. In fact, as the author Richard Heinberg points out, humanity's discovery of fossil fuels and the methods to exploit them was like winning the lottery—a stroke of good fortune, at least for a while. But to what extent can we expect these winnings to support us in the long term? The challenge in answering this is that we don't know how much of a balance is left in the account or, for that matter, how much we won in the first place. Estimates of remaining reserves vary considerably. When determining which reserves are economically or energetically feasible to recover, that variation becomes far wilder. With many signs pointing to imminent declines in global crude oil production—humanity's favorite fossil fuel—it's apparent that at least one account balance is getting too low to be relied on for much longer. Yet we're continuing to spend as if the account was endless. Maybe it's time for a Plan B.

Plan B means doing more with less. It means taking advantage of a wide array of available technologies and design approaches that are currently underutilized. It means getting more utility and more efficiency out of every ounce of fuel we burn or every photon of solar energy we convert to electricity. Oddly, the concept of efficiency has gotten a bad reputation among some economists and environmentalists because of a phenomenon known as the "Jevons paradox," first described by the nineteenth-century British political economist William Jevons.

He contended that when efficiency is increased in any resource-using process, downward pressure is exerted on the price of that resource—for instance, energy. And, because of the laws of supply and demand, reducing the price of something increases demand for it, which in turn increases its use. Often the increase in use due to this "rebound" effect is greater than the initial drop. This helps explain why a twenty-first-century person uses so much more energy than a seventeenth-century Pilgrim or an ancient Babylonian, even though our modern devices allow us to do a given job for a fraction of the energy.[2]

In the context of this book, I believe that Jevons' paradox is ir-relevant, because it assumes a fixed real price of energy and a limitless supply. If we instead see energy supplies as finite and prices as subject to long-term supply-driven increases, the paradox no longer applies, because the natural rise of prices more than offsets the price reductions due to efficiency gains. If the opposite is true—that efficiency gains are so huge that energy prices can continue to fall even in the face of dwindling supplies—then the whole premise of this book is moot. Of course, that possibility is extremely far-fetched. So, to set the record straight, efficiency, in the context of this book, is not about freeing up more energy so that we can buy more and bigger toys; rather, it is about finding a way to keep up with rising energy prices without dramati-cally compromising the way we live.

If we are to maintain our quality of life, there must be a dramatic ramping up of renewable energy resources, something that's outside the scope of this book. But the rate at which we're depleting fossil fuels is currently much faster than the rate at which we're developing new renewable generation capacity, and it's unlikely that the latter will over-take the former any time soon. That leaves energy efficiency to plug the gap, and it means that the rate at which efficiency measures are implemented must be at least as great as the rate of long-term increases in energy prices.

Just as oil and coal are hidden among geologic formations, sources of efficiency are hidden all around us.

Although lots of attention has gone into technological approaches to efficiency, I believe that the biggest source of potential efficiency gains is right under our noses, in the form of our communities. And I also believe that communities committed to restructuring themselves for energy efficiency will be at a big advantage over those that do not. If changes are put in place correctly, they will also make cities more desirable, vibrant, aesthetic, and healthy places to live.

But how do we get there from here? And whose responsibility is it to make these changes?

As energy prices rise, the quickest changes will be made by individuals. Previous experience has shown that individuals adapt quickly—we saw this clearly during the gasoline price spikes in 2008 and in the 1970s, when average vehicle miles traveled plummeted, car pooling increased, thermostats were turned down, and more fuel-efficient cars were purchased en masse. We're also seeing behavior shift quickly in response to rising water rates in places like Los Angeles. The dramatic drops there indicate how quickly adjustments can be made to daily water consumption without significantly affecting the quality of life and, consequently, how much water had been previously used unnecessarily.

Individuals will also increasingly retrofit their homes and appliances as energy prices rise, because the payback period on these investments will shorten and the rewards will grow. The same will be true for industry, their offices, and their manufacturing plants. And the economics will only get better as energy-efficient building practices become more widespread and volume brings down the costs of things like solar hot-water heaters or high-efficiency windows. This will happen even in the absence of government incentives. But that doesn't mean that incentives are unnecessary. First, the absence of incentives is inequitable. Upgrading housing takes capital, even if the payback is quick. Relying on the market alone would leave millions of lower-income homeowners behind. Further, landlords would have relatively little incentive to upgrade rental units whose utility costs are paid by renters, particularly in markets where housing supply is tight. Finally, policies and incentives will make the changeover happen a lot faster, particularly for single-family detached housing, which is at a disadvantage relative to multifamily buildings in terms of efficiency. That means massive amounts of energy that won't be used—and massive amounts of greenhouse gases that won't be emitted—in the interim.

There will no doubt be an important role for private companies that fund energy-saving retrofits, like Transcend Equity, described in Chapter 6. But no entity can possibly substitute for the federal government when it comes to the scale, scope, and reach of efficiency programs. As of late 2010, a wide range of federal incentives were attempting to accelerate in the development of energy-efficiency improvements. These included a 30 percent tax credit on residential insulation, windows, and sealing, capped at $1,500; a similar tax credit for efficient home heating and cooling equipment; a 30 percent tax credit (with no cap) for home or office solar photovoltaic, solar hot water, geothermal, or wind systems; a 30 percent credit (with a cap of $1,000 per installed kilowatt) for home or office fuel cells; a tax deduction of $1.80 per square foot for commercial buildings retrofitted to save at least 50 percent on energy use; and a 10 percent investment tax credit for commercial installation of combined heat and power. A dizzying array of state and local incentives can often significantly sweeten those at the federal level.

These are all valuable incentives, but they could be much better. Further, many of these credits are only temporary, which creates difficulties in scaling up for the contractors who perform this type of work. So, very simply, the federal government needs to invest far more in these incentives and turn them into dependable long-term programs. It will be costly, but the returns on this investment will be far higher than many other federal programs that currently receive orders of magnitude more funding.

Although I'm fairly confident that we'll see significant improvements to the United States' building stock, retrofitting entire metropolitan areas for lower energy metabolism is another matter. Among all the determinants of energy metabolism, this is where the largest savings in energy could be realized. But it's also the hardest to change, and for good reason; there are nearly forty thousand general-purpose local governments in the United States, all separately managing land use with minimal coordination or oversight.

Assuming that getting forty thousand governments to act in unison voluntarily is not realistic, there must be some higher level of government intervention. States are important, but getting fifty of them to act in unison may be almost as difficult as getting the local governments to do so. In my opinion, a federal role is warranted.

Today, a coherent or comprehensive federal policy on cities is nearly nonexistent, and urban issues rank close to the bottom of most people's national-level concerns. But it hasn't always been that way. Federal involvement in cities was considerable starting with the New Deal and going into the Carter administration, although increases in federal funding to municipalities were not always coordinated or accompanied by cohesive policy objectives and programs were often counterproductive. The increasingly chaotic and piecemeal nature of federal urban programs led Richard Nixon to call for a comprehensive national urban policy in 1969. This policy resulted in an increasingly federalist approach that gave local and state government greater discretionary control over programs and resources and shifted a larger share of those resources toward suburbs. The Carter administration called for a new urban policy, known as the New Partnership to Conserve America's Communities, based on targeted aid to places in distress. Although some elements of this plan were implemented, such as enactment of the Urban Development Action Grants program, changes to federal formula funding, and expansion of the reach of the Economic Development Administration, Carter's proposals proved to be "but a brief candle in the strong gusts of conflicting interests," according to William Barnes, of the National League of Cities.[3]

A lack of interest in cities, the failure of many urban programs, and larger problems like recession and inflation put urban policy on the back burner. By the end of Carter's term, his own Commission on a National Agenda for the Eighties conceded that the failure of most revitalization efforts indicated that programs should be aimed more at "people" rather than at "places." This view was taken up a notch in the Reagan administration, as federal programs to aid cities were dramatically downsized. Although Bill Clinton, during his 1992 presidential campaign, promised to change this trajectory with a revamped "urban policy," any attempt at this was abandoned after the administration changed its priority to deficit reduction. The new Republican majority ushered into Congress in 1994 even attempted to close down the Department of Housing and Urban Development (HUD). Nonetheless, Clinton's two HUD secretaries did their best to revitalize federal urban policy by increasing "empowerment zone" grants and by preparing biannual urban policy reports to Congress (a requirement stipulated by Congress in the early 1970s, but given relatively little attention by most administrations). After this, it's generally agreed that, with the exception of Al Gore's occasional mention of "livable cities" in the 2000 presidential election, urban issues for the most part disappeared from presidential discourse. As Barnes writes, "Under Democratic and Republican leaders alike, urban policy has receded into a Washington backwater, and it is unlikely to reemerge as a priority any time soon."[4]

Whether President Obama will reopen the question of federal urban policy has yet to be seen. Although he's called this issue "near and dear to my heart," it hasn't received much attention given two wars, deficits, a recession, and a Republican electoral juggernaut all dogging him. Obama's one major speech to date on urban affairs, however, does shed light on what he considers to be a politically feasible approach to the issue in this day and age.

First, his policy goals are framed in terms of making cities "competitive" and "hotbeds of innovation," buzzwords that signal a break from the traditional Democratic redistribution-oriented urban policy toward one based on economic competitiveness. Second, rather than just talking about cities, he repeatedly refers to "cities and metropolitan areas," perhaps a coded message suggesting that his urban policies are targeted not just at the traditional urban-core constituency but also at suburbs. Third, and logically following from the first two, Obama brings up the challenges associated with unchecked suburban and ex-urban growth—a viewpoint that is also evident in Clinton's Federal Urban Policy Report. He further recognizes that solutions to these problems have to be metropolitan in nature and involve the cooperation of cities and suburbs and that badly designed federal policies are partly to blame—a significant acknowledgment from an American President: "For too long, federal policy has actually encouraged sprawl and congestion and pollution, rather than quality public transportation and smart sustainable development." In response to this perceived need, Obama commissioned what he referred to in the speech as "the first comprehensive interagency review in thirty years on how the federal government approaches and funds urban and metropolitan issues." The review was intended to give a "concentrated, focused, strategic approach to federal efforts to revitalize our metropolitan areas." While this rhetoric may sound sweeping, his concrete proposals are in fact few and poorly funded: the Promise Neighborhoods program, which seeks to improve educational outcomes for disadvantaged children using block-by-block neighborhood strategies, was funded with only $10 million for the 2010 fiscal year; and the Choice Neighborhoods program, which seeks to foster locally initiated and planned affordable housing projects, received an estimated $65 million in funding for that same fiscal year.[5]

As Bruce Katz of the Brookings Institution and Hilary Silver of Brown University both point out, however, a look at Obama's budgetary priorities suggests an implicit "stealth urban policy." Bills like the American Recovery and Reinvestment Act of 2009 and the 2010 budget contain a large number of place-based urban investments designed to drive urban productivity, including investments in education, research and development, infrastructure, and energy efficiency—including a few big-ticket items like high-speed rail. Obama also requested a nearly 11 percent increase in the budget for HUD in 2010, not only to better respond to the housing crisis but also to further investments in areas like rental housing assistance, community block grants, sustainable neighborhood development, energy efficiency, and housing retrofits. He further secured almost $130 million for so-called Regional Innovation Clusters, a program ostensibly targeted at fostering energy-efficiency commercialization, but in the process designed to illustrate a new approach to government involvement in regional economic development. This program would do so through funding pilot "Energy Innovation Hubs," focused on developing new building-efficiency technologies. This, in turn, would promote the development of regional industrial clusters through the local dissemination of newly developed technologies and workforce education.[6]

Remote as the odds may seem, I do believe there will be windows of opportunity for crafting a much more far-reaching and meaningful national urban policy. And surprisingly, many of the needed changes can be accomplished without any major new programs or regulatory authority, but, rather, by reprioritizing investments in existing programs.

At the foundation of any federal urban policy should be a framework for regionalism, which I hope the previous chapter has indicated is worthwhile. Regionalism may sound like a radical departure from the status quo. Many Americans assume that any higher level involvement in local land use is contrary to the American system. But, as Peter Calthorpe and Bill Fulton point out, the federal government already plays at least an indirect role in almost all aspects of community building, through transportation and infrastructure funding, environmental protection, natural hazards protection, and housing policy, among other things. That means that the costs created by bad local planning are borne heavily by the federal government. For instance, uncoordinated local growth that leads to sprawl requires the federally funded construction of billions of dollars of suburban highway infrastructure to ease congestion—funding that otherwise would have gone to something else. If the government is expected to foot the bill for the consequences of poorly thought out local planning, then it should have some say in how those investments relate to local planning. Or, as Calthorpe and Fulton suggest, the federal government should have the right to ensure that its investments are cost-effective; when regions use federal investments effectively, they should be rewarded and when they squander investments on sprawl, they should be penalized. In particular, regions shouldn't be rewarded with increasing amounts of federal largess for sprawling more, as they are now.[7]

Calthorpe and Fulton point out a number of areas of regionalism in which the federal government is already involved but could be much more effective. One of these is locally relevant environmental policies. Acquisition of open space can be an important tool in defining the outer edges of metropolitan areas and setting ultimate "natural boundaries" to growth. In fact, in western states many federally owned parcels of lands contiguous to existing development are often swapped with local jurisdictions for more ecologically important but peripheral land—in the process, helping to establish a harder outer metropolitan border. This process has significant potential to influence urban form.

Various environmental statutes give the federal government regulatory leeway to influence metropolitan land use. The federal government could theoretically make greater use of the Clean Water Act to regulate land use near wetlands and watercourses. The Endangered Species Act also has significant potential to be used for wide-scale ecosystem management. The act does not specifically regulate land use, but designation of a species as endangered, coupled with mapping of core habitat areas, opens up the potential to either shut down development or trigger a Habitat Conservation Plan, which can in turn restrict development on designated lands. This could give regional land-use planning extra leverage in areas where many species are endangered. In California, there are so many endangered species that the state and federal governments have teamed up to address ecosystem-wide planning for affected areas through the Natural Communities Conservation Program. This approach is auspicious but has yet to be applied in a way that fundamentally stops sprawl or fragmentation of these habitats.

A second area of regionalism where Calthorpe and Fulton see promise is housing financing. They see federal housing finance and credit policies as fundamentally driving sprawl and limiting housing choices. Policies from federal entities like the Federal Housing Administration, the Veterans Administration, and the Federal National Mortgage Association (Fannie Mae) have largely promoted easy financing for suburban single-family homes, to the detriment of other housing types (for instance, in 1998, only 1.4 percent of Fannie Mae's loan purchases were for multifamily units). As this book has pointed out numerous times, mixed-used development is a key strategy toward lower energy metabolism, yet federal housing finance regulations do nothing to encourage private financing of these types of projects, leaving them as a miniscule fraction of the secondary mortgage market. As a result, obtaining financing for mixed-use projects can often be difficult. One approach to address this would be the creation of a federal entity similar to Fannie Mae that focuses on buying and reselling portfolios of loans specifically for mixed-use and multifamily real estate. This would redirect billions of dollars of private money into these very badly needed sectors of the real estate industry and could significantly change our cities.

A third area of federal involvement is urban revitalization. As I discussed in Chapter 8, no solution to energy metabolism will be complete without addressing the need for reinvestment and repopulation of the urban core. Most federal revitalization efforts since the New Deal have only made matters worse, by replacing historical structures with substandard and badly designed modern building stock, isolating neighborhoods, creating pockets of poverty, and leaving aesthetic blight. Existing programs within HUD, such as the Community Development Block Grants, the Hope VI housing program, and the federal Empowerment Zone/Enterprise Community program, are increasingly taking a holistic approach to integrated community planning, as opposed to the previous federal approach of dealing with problems in compartmentalized isolation. However, there is still a long way to go. Coordination must increase between federal revitalization efforts and other federal investments, such as transit, other infrastructure, and open space. Greater incentives are needed to bring more private capital into central urban redevelopment. And federal incentives should increase for central-city historic preservation.

Although all these federal roles are extremely important, they pale in comparison to the federal role in transportation. With more than $50 billion per year in federal funds going to metropolitan transportation projects throughout the country, it's not surprising that at the top of Calthorpe and Fulton's list of recommendations is reform in the way federal transportation projects are conceptualized and funded. This massive amount of money could theoretically go a long way toward curbing energy metabolism, but in reality it tends to do the opposite. Federally subsidized highways opened up huge areas of land to development by shrinking travel times and reducing the cost of transportation. All this newly available land gave millions of people the opportunity to own property and homes. But it also served to decentralize cities on a scale never before seen and it made the construction of traditional urban forms nearly impossible under current market conditions. Consequently, future transportation investments were directed away from transit toward maintaining capacity on suburban highways. Put another way, highway subsidies gave people far more access to highways than they were willing to pay for. If urban energy metabolism is to be seriously addressed, this has to change.

Federal transportation priorities are abundantly clear in the most recent (2005) transportation bill, known as SAFETEA-LU (The Safe, Accountable, Flexible, Efficient Transportation Equity Act: A Legacy for Users), under which more than 80 percent of funding went to highways and highway-related expenses, and less than 19 percent went to transit. In the blueprint for the subsequent reauthorization, which has yet to pass Congress as of the middle of 2011, the proposed percentage going to transit is about the same (although $8 billion was included as part of the 2009 American Recovery and Reinvestment Act for intercity rail projects, including high-speed rail). Clearly, the paradigm shift needed to fundamentally change transportation priorities is not going to happen through this legislation any time soon.

Making these needed changes is so difficult because most of our transportation funding now has to go to maintaining a minimum level of service on a highway system that was built over the last half century—a system that is now beginning to deteriorate rapidly. This problem is becoming particularly acute as the Federal Highway Trust Fund becomes increasingly insolvent. And as the nation's highway system ages, those funding needs only get larger. For instance, in 2004 the Federal Highway Administration estimated that 18 percent more funding was needed to keep up with minimum highway maintenance and construction than was needed in 2000.[8] Other funding mechanisms for subsidizing non-automobile modes have also been proposed recently, such as in the Clean, Low-Emission, Affordable, New Transportation Efficiency Act (CLEAN-TEA), which was introduced in Congress in 2009 but has yet to be passed. This act would have set aside 10 percent of funds generated through greenhouse gas emissions auctions under any future cap-and-trade system (which also has not been passed into law as of 2011) to fund a Low Greenhouse Gas Transportation Fund. Metropolitan planning entities would submit applications to the fund, and awards would be made based on projected reductions in greenhouse gas emissions—particularly in the areas of transit, travel demand management, bike-pedestrian facilities, and improvements to the walkability of urban areas. Although the passage of this act would be a positive step, the funding would likely represent only a fraction of what is needed to make any meaningful changes in urban energy metabolism.

The Clear Air Act, which gives the federal government some oversight of regional transportation issues, offers one potentially important mechanism by which federal transportation investments could be retargeted. Regions that are out of attainment with federal air-quality standards are subject to loss of federal highway funding, requirements for more expensive reformulated fuels, and increased permitting oversight for point source polluters. They can no longer freely spend federal transportation funds on new highways that induce sprawl without risking the loss of those funds. Clean Air Act attainment strategies have largely focused on tailpipe emission technology, but the US Environmental Protection Agency is increasingly realizing that, given the integral link between land use and transportation, long-term attainment strategies must also address metropolitan growth. The federal government could take a more active role in these nonattainment districts by requiring centralized transportation infrastructure, such as public transit, over traditional highways.

Another possibility that has been championed by an unlikely mix of both conservative and liberal economists is charging for the use of roads. The federal highway system was designed to operate without a user charge. While this had positive equity effects in terms of giving access to all regardless of income, many economists argue that the system provides more highway services than people are really willing to pay for. This in turn not only facilitated sprawl and congestion (the latter because roads are not rationed by price) but also resulted in insufficient revenues to cover the maintenance of this gargantuan system. It also undercuts the ability of public transit to operate without large subsidies, because subsidies toward automobile use—the main competing mode—are much greater than for transit. Charging for the use of our highways, therefore, seems a potentially auspicious approach to simultaneously addressing the linked problems of highway deterioration and overuse, transit underfunding, decentralizing land use, and energy consumption.

Although this approach certainly raises some equity concerns, it does elicit support from a mix of people on both sides of the ideological spectrum. It's popular with some liberals because it can help redirect subsidies and investments away from automobile infrastructure and toward more energy-efficient alternative modes. And it's popular with some conservatives because it's market-based. Robert Poole, of the libertarian Reason Foundation, wrote in a recent policy-position statement that "the federal government should aggressively lead a national effort to identify a replacement funding source consistent with the principle of users (and beneficiaries) pay. This likely means a move toward a distance-based fee as a replacement for the gas tax, bolstered in the near term by expanded use of tolling and pricing on major urban and inter-city roadways."[9]

A federal philosophy once prevailed that all federal highways would forever remain free; in recent years, however, federal involvement in toll roads and highway privatization has increased significantly. The 1991 Intermodal Surface Transportation Efficiency Act (ISTEA) allowed for 50 percent federal subsidies on both private and public toll roads. The Transportation Infrastructure Finance and Innovation Act (TIFIA) of 1998 introduced a way to use federal funds to leverage private capital to build revenue-producing roads. SAFETEA-LU then required the secretary of transportation to carry out fifteen case studies of toll collection on federal highways between 2005 and 2009. Next came the Department of Transportation's $1 billion Urban Partnerships Congestion Initiative, discussed in Chapter 7, which is implementing experimental congestion-charging schemes in a number of pilot cities. All of this indicates the government's growing acceptance of user fees on highways.[10] This philosophical shift may be exactly what is needed to counter the decades of subsidies that made long commutes and automobile dependence artificially cheap. It may be that the growing acceptance of road charges relates to new technology, like visual license plate recognition, which allows for easy and fair collection of revenues. Whatever the reason, the growing acceptance of this approach represents an incredible opportunity to dramatically shift the energy metabolism of our transport system.

All of these changes to existing federal investments will go a long way. However, if a coordinated regional approach is to be implemented in metropolitan areas, some fundamental institutional changes will also be needed. Top among those is the empowerment of regional governance agencies. Currently, the closest things to federally sanctioned regional planning agencies are the Metropolitan Planning Organizations (MPOs). But even though these agencies are instrumental in targeting federal transportation investments, they have no real influence over land use (with the exception of places like Portland, where they are involved with the urban growth boundaries). This is particularly problematic because transportation investments are generally in response to changes in land use. That is, if a sprawling pattern is allowed to occur in a region, highways are generally built after the fact to service that pattern.

Clearly then, there is a need for a system that coordinates transportation and land use. Such a system is already in place in most large European cities, where nationally empowered regional agencies set goals and requirements that smaller constituent planning entities must meet. To some this may seem like draconian national intervention, but most Europeans I've talked to don't seem to mind at all.

I spoke with Thomas Sick Nielsen, a planning professor at the University of Copenhagen, about the system there, in which the national Ministry of the Environment oversees planning for the greater Copenhagen area and administers its so-called Finger Plan, which gets its name from five radial lines of outward development. The plan stipulates an urban growth boundary and the location of preserved open space. It also provides some guiding principles: for example, that intensive land use be within a certain distance of public transit and that large commercial uses be clustered in a few main areas. Municipal governments are charged with implementing this regional plan and are given considerable leeway for interpretation, including doing their own zoning, but the ministry ensures that these local actions are consistent with the plan. Municipalities that don't agree with a specific stipulation can negotiate with the ministry, which allows for conflict resolution and public participation. However, the ministry is firm about not compromising on the fundamental tenets of the finger structure, and municipalities respect this. According to Nielsen, residents and municipalities are very deferential to the Finger Plan because of its long historical legacy (it originated in the early postwar period) and because "there's a strong tradition of maintaining the Finger Plan structure." Consequently, "we don't really see the American type of conflict where you have some low density suburban development that doesn't want to 'densify.'" Likewise, if someone owns private property that is designated as rural and hence has limited development potential, "it's accepted that it's OK. It has a good location, but it's rural—that's just the way it is." This ministerial oversight of land use is accepted "because it relates to competitiveness. It relates to maintaining a functional capitol area with attractive living conditions and good connections to the airport, and so forth. So it's accepted." In other words, Danes are aware that in sacrificing some autonomy over their land, they're actually getting something in return.[11]

Even though federally enabled regional planning is essential, the answers to urban energy metabolism clearly do not lie just at the federal level. Local, county, regional and state governments are all essential players in finding solutions to this issue. As Daniel Lerch, of the Post Carbon Institute, writes, when it comes to planning for climate and energy insecurity, "a municipal government, with its local experts, local accountability, local information and local interests, has the flexibility, capacity and motivation to address issues in ways that larger governments cannot."[12]

In fact, in today's environment of minimal federal involvement, local governments are increasingly finding themselves taking the lead when it comes to dealing with urban energy metabolism and the related problems of non-point-source greenhouse gas emissions reductions and peak oil preparedness. The Post Carbon Cities initiative of the Post Carbon Institute keeps a database of actions that these governments have taken in response to climate and energy insecurity.[13] Among these are the creation of Peak Oil task forces and the writing of Peak Oil preparedness reports in numerous US cities (e.g., San Francisco; Portland, Oregon; Austin, Texas; Lawrence, Kansas; and Bloomington, Indiana). Dozens of cities have also undertaken climate-change initiatives that have the potential to positively affect energy metabolism, since reducing carbon emissions essentially means reducing energy consumption. Then there are also the thousands of small local actions that are not explicitly related to peak oil or climate change but that help address these problems regardless, from installing bike infrastructure to green building ordinances to mixed-used zoning.

These actions are far too numerous to discuss here, but I hope I've illustrated at least a good cross-section of them—whether they relate to buildings, transportation, neighborhoods, or whole regions. I hope I've also demonstrated that cities can't make needed changes entirely on their own, because land use is regional, and individual cities don't control regions. Energy metabolism is a problem at all levels of society, and everyone needs to contribute to the solution.

As I write this, we're seeing the fallout from previous energy price spikes and the unraveling of a dysfunctional housing market, as places like Rio Vista and Antillean Isles are outright abandoned. In hindsight, we're also seeing the links between energy, housing, and the economy. Cheap energy and cheap credit fueled the construction of too much housing that was too far away from employment and essential services. The overconstruction of housing in turn contributed to the bottom falling out of the housing market, deflating values, and precipitating the current recession we're in. When the house of cards fell, suburbs and exurbs were left with the biggest mess to clean up, in the form of untold numbers of foreclosed properties and abandoned developments.

Current federal policies would do little to prevent this from happening again. Although lending standards have been tightened up somewhat, if the housing market were to heat up once more, there would be little to stop the kind of reckless mass development that drove us into recession. Higher fuel prices—which are likely to follow in the wake of economic recovery—will certainly attenuate that effect. But if we rely simply on increased energy prices to regulate the outward expansion of cities, there will be a tremendous squandering of resources as we invest in areas that have no long-term potential for sustainable settlement—resources that could have gone into making established settlements more efficient and livable in the long term. Furthermore, allowing such boom-bust cycles to occur only adds to instability in the economy.

The fundamental quandary is that heading off these problems requires decisive action now, but taking such action is difficult because it's costly and requires anticipating a problem that is still hypothetical. It's possible, for instance, that current increases in energy prices are just a temporary blip and that long-term prices could actually come down. Highly efficient cars may be invented that use minimal amounts of energy and newly discovered deposits of fossil fuels could boost supplies.

These optimistic outcomes are what most of society has assumed will happen when it comes to energy. And the optimists may be right. But, as I've laid out in the Interludes of this book, the evidence to the contrary is strong. To me, doing nothing presents a far bigger gamble than being overly proactive.

And even if the expectations of the optimists are exceeded and we learn how to make unlimited, costless energy from sand, the investment made in this resiliency will not be in vain, for communities that are energy efficient are, I believe, also better places to live. Even if a two-hour commute involved no fuel cost, it would still take two hours. Even if natural gas cost nothing, a drafty house is still less pleasant and less reliable. Whether we frame the goal in terms of quality of life, economic development, or energy efficiency, I think the result will fundamentally be the same. Good cities are good places to live. But they take work.

Notes

INTRODUCTION

1. The final stretch of the Los Angeles Aqueduct is also here. As is pointed out in Chap. 2, the Los Angeles Aqueduct does not require energy for pumping water uphill, though it did take vast amounts of energy to build. LA's other two major aqueducts do require energy for pumping.

2. Christopher Kennedy, John Cuddihy, and Joshua Engel-Yan, "The Changing Metabolism of Cities," *Journal of Industrial Ecology* 11, no. 2 (2007); Halla R. Sahely, Shauna Dudding, and Christopher A. Kennedy, "Estimating the Urban Metabolism of Canadian Cities: Greater Toronto Area Case Study," *Canadian Journal of Civil Engineering* 30, no. 2 (2003); Peter Newman, "Sustainability and Cities: Extending the Metabolism Model," *Landscape and Urban Planning* 44, no. 4 (1999); Abel Wolman, "The Metabolism of Cities," *Scientific American* 213, no. 3 (1965). Put simply, urban metabolism looks at the inputs of resources and energy relative to the outputs of productivity and waste. When compared on a per person basis, it provides a way of comparing the efficiency of cities.

3. International Energy Agency (IEA) Statistics Division, 2007. Energy Balances of OECD Countries, 2008 ed., and Energy Balances of Non-OECD Countries, 2007 ed. (Paris: IEA). Available at http://data.iea.org/ieastore/default.asp.

4. Phillip Schneider, phone interview with the author, October 7, 2009.

5. Jeanette Boner, "Dealing with the Dead: County Begins to Address 'Zombie Subdivisions,'" *Valley Citizen*, August 18, 2010. http://valleycitizen .com/stories_news_detail.php?pkStories=243.

6. Matthew Haggman, "Housing Crisis Turns South Dade Suburbs into Ghost Towns," *Miami Herald*, May 24, 2009. The figure of one hundred thousand dollars is based on a quotation in the Haggman article from Ronald Shuffield, president of Wooten Maxwell Brokerage.

7. Carolina Reid, "Shuttered Subdivisions: REOS and the Challenges of Neighborhood Stabilization in Suburban Cities" (Boston: Federal Reserve Banks of Boston and Cleveland and the Federal Reserve Board, 2010).

8. Joe Cortright, "Driven to the Brink: How the Gas Price Spike Popped the Housing Bubble and Devalued the Suburbs" (Chicago: CEOs for Cities, 2008).

9. The 2010 Federal Reserve study cited is Raven Molloy and Hui Shan, "The Effect of Gasoline Prices on Household Location" (Washington, D.C.: Federal Reserve Board Division of Research and Statistics and Monetary Affairs, 2010). This paper states that in the long term gasoline prices have less impact on suburban housing prices than on urban housing prices. However, this is mostly consistent with Cortright's results, because it is a longer-term study, and in the longer term, supply adjustments can attenuate price reductions. That is, reductions in suburban construction constrain the supply, which serves to limit the loss in value relative to more urban areas. Consistent with this, they found that metropolitan areas without the supply-constraining response did experience greater suburban price reductions relative to urban. Whether gas prices are found to reduce construction levels or prices in the suburbs, the interpretation of the results is largely the same: demand has gone down. The quotation at the end of the paragraph is from Glenn Setzer, "What Do High Gas Prices Mean for the Housing Market?," *Mortgage News Daily*, April 26, 2006.

10. John Norquist, phone interview with the author, June 22, 2010; all subsequent quotations from Norquist are from this interview.

CHAPTER 1: The 68° City

1. Pat McGlothan, as quoted in Jennifer Warren, "A Company Town Changes Companies—Mining: The Sale of Trona's Major Employer Has Brought Anxiety—and Hope—to the Mojave Desert Town," *Los Angeles Times*, December 13, 1990.

2. M. L. Rafferty Jr., "Schoolhouse in the Inferno," *Saturday Evening Post*, December 5, 1942, 87.

3. For a definition of "Sun Belt," see Robert Lang and Kristopher Rengert, "The Hot and Cold Sunbelts: Comparing State Growth Rates, 1950–2000," Fannie Mae Foundation Census Note (Washington, D.C.: Fannie Mae Foundation, 2001). This study from the Census defines the Sun Belt as warm-weather areas including all states south of 37° latitude: North Carolina, South Carolina, Florida, Georgia, Alabama, Tennessee, Mississippi, Louisiana, Arkansas, Texas, Oklahoma, New Mexico, Arizona, Clark County (Las Vegas) in Nevada, and the ten southernmost counties in California.

4. John Reese, "The Air-Conditioning Revolution," *Saturday Evening Post*, July 9, 1960, 47.

5. Jonah Goldberg, "If You Thought I Hated DC Before . . ." *National Review Online*, July 6, 1999.

6. Information on the conference sponsored by *House and Home* is from Marsha E. Ackermann, *Cool Comfort: America's Romance with Air-Conditioning* (Washington, D.C.: Smithsonian Institution Press, 2002), 117. Reference is made to the June 1952 issue of *House and Home*, 82–111. Information on air-conditioning for the Republican National Convention, the 1952 poll of homebuilders, and the use of air-conditioning prior to 1952 is from Rufus Jarman, "They're Trying to Make Summer Extinct," *Saturday Evening Post*, June 6, 1953, 142–43.

7. The section on driving is from Theodore Pratt, "How to Keep Cool in a Car," *New York Times*, July 5, 1953. The advertisement for refrigeration is from Philip Kerby, "Fires of Heaven," *Saturday Evening Post*, June 15, 1935, 39.

8. The quote from Dick Hughes is found in Arnold Nicholson, "They Lock Hot Weather Out," *Saturday Evening Post*, June 16, 1956, 132. The figures on air-conditioning adoption in Texas and the South in 1966 and 1970 are from Raymond Arsenault, "The End of the Long Hot Summer: The Air-Conditioner and Southern Culture," *Journal of Southern History* 50, no. 4 (1984): 610, 613, based on data from the US Census. The anecdote about keeping car windows rolled up is from Wade Greene, "Air-Conditioning," *New York Times*, July 14, 1974. The 2005 figure on southern air-conditioning is from Stephanie Battles, "Trends in Residential Air-Conditioning Usage from 1978 to 1997" (Washington, D.C.: Energy Information Administration, 2000), http://www.eia.doe.gov/emeu/consumptionbriefs/recs/actrends/recs_ac_trends.html#consumption.

9. Editorial, "The Air-Conditioned Census," *New York Times*, September 6, 1970.

10. Quoted in Joe Alex Morris, "Arizona: Air-Conditioned Desert," *Saturday Evening Post*, June 17, 1961, 31.

11. The figure on Phoenix's manufacturing income is from Daniel Noble, "Motorola Expands in Phoenix," *Arizona Business and Economics Review*, June 1954, 1–2. The Motorola quotation is found in Michael F. Logan, *Desert Cities: The Environmental History of Phoenix and Tucson* (Pittsburgh: University of Pittsburgh Press, 2006), 147.

12. US Department of Commerce National Oceanic and Atmospheric Administration National Environmental Satellite, Data, and Information

Service. Historical Climatology Series 5–1 and 5–2, September 2009, http://lwf.ncdc.noaa.gov/oa/documentlibrary/hcs/hdd.200707–200904 .pdf.

13. Robert Quayle and Henry Diaz, "Heating Degree Day Data Applied to Residential Heating Energy Consumption," *Journal of Applied Meteorology* 19, no. 3 (1980); US Energy Information Administration, Residential Energy Consumption Survey, 2005, http://www.eia.doe.gov/emeu/recs/.

14. Figures on energy savings are from Robert Ayres and Edward Ayres, *Crossing the Energy Divide* (Upper Saddle River, N.J.: Pearson Prentice Hall, 2010), 135. Cost estimates are from Tom Zeller, "Can We Build a Brighter Shade of Green?" *New York Times*, September 25, 2010.

15. Ackermann, *Cool Comfort*, 121. This passage describes the special supplement to the March 1954 issue of *House and Home*

16. "Climate Risk Information" (New York: New York City Panel on Climate Change, 2009); Stanton Hadley et al., "Responses of Energy Use to Climate Change: A Climate Modeling Study," *Geophysical Research Letters* 33 (2006).

17. A. John Arnfield, "Two Decades of Urban Climate Research: A Review of Turbulence, Exchanges of Energy and Water, and the Urban Heat Island," *International Journal of Climatology* 23, no. 1 (2003); Timothy R. Oke, "The Energetic Basis of the Urban Heat-Island," *Quarterly Journal of the Royal Meteorological Society* 108, no. 455 (1982); *Boundary Layer Climates*, 2nd ed. (London: New York: Methuen, 1987); "Urban Climates and Global Environmental Change," in *Applied Climatology: Principles and Practice*, ed. Russell D. Thompson and A. H. Perry (London: New York: Routledge, 1997).

18. Hashem Akbari, M. Pomerantz, and Haider Taha, "Cool Surfaces and Shade Trees to Reduce Energy Use and Improve Air Quality in Urban Areas," *Solar Energy* 70, no. 3 (2001); Hashem Akbari et al., "Cooling Our Communities: A Guidebook on Tree Planting and Light-Colored Surfacing" (Washington, D.C.: US Environmental Protection Agency, Office of Policy Analysis, Climate Change Division, 1992); R. Giridharan and M. Kolokotroni, "Urban Heat Island Characteristics in London during Winter," *Solar Energy* 83 (2009).

19. "Twice the Power at Double the Efficiency: Providing Secure Energy in Texas with CHP" (Houston: Texas Combined Heat and Power Initiative, 2007).

20. The figure of $10 to $35 comes from Haider Taha, Steven Konopacki, and Sasa Gabersek, "Modeling the Meteorological and Energy Effects of

Urban Heat Islands and Their Mitigation: A Ten-Region Study" (Berkeley, Calif.: Lawrence Berkeley National Laboratory, 1996), as referenced in Hashem Akbari, "Shade Trees Reduce Building Energy Use and CO_2 Emissions from Power Plants," *Environmental Pollution* 116 (2002), S121. The 3 percent national reduction figure is from Akbari, Pomerantz, and Taha, "Cool Surfaces and Shade Trees," 301. The figures on northern California savings and the two hundred dollars per tree are from Akbari et al., "Peak Power and Cooling Energy Savings of Shade Trees," *Energy and Buildings* 25, no. 2 (1997). Other sources include Akbari, "Shade Trees Reduce Building Energy Use"; Akbari et al., "Cooling Our Communities."

21. Cynthia Rosenzweig, William Solecki, and Ronald Slosberg, "Mitigating New York City's Heat Island with Urban Forestry, Living Roofs, and Light Surfaces" (Albany: New York State Energy Research and Development Authority, 2006).

22. Figures on the proportion of electricity used for cooling in the UAE and in Masdar City and on demand-side measures are from an interview with Afshin Afshari given in Gerard Hope, "Still Cool," ConstructionWeekOnline.com, November 14, 2010. Information on solar energy production and cooling technology in Masdar City is from Tony Seba, *Solar Trillions: Seven Market and Investment Opportunities in the Emerging Clean Energy Economy* (San Francisco: Tony Seba Group, 2010), 119–22. Estimates of the range of energy savings for district cooling comes from my review of a number of reports, technical documents, and interviews. Different cities have had very different realized savings with district cooling. For instance, in Stockholm it is estimated at 80 percent (see http://www.logstor.com/showpage.php?pageid=5589898), while in Qatar it has been found to be 60 percent (see http://www.powergenworldwide.com/index/display/articledisplay.8258028075.articles.powergenworldwide.distributed-generation.district-energy.2010.11.district-cooling_.html).

23. Goldberg, "If You Thought I Hated DC Before . . ."

24. Arsenault, "The End of the Long Hot Summer," 628.

25. Reese, "The Air-Conditioning Revolution," 100.

INTERLUDE 1: The Big Picture on Rising Energy Prices

1. Jeff Rubin, *Why Your World Is About to Get a Whole Lot Smaller* (New York: Random House, 2009), 20.

2. The quotation from the military report is from the US Joint Forces Command, "The Joint Operating Environment" (Suffolk, Va.: US Joint Forces

Command, 2010), 29; Jeroen van der Veer, quoted during the Asia Oil and Gas Conference in Malaysia, June 8, 2009. The Nobuo Tanaka quotation is from a speech given at the Bridge Forum Dialogue, Luxembourg, April 13, 2011, as quoted in International Energy Agency, "The Age of Cheap Energy Is Over, IEA Executive Director Warns," April 21, 2011, http://www.iea.org/index_info.asp?ID=1928.

3. Carlos Caminada and Jeb Blount, "Petrobras' Tupi Oil Field May Hold Nine Billion Barrels," *Bloomberg*, November 8, 2007.

4. The statement on replacing all fossil fuels with ten thousand nuclear reactors is from the Nobel Prize–winning chemist Richard Smalley, as given in a speech at Rice University in 2004. The statement on wind turbines is from Paul Roberts, *The End of Oil: On the Edge of a Perilous New World* (Boston: Houghton Mifflin, 2005), 205.

CHAPTER 2: The Very Thirsty City

1. Henry A. Wise, *Los Gringos: Or, an Inside View of Mexico and California* (New York: Baker and Scribner, 1849), 39.

2. Zev Yaroslavsky, phone interview with the author, June 23, 2010; all subsequent quotations from Yaroslavsky are from this interview.

3. Actual consumption during the first 278-mile section of the aqueduct with its 6 pumping stations is 3.95 billion kWh. This calculation is based on the US Energy Information Administration estimate that California households use 7,000 kWh annually, considerably less than the national average of 11,000 kWh. Energy consumption data are from California Department of Water Resources, *Management of the California State Water Project*, Bulletin 132-05 (Sacramento: California Department of Water Resources, 2006); all power figures are from 2004 data. Edmonston uses 2.23 billion kWh. See http://www.hwd.com/news/griffenobit.htm. In terms of hydroelectric recovery, of 8.65 billion kWh used for the entire pumping system, my calculations based on data from the California Department of Water Resources indicate that only 2.15 billion kWh are recovered after pumping water uphill. The California Department of Water Resources literature accounts for additional hydroelectric power generated before any water is pumped uphill—that is, from dams in the Sierra Nevada Mountains, where the initial water is impounded—as if it were recovery power for the California Water Project. However, from the perspective of evaluating energy efficiency, this is misleading, because that power would have been generated regardless of whether the Cali-

fornia Aqueduct existed and it is therefore not "recovered" as a result of any uphill pumping. In total, to get from the Sacramento River to the crest of the Tehachapi Mountains, one year's worth of water requires the equivalent energy used by 1.2 million California households—just slightly less than the number in the city of Los Angeles (1.275 million, according to the 2000 Census). If you subtract the power that is recovered after uphill pumping has occurred, there is a net consumption of 6.4 billion kWh, or the equivalent of the power for 900,000 average California homes.

4. Gary Klein, phone interview with the author, March 11, 2009. This figure includes all energy use in the water system, including filtration, treatment, and pumping within cities. Northern California is estimated at 4,000 kWh per megagallon; Southern California at 13,000. The average water energy cost per megagallon for the US is approximately 5,000 kWh. The amount of energy that each additional 1,000 feet of lift adds is about 4,000 kWh per megagallon. The contention that water delivery is the third largest energy need for households comes from Robert Wilkinson, "Methodology for Analysis of the Energy Intensity of California's Water Systems" (Berkeley, Calif.: Lawrence Berkeley Laboratory, 2000).

5. The reported extra costs during the 2000–2001 California energy crisis are according to http://www.reason.org/apr2005/water_wastewater.shtml. The additional pumping costs did not translate into higher prices for ratepayers at the time, because the State Water Project is also a hydroelectric generator, so they also benefit from higher electricity prices. Hence they could at least partially offset their losses due to added pumping costs by gains in electricity-generating revenue. However, if price increases were long-term, unlike in 2000–2001, it is very likely that the added cost would be passed on to ratepayers, as the State Water Project uses more energy than it produces. In other words, its gains as a producer can only offset its added costs as a consumer for a short time. On the point about demand and supply, demand is estimated to outstrip supply by 1.6 million acre-feet annually. Projections are that demand will increase by 15 percent by 2030. In terms of decreased supply from global climate change, according to Stephen Saunders et al., "Hotter and Drier: The West's Changed Climate" (Denver: Rocky Mountain Climate Organization, 2008), the western United States is warming 50 percent faster than the global average, and the Colorado Basin, from which Los Angeles gets much of its water, is warming more than twice as fast. Warming in turn leads to less snowpack, earlier snowmelt, less summer runoff, more evaporation, and

more drought. It is estimated that of the 1.25 million acre-feet of water that Southern California gets from the Colorado River, recent droughts have reduced that amount by 500,000 acre-feet per year.

6. Information on the energy costs of desalination and its limitations is from Quirin Schiermeier, "Purification with a Pinch of Salt," *Nature* 452, no. 7185 (2008): 260–61.

7. Natural Resources Defense Council, "In Hot Water" (2007), http://www .nrdc.org/globalWarming/hotwater/hotwater.pdf. Also see Southern California Association of Governments, "State of the Region" (2006). According to this, consumption levels were almost the same as those in 1990, despite the addition of 3 million people.

8. Western Resource Advocates, "Smart Water: A Comparative Study of Urban Water Use Efficiency across the Southwest" (Boulder: Western Resource Advocates, 2003). Note that California water-use estimates are based on 2006 data and that estimates from other cities are based on 2003–4 data. The German figure is from Statistisches Bundesamt Deutschland, Press Release 377/2009-10-02, and is converted to per household consumption using average German household size of 2.2. Slip 'n Slide is a popular water toy from Wham-O.

9. Douglas E. Kupel, *Fuel for Growth: Water and Arizona's Urban Environment* (Tucson: University of Arizona Press, 2003), 128.

10. Craig Childs, "Phoenix Falling?" *High Country News*, April 13, 2007, 15.

11. The figure on the relative amount of water in Phoenix's reservoir versus Tucson's is from Michael F. Logan, *Desert Cities: The Environmental History of Phoenix and Tucson* (Pittsburgh: University of Pittsburgh Press, 2006), 77. Information on Tucson groundwater pumping is from Kupel, *Fuel for Growth*, 107, 121.

12. From Ray W. Wilson, *Report on Verde River Water Problem*, July 20, 1951, City of Phoenix Archives; as quoted in Kupel, *Fuel for Growth*, 159.

13. Michael Hanemann, "The Central Arizona Project," working paper (University of California, Berkeley Department of Agricultural and Resource Economics, 2002). The project cost over $5 billion.

14. The estimate of 210,000 households is based on the fact that Central Arizona Project's pumps use about 2.8 million megawatts per year. Average residential electricity use is based on the Energy Information Agency's estimate of 1,118 kWh per month for the typical Arizona household. Estimates of residential water use to get the household energy share are from Peter W. Mayer, William B. DeOreo, and AWWA Research Foundation, *Residential End Uses of Water* (Denver: AWWA Research Foundation and American

Water Works Association, 1999). This estimate of water use is based on both indoor and outdoor use. Electricity use is based on the Energy Information Agency's estimate of 1,118 KwH per month for the typical Arizona household. According to the CAP rate schedule at http://www.cap-az.com/includes/media/docs/5-b-ii-Revised-Rate-Schedule-Combined.pdf, the 2010 rate is set at $118 per acre-foot, while the standard pumping energy rate for most clients is set at $45. For out-of-state clients who are part of the water bank, like California and Nevada, this rate is considerably higher.

15. Shaun McKinnon, phone interview with the author, October 21, 2009; all subsequent quotations from McKinnon are from this interview. While per capita water use is high in Phoenix, it is much lower in Tucson because that city had already achieved significant water-use reductions long before the CAP. Because of its limited reservoir capacity and lowering water tables, which led to increased groundwater pumping costs, Tucsonans became accustomed to paying higher water rates and, hence, to enjoying cacti in their front yards instead of Kentucky Bluegrass.

16. California Department of Water Resources, *Management of the California State Water Project*, Bulletin 132–06 (Sacramento: California Department of Water Resources, 2007). According to this bulletin, in 2005 energy generated for the SWP included 1.83 MWh from the Hyatt-Thermalito Hydro-power complex, 1.74 million MWh from recovery plants along the California Aqueduct, and 1.58 million MWh from the Gardner coal-fired power plant.

17. This viewpoint is expressed in a white paper by CAP entitled "The Navajo Generating Station." July 23, 2009, http://www.cap-az.com/includes/media/docs/Navajo-Generating-Station-White-Paper--2-.pdf.

18. Energy Information Administration, "Energy Market and Economic Impacts of Hr 2454, the American Clean Energy and Security Act of 2009" (2009). The energy component of the cost of an acre-foot is about $50, while the total cost is about $120 according to CAP's rate schedule; see http://www.cap-az.com/includes/media/docs/5-b-ii-Revised-Rate-Schedule-Combined.pdf.

19. Matthew Power, "Peak Water: Aquifers and Rivers Are Running Dry: How Three Regions Are Coping," *Wired*, April 21, 2008.

20. Shaun McKinnon, "Five Cities Cash in on Wastewater Deal," *ArizonaCentral.com*, April 1, 2010, http://www.azcentral.com/business/news/articles/2010/04/01/20100401water-paloverde0401.html.

21. Cynthia Barnett, *Mirage: Florida and the Vanishing Water of the Eastern U.S* (Ann Arbor: University of Michigan Press, 2007).

22. H. Eschebach, "Die Gebrauchswasserversorgung Des Antiken Pompeii," *Antike Welt* 2 (1979), as cited in Henning Fahlbusch, "Municipal Water Supply in Antiquity," Roman Aqueducts website, http://www.romanaqueducts .info/webteksten/waterinantiquity.htm.

INTERLUDE 2: Oil Depletion in the United States

1. Paul Roberts, *The End of Oil: On the Edge of a Perilous New World* (Boston: Houghton Mifflin, 2005), 41.

CHAPTER 3: The Very Mobile City

1. Duncan Crary, phone interview with the author, January 22, 2010.
2. The figure relating gasoline consumption to a football field is from "Household Vehicle Energy Use: Latest Data and Trends," US Energy Information Administration (2005). Data relating US consumption to other countries are from the International Energy Agency (IEA) Statistics Division, as summarized in the World Resources Institute's website at earthtrends.wri.org/text/energy-resources/variable-291.html. Sources include the following IEA data sets: Energy Balances of OECD Countries (2008 ed.) and Extended Balances and Energy Balances of Non-OECD Countries (2007 ed.), available at http://data.iea.org/ieastore/default.asp.
3. The "horse and buggy" quote is from Michael P. Regan, "Segway Sets Course for Stock Market," *USA Today*, May 5, 2006. The term "symbol of dorkiness" appears in http://news.cnet.com/8301-17938_105-9670835-1 .html.
4. United State Census Bureau, *American Community Survey*, table S0801 (Washington, D.C.: 2008).
5. Ibid.
6. "Most of Us Still Drive to Work—Alone," US Census Bureau Press Release, June 13, 2007, http://www.census.gov/newsroom/releases/archives/ american_community_survey_acs/cb07-cn06.html.
7. Jeffrey R. Kenworthy, *Indicators of Transport Efficiency in 37 Global Cities: A Report for the World Bank* (Perth, W.A.: Institute for Science and Technology Policy, Murdoch University, 1997); Peter Newman and Jeffrey R. Kenworthy, *Sustainability and Cities: Overcoming Automobile Dependence* (Washington, D.C.: Island Press, 1999). Note that data are from the early 1990s. Unfortunately no newer data on comprehensive international transit ridership are easily available.

8. Data are from Jeffrey R. Kenworthy, Felix B. Laube, and Peter Newman, *An International Sourcebook of Automobile Dependence in Cities, 1960–1990* (Boulder: University Press of Colorado, 1999), and from the US Census Bureau, *American Community Survey*.

9. Daniel B. Hess, "Effect of Free Parking on Commuter Mode Choice: Evidence from Travel Diary Data," *Transit Planning, Intermodal Facilities, and Marketing*, no. 1753 (2001).

10. Hannah Beech, "The Capital of Gridlock," *Time*, February 8, 2008, http://www.time.com/time/specials/2007/article/0,28804,1709961_1711305_1722542,00.html.

11. The first quotation is from Peter Gordon and Harry Richardson, "Prove It: The Costs and Benefits of Sprawl," *Brookings Review*, September 1998, 25. The second is from Peter Gordon and Harry Richardson, "Are Compact Cities a Desirable Planning Goal?" *Journal of the American Planning Association* 63, no. 1 (1997): 98. See also Peter Gordon and Harry Richardson, "The Sprawl Debate: Let Markets Plan," *Publius* 31, no. 3 (2001), for their discussion of the evidence of the density-congestion relationship.

12. Quotation is from Anthony Downs, *Still Stuck in Traffic: Coping with Peak-Hour Traffic Congestion*, James A. Johnson Metro Series (Washington, D.C.: Brookings Institution Press, 2004), 204.

13. Information on the change in average daily vehicle miles traveled comes from Pat Hu, "Summary of Travel Trends: 2001 National Household Travel Survey" (Washington, D.C.: US Department of Transportation Federal Highway Administration, 2004), 12. US land-consumption data come from the US Department of Agriculture Natural Resources Conservation Service's 1997 National Resources Inventory, http://www.nrcs.usda.gov/technical/nri/. Information on foreign comparisons is from Newman and Kenworthy, *Sustainability and Cities*, 84, 94.

14. David Schrank and Tim Lomax, "2009 Urban Mobility Report" (College Station: Texas Transportation Institute, Texas A&M University, 2009).

15. Joe Cortright, "Measuring Urban Transportation Performance" (Chicago: CEOs for Cities, 2010), http://www.ceosforcities.org/work/driven-apart.

16. See R. Cervero, "Road Expansion, Urban Growth, and Induced Travel: A Path Analysis," *Journal of the American Planning Association* 69, no. 2 (2003), for a study of induced growth (increased development) and induced demand (increased traffic volumes) on highways due to road improvements.

17. The estimate of a 25 to 40 percent reduction in miles traveled and a 70 percent decrease in driving trips is based on studies by Robert Dunphy and Kimberly Fisher, "Transportation, Congestion, and Density: New

Insights," *Transportation Research Record*, 1552 (1996); John Holtzclaw, "Explaining Urban Density and Transit Impacts" (San Francisco: Natural Resources Defense Council and Sierra Club, 1991); John Holtzclaw, "Using Residential Patterns and Transit to Decrease Auto Dependence and Costs" (San Francisco: Natural Resources Defense Council and California Home Energy Efficiency Rating Systems, 1994); and Niovi Karathodorou, Daniel Graham, and Robert Noland, "Estimating the Effect of Urban Density on Fuel Demand," *Energy Economics* 32 (2010): 91. The finding of a 2.5 percent increase in miles driven is from *Why Are the Roads So Congested?* (Washington D.C.: Surface Transportation Policy Project, 1999).

18. The first study cited is Edward Glaeser and Matthew Kahn, "The Greenness of Cities," John F. Kennedy School of Government Policy Briefs (Cambridge: Harvard University, 2008). The interpretation I use of that study's results is from Edward Glaeser, *The Triumph of the City* (New York: Penguin, 2011). The second is Karathodorou et al., "Estimating the Effects of Urban Density on Fuel Demand." The relationship between density and per capita fuel use and data on New York area are from Newman and Kennedy, *Sustainability and Cities*, 100–102. Other relevant works by Peter Newman and Jeffrey Kenworthy, with similar findings, include *Cities and Automobile Dependence: A Sourcebook* (Aldershot, UK: Gower, 1989) and "Gasoline Consumption and Cities: A Comparison of US Cities with a Global Survey," *Journal of the American Planning Association* 55, no. 1 (1989).

19. Among the studies critical of Newman and Kenworthy's earlier work are J. A. Gomez-Ibanez, "Global View of Automobile Dependence," Review of Cities and Automobile Dependence: An International Sourcebook, *Journal of the American Planning Association* 57 (1991); and M. J. Breheny, "The Contradiction of the Compact City: A Review," in *Sustainable Development and Urban Form*, ed. M. J. Breheny (London: Pion, 1992). The London study is D. Banister, "Energy Use, Transport, and Settlement Patterns," in *Sustainable Development and Urban Form*, ed. Breheny. The Denver study is J. May and G. Scheuernstuhl, "Sensitivity Analysis for Land Use Transportation and Air Quality," *Transportation Research Record* 1312 (1991).

20. The case for the importance of considering congestion in energy studies is made in the review article by William Anderson et al., "Urban Form, Energy and the Environment: A Review of Issues, Evidence and Policy," *Urban Studies* 33, no. 1 (1996): 26.

21. Reid Ewing, phone interview with the author, December 4, 2009; all subsequent quotations from Ewing are from this interview. The meta-analysis

paper is from Reid Ewing and Robert Cervero, "Travel and the Built Environment," *Journal of the American Planning Association* 76, no. 3 (2010). Another, related review paper from Reid Ewing and Robert Cervero is "Travel and the Built Environment: A Synthesis," *Transportation Research Record*, 1780 (2001). The 2010 study cited is Karathodorou et al., "Estimating the Effect of Urban Density on Fuel Demand."

22. B. H. West et al., "Development and Verification of Light-Duty Modal Emissions and Fuel Consumption Values for Traffic Models" (Washington, D.C.: Oak Ridge National Laboratory, 1999). See also Stacy C. Davis et al., *Transportation Energy Data Book*, 28th ed. (Oak Ridge, Tenn.: Oak Ridge National Laboratory, 2009). Graph is based on West et al., "Development and Verification." This estimate is based on an average of 8 cars from between 1993 and 1997 (I excluded an additional car from 1988). Other estimates give slightly different optimum speeds. For instance, according to the EMFAC 2007 Motor Vehicle Emission Model for California (http://www.arb.ca.gov/msei/onroad/downloads/docs/user_guide_emfac2007.pdf), the optimum speed is closer to 45 mph; see also Reid H. Ewing, *Growing Cooler: Evidence on Urban Development and Climate Change* (Washington, D.C.: ULI, 2008), 27, for graph. In all studies it is acknowledged that the "optimum speed" and the shape of the curve will vary by car size, type, engine, conditions, etc. Furthermore, these average relationships between speed and efficiency may change with vehicle fleet composition. Truck figures are for a dual-tire tractor-trailer and are from Gary Capps et al., "Class-8 Heavy Truck Duty Cycle Project Final Report" (Oak Ridge, Tenn.: Oak Ridge National Laboratory, 2008), as referenced in Davis et al., *Transportation Energy Data Book*, sec. 5, p. 15. Note the statistics described for trucks in the text apply to dual tire tractor single (wide) tire trailers.

23. Helen Jarvis, "Urban Sustainability as a Function of Compromises Households Make Deciding Where and How to Live: Portland and Seattle Compared," *Local Environment* 6, no. 3 (2001): 249–50.

24. Pat Hu, "Summary of Travel Trends: 2001 National Household Travel Survey" (Washington, D.C.: US Department of Transportation Federal Highway Administration, 2004), 16.

25. Jarvis, "Urban Sustainability as a Function of Compromises," 250. This conclusion is based on her research in Portland, Oregon, and Seattle, Washington, and doesn't necessarily generalize to the whole country.

26. Greg Dicum, phone interview with the author, December 5, 2009; all subsequent quotations by Dicum are from this interview.

27. http://www.mtc.ca.gov/maps_and_data/datamart/forecast/ao98/Table S12.htm.
28. Steven Hayward, "Legends of the Sprawl," *Policy Review*, no. 91 (1998): 29.

INTERLUDE 3: Global Oil Depletion

1. The range of peak oil dates as well as the range of remaining recoverable reserve estimates are from Steve Sorrell et al., "Global Oil Depletion: A Review of the Evidence," *Energy Policy* 38, no. 9 (2010).
2. WikiLeaks cites Sadad Al Husseini, a geologist and former executive vice president of exploration of Saudi Aramco (their oil monopoly) in conversation with US embassy personnel. This summary was obtained from Jeff Rubin, "WikiLeaks Reveals Imminent Saudi Oil Peak," *The Globe and Mail*, February 16, 2011.
3. The point about the six largest OPEC producers is from Paul Roberts, *The End of Oil: On the Edge of a Perilous New World* (Boston: Houghton Mifflin, 2005), 48. A good source for information on EROI is Cutler Cleveland and Robert Costanza, "Energy Return on Investment (EROI)," in *Encyclopedia of Earth*, ed. Cutler Cleveland (Washington, D.C.: Environmental Information Coalition, National Council for Science and the Environment, 2010). Figures on US EROI are from Cutler Cleveland, "Net Energy Obtained from Extracting Oil and Gas in the US," *Energy* 30 (2005): 780–81; and Cutler Cleveland et al., "Energy and the US Economy: A Biophysical Perspective," *Science* 225 (1984): 895. Global EROI estimates are from Charles Hall, Sarah Palcher, and Mike Herweyer, "Provisional Results from EROI Assessment," http://www.theoildrum.com/node/3810. The first two estimates are based on empirical data, while the last, for 2008, is based on extrapolation.
4. Kenneth S. Deffeyes, *Beyond Oil: The View from Hubbert's Peak* (New York: Hill and Wang, 2006), 28. The figure on needed infrastructure investment is from International Energy Agency, "World Energy Outlook 2007: Fact Sheet—Oil," OECD/IEA (2007), http://www.iea.org//textbase/papers/2007/fs_oil.pdf.
5. From an interview with Matthew Simmons; retrieved at http://www.oilcrash.com/articles/blackout.htm.
6. The 2008 review of peak oil models and estimates is from Robert Kaufman and Laura Shiers, "Alternatives to Conventional Crude Oil: When,

How Quickly and Market-Driven?" *Ecological Economics* 67, no. 3 (2008). The other review mentioned Sorrell et al., "Global Oil Depletion." The International Energy Agency report referenced is "World Energy Outlook 2010, Executive Summary," 2010, 6.

7. Jeff Rubin, *Why Your World Is About to Get a Whole Lot Smaller* (New York: Random House, 2009), 18.

8. http://blogs.ec.europa.eu/piebalgs/are-we-moving-towards-a-new-oil-crisis/.

9. International Energy Agency, "World Energy Outlook 2008, Executive Summary."

CHAPTER 4: From Dirt Tracks to Interstates

1. Dayton Duncan and Ken Burns, *Horatio's Drive: America's First Road Trip* (New York: Knopf, 2003), 15.

2. Information on studies quantifying the costs of poor roads is from Tom Lewis, *Divided Highways: Building the Interstate Highways, Transforming American Life* (New York: Viking, 1997), 10–11. The point about railroad overbuilding leading to a lack of political will for roads is from Irving B. Holley, *The Highway Revolution, 1895–1925: How the United States Got Out of the Mud* (Durham, N.C.: Carolina Academic Press, 2008), 4, 11.

3. Lewis, *Divided Highways*, 11, 21.

4. Ibid., 18–20

5. Dwight Eisenhower *Report on Transcontinental Trip*, November 1919, Dwight D. Eisenhower Presidential Library, http://www.eisenhower.archives.gov/Research/DigitalDocuments/1919Convoy/New%20PDFs/Principal%20facts.pdf.

6. Dwight D. Eisenhower, *At Ease: Stories I Tell to Friends*, 1st TAB ed., Military Classics Series (Blue Ridge Summit, Pa.: TAB Books, 1988).

7. Richard Weingroff, "The Man Who Changed America, Part 2," *Public Roads*, May–June 2003, http://www.tfhrc.gov/pubrds/03may/05.htm.

8. Lewis, *Divided Highways*, 147. Eisenhower was opposed to intra-urban highways not because of any deeply held urban-planner principles but because he thought intracity transportation was the business of local and state governments.

9. All quotations and paraphrasing of the record in this paragraph are from the following presidential meeting notes: Memorandum for the Record: Meeting in the President's Office, Interim Report on the Interstate

Highway Program, April 6, 1960. See source: http://www.fhwa.dot.gov/infrastructure/bragdon2.cfm

10. Lewis, *Divided Highways*, 153.

11. Raymond A. Mohl, "Stop the Road: Freeway Revolts in American Cities," *Journal of Urban History* 30, no. 5 (2004).

12. Chris Carlsson, "The Freeway Revolt," FoundSF.org, http://foundsf.org/index.php?title=The_Freeway_Revolt.

13. M. Berman, *All That Is Solid Melts into Air: The Experience of Modernity* (New York: Penguin, 1988), 290.

14. Mohl, "Stop the Road," 676.

15. William Bronson, "Home Is a Freeway," *Cry California*, 1966; reprinted in *Los Angeles: Biography of a City*, ed. John Caughy and LaRee Caughy (Berkeley: University of California Press, 1977), 433–37.

16. Noelle Sullivan, *It Happened in Southern California* (Helena, Mont.: Twodot, 1996), 98.

17. Millard Bailey, "Getting Somewhere," *Los Angeles Times*, June 18, 1926.

18. Los Angeles has the worst fuel rankings in terms of both aggregate (383 million gallons) and per capita (57 gallons) consumption. In terms of per capita fuel consumption by region, the figure for Los Angeles of 485 gallons per person per year comes from Ping Chang, *State of the Region 2007* (Los Angeles: Southern California Area Governments, 2007). New York City's estimate is 146, and San Francisco's is 238. These figures are from Mark Ginsberg and Mark Strauss, "New York City—A Case Study in Density after 9/11," Density Conference (Boston, 2003). Presentation.

19. The Brookings report mentioned is Marilyn Brown, Frank Southworth, and Andrea Sarzynski, *Shrinking the Carbon Footprint of Metropolitan America*, Metropolitan Policy Program (Washington, D.C.: Brookings Institution, 2008). This methodology used even more stringent criteria in determining "developable land" for the land denominator in the calculation of population density. The Census Bureau assigns the Los Angeles region sixth place nationally, above the New York region. The Ewing reference mentioned is Reid Ewing, Rolf Pendall, and Don Chen, *Measuring Sprawl and Its Impacts*, vol. 1 (Washington, D.C.: Smart Growth America, 2002).

20. The points about garden cities and outlying Westside towns getting big are from Jeremiah B. C. Axelrod, *Inventing Autopia: Dreams and Visions of the Modern Metropolis in Jazz Age Los Angeles* (Berkeley: University of California Press, 2009). Information on the extent of construction in downtown is from Richard W. Longstreth, *City Center to Regional Mall:*

Architecture, the Automobile, and Retailing in Los Angeles, 1920–1950 (Cambridge: MIT Press, 1997).

21. The figures on automobiles per resident are from Scott L. Bottles, *Los Angeles and the Automobile: The Making of the Modern City* (Berkeley: University of California Press, 1987), 92–93. The figure on the number of cars commuting each day into Los Angeles is from Kevin Starr, *Material Dreams: Southern California through the 1920s, Americans and the California Dream* (New York: Oxford University Press, 1990), 79. The Bliven quotations are from Bruce Bliven, "Los Angeles: The City That Is Bacchanalian—In a Nice Way," *New Republic*, July 13, 1927, 197.

22. Donald Baker, "The Present Problem," paper presented at the Conference on the Rapid Transit Question, Los Angeles, January 21, 1930, 6–7. The figure that a quarter of activity was taking place outside of the established business districts is from Howard J. Nelson, *The Los Angeles Metropolis* (Dubuque, Iowa: Kendall/Hunt Pub. Co., 1983). Information about the leapfrog pattern is from Axelrod, *Inventing Autopia*, 214. The fact that large, centrally placed parking lots went up comes from Longstreth, *City Center to Regional Mall*, 174.

23. Axelrod, *Inventing Autopia*, 297.

24. Automobile Club of Southern California, *Traffic Survey, Los Angeles Metropolitan Area, 1937* (Los Angeles: Automobile Club, 1938), 7–8, 12.

25. Robert Gottlieb, *Reinventing Los Angeles: Nature and Community in the Global City* (Cambridge: MIT Press, 2007), 175.

26. Frank J. Taylor, "The Word's Worst Traffic Tangle," *Saturday Evening Post*, March 13, 1954, 42.

27. Eric Morris, "Los Angeles Transportation Facts and Fiction: Freeways," *Los Angeles Times*, February 29, 2009.

28. John Nordquist, interview with the author, June 22, 2010.

INTERLUDE 4: Tar Sands

1. US Energy Information Administration; based on data available at http://www.eia.doe.gov/emeu/aer/txt/ptb0103.html.

2. The figure of 200 billion barrels is from Peter Tertzakian, *A Thousand Barrels a Second: The Coming Oil Break Point and the Challenges Facing an Energy Dependent World* (New York: McGraw-Hill, 2006), 203. Getting at the exact EROI for tar sands is very difficult. The 1:5 EROI estimate is for strip-mined tar sands (Charles Hall, A. Gupta, and Mike Herweyer, "Unconvential Oil: Tar Sands and Shale Oil—EROI on the Web, Part 3 of

6," http://www.theoildrum.com/node/3839). The 1:9 estimate, from a different study, is for the newer and less destructive toe-to-heel air-injection method, although there is considerable variation in the EROI value depending on what components of energy input are included in the accounting (David Murphy, "EROI Update: Preliminary Results Using Toe-to-Heel Air Injection," http://netenergy.theoildrum.com/node/5183).

CHAPTER 5: Transit Wars

1. Collected from Clifton Hood, *722 Miles: The Building of the Subways and How They Transformed New York* (New York: Simon and Schuster, 1993); Peter Kihss, "Kozlov Sees City in 77-Minute Tour," *New York Times*, July 13, 1959; "Kozlov Denounces New York Subway: Urges Rebuilding It," *New York Times*, July 26, 1959.

2. Hood, *722 Miles*, 259.

3. The way transit systems affect urban form is dealt with in Peter Newman and Jeffrey Kenworthy, *Sustainability and Cities: Overcoming Automobile Dependence* (Washington, D.C.: Island Press, 1999). The CEOs for Cities report is Joe Cortright, *New York City's Green Dividend* (Chicago: CEOs for Cities, 2010). The figures cited from that report are from p. 1, except for the figure of 57 percent transit share, which comes from the US Census Bureau's American Community Survey statistics, p. 7.

4. Hood, *722 Miles*, 27.

5. Information about how Van Wyck and others tried to hobble the chances for transit are from Ray Stannard Baker, "The Subway Deal," *McClure's Magazine*, March 1905. Information on how John B. McDonald and August Belmont collaborated to form the IRT is from Hood, *722 Miles*, 27, 59, 64–71.

6. Quotation is from Baker, "Subway Deal," 462. The figure of 350,000 riders is from Hood, *722 Miles*, 96.

7. Hood, *722 Miles*, 123–24.

8. Ibid., 124–36.

9. Ibid., 136–58; Vivian Heller, *The City Beneath Us: Building the New York Subways* (New York: Norton, 2004), 28–31.

10. Information on the city's Transportation Administration study is from Iver Peterson, "City Team Cites Subway Decline," *New York Times*, January 31, 1970. Information on the 1975 report is from Edward Burks, "Subway Ridership Lowest since '18; Off 20% in Decade," *New York Times*,

April 6, 1975. Figures on dropping ridership in 1976–77 and its extrapolation are from Mark Feinman, "The New York City Transit Authority in the 1970s," NYCsubway.org (2002), http://www.nycsubway.org/articles/history-nycta1970s.html.

11. Edward Burks, "15 Busiest Subway Stations Show Big Decline in Riders," *New York Times*, November 10, 1975.

12. Newman and Kenworthy, *Sustainability and Cities*, table 3.10.

13. Frederick Olmsted, Harland Bartholomew, and Charles Cheney, *Major Traffic Street Plan of Los Angeles* (Los Angeles: Traffic Commission of the City and County of Los Angeles, 1924).

14. The view of Pacific Electric executives that the Hollywood subway would be the foundation for a long-term plan of transit and vertical growth is from Jeremiah Axelrod, *Inventing Autopia: Dreams and Visions of the Modern Metropolis in Jazz Age Los Angeles* (Berkeley: University of California Press, 2009), 176–77. The Pontius quote is from the *Los Angeles Examiner*, March 28, 1926, as quoted in Axelrod, *Inventing Autopia*, 348, n. 24.

15. "The seed of a vast subterranean system" is from Spencer Crump, *Ride the Big Red Cars: How Trolleys Helped Build Southern California*, 1st ed. (Los Angeles: Crest Publications, 1962), 151–52; as quoted in Axelrod, *Inventing Autopia*, 178. Information on the charter change is from Axelrod, 176–80.

16. The "future city population of 3,000,000" is from Past Visions of LA's Transportation Future, LA Metro, http://www.metro.net/about/library/archives/visions-studies/mass-rapid-transit-concept-maps/. "Future orderly development" is from Kelker, De Leuw and Company, "Report on Comprehensive Rapid Transit Plan for the City and County of Los Angeles" (1930), as quoted in J. Ogden Marsh, "A Digest and Simple Statement of the High Lights of the Kelker DeLeuw Report," *Conference on the Rapid Transit Question*, Los Angeles, 1930, 17.

17. The "unequalled position" quotation is from Kelker, De Leuw, "Report on Comprehensive Rapid Transit Plan," as quoted in Marsh, "High Lights of the Kelker DeLeuw Report," 17. The point about garden communities is from David Brodsly, *L.A. Freeway: An Appreciative Essay* (Berkeley: University of California Press, 1981), 153; Baker, "The Present Problem," 7.

18. Axelrod, *Inventing Autopia*, 179–83.

19. The rumors that Chandler had real estate holdings is from Starr, *Material Dreams*, 108. An example of the *Los Angeles Times'* language is found in "Let 'Em Walk!," February 14, 1926.

20. Information about the political expediency of putting the plan to referendum is from Scott L. Bottles, *Los Angeles and the Automobile: The Making of the Modern City* (Berkeley: University of California Press), 143. "The future form of urbanism" is from Axelrod, *Inventing Autopia*, 184.

21. Brodsly, *L.A. Freeway*, 155.

22. Los Angeles County Regional Planning Commission, "Report of a Highway Traffic Survey in the County of Los Angeles" (Los Angeles: Regional Planning Commission, 1937), 4.

23. City of Stockholm, "Stockholm: Application for European Green Capital Award," http://international.stockholm.se/PageFiles/145186/application_european_green_capital.pdf (2008), http://international.stockholm.se/PageFiles/145186/application_european_green_capital.pdf.

24. Data on miles traveled are from Newman and Kenworthy, *Sustainability and Cities*, table 3.10. Mode split information for Stockholm is from City of Stockholm (2008), 15.

25. The 90 percent figure is from City of Stockholm (2008), 15. Land ownership statistics are from Robert Cervero, *The Transit Metropolis: A Global Inquiry* (Washington, D.C.: Island Press, 1998), 112.

26. Facebook, 2010 Tax Day Tea Party (Group), retrieved May 3, 2011, from http://www.facebook.com/note.php?note_id=108328685861105.

INTERLUDE 5: Coal

1. Oscar P. R. van Vliet, Andre P. C. Faaij, and Wim C. Turkenburg, "Fischer-Tropsch Diesel Production in a Well-to-Wheel Perspective: A Carbon, Energy Flow and Cost Analysis," *Energy Conversion and Management* 50, no. 4 (2009).

2. Energy Watch Group, "Coal: Resources and Future Production" (Berlin, Germany: Energy Watch Group, 2007), 4.

3. Energy Information Administration, "Emission of Greenhouse Gases in the United States, 1985–1990" (1993), 16.

4. Bert Metz et al., *Special Report on Carbon Dioxide Capture and Storage*, Intergovernmental Panel on Climate Change (Cambridge: Cambridge University Press, 2005). According to this report, pulverized coal-based electricity would go from the 2002 baseline of 4–5 cents per kWh to 6–10 cents per kWh. However, that increase would go down to 5–8 cents per kWh if sequestration was combined with enhanced oil-recovery techniques.

CHAPTER 6: The Building Energy Diet

1. Ed Begley Jr. interview with the author, December 22, 2009, Studio City, California; all subsequent quotations by Begley are from this interview.

2. Energy source data for buildings are from the US Energy Information Administration, "Annual Energy Review, 2008," Department of Energy/ Energy Information Administration (2009), 38–39. The figure on the amount of coal needed to keep a lightbulb burning is from Electropaedia, http://www.mpoweruk.com/energy_efficiency.htm and is for a 100-watt bulb.

3. Energy savings from negawatts are from the International Energy Agency, "World Energy Outlook 2006" (2006). The "cities are the Saudi Arabia of energy efficiency" quotation is from Douglas Foy and Robert Healy, "Cities Are the Answer," *Boston Globe*, April 4, 2007.

4. Diana Farrell et al., "The Case for Investing in Energy Productivity" (San Francisco: McKinsey Global Institute, 2008), 11.

5. Marshini Chetty, David Tran, and Rebecca Grinter, "Getting to Green: Understanding Resource Consumption in the Home," in *UbiComp 2008 Conference Proceedings* (Seoul, South Korea: Association for Computer Machinery, 2008), 244.

6. Paul Scheckel, interview with the author, May 24, 2010, Burlington, Vermont; all subsequent quotations from Scheckel are from this interview.

7. Matthew Wald, "Efficiency, Not Just Alternatives, Is Promoted as an Energy Saver," *New York Times*, May 29, 2007.

8. Marc Gerken, as quoted in "Vermont Energy Investment Corporation to Create 'Efficiency Smart Power Plant' for American Municipal Power Members in Six States," Vermont Energy Investment Corporation and AMP Public Power Press Release, June 14, 2010. http://amppartners.org/newsroom/vermont-energy-investment-corporation-to-create-%E2%80%9Cefficiency-smart-power-plant%E2%80%9D-for-amp-members-in-six-states/.

9. See Kate Galbraith, "Energy Efficiency the Green Mountain Way," *New York Times*, October 8, 2008. Information on the National Energy Efficiency Scorecard is from Maggie Eldridge et al., "The 2009 State Energy Efficiency Scorecard" (Washington, D.C.: American Council for an Energy Efficiency Economy, 2009), iv, 9, 11.

10. Efficiency Vermont, "Annual Report" (Burlington, Vt.: Efficiency Vermont, 2008).

11. Blair Hamilton, interview with the author, May 24, 2010, Burlington, Vermont; all subsequent quotations from Hamilton are from this interview.

12. Mitchell Schnurman, "A Game-Changer for a Green Economy Is Closer Than You Think," *Fort Worth Star-Telegram*, March 9, 2010.

13. Quoted in Lindsay Riddell, "PACE Energy Efficiency Programs Suspended," *San Francisco Business Times*, June 11, 2010.

14. Figures on existing commercial PACE programs and projects are from Lawrence Berkeley Lab, Clinton Climate Initiative, and Renewable Funding, "Property Assessed Clean Energy (PACE) Financing: Update on Commercial Programs," policy brief, March 2011. The $2.5 billion figure is from "PACE Financing for Commercial Buildings to Reach $2.5 Billion Annually by 2015," Pike Research Press Release, June 21, 2010. http://www.pikeresearch.com/newsroom/pace-financing-for-commercial-buildings-to-reach-2-5-billion-annually-by-2015.

15. Sean Patrick Neill, interview with the author, May 12, 2011; all subsequent quotations by Neill are from this interview.

16. Murat Armbruster, interview with the author, May 9, 2011.

17. Information on Barcelona's solar ordinance is from http://www.c40cities.org/bestpractices/renewables/barcelona_solar.jsp. Household electricity use based on http://earthtrends.wri.org/text/energy-resources/variable-574.html.

18. American Institute of Architects, "Local Leaders in Sustainability: Green Incentives" (Washington, D.C.: American Institute of Architects, 2009).

19. The 2008 survey is from Turner Construction, "Green Building Market Barometer" (New York: Turner Construction, 2008), http://www.turnerconstruction.com/Uploads/Documents/Turrner_2008_Green_Building_Market_Barometer.pdf. Information on the Rosenberg Real Estate Equity Funds Study is from Andrew Nelson, "The Greening of US Investment Real Estate: Market Fundamentals, Prospects, and Opportunities" (San Francisco: Rosenberg Real Estate Equity Funds Research Report, 2007). That LEED is the most common municipal certification system is from Joan Fitzgerald, *Emerald Cities: Urban Sustainability and Economic Development* (New York: Oxford University Press, 2010), 83–85.

20. The study on LEED building-energy performance is from Henry Gifford, "A Better Way to Rate Green Buildings," *Northeast Sun*, Spring (2009). According to his study, the US Green Building Council relies on the database of the Commercial Buildings Energy Consumption Survey (CBECS) for comparison of energy-use statistics, though the council uses buildings from all construction years, even before 1920. It also uses the median to summarize energy use per square foot for LEED buildings, while compar-

ing them to mean values for the CBECS survey, which is not "apples to apples." According to Gifford, if you use only similar vintage buildings for comparison, with only mean values, the LEED buildings that responded to his survey use 29 percent more energy than comparable buildings without certification. Information on the USGBC's internal study of energy performance and on data requirements is from Mireya Navarro, "Some Buildings Not Living Up to Green Label," *New York Times*, August 30, 2009. Information on new requirements is from Tristan Roberts, "Your Guide to the New Draft of LEED," Environmental Building News Blog, November 8, 2010, http://www.buildinggreen.com/auth/article .cfm/2010/11/8/Your-Guide-to-the-New-Draft-of-LEED-2012-public-comment-USGBC/.
21. City of New York, "Greater, Greener Buildings Plan" (2010), http://www .nyc.gov/html/planyc2030/downloads/pdf/greener_greater_buildings_ final.pdf.
22. LA Department of Water and Power, "LADWP Applauds Its Customers, February Marks Lowest Recorded Water Use in 32 Years," Los Angeles Department of Water and Power (2010), http://www.piersystem.com/go/ doc/1475/499743/.
23. Zev Yaroslavsky, phone interview with the author, June 23, 2010.

INTERLUDE 6: Natural Gas

1. http://www.pickensplan.com/didyouknow/.
2. Information on the peaking of US gas production and gas found per foot drilled is from Walter Yongquist and Richard Duncan, "North American Natural Gas: Data Show Supply Problems," *Natural Resources Research* 12, no. 4 (2003). The 30,000 wells figure is from J. David Hughes, *Will Natural Gas Fuel America in the Twenty-First Century?* (Santa Rosa, Calif.: Post Carbon Institute, 2011), 18. The figure on pipeline length is from the US Energy Information Administration, "About US Natural Gas Pipelines," http://www.eia.doe.gov/pub/oil_gas/natural_gas/analysis_publications/ ngpipeline/index.html.
3. An example of shale being referred to as "a revolution" is from Daniel Yergin and Robert Ineson, "America's Natural Gas Revolution," *Wall Street Journal*, November 2, 2009. Figures on reserve changes are from US Energy Information Administration, Office of Oil, Gas and Coal Supply Statistics, "Summary: US Crude Oil, Natural Gas, and Natural Gas Liquids Proved Reserves 2009" (Washington, D.C.: US Energy Information

Administration, 2010), 1, 3. The quadrupling figure is from Hughes, *Will Natural Gas Fuel America?*, 29.

4. The 20 percent reduction figure is from Hughes, *Will Natural Gas Fuel America?*, 30. The difference between the 2010 and 2011 forecasts is from Hughes, 31, and is based on data from the US Energy Information Administration.

5. US House of Representatives Committee on Energy and Commerce, *Chemicals Used in Hydraulic Fracturing*, 112th Congress, 2011.

6. Ian Urbina, "Regulation Lax as Gas Wells' Tainted Water Hits Rivers," *New York Times*, February 26, 2011. This article links to a database of public documents that give extensive evidence of official concern over water quality impacts, at http://www.nytimes.com/interactive/2011/02/27/us/natural-gas-documents-1.html#document/p1/a9895.

7. Production decline figures are from Hughes, *Will Natural Gas Fuel America?*, 25, whose data come from Chesapeake Energy, "2010 Institutional Investor and Analyst Meeting," (Oklahoma City, 2010), http://phx.corporateir.net/External.File?item=UGFyZW50SUQ9NjYwMTd8Q2hpbGRJRD0tMXxUeXBlPTM=&t=1, p. 54. The point about extrapolation is from Hughes, *Will Natural Gas Fuel America?*, 25–26, based on information from Arthur E. Berman, "Shale Gas—Abundance or Mirage? Why the Marcellus Shale Will Disappoint Expectations," presented at the Association for the Study of Peak Oil and Gas, USA 2010 World Oil Conference, Washington, D.C., October 8, 2010, http://www.aspousa.org/2010presentationfiles/10-8-2010_aspousa_NaturalGas_Berman_A.pdf.

8. That isolated gas fields tend to be economically unrecoverable is from Deffeyes, *Beyond Oil: The View from Hubbert's Peak* (New York: Hill and Wang, 2006), 53. The 60 percent figure is from Julian Darley, *High Noon for Natural Gas: The New Energy Crisis* (White River Junction, Vt.: Chelsea Green Publishing, 2004), 59.

9. The cost of the LNG Train is from Darley, *High Noon for Natural Gas*, 59; information on energy return on investment for the LNG Train is from p. 60. According to Darley, the process of turning 1,000 cubic feet of gas into LNG requires between 80 and 130 cubic feet of gas. Figures on the share of imported LNG and number of ports are from Deffeyes, *Beyond Oil*, 78.

10. Colin Campbell, "The Assessment and Importance of Oil Depletion," in *The Final Energy Crisis*, ed. Andrew McKillop and Sheila Newman (London: Pluto Press, 2005), 43.

CHAPTER 7: Smart Mobility

1. Statistics on bike ownership are from Alyse Nelson, "Livable Copenhagen: The Design of a Bicycle City," Center for Public Space Research and University of Washington (2006), 4; on Danish car ownership, from Jim Brewer et al., "Geometric Design Practices for European Roads," US-DOT Federal Highway Administration (2001), 25; on daily ridership for all trips and car ownership in Copenhagen, from Andrea Ramage, Patricia Chase, and Jayson Antonoff, "Scandinavian Lessons in Mobility," (presentation to the Seattle Department of Transportation, Seattle, Wash., September 14, 2004), http://www.i-sustain.com/index.php?option=com_docman&task=doc_details&gid=51&Itemid=308. Slide 27; on Copenhagen's bicycle and car commute mode share and cycle infrastructure, from City of Copenhagen, "Bicycle Account" (2008), kk.sites.itera.dk/apps/kk_publikationer/pdf/679_a4jBCZL3Xz.pdf, 7–9. Mode shares for American cities are from the American Community Survey of the US Census, 2008.

2. According to C40 Cities Climate Leadership Group (http://www.c40 cities.org/bestpractices/transport/copenhagen_bicycles.jsp).

3. Mikael Colville-Andersen, interview with the author, Copenhagen, Denmark, May 17, 2010; all subsequent quotations from Colville-Andersen are from this interview.

4. City of Copenhagen, "Bicycle Account" (2006), http://kk.sites.itera.dk/apps/kk_publikationer/pdf/464_Cykelregnskab_UK.%202006.pdf, p. 6.

5. The film with the interviews is Michael Thomas, *Copenhagen: City of Cyclists* (Copenhagen, Denmark: Copenhagen City Council Department of Roads and Parks, 2003), documentary web video, http://video.google.com/videoplay?docid=-5092322980326147472#. The attitude of biking as "hygge" is also mentioned in Marc Santos Canals, Antoine Pinaud, and Janneau Thibaut, "Copenhagen: How Bicycles Can Become an Efficient Means of Public Transportation," Roskilde University, Geography Department, working paper (2006).

6. Cycle Chic Blog; "Cycle Chic Origins," blog entry by Mikael Colville-Andersen, http://www.copenhagencyclechic.com/2007/06/cycle-chic-origins.html.

7. For a review of literature on perceptions of bike safety, see Conor C. Reynolds et al., "The Impact of Transportation Infrastructure on Bicycling Injuries and Crashes: A Review of the Literature," *Environ Health* 8 (2009).

Some of the original studies include A. Carver et al., "How Do Perceptions of Local Neighborhood Relate to Adolescents' Walking and Cycling?" *American Journal of Health Promotion* 20, no. 2 (2005); Robert B. Noland, "Perceived Risk and Modal Choice: Risk Compensation in Transportation Systems," *Accident Analysis and Prevention* 27, no. 4 (1995); and M. Winters and K. Teschke, "Route Preferences among Adults in the near Market for Bicycling: Findings of the Cycling in Cities Study," *American Journal of Health Promotion* 25, no. 1 (2010). The survey of Copenhagen residents is from Søren Jensen, Claus Rosenkilde, and Niels Jensen, "Road Safety and Perceived Risk of Cycle Facilities in Copenhagen" (Lyngby: Trafitec and City of Copenhagen, 2007), 7–8.

8. Studies on the "safety in numbers" effect include Peter L. Jacobsen, "Safety in Numbers: More Walkers and Bicyclists, Safer Walking and Bicycling," *Injury Prevention* 9, no. 3 (2003); Dorothy L. Robinson, "Safety in Numbers in Australia: More Walkers and Bicyclists, Safer Walking and Bicycling," *Health Promotion Journal of Australia* 16, no. 1 (2005); and G. Vandenbulcke et al., "Mapping Bicycle Use and the Risk of Accidents for Commuters Who Cycle to Work in Belgium," *Transport Policy* 16, no. 2 (2009). Findings on the relationship between cycling injuries and distance ridden in Copenhagen are from Municipality of Copenhagen, "Cycle Policy 2002–2012," Municipality of Copenhagen, Roads and Parks Department (2002). The point about drivers' experience relative to bikers' is from Mikko Rasanen and Heikki Summala, "Attention and Expectation Problems in Bicycle-Car Collisions: An In-Depth Study," *Accident Analysis and Prevention* 30, no. 5 (1998).

9. Perceptions of safety among Copenhagen cyclists is from Jensen, Rosenkilde, and Jensen, "Road Safety and Perceived Risk," 7. Examples of literature showing that on-road marked bike lanes improve safety include William E. Moritz, "Adult Bicyclists in the United States: Characteristics and Riding Experience in 1996," *Bicycle and Pedestrian Research* 1998, no. 1636 (1998); and Gregory B. Rodgers, "Factors Associated with the Crash Risk of Adult Bicyclists," *Journal of Safety Research* 28, no. 4 (1997). The point about separated, recreational paths is from Lisa Aultman-Hall and F. L. Hall, "Ottawa-Carleton Commuter Cyclist On- and Off-Road Incident Rates," *Accident Analysis and Prevention* 30, no. 1 (1998); and Moritz, "Adult Bicyclists in the United States."

10. Information on the Arroyo Seco Cycleway is from Mikael Coleville-Andersen, "Bottleneck Blog: Bikes, Copenhagen and Disneyland: What

We Have in Common," *Los Angeles Times*, August 8, 2008. In the 1980s, the County of Los Angeles put in a two-mile cycle path in the bottom of the cement-lined Arroyo Seco stream channel, an idea of dubious environmental value. Currently a plan is under consideration, spearheaded by the Arroyo Seco Foundation, to develop the Arroyo Seco Greenway, which would include a bikeway intended to provide a serious alternative to car commuting. See http://www.arroyoseco.org/bikepath2010.htm.

11. According to statistics from the Stockholm County Council, Office of Regional Planning, as accessed in the following presentation: Hans Hede, "Transport Planning in the Stockholm Region," presented to the METREX/Moscow International Workshop, Moscow, June 2006.

12. Daniel Firth, "Stockholm's Transport Profile, 2010," internal presentation slides from the City of Stockholm Transport Administration, 2010. Note that the dollar figure given is converted from Euros. The amount given was €300 and €800 million.

13. For an explanation of the economic fundamentals of congestion pricing and an analysis of the debates among economists about it, see Robin Lindsey, "Do Economists Reach a Conclusion on Road Pricing? The Intellectual History of an Idea," *Econ Journal Watch* 3, no. 2 (2006). According to Lindsey, there is general agreement among economists that the concept works, but much debate about the specifics, such as how to set tolls, cover costs, and spend revenues.

14. Oslo and other Norwegian cities, such as Bergen and Trondheim, have electronic urban tolling. This was initially implemented only to raise revenues to finance road infrastructure and does not currently have the other characteristics of congestion pricing. As of this time, Norway is considering converting these systems to full-fledged congestion pricing.

15. An amendment to the Swedish Constitution is being considered currently that would change this. Under the new proposed Constitution, a regional agency would be responsible for taxes such as this.

16. Daniel Firth, interview with the author, May 18, 2010, Stockholm, Sweden; all subsequent quotations by Firth are from this interview.

17. Data on the results of the program come from personal communications with Firth as well as from the following references: Firth, "Analysis of Traffic in Stockholm—with Special Focus on the Effects of the Congestion Tax, 2005–2008" (Stockholm: City of Stockholm Traffic Administration, 2009), http://www.stockholm.se/PageFiles/70349/Sammanfattning%20 eng%20090918_.pdf; and Lars Burman and Christer Johansson, "The

Effects of the Congestion Tax on Emissions and Air Quality," (Stockholm: Stockholm Environment and Health Administration, 2009), http://slb .nu/slb/rapporter/pdf8/slb2010_006.pdf.

18. Gasoline deliveries decreased while diesel increased by about the same amount during this period, probably because some diesel vehicles were exempt from the congestion tax for a certain period.

19. See, e.g., Timothy Beatley, *Green Urbanism: Learning from European Cities* (Washington, D.C.: Island Press, 2000), 163.

20. A listing of the details of each demonstration program for the Urban Partnership is given at http://www.upa.dot.gov.

21. Nicholas Confessore, "Congestion Pricing Plan Dies in Albany: City Room Blog," *New York Times*, April 7, 2008.

22. Joel Epstein, "Moving L.A.: There's a Train a Comin," *Huffington Post*, February 10, 2010. Comments come in response to Sam Allen, "Los Angeles Ranks High in 'Commuter Pain' Study, but Things Could Be Worse: L.A. Now," *Los Angeles Times,* June 30, 2010. The survey in question is: IBM, "The Globalization of Traffic Congestion: IBM 2010 Commuter Pain Survey" (2010), http://www-03.ibm.com/press/us/en/attachment/32017.wss? fileId=ATTACH_FILE1&fileName=Globalization%20of%20Traffic.pdf.

23. Cost savings due to the 30/10 plan would be relative to original cost proposals under Measure R, according to Deputy Mayor Jaime de la Vega, as quoted in Tim Rutten, "Mayor Antonio Villaraigosa's 30/10 Plan: Moving Forward," *Los Angeles Times*, June 9, 2010. The estimates on reductions in fuel use and emissions are from http://www.metro.net/projects/30–10/.

24. Zev Yaroslavsky, interview with the author, June 23, 2010; all subsequent quotations from Yaroslavsky are from this interview. The information on Yaroslavsky's commute is from Steve Hymon, "Bottleneck Blog: On the Subway with Zev," *Los Angeles Times*, July 9, 2008.

25. The explanation for Yaroslavsky's vote is given in his interview in Hymon, "Bottleneck Blog." The ballot measure in 1998 barred county sales-tax revenues from previously passed Propositions A (1980) and C (1990), the main source of capital for the MTA, from being used for subway tunneling, although other subway costs were allowed (see http://www.metro.net/ about/financebudget/taxes/). The federal bill ban on tunneling through the mid-Wilshire district was sponsored by Congressman Henry Waxman in 1985 in response to a methane explosion in the Fairfax District. Following a report from an expert panel, he sponsored legislation overturning it in 2007. The final quotation is from Robert Sechler, "The Seven

Eras of Rapid Transit Planning in Los Angeles," The Electric Railway Historical Association of Southern California (1999), http://www.erha.org/seveneras.htm.

26. Happiness surveys include the "World Values Survey" (Stockholm: World Values Survey Association, 2008), www.worldvaluessurvey.org and the World Map of Happiness, described in Adrian White, "A Global Projection of Subjective Well-being: A Challenge to Positive Psychology?" *Psychtalk* 56: 17–20; the competitiveness survey is from International Institute for Management Development, "World Competitiveness Yearbook, 2009" (Lausanne, Switzerland: IMD, 2009).

INTERLUDE 7: Biofuels

1. Figures on the share of renewables are from the US Energy Information Administration, http://www.eia.gov/totalenergy/data/monthly/query/mer_data.asp?table=T01.01 and http://www.eia.doe.gov/cneaf/electricity/epm/epmxlfilees1_b.xls.

2. See David Murphy, "EROI Update: Preliminary Results Using Toe-to-Heel Air Injection," The Oil Drum blog, March 18, 2009, http://netenergy.theoildrum.com/node/5183. For the effect of natural gradients on the net energy profits from corn ethanol, see David Murphy, "The Effect of Natural Gradients on the Net Energy Profits from Corn Ethanol," The Oil Drum blog, January 13, 2009, http://netenergy.theoildrum.com/node/4910.

3. That mass cultivation of corn for biofuels increases water pollution is from S. D. Donner and C. J. Kucharik, "Corn-Based Ethanol Production Compromises Goal of Reducing Nitrogen Export by the Mississippi River," *Proceedings of the National Academy of Sciences of the United States of America* 105, no. 11 (2008). That it has a worse greenhouse gas footprint than gasoline is from Timothy Searchinger et al., "Use of US Croplands for Biofuels Increases Greenhouse Gases through Emissions from Land-Use Change," *Science* 319, no. 5867 (2008). The figure on the energy return on investment for switchgrass is from Marty R. Schmer et al., "Net Energy of Cellulosic Ethanol from Switchgrass," *Proceedings of the National Academy of Sciences of the United States of America* 105, no. 2 (2008). Figures on the amount of land needed for biofuel cultivation to offset 25 percent of petroleum use are from Maywa Montenegro, "The Numbers Behind Ethanol, Cellulosic Ethanol and Biodiesel in the US," *Grist Magazine*, December 4, 2006.

CHAPTER 8: Reinventing Neighborhoods

1. Downtown Partnership of Baltimore, 2010 Quarterly Newsletter, winter/ spring issue.

2. The characterization of Sandtown as being replete with services, musicians, etc., is from Anne Haddad, "Sandtown-Winchester," *Urbanite Baltimore*, November 1, 2004. The figure of 42,000 vacant units is from the US Census, which defines vacant to include habitable structures. The 15,000 figure is from the City of Baltimore and Baltimore Neighborhood Indicators Alliance and is meant to include dilapidated structures. See http://www.ubalt.edu/bnia/indicators/DailyRecordVS3.html.

3. The report from the EPA cited is Hagler Bailly Services Inc. and Criterion Planners/Engineers, "The Transportation and Environmental Impacts of Infill Versus Greenfield Development," (Washington, D.C.: US Environmental Protection Agency, 1999). That industrial infill is outperforming suburban industrial real estate is from David Twist and Aaron Binkley, "A.M.B. Infill Strategy," research paper (San Francisco: AMB Property Corporation, 2010), www.amb.com/assets/infill_research.pdf.

4. Michael Pagano and Ann Bowman, "Vacant Land in Cities: An Urban Resource" (Washington, D.C.: Brookings Institution, Center on Urban and Metropolitan Policy, 2000).

5. The figure on the percentage of Americans living in large cities is from Edward. L. Glaeser and Jesse M. Shapiro, "Urban Growth in the 1990s: Is City Living Back?" *Journal of Regional Science* 43, no. 1 (2003). The Cleveland statistic is from Fred Smith, "Decaying at the Core: Urban Decline in Cleveland, Ohio," *Research in Economic History* 21 (2003). The statistic on vacant lots in Detroit is from Deborah Popper and Frank Popper, "Smart Decline in Post-Carbon Cities," in *The Post Carbon Reader: Managing the 21st Century's Sustainability Crises*, ed. R. Heineberg and D. Lerch (Healdsburg, Calif.: Watershed Media, 2010), 318.

6. The −8 percent figure is from Arthur C. Nelson and Kathy T. Young, "Limited Role of Downtowns in Meeting Metropolitan Housing Needs," *Journal of Urban Planning and Development* 134, no. 1 (2008). That the balance of population didn't significantly change is from J. Dannes, "Collateral Damage: Unintended Consequences of Urban Renewal in Baltimore, Maryland," http://shepherd.wlu.edu/PDF_files/Consequences%20of%20Baltimore%20Urban%20renewal.pdf.

7. Stellan Fryxell, interview with the author, May 19, 2010, Stockholm, Sweden; all subsequent quotations from Fryxell are from this interview.

8. Erik Freudenthal, interview with the author, May 19, 2010, Stockholm, Sweden; all subsequent quotations from Freudenthal are from this interview.

9. Finding of 5 percent cost increases is from Tommy Kjellgren and Agneta Persson, "Energy Efficiency and Environmental Awareness Integrated in the Everyday Living," in *Proceedings of the European Council for an Energy Efficient Economy*, 2001 Summer Study (Stockholm: European Council for an Energy Efficient Economy, 2001). Quotations in this paragraph are from Lars Gärde, interview with the author, May 19, 2010, Stockholm, Sweden; all subsequent quotations from Gärde are from this interview.

10. Karolina Brick, "Report Summary: Follow Up of Environmental Impact in Hammarby Sjöstad: Sickla Udde, Sickla Kaj, and Proppen" (Stockholm: Grontmij AB 2008), www.hammarbysjostad.se/inenglish/pdf/Grontmij%20Report%20eng.pdf.

11. This according to a survey from the Swedish Property Federation, cited in Peter V. Simpson, "Two-Year Wait for Stockholm Flat: Report," *The Local*, February 8, 2010.

12. John Norquist, interview with the author, June 22, 2010; all subsequent quotations from Norquist are from this interview.

13. From LEED-ND's "Fact Sheet"; available from http://www.usgbc.org/ShowFile.aspx?DocumentID=6423.

14. Sophie Lambert, interview with the author, June 25, 2010; all subsequent quotations from Lambert are from this interview. The "smart location" prerequisite quotation is from US Green Building Council, Congress for the New Urbanism, and Natural Resources Defense Council, "LEED 2009 for Neighborhood Development" (Washington, D.C.: US Green Building Council, 2009), 1.

15. See "LEED 2009 for Neighborhood Development," 1–9, for a full description of rules.

16. Kaid Benfield, phone interview with the author, June 25, 2010; all subsequent quotations from Benfield are from this interview.

17. Speech by HUD secretary Shaun Donovan to the Congress for the New Urbanism, Atlanta, Ga., May 21, 2010; transcript from http://www.cnu.org/node/3555.

18. Llewellyn Wells, interview with the author, September 8, 2010; all subsequent quotations from Wells are from this interview.

INTERLUDE 8: Nuclear

1. Robert L. Evans, *Fueling Our Future: An Introduction to Sustainable Energy* (Cambridge: Cambridge University Press, 2007), 116.

2. OECD Nuclear Energy Agency, International Atomic Energy Agency, and NetLibrary Inc., "Uranium 2005 Resources, Production, and Demand: A Joint Report" (Paris: Nuclear Energy Agency, Organisation for Economic Co-operation and Development, 2006); http://www.netLibrary.com/urlapi.asp?action=summary&v=1&bookid=170180.

3. Information on the fission products left in the waste and low rates of conversion for fast reactors is from Public Citizen, "Fast Reactors: Unsafe, Uneconomical, and Unable to Resolve the Problems of Nuclear Power," http://www.citizen.org/documents/FastReactors.pdf. The quotation is from an interview with Dr. Matthew Bunn in Clementine Fullias, "Cancelling the Yucca Mountain Repository Will Throw the Entire Nuclear Waste Management Program into Doubt," Scitizen, June 15, 2009, http://scitizen .com/stories/future-energies/2009/06/Cancelling-the-Yucca-Mountain-repository-will-throw-the-entire-nuclear-waste-management-program-into-doubt/.

4. The 2002 report cited on financial feasibility is Scully Capital Systems, "Business Case for New Nuclear Power Plants," presentation prepared for the US Department of Energy Office of Nuclear Energy, October 2002. Quotation is from "Cancelling the Yucca Mountain Repository," interview with Dr. Matthew Bunn.

5. According to Andrew Oswald, an economist at the University of Warwick, as referenced in Mark Peplow, "Hydrogen Economy Looks out of Reach," *Nature News*, online, October 7, 2004, www.nature.com/news/2004/041004/full/041004–13.html.

CHAPTER 9: The Very Regional City

1. Lewis Mumford, "The Fourth Migration," *Survey Graphic* 54, no. 3 (1925).

2. Philip D'Anieri, "A 'Fruitful Hypothesis'? The Regional Planning Association of America's Hopes for Technology," *Journal of Planning History* 1, no. 4 (2002): 284. An example of Mumford's later work, in which he acknowledges the failure of the suburban model, is Lewis Mumford, *The City in History: Its Origins, Its Transformations, and Its Prospects*, 1st ed. (New York: Harcourt, 1961); see his final chapter.

3. Carl Sussman, *Planning the Fourth Migration: The Neglected Vision of the Regional Planning Association of America* (Cambridge: MIT Press, 1976), 44.

4. The concept of a fifth migration is presented in Robert Fishman, "The Fifth Migration," *Journal of the American Planning Association* 71, no. 4 (2005). "Unslumming" is from Jane Jacobs, *The Death and Life of Great American Cities* (New York: Random House, 1961).

5. On the 1990s as the decade when property values and population shares began to rise for central cities, see Nelson and Young, "Limited Role of Downtowns in Meeting Metropolitan Housing Needs." On metropolitan growth rates since 2006, see William Frey, "Population and Migration," in *The State of Metropolitan America* (Washington, D.C.: Brookings Institution, 2010), and William Frey, "Texas Gains, Suburbs Lose in 2010 Census Preview" (Washington, D.C.: Brookings Institution, 2010), http://www.brookings.edu/opinions/2010/0625_population_frey.aspx#. The study on the "reversal phenomenon" is from James Hughes and Joseph Seneca, "The Beginning of the End of Sprawl?" (Rutgers, N.J.: Rutgers University, Edward J. Bloustein School of Planning and Public Policy, 2004).

6. Joe Cortright, "Driven to the Brink: How the Gas Price Spike Popped the Housing Bubble and Devalued the Suburbs" (Chicago: CEOs for Cities, 2008), 21.

7. Jonathan Levine, *Zoned Out: Regulation, Markets, and Choices in Transportation and Metropolitan Land-Use* (Washington, D.C.: Resources for the Future, 2005), 2–3.

8. John Norquist, interview with the author, June 22, 2010. Emily Talen and Gerrit Knaap, "Legalizing Smart Growth: An Empirical Study of Land-Use Regulation in Illinois," *Journal of Planning Education and Research* 22, no. 4 (2003).

9. Levine, *Zoned Out*, 73. Levine cites a number of studies supporting this contention on p. 52, including, among others, Daniel P. McMillen and John F. McDonald, "A Markov-Chain Model of Zoning Change," *Journal of Urban Economics* 30, no. 2 (1991); James R. White, "Large Lot Zoning and Subdivision Costs: A Test," *Journal of Urban Economics* 23, no. 3 (1988); James A. Thorson, "Zoning Policy Changes and the Urban Fringe Land Market," *Journal of the American Real Estate and Urban Economics Association* 22, no. 3 (1994); and Richard B. Peiser, "Density and Urban Sprawl," *Land Economics* 65, no. 3 (1989). Studies that have found that constraining the land market can lead to sprawl include John I. Carruthers

and G. F. Ulfarsson, "Fragmentation and Sprawl: Evidence from Interregional Analysis," *Growth and Change* 33, no. 3 (2002); Anthony Downs, "Some Realities about Sprawl and Urban Decline," *Housing Policy Debate* 10, no. 4 (1999); and Rolf Pendall, "Do Land-Use Controls Cause Sprawl?" *Environment and Planning B-Planning and Design* 26, no. 4 (1999). The 1999 study cited is Pendall, "Do Land-Use Controls Cause Sprawl?" The figure on amount of land at different densities is from David M. Theobald, "Land-Use Dynamics beyond the American Urban Fringes," *Geographical Review* 91, no. 3 (2001).

10. See the following four sources by William A. Fischel: "Why Are There NIMBYs?" *Land Economics* 77, no. 1 (2001); *The Homevoter Hypothesis: How Home Values Influence Local Government Taxation, School Finance, and Land-Use Policies* (Cambridge: Harvard University Press, 2001); "An Economic History of Zoning and a Cure for Its Exclusionary Effects," *Urban Studies* 41, no. 2 (2004); and *The Economics of Zoning Laws: A Property Rights Approach to American Land Use Controls* (Baltimore: John Hopkins University Press, 1985).

11. This is known as the "Tiebout-Hamilton model." See Bruce Hamilton, "Capitalization of Intrajurisdictional Difference in Local Tax Prices," *American Economic Review* 66, no. 5 (1976); and Charles Tiebout, "The Pure Theory of Local Expenditures," *Journal of Political Economy* 64 (1956).

12. David Rusk, *Cities without Suburbs: A Census 2000 Update*, 3rd ed. (Washington, D.C.: Woodrow Wilson Center Press, 2003).

13. Robert C. Ellickson and A. Dan Tarlock, *Land-Use Controls: Cases and Materials, Law School Casebook Series* (Boston: Little, Brown, 1981).

14. Information on Houston rights-of-way and intersections is from Michael Lewyn, "Zoning without Zoning," Planetizen, http://www.planetizen.com/node/109. Information on lane miles is from US DOT, http://www.fhwa.dot.gov/policyinformation/statistics/2007/hm72.cfm.

15. For the Pew survey, see Paul Taylor et al., "For Nearly Half of America, Grass Is Greener Somewhere Else" (Washington, D.C.: Pew Research Center, 2009). Information on attitudes of potential homebuyers is from Belden, Russonello, and Stewart, *2004 National Community Preference Survey* (Washington, D.C.: Smart Growth America, 2004).

16. Peter Calthorpe and William B. Fulton, *The Regional City: Planning for the End of Sprawl* (Washington, D.C.: Island Press, 2001).

17. Frank J. Popper, "Understanding American Land-Use Regulation since 1970: A Revisionist Interpretation," *Journal of the American Planning Association* 54, no. 3 (1988): 299.

18. Wilbur Smith Associates, *Noteworthy MPO Practices in Transportation: Land Use Planning Integration* (Washington, D.C.: Association of Metropolitan Planning Organizations, 2004).

19. http://narc.org/regional-councils-mpos/what-is-a-regional-council.html.

20. Peter Newman, Timothy Beatley, and Heather Boyer, *Resilient Cities: Responding to Peak Oil and Climate Change* (Washington, D.C.: Island Press, 2009), 145.

21. Yan Song and Gerrit J. Knaap, "Measuring Urban Form: Is Portland Winning the War on Sprawl?" *Journal of the American Planning Association* 70, no. 2 (2004).

22. The study that reported the increase in density of new housing was Carl Abbot, "Planning a Sustainable City," in *Urban Sprawl: Causes, Consequences, and Policy Responses*, ed. Gregory D. Squires (Washington, D.C.: Urban Institute Press, 2002). The point about Clark County as a "safety valve" is from Myung-Jin Jun, "The Effects of Portland's Urban Growth Boundary on Urban Development Patterns and Commuting," *Urban Studies* 41, no. 7 (2004). Note that Jun and many others also write about another potential pitfall of UGBs, which is regionally increased housing prices. Although some studies have suggested that Portland's UGB raises prices, another study by Jun ("The Effects of Portland's Urban Growth Boundary on Housing Prices," *Journal of the American Planning Association* 72, no. 2 [2006]), which is among the most statistically sophisticated, found no such effect. Information on "leakage" is from Douglas Porter, *Managing Growth in America's Communities* (Washington, D.C.: Island Press, 2009), 84.

23. Porter, *Managing Growth*, 82–83.

24. See, e.g., Calthorpe and Fulton, *The Regional City*, 273.

25. Dollar estimates for Measure 37 are from http://www.bendbulletin.com/apps/pbcs.dll/article?AID=/20071003/NEWS0107/710030412/1001&nav_category=. Information on the expected and actual effects of Measure 37 is from James Holman, "Measure 49 Scales Back Rural Housing Development," *The Oregonian*, June 19, 2007.

26. Marc Pisano, interview with the author, January 9, 2009; all subsequent quotations from Pisano are from this interview.

27. Robert Lang, *Edgeless Cities: Exploring the Elusive Metropolis*, Brookings Metro Series (Washington, D.C.: Brookings Institution, 2003), 10, 55.

28. Christopher B. Leinberger, *The Option of Urbanism: Investing in a New American Dream* (Washington, D.C.: Island Press, 2008

29. Ali Modarres, "Polycentricity, Commuting Pattern, Urban Form: The Case of Southern California," *International Journal of Urban and Regional Research*. In press.

30. The common characteristics of successful urban villages are given in Newman and Kenworthy, *Sustainability and Cities: Overcoming Automobile Dependence* (Washington, D.C.: Island Press, 1999), 165–72. On subcenter specialization, see Christopher Leinberger and Charles Lockwood, "How Business Is Reshaping America," *Atlantic Monthly*, October 1986; note that although this article is more than twenty years old, the characterization of subcenter specialization still holds.

31. Ellen Dunham-Jones and June Williamson, *Retrofitting Suburbia: Urban Design Solutions for Redesigning Suburbs* (Hoboken, N.J.: John Wiley 2009), 207–8.

32. Lang, *Edgeless Cities*, 30–31.

33. Mumford, *The City in History*, 519.

34. Blog posting is from William B. Fulton, "What's the Difference between Glendale and Palmdale? Don't Ask Joel Kotkin," California Planning and Development Report, July 7, 2008. The Leinberger article is Christopher Leinberger, "The Next Slum?" *Atlantic Monthly*, March 2008. The Kotkin opinion piece is from Joel Kotkin, "Suburbia's Not Dead," *Los Angeles Times*, July 6, 2008.

INTERLUDE 9: Renewable Energy Generation

1. The figure on wind and solar generation's percentage share is from the US Energy Information Administration, http://www.eia.doe.gov/cneaf/ electricity/epm/epmxlfilees1_b.xls. The figure regarding coal-plant equivalency of all installed solar in 2004 is from Paul Roberts, *The End of Oil* (Boston: Houghton Mifflin, 2005), 191. The figures on the percentage of generation accounted for by renewables in the United States is from http://www.eia .doe.gov/cneaf/electricity/epm/epmxlfilees1_a.xls and http://www.eia.doe .gov/cneaf/electricity/epa/epates.html. The figure on the share of different renewables is from http://www.eia.doe.gov/cneaf/solar.renewables/page/ table3.html. The figure on 350,000 households is from Matthew Wald and Tom Zeller, "Cost of Green Power Makes Projects Tougher Sell," *New York Times*, November 7, 2010. The figure on a million wind turbines is from Roberts, *End of Oil*, 205.

2. Solar energy prices by month are updated at http://www.solarbuzz .com/facts-and-figures/retail-price-environment/solar-electricity-prices.

Total average electricity rates are available at http://www.eia.doe.gov/cneaf/electricity/epm/table5_3.html and at http://www.eia.doe.gov/cneaf/electricity/epm/table5_6_a.html for a state-by-state breakdown.

3. The figure on wind power costing 50 percent more than coal is from Matthew Wald, "Cost Works against Alternative and Renewable Energy Source in Time of Recession," *New York Times*, March 28, 2009. The EPRI studies cited are referenced in the *Times* article. To calculate the cost comparison of solar photovoltaics with conventional power, solar generation costs were from http://www.solarbuzz.com/facts-and-figures/retail-price-environment/solar-electricity-prices and average electricity rates were from http://www.eia.doe.gov/cneaf/electricity/epm/table5_3.html and http://www.eia.doe.gov/cneaf/electricity/epm/table5_6_a.html.

4. The percentage of time that solar cells can work is from Roberts, *End of Oil*, 194; that for wind is from p. 202. The German capacity factor is from http://www.leonardo-energy.org/capacity-factor-wind-power.

5. Roberts, *End of Oil*, 203.

6. Brent Barker, "Pathways to the Full Portfolio," *EPRI Journal*, March 2007, 24.

7. Peter Meisen and Oliver Pochert, "A Study of Very Large Solar Desert Systems with the Requirements and Benefits to Those Nations Having High Solar Irradiation Potential" (San Diego: Global Energy Network Institute, 2006).

8. The land footprint of a wind farm and coal plant is from Roberts, *End of Oil*, 20. The figure of how many square miles of solar or wind a city of a million people would need is from US Department of the Interior, Minerals Management Service (http://www.mms.gov/). The figure for the entire United States is from John A. Turner, "A Realizable Renewable Energy Future," *Science* 285, no. 5433 (1999): 687. This analysis was conducted using 1997 data on electricity demand. I have updated their calculation to demand data for 2008, which is approximately 25 percent higher. The 2005 analysis on rooftop solar is from Ross McCluney, "Renewable Energy Limits," in *The Final Energy Crisis*, ed. Andrew McKillop and Shelia Newman (London: Ann Arbor Pluto, 2005), 153–75.

9. As quoted in Brian Schimmoller, "Electricity Solutions for a Carbon-Constrained Future," *EPRI Journal*, Fall 2007, 7.

10. The figure on fuel-cell cars getting three times the fuel efficiency of gasoline cars is from Roberts, *End of Oil*, 73. The fact that near-term hydrogen cars could be modified internal combustion vehicles is from John Turner, "A Realizable Energy Future," *Science* 285, no. 5428 (1999): 689.

11. US Department of Energy Hydrogen Program, "Distributed Hydrogen Production from Wind," http://www.hydrogen.energy.gov/well_wheels_analysis.html.

12. The report referenced is Diana Bauer et al., "Critical Materials Strategy" (Washington, D.C.: US Department of Energy, 2010). Information on rare-earth mineral vulnerability also comes from Keith Bradsher, "US Called Vulnerable to Rare Earth Shortages," *New York Times*, December 15, 2010, and from Anil Das, "2011 Spells Desperate Search for Rare Earth Minerals," *International Business Times*, January 7, 2011.

CHAPTER 10: The Very Efficient City

1. "Energy slave" figures come from a variety of sources, including Stephen Vickers Boyden, *Western Civilization in Biological Perspective: Patterns in Biohistory* (Oxford: Clarendon Press, 1987); Michael S. Common and Sigrid Stagl, *Ecological Economics: An Introduction* (Cambridge: Cambridge University Press, 2005); and Richard Heinberg, *The Party's Over: Oil, War and the Fate of Industrial Societies*, 2nd ed. (Gabriola Island, B.C.: New Society Publishers, 2005). The Nordhaus article is William Nordhaus, "Do Real-Output and Real-Wage Measures Capture Reality? The History of Lighting Suggests Not," in *The Economics of New Goods: Studies in Income and Wealth*, National Bureau of Economic Research Series vol. 58, ed. Timothy F. Bresnahan and Robert J. Gordon (Chicago: University of Chicago Press, 1997). American energy-slave equivalence comes from Boyden, *Western Civilization*, 196; the figure on minimum wage equivalence comes from Heinberg, *The Party's Over*, 272.

2. William Stanley Jevons and Alfred William Flux, *The Coal Question: An Inquiry Concerning the Progress of the Nation, and the Probable Exhaustion of Our Coal-Mines*, 3d rev. ed., Reprints of Economic Classics (New York: A. M. Kelley, 1965).

3. The quotation is from William R. Barnes, "Beyond Federal Urban Policy," *Urban Affairs Review* 40, no. 5 (2005): 578. Information on the evolution of federal urban policy comes from Barnes and from Hillary Silver, "Obama's Urban Policy: A Symposium," *City and Community* 9, no. 1 (2010).

4. Barnes, "Beyond Federal Urban Policy," 576.

5. The Obama speech on urban affairs was given on July 13, 2009, Urban and Metropolitan Policy Roundtable, Washington, D.C.

6. Bruce Katz, "Obama's Metro Presidency," *City and Community* 9, no. 1 (2010); Silver, "Obama's Urban Policy."

7. Peter Calthorpe and William B. Fulton, *The Regional City: Planning for the End of Sprawl* (Washington, D.C.: Island Press, 2001), 88.

8. Thomas L. Karnes, *Asphalt and Politics: A History of the American Highway System* (Jefferson, N.C.: McFarland, 2009), 163.

9. Robert Poole, "Policy Strategies for US Surface Transportation Funding Reauthorization" (Washington, D.C.: Reason Foundation, 2010).

10. Karnes, *Asphalt and Politics*, 165. He mentions a Government Accountability Office report which states that federal programs are increasingly receptive to private-sector participation in highways.

11. Thomas Sick Nielsen, interview with the author, May 17, 2010, Copenhagen, Denmark.

12. Daniel Lerch, "Post-Carbon Cities: Planning for Energy and Climate Uncertainty" (Santa Rosa, Calif.: Post-Carbon Institute, 2007), 27.

13. For the list, see http://postcarboncities.net/actions/table?sort=desc&order=Population.

Select Bibliography

Abbot, Carl. "Planning a Sustainable City." In *Urban Sprawl: Causes, Consequences, and Policy Responses*, edited by G. D. Squires. Washington, D.C.: Urban Institute Press, 2002.

Ackermann, Marsha E. *Cool Comfort: America's Romance with Air-Conditioning*. Washington, D.C.: Smithsonian Institution Press, 2002.

"The Air-Conditioned Census." Editorial. *New York Times*, September 6, 1970.

Akbari, Hashem. "Shade Trees Reduce Building Energy Use and CO_2 Emissions from Power Plants." *Environmental Pollution* 116 (2002): S119–S126.

Akbari, Hashem, Susan Davis, Sofia Dorsano, Joe Huang, and Steven Winnett. "Cooling Our Communities: A Guidebook on Tree Planting and Light-Colored Surfacing." Washington, D.C.: US Environmental Protection Agency, Office of Policy Analysis, Climate Change Division, 1992.

Akbari, Hashem, Dan M. Kurn, Sarah E. Bretz, and James W. Hanford. "Peak Power and Cooling Energy Savings of Shade Trees." *Energy and Buildings* 25, no. 2 (1997): 139–48.

Akbari, Hashem, M. Pomerantz, and Haider Taha. "Cool Surfaces and Shade Trees to Reduce Energy Use and Improve Air Quality in Urban Areas." *Solar Energy* 70, no. 3 (2001): 295–310.

Allen, Sam. "Los Angeles Ranks High in 'Commuter Pain' Study, but Things Could Be Worse: L.A. Now." *Los Angeles Times*, June 30, 2010.

American Council for an Energy Efficiency Economy. "The 2009 State Energy Efficiency Scorecard." Washington, D.C., 2009.

American Institute of Architects. "Local Leaders in Sustainability-Green Incentives." Washington, D.C.: American Institute of Architects, 2009.

Anderson, William, et al. "Urban Form: Energy and the Environment: A Review of Issues, Evidence and Policy." *Urban Studies* 33, no. 1 (1996): 7–35.

Arnfield, A. John. "Two Decades of Urban Climate Research: A Review of Turbulence, Exchanges of Energy and Water, and the Urban Heat Island." *International Journal of Climatology* 23, no. 1 (2003): 1–26.

Arsenault, Raymond. "The End of the Long Hot Summer: The Air-Conditioner and Southern Culture." *Journal of Southern History* 50, no. 4 (1984): 597–628.

Aultman-Hall, Lisa, and F. L. Hall. "Ottawa-Carleton Commuter Cyclist On- and Off-Road Incident Rates." *Accident Analysis and Prevention* 30, no. 1 (1998): 29–43.

Automobile Club of Southern California. *Traffic Survey: Los Angeles Metropolitan Area, 1937*. Los Angeles: Automobile Club, 1938.

Axelrod, Jeremiah B. C. *Inventing Autopia: Dreams and Visions of the Modern Metropolis in Jazz Age Los Angeles*. Berkeley: University of California Press, 2009.

Baker, Donald. "The Present Problem." Paper presented at the Conference on the Rapid Transit Question, Los Angeles, January 21, 1930.

Baker, Ray Stannard. "The Subway Deal." *McClure's Magazine*, March 1905, 451–69.

Banister, D. "Energy Use, Transport, and Settlement Patterns." In *Sustainable Development and Urban Form*, edited by M. J. Breheny. London: Pion, 1992.

Barker, Brent. "Pathways to the Full Portfolio." *EPRI Journal*, March 2007.

Barnes, William R. "Beyond Federal Urban Policy." *Urban Affairs Review* 40, no. 5 (2005): 575–89.

Barnett, Cynthia. *Mirage: Florida and the Vanishing Water of the Eastern U.S.* Ann Arbor: University of Michigan Press, 2007.

Battles, Stephanie. "Trends in Residential Air-Conditioning Usage from 1978 to 1997." Washington, D.C.: Energy Information Administration, 2000.

Bauer, Diana, et al. "Critical Materials Strategy." Washington, D.C.: US Department of Energy, 2010.

Beatley, Timothy. *Green Urbanism: Learning from European Cities*. Washington, D.C.: Island Press, 2000.

Belden, Russonello, and Stewart. *2004 National Community Preference Survey*. Washington, D.C.: Smart Growth America, 2004.

Bottles, Scott L. *Los Angeles and the Automobile: The Making of the Modern City*. Berkeley: University of California Press, 1987.

Boyden, Stephen Vickers. *Western Civilization in Biological Perspective: Patterns in Biohistory*. Oxford: Clarendon Press, 1987.

Bradsher, Keith. "U.S. Called Vulnerable to Rare Earth Shortages." *New York Times*, December 15, 2010.

Breheny, M. J. "The Contradiction of the Compact City: A Review." In *Sustainable Development and Urban Form*, edited by M. J. Breheny. London: Pion, 1992.

Brewer, Jim, et al. "Geometric Design Practices for European Roads." Washington, D.C.: US Department of Transportation, 2001.

Brick, Karolina. "Report Summary: Follow-Up of Environmental Impact in Hammarby Sjöstad: Sickla Udde, Sickla Kaj, and Proppen." Stockholm: Grontmij AB, 2008.

Brodsly, David. *L.A. Freeway: An Appreciative Essay*. Berkeley: University of California Press, 1981.

Bronson, Willsam. "Home Is a Freeway." *Cry California*, Summer 1966, 8–13.

Brown, Marilyn, Frank Southworth, and Andrea Sarzynski. *Shrinking the Carbon Footprint of Metropolitan America*. Washington, D.C.: Brookings Institution, 2008.

Burks, Edward. "15 Busiest Subway Stations Show Big Decline in Riders." *New York Times*, November 10, 1975.

———. "Subway Ridership Lowest since '18: Off 20% in Decade." *New York Times*, April 6, 1975.

Burman, Lars, and Christer Johansson. "The Effects of the Congestion Tax on Emission and Air Quality." Stockholm: Stockholm Environment and Health Administration, 2009.

Calthorpe, Peter, and William B. Fulton. *The Regional City: Planning for the End of Sprawl*. Washington, D.C.: Island Press, 2001.

Caminada, Carlos, and Jeb Blount. "Petrobras' Tupi Oil Field May Hold 9 Billion Barrels." *Bloomberg*, November 8, 2007.

Campbell, Colin. "The Assessment and Importance of Oil Depletion." In *The Final Energy Crisis*, edited by A. McKillop and S. Newman. London: Pluto Press, 2005.

Carruthers, John I., and G. F. Ulfarsson. "Fragmentation and Sprawl: Evidence from Interregional Analysis." *Growth and Change* 33, no. 3 (2002): 312–40.

Carver, A., J. Salmon, K. Campbell, L. Baur, S. Garnett, and D. Crawford. "How Do Perceptions of Local Neighborhood Relate to Adolescents' Walking and Cycling?" *American Journal of Health Promotion* 20, no. 2 (2005): 139–47.

Cervero, R. "Road Expansion, Urban Growth, and Induced Travel: A Path Analysis." *Journal of the American Planning Association* 69, no. 2 (2003): 145–63.

Cervero, Robert. *The Transit Metropolis: A Global Inquiry*. Washington, D.C.: Island Press, 1998.

Chetty, Marshini, David Tran, and Rebecca Grinter. "Getting to Green: Understanding Resource Consumption in the Home." *UbiComp 2008 Conference Proceedings*, Seoul, South Korea, September 2008.

Childs, Craig. "Phoenix Falling?" *High Country News*, April 13, 2007.

City of Stockholm Traffic Administration. "Analysis of Traffic in Stockholm— with Special Focus on the Effects of the Congestion Tax, 2005–2008." Stockholm: City of Stockholm Traffic Administration, 2009.

Cleveland, Cutler. "Net Energy Obtained from Extracting Oil and Gas in the Us." *Energy* 30 (2005): 769–82.

Cleveland, Cutler, and Robert Costanza. "Energy Return on Investment (Eroi)." In *Encyclopedia of Earth*, edited by C. Cleveland. Washington, D.C.: Environmental Information Coalition, National Council for Science and the Environment, 2010.

Cleveland, C., R. Costanza, A. Hall, and R. Kaufman. "Energy and the US Economy: A Biophysical Perspective." *Science* 225 (1984): 890–97.

Coleville-Andersen, Mikael. "Bottleneck Blog: Bikes, Copenhagen and Disneyland: What We Have in Common." *Los Angeles Times*, August 8, 2008.

Common, Michael S., and Sigrid Stagl. *Ecological Economics: An Introduction*. Cambridge: Cambridge University Press, 2005.

Confessore, Nicholas. "Congestion Pricing Plan Dies in Albany—City Room Blog." *New York Times*, April 7, 2008.

Cortright, Joe. *Driven to the Brink: How the Gas Price Spike Popped the Housing Bubble and Devalued the Suburbs*. Chicago: CEOs for Cities, 2008.

———. *Measuring Urban Transportation Performance*. Chicago: CEOs for Cities, 2010.

———. *New York City's Green Dividend*. Chicago: CEOs for Cities, 2010.

Crump, Spencer. *Ride the Big Red Cars: How Trolleys Helped Build Southern California*. 1st ed. Los Angeles: Crest Publications, 1962.

D'Anieri, Philip. "A 'Fruitful Hypothesis'? The Regional Planning Association of America's Hopes for Technology." *Journal of Planning History* 1, no. 4 (2002): 279–89.

Darley, Julian. *High Noon for Natural Gas: The New Energy Crisis*. White River Junction, Vt.: Chelsea Green Publishing, 2004.

Das, Anil. "2011 Spells Desperate Search for Rare Earth Minerals." *International Business Times*, January 7, 2011.

Davis, Stacy C., et al. *Transportation Energy Data Book*. 29th ed. Oak Ridge, Tenn.: Oak Ridge National Laboratory, 2010.

Deffeyes, Kenneth S. *Beyond Oil: The View from Hubbert's Peak*. New York: Hill and Wang, 2006.

Donner, S. D., and C. J. Kucharik. "Corn-Based Ethanol Production Compromises Goal of Reducing Nitrogen Export by the Mississippi River." *Proceed-*

ings of the National Academy of Sciences of the United States of America 105, no. 11 (2008): 4513–18.

Downs, Anthony. "Some Realities about Sprawl and Urban Decline." *Housing Policy Debate* 10, no. 4 (1999): 955–74.

———. *Still Stuck in Traffic: Coping with Peak-Hour Traffic Congestion.* James A. Johnson Metro Series. Washington, D.C.: Brookings Institution, 2004.

Dunham-Jones, Ellen, and June Williamson. *Retrofitting Suburbia: Urban Design Solutions for Redesigning Suburbs.* Hoboken, N.J.: John Wiley, 2009.

Dunphy, Robert, and Kimberly Fisher. "Transportation, Congestion, and Density: New Insights." *Transportation Research Record* 1552 (1996): 89–96.

Efficiency Vermont. "Annual Report." Burlington, Vt.: Efficiency Vermont, 2008.

Eisenhower, Dwight D. *At Ease: Stories I Tell to Friends.* 1st TAB ed. Military Classics Series. Blue Ridge Summit, Penn.: TAB Books, 1988.

Ellickson, Robert C., and A. Dan Tarlock. *Land-Use Controls: Cases and Materials.* Law School Casebook Series. Boston: Little, Brown, 1981.

Energy Information Administration. "Emission of Greenhouse Gases in the United States, 1985–1990." Washington, D.C.: Energy Information Administration, 1993.

———. "Energy Market and Economic Impacts of HR 2454, the American Clean Energy and Security Act of 2009." Washington, D.C.: Energy Information Administration, 2009.

Energy Watch Group. "Coal: Resources and Future Production." Berlin: Energy Watch Group, 2007.

Epstein, Joel. "Moving L.A.: There's a Train a Comin'." *Huffington Post*, February 10 2010.

Eschebach, H. "Die Gebrauchswasserversorgung Des Antiken Pompeii." *Antike Welt* 2 (1979): 3–24.

Evans, Robert L. *Fueling Our Future: An Introduction to Sustainable Energy.* Cambridge: Cambridge University Press, 2007.

Ewing, Reid H. *Growing Cooler: Evidence on Urban Development and Climate Change.* Washington, D.C.: Urban Land Institute, 2008.

Ewing, Reid, and Robert Cervero. "Travel and the Built Environment." *Journal of the American Planning Association* 76, no. 3 (2010): 265–94.

———. "Travel and the Built Environment: A Synthesis." *Transportation Research Record*, 1780 (2001): 87–114.

Ewing, Reid, Rolf Pendall, and Donald Chen. "Measuring Sprawl and Its Impacts." Washington, D.C.: Smart Growth America, 2003.

———. "Measuring Sprawl and Its Transportation Impacts." *Travel Demand and Land Use 2003*, no. 1831 (2003): 175–83.

Farrell, Diana, Jaana Remes, Florian Bressand, Mark Laabs, and Anjan Sundaram. "The Case for Investing in Energy Productivity." San Francisco: McKinsey Global Institute, 2008.

Feinman, Mark. "The New York City Transit Authority in the 1970s" (2002); http://www.nycsubway.org/articles/history-nycta1970s.html.

Fischel, William A. "An Economic History of Zoning and a Cure for Its Exclusionary Effects." *Urban Studies* 41, no. 2 (2004): 317–40.

———. *The Economics of Zoning Laws: A Property Rights Approach to American Land Use Controls*. Baltimore: John Hopkins University Press, 1985.

———. *The Homevoter Hypothesis: How Home Values Influence Local Government Taxation, School Finance, and Land-Use Policies*. Cambridge: Harvard University Press, 2001.

———. "Why Are There NIMBYs?" *Land Economics* 77, no. 1 (2001): 144–52.

Fishman, Robert. "The Fifth Migration." *Journal of the American Planning Association* 71, no. 4 (2005): 357–66.

Fitzgerald, Joan. *Emerald Cities: Urban Sustainability and Economic Development*. New York: Oxford University Press, 2010.

Foucher, Sam. "Peak Oil Update—August 2008: Production Forecasts and Eia Production Numbers." http://www.theoildrum.com/node/3720.

Foy, Douglas, and Robert Healy. "Cities Are the Answer." *Boston Globe*, April 4, 2007.

Frey, William. "Population and Migration." In *The State of Metropolitan America*. Washington, D.C.: Brookings Institution, 2010.

Fullias, Clementine. "Cancelling the Yucca Mountain Repository Will Throw the Entire Nuclear Waste Management Program into Doubt." Interview with Dr. Matthew Bunn. Scitizen.com, June 15, 2009.

Fulton, William B. "What's the Different between Glendale and Palmdale? Don't Ask Joel Kotkin." California Planning and Development Report, July 7, 2008, http://www.cp-dr.com/node/2069.

Galbraith, Kate. "Energy Efficiency the Green Mountain Way." *New York Times*, October 8, 2008.

Gifford, Henry. "A Better Way to Rate Green Buildings." *Northeast Sun*, Spring 2009.

Glaeser, Edward. *The Triumph of the City*. New York: Penguin Press, 2011.

Glaeser, Edward, and Matthew Kahn. "The Greenness of Cities." Cambridge: Harvard University, John F. Kennedy School of Government Policy Briefs, 2008.

Glaeser, Edward L., and Jesse M. Shapiro. "Urban Growth in the 1990s: Is City Living Back?" *Journal of Regional Science* 43, no. 1 (2003): 139–65.

Goldberg, Jonah. "If You Thought I Hated D.C. Before . . ." *National Review*, July 6, 1999.

Gomez-Ibanez, J. A. "A Global View of Automobile Dependence: A Review of Cities and Automobile Dependence: An International Sourcebook." *Journal of the American Planning Association* 57, no. 3 (1991): 376–79.

Gottlieb, Robert. *Reinventing Los Angeles*. Cambridge: MIT Press, 2007.

Greene, Wade. "Air-Conditioning." *New York Times*, July 14, 1974.

Haddad, Anne. "Sandtown-Winchester." *Urbanite Baltimore*, November 1, 2004.

Hagler Bailly Services Inc., and Criterion Planners/Engineers. "The Transportation and Environmental Impacts of Infill Versus Greenfield Development." Washington, D.C.: US Environmental Protection Agency, 1999.

Hall, Charles, A. Gupta, and Mike Herweyer. "Unconvential Oil: Tar Sands and Shale Oil: EROI on the Web, Part 3 of 6." http://www.theoildrum.com/node/3839.

Hall, Charles, Sarah Palcher, and Mike Herweyer. "Provisional Results from EROI Assessment." http://www.theoildrum.com/node/3810.

Hamilton, Bruce. "Capitalization of Intrajurisdictional Difference in Local Tax Prices." *American Economic Review* 66, no. 5 (1976): 743–53.

Hanemann, Michael. "The Central Arizona Project." Working paper. Berkeley: Department of Agriculture and Resource Economics, 2002.

Hayward, Steven. "Legends of the Sprawl." *Policy Review*, no. 91 (1998): 26–32.

Heinberg, Richard. *The Party's Over: Oil, War and the Fate of Industrial Societies*. 2nd ed. Gabriola Island, B.C.: New Society Publishers, 2005.

Hess, Daniel B. "Effect of Free Parking on Commuter Mode Choice: Evidence from Travel Diary Data." *Transit Planning, Intermodal Facilities, and Marketing*, no. 1753 (2001): 35–42.

Holley, Irving B. *The Highway Revolution, 1895–1925: How the United States Got out of the Mud*. Durham, N.C.: Carolina Academic Press, 2008.

Holman, James. "Measure 49 Scales Back Rural Housing Development." *The Oregonian*, June 19, 2007.

Holtzclaw, John. "Explaining Urban Density and Transit Impacts." San Francisco: Natural Resources Defense Council and Sierra Club, 1991.

———. "Using Residential Patterns and Transit to Decrease Auto Dependence and Costs." San Francisco: Natural Resources Defense Council and California Home Energy Efficiency Rating Systems, 1994.

Hood, Clifton. *722 Miles: The Building of the Subways and How They Trans-formed New York*. New York: Simon and Schuster, 1993.

Hu, Pat. "Summary of Travel Trends: 2001 National Household Travel Survey." Washington, D.C.: US Department of Transportation, 2004.

Hughes, J. David. *Will Natural Gas Fuel America in the Twenty-First Century?* Santa Rosa, Calif.: Post Carbon Institute, 2011.

Hughes, James, and Joseph Seneca. *The Beginning of the End of Sprawl?* Rutgers, N.J.: Edward J. Bloustein School of Planning and Public Policy, Rutgers University, 2004.

Hymon, Steve. "Bottleneck Blog: On the Subway with Zev." *Los Angeles Times*, July 9, 2008.

International Energy Agency. "World Energy Outlook 2007." Paris: International Energy Agency, Organisation for Economic Co-operation and Development, 2007.

Jacobs, Jane. *The Death and Life of Great American Cities*. New York: Random House, 1961.

Jacobsen, Peter L. "Safety in Numbers: More Walkers and Bicyclists, Safer Walking and Bicycling." *Injury Prevention* 9, no. 3 (2003): 205–9.

Jarman, Rufus. "They're Trying to Make Summer Extinct." *Saturday Evening Post*, June 6, 1953, 142–46.

Jensen, Søren, Claus Rosenkilde, and Niels Jensen. "Road Safety and Perceived Risk of Cycle Facilites in Copenhagen." Lyngby: City of Copenhagen and Trafitec, 2007.

Jevons, William Stanley, and Alfred William Flux. *The Coal Question: An Inquiry Concerning the Progress of the Nation, and the Probable Exhaustion of Our Coal-Mines*. 3d rev. ed. Rpt. Economic Classics. New York: A. M. Kelley, 1965.

Jun, Myung-Jin. "The Effects of Portland's Urban Growth Boundary on Housing Prices." *Journal of the American Planning Association* 72, no. 2 (2006): 239–43.

———. "The Effects of Portland's Urban Growth Boundary on Urban Development Patterns and Commuting." *Urban Studies* 41, no. 7 (2004): 1333–48.

Karathodorou, Niovi, Daniel Graham, and Robert Noland. "Estimating the Effect of Urban Density on Fuel Demand." *Energy Economics* 32 (2010): 86–92.

Karnes, Thomas L. *Asphalt and Politics: A History of the American Highway System*. Jefferson, N.C.: McFarland, 2009.

Katz, Bruce. "Obama's Metro Presidency." *City and Community* 9, no. 1 (2010): 23–31.

Kennedy, Christopher, John Cuddihy, and Joshua Engel-Yan. "The Changing Metabolism of Cities." *Journal of Industrial Ecology* 11, no. 2 (2007): 43–59.

Kenworthy, Jeffrey R. *Indicators of Transport Efficiency in Thirty-Seven Global Cities: A Report for the World Bank*. Perth, W.A.: Institute for Science and Technology Policy, Murdoch University, 1997.

Kenworthy, Jeffrey R., Felix B. Laube, and Peter Newman. *An International Sourcebook of Automobile Dependence in Cities, 1960–1990*. Boulder: University Press of Colorado, 1999.

Kerby, Philip. "Fires of Heaven." *Saturday Evening Post*, June 15, 1935, 39.

Kihss, Peter. "Kozlov Sees City in Seventy-Seven-Minute Tour." *New York Times*, July 13, 1959.

Kotkin, Joel. "Suburbia's Not Dead." *Los Angeles Times*, July 6, 2008.

"Kozlov Denounces New York Subway; Urges Rebuilding It." *New York Times*, July 26, 1959.

Kupel, Douglas E. *Fuel for Growth: Water and Arizona's Urban Environment*. Tucson: University of Arizona Press, 2003.

Lang, Robert. *Edgeless Cities: Exploring the Elusive Metropolis*. Brookings Metro Series. Washington, D.C.: Brookings Institution, 2003.

Lang, Robert, and Kristopher Rengert. "The Hot and Cold Sunbelts: Comparing State Growth Rates, 1950–2000." Fannie Mae Foundation Census Note. Washington, D.C.: Fannie Mae Foundation, 2001.

Leinberger, Christopher. "The Next Slum?" *Atlantic Monthly*, March 2008.

———. *The Option of Urbanism: Investing in a New American Dream*. Washington, D.C.: Island Press, 2008.

Leinberger, Christopher, and Charles Lockwood. "How Business Is Reshaping America."*Atlantic Monthly*, March 1986, 43–52.

Lerch, Daniel. "Post-Carbon Cities: Planning for Energy and Climate Uncertainty." Santa Rosa, Calif.: Post-Carbon Institute, 2007.

"Let 'Em Walk!" *Los Angeles Times*, February 14, 1926.

Levine, Jonathan. *Zoned Out: Regulation, Markets, and Choices in Transportation and Metropolitan Land-Use*. Washington, D.C.: Resources for the Future, 2005.

Lewis, Tom. *Divided Highways: Building the Interstate Highways, Transforming American Life*. New York: Viking, 1997.

Lewyn, Michael. "Zoning without Zoning." Planetizen, http://www.planet izen.com/node/109.

Lindsey, Robin. "Do Economists Reach a Conclusion on Road Pricing? The Intellectual History of an Idea." *Econ Journal Watch* 3, no. 2 (2006): 292–379.

Logan, Michael F. *Desert Cities: The Environmental History of Phoenix and Tucson*. History of the Urban Environment. Pittsburgh: University of Pittsburgh Press, 2006.

Longstreth, Richard W. *City Center to Regional Mall: Architecture, the Automobile, and Retailing in Los Angeles, 1920–1950*. Cambridge: MIT Press, 1997.

Los Angeles County Regional Planning Commission. "Report of a Highway Traffic Survey in the County of Los Angeles." Los Angeles: Regional Planning Commission, 1937.

Mayer, Peter W., William B. DeOreo, and AWWA Research Foundation. *Residential End Uses of Water*. Denver, Colo.: AWWA Research Foundation and American Water Works Association, 1999.

McCluney, Ross. "Renewable Energy Limits." In *The Final Energy Crisis*, edited by A. McKillop and S. Newman. London: Ann Arbor Pluto, 2005.

McKinnon, Shaun, "Five Cities Cash in on Wastewater Deal." *ArizonaCentral.com*, April 1, 2010.

McMillen, Daniel P., and John F. McDonald. "A Markov-Chain Model of Zoning Change." *Journal of Urban Economics* 30, no. 2 (1991): 257–70.

Meisen, Peter, and Oliver Pochert. "A Study of Very Large Solar Desert Systems with the Requirements and Benefits to Those Nations Having High Solar Irradiation Potential." San Diego: Global Energy Network Institute, 2006.

Metz, Bert. *Special Report on Carbon Dioxide Capture and Storage*, Intergovernmental Panel on Climate Change. Cambridge: Cambridge University Press, 2005.

Modarres, Ali. "Polycentricity, Commuting Pattern, Urban Form: The Case of Southern California." *International Journal of Urban and Regional Research* In press (2010).

Mohl, Raymond A. "Stop the Road: Freeway Revolts in American Cities." *Journal of Urban History* 30, no. 5 (2004): 674–706.

Montenegro, Maywa. "The Big Three: The Numbers behind Ethanol, Cellulosic Ethanol and Biodiesel in the US." *Grist Magazine*, December 2006, http://www.grist.org/article/montenegro.

Moritz, William E. "Adult Bicyclists in the United States: Characteristics and Riding Experience in 1996." *Bicycle and Pedestrian Research 1998*, no. 1636 (1998): 1–7.

Morris, Eric. "Los Angeles Transportation Facts and Fiction: Freeways." *Los Angeles Times*, February 29, 2009.

Morris, Joe Alex. "Arizona: Air-Conditioned Desert." *Saturday Evening Post*, June 17, 1961, 30–64.

Mumford, Lewis. *The City in History: Its Origins, Its Transformations, and Its Prospects.* 1st ed. New York: Harcourt, 1961.

———. "The Fourth Migration." *Survey Graphic* 54, no. 3 (1925): 130–33.

Municipality of Copenhagen. "Cycle Policy 2002–2012." Municipality of Copenhagen: Roads and Parks Department, 2002.

Murphy, David. "EROI Update: Preliminary Results Using Toe-to-Heel Air Injection." March 18, 2009, http://netenergy.theoildrum.com/node/5183.

Navarro, Mireya. "Some Buildings Not Living Up to Green Label." *New York Times*, August 30, 2009.

Nelson, Alyse. "Livable Copenhagen: The Design of a Bicycle City." Seattle and Copenhagen: Center for Public Space Research and University of Washington, 2006.

Nelson, Andrew. *The Greening of U.S. Investment Real Estate: Market Fundamentals, Prospects, and Opportunities.* San Francisco: Rosenberg Real Estate Equity Funds Research Report, 2007.

Nelson, Arthur C., and Kathy T. Young. "Limited Role of Downtowns in Meeting Metropolitan Housing Needs." *Journal of Urban Planning and Development* 134, no. 1 (2008): 1–8.

Nelson, Howard J. *The Los Angeles Metropolis.* Dubuque, Iowa: Kendall/Hunt Publishing, 1983.

New York City Panel on Climate Change. "Climate Risk Information." New York: New York City Panel on Climate Change, 2009.

Newman, Peter. "Sustainability and Cities: Extending the Metabolism Model." *Landscape and Urban Planning* 44, no. 4 (1999): 219–26.

Newman, Peter, Timothy Beatley, and Heather Boyer. *Resilient Cities: Responding to Peak Oil and Climate Change.* Washington, D.C.: Island Press, 2009.

Newman, Peter, and Jeffrey R. Kenworthy. *Cities and Automobile Dependence: A Sourcebook.* Aldershot, UK: Gower, 1989.

———. "Gasoline Consumption and Cities: A Comparison of US Cities with a Global Survey." *Journal of the American Planning Association* 55, no. 1 (1989): 24–37.

———. *Sustainability and Cities: Overcoming Automobile Dependence.* Washington, D.C.: Island Press, 1999.

Nicholson, Arnold. "They Lock Hot Weather Out." *Saturday Evening Post*, June 16, 1956.

Noble, Daniel. "Motorola Expands in Phoenix." *Arizona Business and Economics Review* (1954): 1.

Noland, Robert B. "Perceived Risk and Modal Choice: Risk Compensation in Transportation Systems." *Accident Analysis and Prevention* 27, no. 4 (1995): 503–21.

Nordhaus, William. "Do Real-Output and Real-Wage Measures Capture Reality? The History of Lighting Suggests Not." In *The Economics of New Goods: Studies in Income and Wealth*, vol. 58, edited by T. F. Bresnahan and R. J. Gordon. Chicago: University of Chicago Press, 1997.

OECD Nuclear Energy Agency, International Atomic Energy Agency, and NetLibrary Inc. "Uranium 2005 Resources, Production, and Demand: A Joint Report." Paris: Nuclear Energy Agency, Organisation for Economic Co-operation and Development, 2006.

Oke, Timothy R. *Boundary Layer Climates*. 2nd ed. London: Methuen, 1987.

———. "The Energetic Basis of the Urban Heat-Island." *Quarterly Journal of the Royal Meteorological Society* 108, no. 455 (1982): 1–24.

———. "Urban Climates and Global Environmental Change." In *Applied Climatology: Principles and Practice*, edited by R. D. Thompson and A. H. Perry. London: Routledge, 1997.

Olmsted, Frederick, Harlan Bartholomew, and Charles Cheney. "Major Traffic Street Plan of Los Angeles." Los Angeles: Traffic Commission of the City and County of Los Angeles, 1924.

Pagano, Michael, and Ann Bowman. "Vacant Land in Cities: An Urban Resource." Washington, D.C.: Brookings Institution Center on Urban and Metropolitan Policy, 2000.

Peiser, Richard B. "Density and Urban Sprawl." *Land Economics* 65, no. 3 (1989): 193–204.

Pendall, Rolf. "Do Land-Use Controls Cause Sprawl?" *Environment and Planning B-Planning and Design* 26, no. 4 (1999): 555–71.

Peplow, Mark. "Hydrogen Economy Looks Out of Reach." *Nature News*, October 7, 2004.

Peterson, Iver. "City Team Cites Subway Decline." *New York Times*, January 31, 1970.

Poole, Robert. "Policy Strategies for US Surface Transportation Funding Reauthorization." Washington, D.C.: Reason Foundation, 2010.

Popper, Deborah, and Frank Popper. "Smart Decline in Post-Carbon Cities." In *The Post Carbon Reader: Managing the Twenty-First Century's Sustainability Crises*, edited by R. Heineberg and D. Lerch. Healdsburg, Calif.: Watershed Media, 2010.

Popper, Frank. "Understanding American Land-Use Regulation since 1970: A Revisionist Interpretation." *Journal of the American Planning Association* 54, no. 3 (1988): 291–301.

Porter, Douglas. *Managing Growth in America's Communities.* Washington, D.C.: Island Press, 2009.

Power, Matthew. "Peak Water: Aquifers and Rivers Are Running Dry. How Three Regions Are Coping." *Wired,* April 21, 2008, 132.

Pratt, Theodore. "How to Keep Cool in a Car." *New York Times,* July 5, 1953.

Rasanen, Mikko, and Heikki Summala. "Attention and Expectation Problems in Bicycle-Car Collisions: An In-Depth Study." *Accident Analysis and Prevention* 30, no. 5 (1998): 657–66.

Reese, John. "The Air-Conditioning Revolution." *Saturday Evening Post,* July 9, 1960, 47–100.

Reynolds, Conor C., M. Anne Harris, Kay Teschke, Peter A. Cripton, and Meghan Winters. "The Impact of Transportation Infrastructure on Bicycling Injuries and Crashes: A Review of the Literature." *Environ Health* 8 (2009): 47.

Riddell, Lindsay. "PACE Energy Efficiency Programs Suspended." *San Francisco Business Times,* June 11, 2010.

Roberts, Paul. *The End of Oil: On the Edge of a Perilous New World.* Boston: Houghton Mifflin, 2005.

Robinson, Dorothy L. "Safety in Numbers in Australia: More Walkers and Bicyclists, Safer Walking and Bicycling." *Health Promotion Journal of Australia* 16, no. 1 (2005): 47–51.

Rodgers, Gregory B. "Factors Associated with the Crash Risk of Adult Bicyclists." *Journal of Safety Research* 28, no. 4 (1997): 233–41.

Rosenzweig, Cynthia, William Solecki, and Ronald Slosberg. "Mitigating New York City's Heat Island with Urban Forestry, Living Roofs, and Light Surfaces." Albany: New York State Energy Research and Development Authority, 2006.

Rubin, Jeff. *Why Your World Is About to Get a Whole Lot Smaller.* New York: Random House, 2009.

Rusk, David. *Cities without Suburbs: A Census 2000 Update.* 3rd ed. Washington, D.C.: Woodrow Wilson Center Press, 2003.

Rutten, Tim. "Mayor Antonio Villaraigosa's 30/10 Plan: Moving Forward." *Los Angeles Times,* June 9, 2010.

Sahely, Halla R., Shauna Dudding, and Christopher A. Kennedy. "Estimating the Urban Metabolism of Canadian Cities: Greater Toronto Area Case Study." *Canadian Journal of Civil Engineering* 30, no. 2 (2003): 468–83.

Santos Canals, Marc, Antoine Pinaud, and Janneau Thibaut. "Copenhagen: How Bicycles Can Become an Efficient Means of Public Transportation." Working paper, Geography Department, Roskilde University. Roskilde, Denmark: Roskilde University, 2006.

Saunders, Stephen, Charles Montgomery, Tom Easley, and Theo Spencer. "Hotter and Drier: The West's Changed Climate." Denver: Rocky Mountain Climate Organization, 2008.

Schiermeier, Quirin. "Purification with a Pinch of Salt." *Nature* 452, no. 7185 (2008): 260–61.

Schimmoller, Brian. "Electricity Solutions for a Carbon-Constrained Future." *EPRI Journal*, Fall 2007.

Schmer, Marty R., Kenneth P. Vogel, R. B. Mitchell, and Richard K. Perrin. "Net Energy of Cellulosic Ethanol from Switchgrass." *Proceedings of the National Academy of Sciences of the United States of America* 105, no. 2 (2008): 464–69.

Schnurman, Mitchell. "A Game-Changer for a Green Economy Is Closer Than You Think." *Fort Worth Star-Telegram*, March 9, 2010.

Schrank, David, and Tim Lomax. "2009 Urban Mobility Report." College Station: Texas Transportation Institute, Texas A&M University, 2009.

Searchinger, Timothy, et al. "Use of U.S. Croplands for Biofuels Increases Greenhouse Gases through Emissions from Land-Use Change." *Science* 319, no. 5867 (2008): 1238–40.

Seba, Tony. *Solar Trillions: Seven Market and Investment Opportunities in the Emerging Clean Energy Economy.* San Francisco: Tony Seba Group, 2010.

Sechler, Robert. "The Seven Eras of Rapid Transit Planning in Los Angeles." Los Angeles: The Electric Railway Historical Association of Southern California, 1999.

Setzer, Glenn. "What Do High Gas Prices Mean for the Housing Market?" *Mortgage News Daily*, April 25, 2006.

Silver, Hillary. "Obama's Urban Policy: A Symposium." *City and Community* 9, no. 1 (2010): 3–12.

Simpson, Peter V. "Two Year Wait for Stockholm Flat: Report." *The Local*, February 8, 2010.

Smith, Fred. "Decaying at the Core: Urban Decline in Cleveland, Ohio." *Research in Economic History* 21 (2003): 135–84.

Song, Yan, and Gerrit J. Knaap. "Measuring Urban Form: Is Portland Winning the War on Sprawl?" *Journal of the American Planning Association* 70, no. 2 (2004): 210–25.

Starr, Kevin. *Material Dreams: Southern California through the 1920s, Americans and the California Dream.* New York: Oxford University Press, 1990.

Sullivan, Noelle. *It Happened in Southern California.* Helena, Mont.: Twodot, 1996.

Surface Transportation Policy Project. "Why Are the Roads so Congested?" Washington D.C.: Surface Transportation Policy Project, 1999.

Sussman, Carl. *Planning the Fourth Migration: The Neglected Vision of the Regional Planning Association of America.* Cambridge: MIT Press, 1976.

Taha, Haider, Steven Konopacki, and Sasa Gabersek. "Modeling the Meteorological and Energy Effects of Urban Heat Islands and Their Mitigation: A Ten-Region Study." Berkeley, Calif.: Lawrence Berkeley Laboratory, 1996.

Talen, Emily, and Gerrit Knaap. "Legalizing Smart Growth: An Empirical Study of Land Use Regulation in Illinois." *Journal of Planning Education and Research* 22, no. 4 (2003): 345–59.

Taylor, Frank J. "The Word's Worst Traffic Tangle." *Saturday Evening Post,* March 13, 1954, 42–112.

Taylor, Paul, Rich Morin, Kim Parker, D'Vera Cohn, and Wendy Wang. "For Nearly Half of America, Grass Is Greener Somewhere Else." Washington, D.C.: Pew Research Center, 2009.

Tertzakian, Peter. *A Thousand Barrels a Second: The Coming Oil Break Point and the Challenges Facing an Energy Dependent World.* New York: McGraw-Hill, 2006.

Theobald, David M. "Land-Use Dynamics Beyond the American Urban Fringes." *Geographical Review* 91, no. 3 (2001): 544–64.

Thorson, James A. "Zoning Policy Changes and the Urban Fringe Land Market." *Journal of the American Real Estate and Urban Economics Association* 22, no. 3 (1994): 527–38.

Tiebout, Charles. "The Pure Theory of Local Expenditures." *Journal of Political Economy* 64 (1956): 416–24.

Turner, John A. "A Realizable Renewable Energy Future." *Science* 285, no. 5428 (1999): 687–98.

Turner Construction. "Green Building Market Barometer." http://www.turner construction.com/greenbuildings, 2008.

US Energy Information Administration. "Annual Energy Review, 2008." Washington, D.C.: Department of Energy, Energy Information Administration, 2009.

———. "Household Vehicle Energy Use: Latest Data and Trends." Washington, D.C.: US Energy Information Administration, 2005.

US Green Building Council, Congress for the New Urbanism, and Natural Resources Defense Council. "LEED 2009 for Neighborhood Development." Washington, D.C.: US Green Building Council, 2009.

US Joint Forces Command. "The Joint Operating Environment." Suffolk, Va.: US Joint Forces Command, 2010.

van Vliet, Oscar P. R., Andre P. C. Faaij, and Wim C. Turkenburg. "Fischer-Tropsch Diesel Production in a Well-to-Wheel Perspective: A Carbon, Energy Flow and Cost Analysis." *Energy Conversion and Management* 50, no. 4 (2009): 855–76.

Vandenbulcke, G., et al. "Mapping Bicycle Use and the Risk of Accidents for Commuters Who Cycle to Work in Belgium." *Transport Policy* 16, no. 2 (2009): 77–87.

Wald, Matthew. "Cost Works against Alternative and Renewable Energy Source in Time of Recession." *New York Times*, March 28, 2009.

———. "Efficiency, Not Just Alternatives, Is Promoted as an Energy Saver." *New York Times*, May 29, 2007.

Wald, Matthew, and Tom Zeller. "Cost of Green Power Makes Projects Tougher Sell." *New York Times*, November 7, 2010.

Warren, Jennifer. "A Company Town Changes Companies—Mining: The Sale of Trona's Major Employer Has Brought Anxiety—and Hope—to the Mojave Desert Town." *Los Angeles Times*, December 13, 1990.

Weingroff, Richard. "The Man Who Changed America, Part 2." Washington D.C.: US Department of Transportation, Federal Highway Administration, 2003.

West, B. H., R. N. McGill, J. W. Hodgson, S. S. Sluder, and D. E. Smith. "Development and Verification of Light-Duty Modal Emissions and Fuel Consumption Values for Traffic Models." Oak Ridge, Tenn.: Oak Ridge National Laboratory, 1999.

Western Resource Advocates. "Smart Water: A Comparative Study of Urban Water Use Efficiency across the Southwest." Boulder, Colo.: Western Resource Advocates, 2003.

White, James R. "Large Lot Zoning and Subdivision Costs: A Test." *Journal of Urban Economics* 23, no. 3 (1988): 370–84.

Wilbur Smith Associates. "Noteworthy MPO Practices in Transportation–Land Use Planning Integration." Washington, D.C.: Association of Metropolitan Planning Organizations, 2004.

Wilkinson, Robert. "Methodology for Analysis of the Energy Intensity of California's Water Systems." Berkeley, Calif.: Lawrence Berkeley Laboratory, 2000.

Winters, M., and K. Teschke. "Route Preferences among Adults in the Near Market for Bicycling: Findings of the Cycling in Cities Study." *American Journal of Health Promotion* 25, no. 1 (2010): 40–47.

Wise, Henry A. *Los Gringos: Or, an Inside View of Mexico and California.* New York: Baker and Scribner, 1849.

Wolman, Abel. "The Metabolism of Cities." *Scientific American* 213, no. 3 (1965): 179–90.

Yongquist, Walter, and Richard Duncan. "North American Natural Gas: Data Show Supply Problems." *Natural Resources Research* 12, no. 4 (2003): 229–40.

Index

Note: Illustrations are indicated by page numbers in italic type.

Gärde, Lars, 219, 224
garden cities, 106, 132, 267
Gaskins, Shirley, 117
gasoline consumption, 61, 70–74,
103–4, 312n18. *See also* natural gas
gasoline prices, suburban housing in
relation to, 7–8, 298n9
Geesman, John, 273
Georgia, 53
German highways, 94–95
Gifford, Henry, 318n20
Global Warming Solutions Act (Cali-
fornia), 34
Goldberg, Jonah, 14, 29
Goldschmidt, Neil, 101
Gordon, Peter, 67–68
Gore, Albert, Jr., 284
Gore, Albert, Sr., 96
Gottlieb, Robert, 110–11
government. *See* federal government
Green Accounts for Public Buildings
program, 168–69
Greener, Greater Buildings Plan, 171
Greenfield development, 228–29
greenhouse gas regulations, 33–34,
47–48, 143, 167
Green Lease, 172
Green Mountain Coffee Roasters, 162
growth boundaries, 257–61, 293

Haas, Pedro, 156
Habitat for Humanity, 237
Hamilton, Blair, 160, 162–64, 167
Hammarby Sjöstad, Stockholm,
Sweden, 215–25, *217, 219, 221, 222,
224*
Hayward, Steven, 82
Hearth and Home at Liberty, Rio
Vista, California, 5
heating degree days (HDDs), 20–21

heating systems efficiency, 25–26
Heinberg, Richard, 279
helmets, bicycle, 191–92
Hewitt, Abram, 120
Highway Act (1921), 93
highway revolts, 99–102, 112
highways, 89–114; cross-country travel,
89–92; emergence of, 92–94; fees
for use of, 291–92; interstate, 91–92,
94–99; in Los Angeles, 102–12;
maintenance of, 290; opposition
to, 99–102, 112; urban planning
and, 96–102, 113–14, 311n8. *See also*
automobiles
Highway Traffic Survey (Los Angeles
County Regional Planning Com-
mission), 136
Hines, Paul, 25
Holiday, Billie, 211
Home Depot Foundation, 237
Hope VI housing program, 288
House and Home (magazine), 15
housing design: environmentally
conscious, 147–52, 154–56, 218–20;
passive, 21–22; in Sun Belt, 22
housing financing, 163–65, 288
housing prices, 6–7, 252
Houston, Texas, 204, 252
Howard, Ebenezer, 139, 267
Howe, Con, 173, 264–65
HSBC, 226
Hubbert, M. King, 57–58
Hubbert's Curve, *57,* 57–58
Hudson and Manhattan Railroad, 123
Hughes, Dick, 16
humidity, 22
Hurricane Katrina, 53
hydroelectric energy, 207
hydrogen, for energy storage, 274–75
hygge, 188

and, 65–66, 76–77; urban villages
and, 265–66. *See also* elevated
trains; rail transit; streetcars;
subways
Public Works Administration, 94
pumping: of aqueduct water, 39–42,
44–52; of flood water, 53–54; of
groundwater, 44–45, 53

Quebec, 179

rail transit, 63–64, 118; in Los Angeles,
107, 127–37, *128, 133;* in Stockholm, 138–40, *139,* 193–94, 197.
See also elevated trains; streetcars;
subways
Rapid Transit Act (New York, 1894),
121–22
rare-earth minerals, 275–76
Reagan, Ronald, 284
real-estate owned properties (REOs), 7
redevelopment. *See* urban
redevelopment
reflective roofs, 26–27
refrigeration, 16
regional councils, 256
Regional Greenhouse Gas Initiative
(RGGI), 34
Regional Heat Island Initiative, New
York City, 27
Regional Innovation Clusters, 286
regional planning: challenges facing,
254–55, 261–62; federal government
and, 286–94; and growth boundaries, 257–61; ideal vision of, 244–45;
institutional structure for, 255–56,
292–93; language of, 267–68; in
Oregon, 256–62; political factors
affecting, 261; polycentric model in,
263–66; and sprawl, 258

Regional Planning Association of
America, 244–45
renewable energy, 207, 269–76. *See
also* solar energy; wind energy
rent control, 225
Residential Energy Consumption
Survey, 21
Residential Energy Demand Tempera-
ture Index, 20–21
reurbanization, 245–47
Richardson, Harry, 67–68
Rio Vista, California, 5
roads. *See* highways
Rocky Mountain Institute, 171
Roman aqueducts, 54–55
roofs, reflective, 26–27
Roosevelt, Franklin Delano, 94
Roosevelt, Theodore, 120
RTC. *See* Board of Rapid Transit Rail-
road Commissioners
Rubin, Jeff, 32, 85
Rust Belt, 211, 213

Safe Drinking Water Act, 48
SAFETEA-LU, 289, 292
safety valves, in development, 258
Sandtown-Winchester neighborhood,
Baltimore, 210–12, 237–38
San Francisco, California: highway
revolt in, 100; walkability of, 79–81
Santa Fe Railroad, 132–34
São Paulo, Brazil, 66–67, 74–75, *75,*
77–78
Sarasota, Florida, 260
satellite towns, 139
Saturday Evening Post (magazine), 14,
111–12
Saudi Arabia, 83
Scheckel, Paul, 173
Schneider, Phillip, 4–5

200; population density and, 67–70, 76; pricing based on, 194–200; in São Paulo, 66–67, 75–76; in Stockholm, 194–97

Traffic Survey Plan (Automobile Club of Southern California), 109–11, *111*

trains, commuter, 63–64

Transcend Equity, 166

Transfers of Development Rights (TDRs), 262

transit-oriented developments (TODs), 257

transportation, 59–82; energy factors concerning, 61; federal government role in, 289–92; fuel consumption by, 70–74; land use coordinated with, 293; population density and, 67–71, 76; trip lengths, 67–68. *See also* automobiles; commuting; highways; public transit

Transportation Infrastructure Finance and Innovation Act, 292

Transverse Range, California, 37

trees, temperature-moderating effects of, 26–27

Triborough System, 123

trip lengths, 67–68, 70. *See also* vehicle miles traveled

Trona, California, 13–14

Tucson, Arizona, 42, 44–45, 48, 305n15

Tunnelbana, 138, 139

Union Pacific Railroad, 132–34

United Arab Emirates, 28

United Nations Intergovernmental Panel on Climate Change, 143

United States: bike commuting in, 189–93; coal reserves in, 142; congestion charging in, 198–200;

energy efficiency regulations in, 169–73; gas consumption in, 61; natural gas in, 176–77; oil sources in, 56, 58; public transit in, 64, 118; roads in, 92

unslumming, 246

urban areas. *See* cities; urban planning

Urban Development Action Grants program, 283

urban energy metabolism: defined, 3; economic significance of, 3–4; factors influencing, 3; local government responses to, 294–95; regional planning and, 257; transportation's effect on, 64

urban growth boundaries, 257–59, *260*, 293

urban heat island effect, 23–24, 26–27

urban metabolism, 2–3, 297n2

Urban Mobility Report, 68–69

Urban Partnerships Congestion Initiative, 198–99, 292

urban planning: and automobiles, 79; centeredness, 76, 105; choice and, 114, 137, 204, 223; Copenhagen, 293–94; economic impact of, 8; Hammarby Sjöstad, 215–25; highways and, 96–102, 113–14, 311n8; infill development, 229–30, 262–68; LoDo, 230–34; Los Angeles, 104–13, 127, 129–38, 263–65; neighborhoods, 215–38; opposition to, 81–82; and public transit, 65–66, 76–77; São Paulo, 77–78; Stockholm, 193–94; in United States, 225–30. *See also* zoning

urban policy, federal, 283–86

urban redevelopment: Baltimore, 212–15; Hammarby Sjöstad, 215–25; inter-building coordination in,

HD 9502 .A2 T76 2012
Troy, Austin.
The very hungry city